PENGUIN BOOKS

# CHOOSE YOUR BABY'S NAME

Rosalind Fergusson was born in Liverpool in 1953 and obtained her degree in French from Exeter University. From there she took a teaching certificate and became an assistant teacher at a school in West Sussex. From 1978 to 1984 she worked for Market House Books where she trained as an assistant editor and lexicographer and rose to the position of Senior Editor. During this time she worked on a range of books, particularly dictionaries. Since leaving Market House Books she has worked as a freelance editor.

Her other publications include *The Mr Men Word Books* (1979), *Pan's English–French Dictionary* (1982), *The Penguin Dictionary of Proverbs* (1983) and *The Penguin Rhyming Dictionary* (1985). Rosalind Fergusson has also edited and co-edited a number of dictionaries and reference books and has contributed to Secker and Warburg's *Dictionary of British History* (1981) and Longman's *Dictionary of Twentieth Century Biography* (1985) among others.

Rosalind Fergusson is married and lives in Southbourne. Her leisure interests include walking, photography and music.

D0207668

# CHOOSE YOUR BABY'S NAME

## A DICTIONARY OF FIRST NAMES

### Rosalind Fergusson

Market House Books Limited

PENGUIN BOOKS

Penguin Books Ltd, Harmondsworth, Middlesex, England
Viking Penguin Inc., 40 West 23rd Street, New York, New York 10010, U.S.A.
Penguin Books Australia Ltd, Ringwood, Victoria, Australia
Penguin Books Canada Limited, 2801 John Street, Markham, Ontario, Canada L3R 1B4
Penguin Books (N.Z.) Ltd, 182–190 Wairau Road, Auckland 10, New Zealand

First published 1987

Copyright © Market House Books Ltd, 1987
All rights reserved

Reproduced, printed and bound in Great Britain by
Hazell Watson & Viney Limited,
Member of the BPCC Group,
Aylesbury, Bucks
Typeset in Times by Market House Books Ltd, Aylesbury

# PREFACE

This dictionary provides a selection of some three thousand first names used in English-speaking countries. Some of these are no older than the present century, while others date back to the Old Testament; some have been adopted from foreign sources, others have their roots in the languages of the earliest settlers and inhabitants of the British Isles.

Until the Norman Conquest most first names were of Celtic or Anglo-Saxon origin. The former were often nicknames relating to the bearer's physical characteristics; the latter, like other Germanic names, were often compounded from two name elements (*Alfred*, for example, literally means 'elf counsel'). Few Anglo-Saxon names survived the eleventh century in their original form; many of the names introduced by the Normans, however, were derived from Old German equivalents of the Anglo-Saxon names they replaced.

The next significant development took place after the Reformation: names with Roman Catholic associations, such as those of non-bibilical saints, ceased to be popular and new names were culled from the Bible, especially the Old Testament. The Puritans also made use of a variety of abstract nouns, such as *Faith*, *Grace* and *Prudence*, in christening their girl babies. The nineteenth century saw the revival of a number of older names and an increase in the use of surnames, especially those of aristocratic families, as first names; towards the end of the century it became fashionable to call girls after flowers, jewels or the months of spring (*April*, *May* and *June*). During the twentieth century, show business, particularly the cinema and television, has been a major influence on the choice of first names.

The entries in this dictionary provide a range of information. The entry begins by listing the most common spellings of the name in their order of frequency; this is followed, if there is likely to be any doubt as to its pronunciation, by a phonetic transcription of the name (see the Pronunciation Guide) and an indication of its gender. The entry itself deals with the origin and meaning of the name (for names of uncertain or disputed derivation several possible interpretations may be given), its history, and any associations it may have, favourable or otherwise, including mention of famous bearers of the name in fact or fiction. At the end of the entries a list of variants, diminutives, and feminine or masculine forms of the name is given. (For the purposes of this dictionary a variant is a derivative that is firmly established as a name in its own right; a diminutive is any pet form of the name, whether or not it is used independently.)

R.F.
1986

# FIRST NAMES –
# PRONUNCIATION GUIDE

The stressed syllable in a name of two or more syllables is shown in *italic type*.

| | | | | |
|---|---|---|---|---|
| a | *as in* bat [bat] | | l | *as in* leg [leg] |
| ă | *as in* arrest [ărest] | | m | *as in* mop [mop] |
| ah | *as in* calf [kahf] | | n | *as in* nail [nayl] |
| air | *as in* dare [dair] | | o | *as in* bog [bog] |
| ar | *as in* heart [hart] | | ŏ | *as in* hillock [*hil*ŏk] |
| aw | *as in* fall [fawl] | | ō | *as in* coal [kōl] |
| ay | *as in* plate [playt] | | oi | *as in* toy [toi] |
| b | *as in* big [big] | | oo | *as in* rue [roo] |
| ch | *as in* chop [chop] | | oor | *as in* poor [poor] |
| d | *as in* dug [dug] | | or | *as in* tore [tor] |
| dh | *as in* this [dhis] | | ōw | *as in* spout [spowt] |
| e | *as in* tell [tel] | | p | *as in* pig [pig] |
| ĕ | *as in* open [*ō*pĕn] | | r | *as in* run [run] |
| ee | *as in* meat [meet] | | s | *as in* sit [sit] |
| eer | *as in* dear [deer] | | sh | *as in* shoe [shoo] |
| er | *as in* third [therd] | | t | *as in* top [top] |
| ew | *as in* tube [tewb] | | th | *as in* thing [thing] |
| ewr | *as in* pure [pewr] | | u | *as in* cup [kup] |
| f | *as in* fog [fog] | | ŭ | *as in* crocus [*krō*kŭs] |
| g | *as in* gate [gayt] | | uu | *as in* book [buuk] |
| h | *as in* hat [hat] | | v | *as in* van [van] |
| i | *as in* will [wil] | | w | *as in* wig [wig] |
| ĭ | *as in* pencil [*pen*sĭl] | | y | *as in* yell [yel] |
| ī | *as in* try [trī] | | yoo | *as in* unit [*yoo*nit] |
| j | *as in* jump [jump] | | yoor | *as in* urine [*yoor*in] |
| k | *as in* cot [kot] | | yr | *as in* mire [myr] |
| ks | *as in* fix [fiks] | | z | *as in* zeal [zeel] |
| kw | *as in* quite [kwīt] | | zh | *as in* vision [*vizh*ŏn] |

# A

**Aaron** [*air*ŏn] (m) a name of Hebrew or Egyptian origin, possibly meaning 'high mountain'. The Aaron of the Old Testament, the brother of Moses and first high priest of the Israelites, is remembered for the miraculous blossoming of his staff or rod (Numbers 17:8). The name became popular in English-speaking countries after the Reformation.

**Abbey, Abbie, Abby** diminutives of **Abigail**.

**Abe** a diminutive of **Abel**, **Abraham**, or **Abram**.

**Abel** (m) a biblical name that may mean 'son' or 'breath'. Abel was the son of Adam and Eve, killed by his elder brother Cain in a fit of jealousy (Genesis 4:8). The name has been in use since the Middle Ages and was popular in the 17th century.
Diminutive **Abe**.

**Abigail** (f) from Hebrew, meaning 'father rejoiced' (sometimes interpreted as 'father's joy'). In the Old Testament Abigail was the intelligent and beautiful wife of King David; in Beaumont and Fletcher's play *The Scornful Lady* (1616) the name was given to a lady's maid and ultimately degenerated into a slang term with this meaning. First popular in the 16th century, the name was revived in the 1970s.
Diminutives: **Abbey, Abbie, Abby, Gail, Gale, Gayle**.

**Abner** (m) from Hebrew, meaning 'father is light'. In the Old Testament Abner was the cousin of Saul and commander of his army. The name became fashionable after the Reformation and was popularized in the USA in the 20th century by 'Li'l Abner', the hero of a comic strip by cartoonist Al Capp.

**Abraham** (m) from Hebrew, meaning 'father of a multitude'. Abraham was the first of the Old Testament patriarchs, his name being changed from **Abram** when it was revealed that he would be the father of the Hebrew nation (Genesis 17:5). One of the many Old Testament names that became fashionable after the Reformation, *Abraham* was further popularized in the 19th century by the US president Abraham Lincoln.
Diminutives: **Abe, Bram, Ham**.

**Abram** (m) from Hebrew, meaning 'high father'; the original name of the Old Testament patriarch **Abraham**.
Diminutive: **Abe**.

**Absalom** (m) from Hebrew, meaning 'the father is peace' or 'father of peace'; the son of King David in the Old Testament. The name became popular in the 12th century, often in the French form *Absolon*: this spelling was used by Chaucer for a character in his *Miller's Tale*.

# Absolon

**Absolon** see **Absalom**.

**Ada** (f) introduced into Britain from Germany in the late 18th century. The origin of the name is uncertain: it may be derived from the Old German name *Eda* or *Etta*, meaning 'happy', or it may simply be a diminutive of **Adela**, **Adelaide**, or **Adeline**. See also **Adah**.

**Adah** (f) from a Hebrew word meaning 'ornament'; the name of two Old Testament women, wives of Lamech and Esau. The name has been used occasionally in English-speaking countries since the 16th century; it is sometimes erroneously associated with **Ada**.

**Adair** [ădair] (m) a Scottish name of uncertain origin: it may be from Gaelic, meaning 'oak tree ford', or it may simply be a variant of **Edgar**. The name has been in use for many hundreds of years, both as a surname and as a first name.

**Adam** (m) from Hebrew, meaning 'red': a reference either to the colour of the skin or to the red earth from which the Adam of the Old Testament, the father of the human race, was created (Genesis 2:7). St Adamnan, an Irish saint of the 7th century and the biographer of St Columba, was an early bearer of the name: *Adamnan* means 'little Adam'. One of the most common names of the 13th century, *Adam* was further popularized in the mid-19th century by George Eliot's novel *Adam Bede* and became fashionable again in the late 1960s.
Variant: **Edom**.
Feminine form: **Adamina**.

**Adamina** the feminine form of **Adam**.

**Adamnan** see **Adam**.

**Addie, Addy** diminutives of **Adela**, **Adelaide**, or **Adeline**.

**Adela** (f) from Old German *athal* 'noble'. The name was introduced into Britain at the time of the Norman Conquest and was borne by one of the daughters of King William I.
Variant: **Adele**.
Diminutives: **Ada, Addie, Addy, Della**.
Related names: **Adeline, Ethel**.

**Adelaide** (f) from the Old German name *Adalheidis*, meaning 'nobility', derived from *athal* 'noble' and *haidu* '-hood' and rendered in modern German as *Adelheid* (see **Heidi**). *Adelaide* was originally the French form of the name; it was popularized in Britain in the early 19th century by King William IV's consort, Queen Adelaide, after whom the capital of South Australia was named.
Diminutives: **Ada, Addie, Addy**.
Related names: **Alice, Heidi**.

2

**Adele** a variant of **Adela**, from the French form of the name.

**Adelheid** see **Adelaide, Heidi**.

**Adelina** the Latinized form of **Adeline**.

**Adeline** (f) from Old German *athal* 'noble'. The name first appeared in the Domesday Book of 1086 and remained in use throughout the Middle Ages; it was also popular in the 19th century.
Variant: **Adelina**.
Diminutives: **Ada, Addie, Addy, Alina, Aline**.
Related names: **Adela, Ethel**.

**Adlai** [*ad*lay] (m) from Hebrew, meaning 'my ornament'. Mentioned in the Old Testament, the name is generally associated with the 20th-century US statesman Adlai Stevenson.

**Adolf, Adolph, Adolphe** [*ad*olf, (US) *ay*dolf] variants of **Adolphus**. *Adolf*, the German form of the name, is generally associated with the 20th-century German dictator Adolf Hitler.

**Adolphus** (m) from the Old German name *Adalwolf*, derived from *athal* 'noble' and *wolfa* 'wolf'; rendered in Old English as *Aethelwulf*. *Adolphus*, a Latinized form of the name used by German royal families in the 17th and 18th centuries, was introduced into Britain by the Hanoverians.
Variants: **Adolf, Adolph, Adolphe**.

**Adrian** (m) from Latin *Hadrianus* 'of Adria' or 'of the Adriatic' (Adria is the Italian town that gave its name to the Adriatic Sea). One of the earliest bearers of the name was the Roman emperor Hadrian, who ordered the building of the famous wall across northern England. The name was also borne by three saints and a number of popes, including Nicholas Breakspear (Adrian IV), the only English pope, who may have been responsible for the introduction of the name into Britain in the late 12th century. It was used only occasionally until the mid-20th century, when it became very popular; in the early 1980s it was given by Sue Townsend to the adolescent hero of *The Secret Diary of Adrian Mole, Aged 13$^3$/$_4$*.
Variant: **Hadrian**.
Feminine forms: **Adriana, Adrianne, Adrienne**.

**Adrienne, Adrianne, Adriana** feminine forms of **Adrian**. *Adrienne*, the French feminine form of the name, became popular in English-speaking countries in the mid-20th century.

**Aeneas** [ee*neeas*] (m) from Greek, meaning 'praiseworthy'. The name of the Trojan hero of Virgil's *Aeneid*, *Aeneas* has been in infrequent use since the Renaissance. It is sometimes used in Scotland as a translation of the Gaelic name *Aonghus* (see **Angus**).

**Afra** the name of an early Christian martyr; of uncertain origin. It is sometimes used as a variant spelling of **Aphra**.

3

# Agacia

**Agacia** see **Agatha**.

**Agatha** (f) from Greek, meaning 'good'. The name was borne by a Christian martyr of the 3rd century, St Agatha, and was popular throughout the Middle Ages, sometimes in the Latinized form *Agacia*. The most famous bearer of the name in the 20th century was the British detective-story writer Agatha Christie.
Diminutive: **Aggie**.

**Aggie** a diminutive of **Agatha** or **Agnes**.

**Agnes** (f) from Greek, meaning 'pure' or 'chaste'; sometimes erroneously associated with Latin *agnus* 'lamb'. St Agnes was a Christian martyr of the 3rd century; the rites and superstitions connected with her feast day (21st January) are described in Keats' poem 'The Eve of St Agnes'. The name was popular until the Reformation, when saints' names not mentioned in the Bible fell from favour. It was revived in the 19th century and has remained in use since then.
Variants: **Agneta, Anis, Annice, Annis, Inez, Senga**.
Diminutives: **Aggie, Nessa, Nessie, Nest, Nesta**.

**Agneta** a variant of **Agnes**.

**Aidan** (m) from Irish Gaelic, meaning 'little fire'. The name was borne by a famous Irish monk of the 7th century; it was revived in the early 19th century and remains in regular use.
Feminine equivalent: **Ethne**.

**Aileen** a variant of **Eileen**, particularly popular in Scotland.

**Ailie** a Scottish diminutive of **Ailis, Ailsa**, or **Alison**.

**Ailis** the Scottish Gaelic form of **Alice**.
Diminutive: **Ailie**.

**Ailith** a variant of **Aldith**.

**Ailsa** (f) from *Ailsa Craig*, the name of a rocky islet in the Firth of Clyde, Scotland. Its use as a first name has spread from Scotland to other parts of Britain and the English-speaking world. The name is sometimes interpreted or used as a Scottish variant of **Elsa**.
Diminutive: **Ailie**.

**Aimee** a variant of **Amy**, from the French form of the name.

**Aine** a variant of **Ethne**. According to Irish legend, Aine is the queen of the fairies in South Munster.

**Ainslie, Ainsley** (m *or* f) from a surname derived from the Nottinghamshire place name *Annesley*.

**Aisling** [*ash*ling] (f) an Irish name, meaning 'dream' or 'vision'.
Variant: **Aislinn**.

**Aislinn** a variant of **Aisling**.

**Aithne** a variant of **Ethne**.

**Al** a diminutive of several masculine names beginning with *Al*-, notably **Alan** and **Alistair**.

**Alain** the French form of **Alan**.

**Alan, Allan, Allen, Alun** (m) a Celtic name of uncertain derivation: possible interpretations include 'harmony', 'stone', or 'noble'. Originally borne by a Welsh and Breton saint, the name was reintroduced into Britain at the time of the Norman Conquest by a number of French noblemen, notably Alain le Roux, who later became Earl of Richmond. The name remained popular throughout the Middle Ages and was given to a character in the Robin Hood legend, Allen a Dale; it was revived in the 19th century and has been in frequent use in English-speaking countries since then.
Variant: **Alain**.
Diminutives: **Al, Allie, Ally**.
Feminine forms: **Alana, Alanna**.

**Alana, Alanna** (f) a name of uncertain origin: it may be derived from the Irish Gaelic word for 'child' or it may simply be a feminine form of **Alan**.
Diminutives: **Lana**.

**Alaric** (m) from Old German, meaning 'noble ruler'. The most famous bearer of the name was Alaric I, a Visigoth king who conquered Rome in the early 5th century.

**Alasdair, Alastair** see **Alistair**.

**Alban** (m) from Latin *Albanus* 'of Alba' (referring to the ancient Latin city of Alba Longa), ultimately from *albus* 'white'. St Alban, after whom the Hertfordshire city of St Albans is named, was the first British martyr. The name was revived in the 19th century and has been used occasionally since then.
Variants: **Albany, Albin**.

**Albany** (m) a name of uncertain origin: it may be derived from a former name for northern Scotland or it may simply be a variant of **Alban**.

**Alberic** see **Aubrey**.

**Albert** (m) from the Old German name *Adalbert*, derived from *athal* 'noble' and *berhta* 'bright'. Its Old English equivalent, *Aethelbeorht* (see **Ethelbert**), was replaced after the Norman Conquest by the French *Aubert* and the Latinized form *Albertus*; the latter survived in northern Britain as *Halbert*. On the marriage of Queen Victoria to Prince Albert of Saxe-Coburg-Gotha in 1840 the name became popular throughout the English-speaking world; it remained in frequent use in the early 20th century.
Diminutives: **Al, Bert, Bertie**.
Feminine forms: **Alberta, Albertina, Albertine**.

**Alberta, Albertine, Albertina** feminine forms of **Albert**. The Canadian province was named after Princess Louise Alberta, daughter of Queen Victoria and Prince Albert and wife of a former governor general of Canada.

**Albin** (m) from the Latin name *Albinus*, derived from *albus* 'white'. The name is sometimes regarded as a variant of **Alban**.
Feminine forms: **Albina, Albinia**.

**Albina** a feminine form of **Albin**, borne by a 3rd-century saint. The name was popular in Britain in the 17th and 18th centuries.

**Albinia** a feminine form of **Albin**, introduced into Britain from Italy in the early 17th century. The name was frequently used by members of the aristocratic Cecil family and their descendants.

**Albreda** (f) from an Old German name meaning 'elf counsel', the equivalent of the Old English name *Aelfraed* (see **Alfred**). Introduced into Britain at the time of the Norman Conquest, the name *Albreda* was originally given to children of either sex. It gradually came to be regarded as a feminine name and was fairly common until the 15th century.
Variant: **Elvira**.

**Alda** the feminine form of **Aldo**.

**Alden** a variant of **Aldwyn**.

**Aldhelm** (m) from the Old English name *Ealdhelm*, a compound of *eald* 'old' and *helm* 'helmet'. The name was rarely used after the Norman Conquest until its revival in the 19th century.

**Aldis** a variant of **Aldo**.

**Aldith** (f) from the Old English name *Ealdgyth*, a compound of *eald* 'old' and *gyth* 'battle'. It remained in use after the Norman Conquest, unlike a number of other Anglo-Saxon names, but has rarely been used since the 14th century.
Variant: **Ailith**.

**Aldo** (m) originally an Old German name, derived from *ald* 'old'; borne by an 8th-century saint. *Aldo* has been popular in Italy for many years and is used in the English-speaking world by US families of Italian descent.
Variants: **Aldis, Aldous, Aldus**.
Feminine form: **Alda**.

**Aldous, Aldus** variants of **Aldo**, of which *Aldus* is the Latinized form. The name has been in use in Britain since the Middle Ages, its most famous bearer in modern times being the 20th-century British novelist Aldous Huxley.

**Aldred** (m) from the Old English name *Ealdraed*, a compound of *eald* 'old' and *raed* 'counsel'. The name was fairly common before the Norman Conquest and was revived in the 19th century.
Variant: **Eldred**.

Feminine form: **Aldreda**

**Aldreda** the feminine form of **Aldred**.

**Aldus** see **Aldo, Aldous**.

**Aldwyn, Aldwin** (m) from the Old English name *Ealdwine*, a compound of *eald* 'old' and *wine* 'friend'. The name was fairly common in the Middle Ages and has been used occasionally since then.
Variant: **Alden**.

**Alec** a diminutive of **Alexander**, often used as a name in its own right. It was popularized in the mid-20th century by the British actor Sir Alec Guinness.

**Aled** [*al*ed] (m) a Welsh name, meaning 'offspring'.
Feminine form: **Aledwen**.

**Aledwen** the feminine form of **Aled**.

**Alethea** [al*ĕthee*ă, ă*lee*thiă] (f) from Greek, meaning 'truth'. The name became fashionable in the early 17th century, possibly as a result of the future King Charles I's courtship of the Spanish infanta Maria Aletea, and has been used occasionally since then. It is sometimes confused with **Althea**.

**Alex** a diminutive of **Alexander** or **Alexandra**.

**Alexa** a feminine form of **Alexander**.

**Alexander** (m) from Greek, meaning 'defender of men'. One of the earliest and most famous bearers of the name was Alexander the Great, the Macedonian king of the 4th century BC who gave his name to the Egyptian city of Alexandria; it has also been borne by eight popes, three Russian emperors, and a number of other prominent historical figures. The name has been in frequent use in Britain since the Middle Ages: it was popularized in Scotland by three Scottish kings of the 12th and 13th centuries and in England by the *Roman d'Alexandre*, a medieval French romance. See also **Alexis**.
Variants: **Alasdair, Alastair, Alistair, Sacha**.
Diminutives: **Alec, Alex, Alick, Lex, Sandy**.
Feminine forms: **Alexa, Alexandra, Alexia**.

**Alexandra** a feminine form of **Alexander**. The name has been in use in Britain since the early 13th century; it became particularly fashionable after the marriage of the future King Edward VII to Princess Alexandra of Denmark in 1863.
Variants: **Alexandria, Alexandrina, Sandra**.
Diminutives: **Alex, Alix, Zandra**.

**Alexandria, Alexandrina** variants of **Alexandra**. *Alexandrina* was the first name of Queen Victoria.

# Alexia

**Alexia** a feminine form of **Alexander**.

**Alexis** (m *or* f) from Greek, meaning 'defender' or 'helper'; sometimes regarded as a variant, diminutive, or feminine form of **Alexander**. Originally a Russian masculine name, it became popular in Britain and the USA in the early 20th century and is now given to children of either sex.

**Alf, Alfie** diminutives of **Alfred**.

**Alfonso** see **Alphonso**.

**Alfred** (m) from the Old English name *Aelfraed*, a compound of *aelf* 'elf' and *raed* 'counsel'; sometimes associated with *Ealdfrith* or *Alfrid*, meaning 'old peace'. After the Norman Conquest *Alfred* was largely superseded by its variant forms and was little used for several hundred years until its revival in the 18th century. Famous bearers of the name include Alfred the Great, the 9th-century king traditionally accused of burning the cakes, and the 19th-century poet Lord Tennyson.
Variants: **Alured, Avery**.
Diminutives: **Alf, Alfie, Fred**.
Feminine form: **Alfreda**.
Related name: **Albreda**.

**Alfreda** a variant of **Elfreda** or the feminine form of **Alfred**.

**Algar** (m) from the Old English name *Aelfgar*, a compound of *aelf* 'elf' and *gar* 'spear'. The name was fairly common in the Middle Ages, giving rise to the surname *Elgar*, among others. It has been used only occasionally since its revival in the 19th century.
Variant: **Alger**.

**Alger** a variant of **Algar**. Alger Hiss, a US government official accused of spying for the USSR in the 1930s, is the most famous bearer of the name in modern times.

**Algernon** (m) from Norman French, meaning 'with whiskers'; a nickname borne by two companions of William the Conqueror who wore moustaches at a time when most Normans were clean-shaven: Eustace II, Count of Boulogne, and William de Percy, founder of the aristocratic Percy family. From the late 15th century the name was frequently given to members of the Percy family and their descendants; it came into more general use in the 19th century.
Diminutives: **Algie, Algy**.

**Algie, Algy** diminutives of **Algernon**.

**Alice, Alys** (f) from the Old German name *Adalheidis*, meaning 'nobility'; see **Adelaide**. The name *Alice* has been in regular use in Britain since the 12th century; in 1865 its popularity increased with the publication of Lewis Carroll's *Alice's Adventures in Wonderland*.
Variants: **Ailis, Alicia, Alison, Alix, Allison**.
Diminutives: **Allie, Ally**.

Related names: **Adelaide, Heidi.**

**Alicia** the Latinized form of **Alice.**

**Alick** a diminutive of **Alexander.**

**Aline, Alina** diminutives of **Adeline.**
Variants: **Arleen, Arlene, Arline.**

**Alison, Allison** variants of **Alice.** Originally a French diminutive of *Alice*, dating back to the 13th century, *Alison* is now used as a name in its own right and is particularly popular in Scotland.
Diminutives: **Ailie, Allie, Ally.**

**Alistair, Alasdair, Alastair** variants of **Alexander.** *Alasdair* is the original Scottish Gaelic form of the name.
Diminutives: **Al, Allie, Ally.**

**Alix** a variant of **Alice,** of French origin. The name is also used as a diminutive of **Alexandra.**

**Allan** see **Alan.**

**Allegra** (f) an Italian word meaning 'cheerful' or 'lively'; its use as a first name in English-speaking countries was probably influenced by the musical term *allegro*. The poet Byron gave the name to an illegitimate daughter born in 1817; it has been used occasionally since then.

**Allen** see **Alan.**

**Allie** see **Ally.**

**Allison** see **Alison.**

**Ally, Allie** diminutives of a number of masculine and feminine names beginning with *Al-*, notably **Alan, Alistair, Alice,** and **Alison.**

**Alma** (f) possibly from Latin, meaning 'kind', or from Italian, meaning 'soul'. The name was rarely used until the Battle of Alma (1854) in the Crimean War, after which it became very fashionable.

**Aloisia** see **Aloysia.**

**Alonso, Alonzo** variants of **Alphonso.**
Diminutive: **Lonnie.**

**Aloysia, Aloisia** feminine forms of **Aloysius.**
Variants: **Eloise, Eloisa.**

**Aloysius** [alō*ish*ŭs] a variant of **Louis,** from the Provençal form of the name. It has been used by Roman Catholics in Britain since the 16th century, in honour of the Italian saint Aloysius of Gonzaga (1568–91).
Feminine forms: **Aloisia, Aloysia.**

**Alphonse** a variant of **Alphonso;** the full name of the gangster Al Capone.

**Alphonsine** the feminine form of **Alphonso.**

**Alphonso, Alfonso** (m) from the Old German name *Adalfuns,* derived from *athàl* 'noble' and *funsa* 'ready'. The name has been in use in Spain since the 7th century; it is occasionally found in Britain and the USA.

# Alphonsus

Variants: **Alonso, Alonzo, Alphonse, Alphonsus.**
Feminine form: **Alphonsine.**

**Alphonsus** a variant of **Alphonso.**

**Althea** (f) from Greek, meaning 'wholesome'; ultimately from the verb 'to heal'. (*Althaia* was the Greek name for the marsh mallow plant, valued for its healing powers; its Latin name is *Althaea officinalis*.) In Greek mythology Althea was the mother of Meleager, whose heroic exploits are related in the *Iliad*. The name was popularized in the mid-17th century by Richard Lovelace's poem 'To Althea, from Prison' and remains in regular use. See also **Alethea.**

**Alun** the Welsh form of **Alan.**

**Alured** a variant of **Alfred**, from the Latinized form of the name.

**Alva** (f) a feminine form of **Alvin.**

**Alva** (m) probably from Hebrew, meaning either 'brightness' or 'exalted'; mentioned in the Old Testament in the form *Alvah*. The name was borne by the prolific US inventor Thomas Alva Edison (1847–1931), who is generally remembered for the development of the electric light bulb.

**Alvah** see **Alva** (m).

**Alvar** (m) from Old English, meaning 'elf army'. The name appears in the Domesday Book of 1086; it was revived in Britain in the mid-20th century, when it was born by the newscaster Alvar Liddell.

**Alvie** a diminutive of **Alvin** or **Alvina.**

**Alvin** (m) from one of two Old English names, *Aethelwine* or *Aelfwine*, compounds of *aethel* 'noble' or *aelf* 'elf' and *wine* 'friend'. The various forms of the name that were in existence after the Norman Conquest gave rise to a number of surnames, which were subsequently readopted as first names.
Variants: **Alwyn, Aylwin, Elvin, Elwyn.**
Diminutive: **Alvie.**
Feminine forms: **Alva, Alvina.**

**Alvina** a feminine form of **Alvin.**
Diminutive: **Alvie.**

**Alvis** (m) a name of uncertain origin. It may be from a Scandinavian language, meaning 'all-wise', a theory supported by the occurrence of the name in Norse mythology; its use in the 20th century was possibly influenced by the Alvis motor car.
Variant: **Elvis.**

**Alwyn** a variant of **Alvin.**

**Alys** the Welsh form of **Alice.**

**Amabel** (f) from Latin *amabilis* 'lovable'. The name was in frequent use during the Middle Ages and enjoyed a brief revival in the 19th century; it was eventually superseded by its diminutive form **Mabel.**

Variants: Annabel, Annabella, Annabollo, Arabella
Diminutives: Bel, Bell, Belle, Mabel, Mabella, Mabelle, Mable.

**Amalia** the Italian form of **Amelia**.

**Amalie** the German form of **Amelia**.

**Amanda** (f) from Latin, meaning 'lovable' or 'worthy of love'. The name may have been in existence since the Middle Ages, though many scholars believe it to have been invented in the late 17th century by the British dramatist Colley Cibber for a character in his play *Love's Last Shift*. It subsequently featured in a number of other literary works, notably in Noel Coward's *Private Lives*, and was regularly used as a first name, becoming particularly popular in the mid-20th century.
Diminutive: **Mandy**.

**Amaryllis** (f) a name frequently given to country girls in the works of Virgil, Ovid, and other classical poets and in pastoral poems of the 17th century, such as Milton's *Lycidas*. It is rarely used in modern times, being more readily associated with the genus of lily-like plants that bears the same name.

**Amata** a Latinized form of **Amy**.

**Amber** (f) from the name of the yellowish resin used to make jewellery and ornaments; one of a number of jewel names that became fashionable in the 19th century. It was further popularized in the mid-20th century by the US writer Kathleen Winsor's novel *Forever Amber* (1944).

**Ambrose** (m) from Greek, meaning 'immortal'. Famous bearers of the name include St Ambrose, Bishop of Milan in the 4th century, and the 5th-century British military leader Ambrosius Aurelianus, a possible prototype of King Arthur. *Ambrosius*, the Latinized form of the name, also occurs in Arthurian legend in connection with the wizard **Merlin**. The name has been in regular use in Britain since the 11th century but has never been common.
Variant: **Emrys**.
Feminine forms: **Ambrosina, Ambrosine**.

**Ambrosine, Ambrosina** feminine forms of **Ambrose**, of French origin.

**Ambrosius** see **Ambrose**.

**Amelia** (f) possibly from the Old German name *Amalburga*, ultimately from *amal* 'labour'; influenced by the Latin name *Aemilia* (see **Emily**). *Amelia* was rarely used in Britain before the 18th century, when it was popularized by the Hanoverians, notably King George III's daughter Princess Amelia, and by Henry Fielding's novel of the same name; it remained in regular use in English-speaking countries until the end of the 19th century.
Variants: **Amalia, Amalie, Emily**.
Diminutives: **Millie, Milly**.

# Amias

Related name: **Emmeline.**

**Amias** see **Amyas.**

**Amice** (f) a name of uncertain origin: it may be a French form of the Latin name *Amica*, meaning 'friend', or it may simply be a variant of **Amy.**
Variant: **Amicia.**

**Amicia** the Latinized form of *Amice.*

**Aminta** (f) a literary invention of the 17th century, possibly inspired by a Greek name meaning 'protector'.
Diminutive: **Minty.**

**Amos** (m) from Hebrew, meaning 'carried'. Amos was an Old Testament prophet of the 8th century BC; the name was revived after the Reformation and remained in regular use until the early 20th century.

**Amy** (f) from the Old French name *Amée*, ultimately from Latin *amatus* 'loved'. The name has been in use since the 13th century, when a Latinized form was popularized by St Amata of Bologna. Its return to fashion in the 19th century was probably influenced by the novels *Kenilworth*, by Sir Walter Scott, and *Little Women*, by Louisa M. Alcott, both of which featured a leading character called Amy. Although *Little Women* was written by an American, the name did not become popular in the USA until the latter half of the 20th century, when it also enjoyed a revival in Britain.
Variants: **Aimee, Amata, Amice, Amicia.**
Masculine equivalent: **Amyas.**
Related name: **Esme.**

**Amyas, Amias** [*ay*miăs] (m) from the Old French name *Amé*, ultimately from Latin *amatus* 'loved'. The name dates back at least to the 12th century and was used by the British writer Charles Kingsley for the hero of his novel *Westward Ho!* (1855).
Feminine equivalent: **Amy.**
Related name: **Esme.**

**Anastasia** (f) from Greek, meaning 'resurrection'. One of the earliest bearers of the name was the 4th-century martyr St Anastasia, whose festival coincides with Christmas Day. In modern times, however, the name is generally associated with a daughter of Tsar Nicholas II, the last emperor of Russia, who may have survived the massacre of her family in 1918. The name has been used in the British Isles, especially Ireland, since the 13th century, sometimes occurring in the forms *Anstey* or *Anstice*; it eventually spread to other parts of the English-speaking world and remains in occasional use.
Diminutives: **Stacey, Stacy.**

**Ancel** see **Lancelot**.

**André** the French form of **Andrew**, occasionally used in English-speaking countries.

**Andrea** a feminine form of **Andrew**, dating back to the 17th century.

**Andreas** a variant of **Andrew**.

**Andrée** the French feminine form of **Andrew**, occasionally used in English-speaking countries.

**Andrew** (m) from Greek, meaning 'manly'. One of the earliest and most famous bearers of the name was St Andrew, an apostle of Jesus Christ who later became patron saint of Scotland and gave his name to the Scottish city of St Andrews; the name has consequently been popular in that country for many hundreds of years. It was in frequent use throughout Britain during the Middle Ages and subsequently spread to the USA, where it was borne by two presidents, Andrew Jackson (1767–1845) and Andrew Carnegie (1835–1919). In the latter half of the 20th century, after the birth of Queen Elizabeth II's third child, Prince Andrew, in 1960, it was one of the most common boys' names in the English-speaking world.
Variants: **André**, **Andreas**.
Diminutives: **Andy**, **Drew**.
Feminine forms: **Andrea**, **Andrée**.

**Andy** a diminutive of **Andrew**, sometimes used as a name in its own right.

**Aneira** the feminine form of **Aneurin**.

**Aneurin, Aneirin** [ănyrin] (m) a Welsh name of uncertain origin: it may be derived from the Latin name *Honorius*, meaning 'man of honour', or from Welsh *eur* 'gold'. Famous bearers of the name include a Welsh poet of the 6th century and the 20th-century Labour politician Aneurin Bevan, architect of Britain's National Health Service.
Diminutive: **Nye**.
Feminine form: **Aneira**.
Related name: **Honor**.

**Angel** (m *or* f) from Greek, meaning 'messenger' or 'angel'. Popularized as a masculine name in Sicily by a 13th-century saint, *Angel* did not reach Britain until the 16th century; it fell from favour in the 17th century, as a result of the Puritans' disapproval of the name, and has rarely been used since then. Its most famous bearer is the fictional character Angel Clare, hero of Thomas Hardy's novel *Tess of the D'Urbervilles* (1891). *Angel* is sometimes used as a feminine name in place of **Angela**.
Variant: (m) **Angelo**.
Feminine form: **Angela**.

**Angela** the feminine form of **Angel**. The name was borne by an Italian saint, Angela Merici, foundress of the Ursuline order of nuns at Brescia in 1535,

and was introduced into Britain in the 17th century. Little used until the 19th century, it has been popular throughout the English-speaking world since the 1920s.
Variants: **Angelina, Angeline**.
Diminutive: **Angie**.

**Angelica** (f) from Latin *angelicus* 'angelic'. The name occurs in the Italian poet Ariosto's epic *Orlando Furioso* (1532), which deals in part with the love of Charlemagne's paladin Orlando (Roland) for Angelica. It was popular in Britain in the 18th century and remains in occasional use.
Variant: **Angelique**.
Diminutive: **Angie**.

**Angelina, Angeline** variants of **Angela**. Originally an Italian diminutive of the name, *Angelina* was popular in the 19th century; it was superseded in the 1930s by the French form, *Angeline*.

**Angelique** a variant of **Angelica**, from the French form of the name.

**Angelo** the Italian form of **Angel** (m). The name is sometimes found in English-speaking countries, particularly in US families of Italian descent.

**Angharad** (f) from Welsh, meaning 'much loved'. The name features in the *Mabinogion*, a collection of medieval Welsh folk tales; its most famous bearer in modern times is the Welsh actress Angharad Rees.

**Angie** a diminutive of **Angela** or **Angelica**.

**Angus** (m) from the Gaelic name *Aonghus*, meaning 'one choice'. Once popular in Ireland, the name is now generally associated with Scotland, where it has also been given to a breed of black cattle, the Aberdeen Angus, and to a former Tayside county. See also **Aeneas**.

**Anis, Annis, Annice** variants of **Agnes**, reflecting an early pronunciation of the name; sometimes erroneously associated with **Ann**.

**Anita** a variant of **Ann**. Originally a Spanish diminutive of the name, *Anita* became popular throughout the English-speaking world in the mid-20th century.

**Ann, Anne** variants of **Hannah**. The name was introduced into Britain in the 13th century as a development of **Anna** and was popularized in the 14th century by the cult of St Anne; it has been in frequent use at all levels of society throughout the English-speaking world since the early 16th century. The form of the name varies with fashion: 19th-century parents favoured the English spelling, *Ann*, whereas in the mid-20th century *Anne*, the French form, was more common. Royal bearers of the name include two of the wives of King Henry VIII, Anne Boleyn and Anne of Cleves; Queen Anne, the last monarch of the Stuart dynasty; and Princess Anne, daughter of Queen Elizabeth II.
Variants: **Anita, Annette, Annika, Anouska, Nancy, Nanette, Nina**.
Diminutives: **Annie, Nan, Nanny**.

**Anna** a variant of **Hannah**, of Greek origin. Anna was the sister of Dido, Queen of Carthage, in Virgil's *Aeneid*; the name was also borne by a New Testament prophetess and, according to an apocryphal gospel, by the mother of the Virgin Mary, known in English-speaking countries as St Anne. The name was very popular in the Byzantine Empire and gradually spread to other parts of Europe, entering Britain in the 13th century (see **Ann**). As the Latinized form of *Ann*, *Anna* became fashionable in the English-speaking world in the 19th century and has remained in regular use since then. The British actress Dame Anna Neagle, whose real name is Marjorie Wilcox, is one of the most famous bearers of the name in the 20th century.

Variant: **Anya**.

**Annabel, Annabelle** variants of **Amabel**, sometimes erroneously associated with **Ann**. *Annabel* has been common in Scotland, where it occasionally appears in the form *Annaple*, since the Middle Ages; it was borne by the mother of King James I of Scotland, Annabel Drummond. The popularity of Edgar Allan Poe's poem 'Annabel Lee' helped to spread the name to the rest of the English-speaking world in the 19th century; the form *Annabelle* has been in use since the mid-20th century.

Variant: **Annabella**.

Diminutives: **Bel, Bell, Belle**.

**Annabella** the Latinized form of **Annabel**; a variant of **Amabel**. The name is sometimes erroneously interpreted as a compound of **Anna** and Latin *bella* 'beautiful'.

Diminutive: **Bella**.

**Annabelle** see **Annabel**.

**Annalisa** a variant of **Anneliese**.

**Annaple** see **Annabel**.

**Anne** see **Ann**.

**Anneliese** (f) a German name, derived from a compound of **Anna** and *Liesa* (a German diminutive of **Elizabeth**).

Variant: **Annalisa**.

**Annette** a variant of **Ann**; originally a French diminutive of the name.

**Annice** see **Anis**.

**Annie** a diminutive of **Ann**, often used as an independent name in the late 19th century. The name has been popularized in music by the traditional folk song 'Annie Laurie' and, more recently, by the US singer and songwriter John Denver's 'Annie's Song'; it also featured in the musicals *Annie Get Your Gun*, the story of the US markswoman Annie Oakley (1860–1926), and *Annie*, based on the US cartoonist Harold Gray's comic strip 'Little Orphan Annie'.

# Annika

**Annika** a variant of **Ann**; originally a Swedish diminutive of the name.

**Annis** see **Anis**.

**Annora** a variant of **Honor**; sometimes erroneously associated with **Ann**. One of the most common forms of the name in the Middle Ages, it has been in occasional use since the Reformation.

**Anona** (f) a name of uncertain origin: it may be from Latin *annona* 'grain harvest' or it may be a compound of **Ann** and **Nona**. Its most famous bearer is the British radio personality Anona Winn.

**Anouska** a variant of **Ann**; originally a Russian diminutive of the name.

**Ansel, Ansell** variants of *Ancel* (see **Lancelot**) or **Anselm**.

**Anselm** (m) from the Old German name *Ansehelm*, derived from *ansi* 'god' and *helma* 'helmet'. The name was introduced into Britain by St Anselm, who became Archbishop of Canterbury in 1093; it was revived in the 19th century but has been used only occasionally since then.
Variants: **Ansel, Ansell**.
Feminine form: **Anselma**.

**Anselma** the feminine form of **Anselm**.

**Anstice, Anstey** see **Anastasia**.

**Anthea** (f) from Greek, meaning 'flowery'. One of the titles borne by the goddess Hera in Greek mythology, the name was revived in the 17th century by the pastoral poets. It was in regular use in Britain in the mid-20th century.

**Anthony** [antŏni, (US) anthŏni], **Antony** (m) from the Roman clan name *Antonius*, of unknown origin. The spelling *Anthony* dates back to the 17th century, when the name was erroneously associated with Greek *anthos* 'flower'. One of the earliest bearers of the name was the Roman triumvir Mark Antony, whose love for the Egyptian queen Cleopatra was immortalized by Shakespeare in the play *Antony and Cleopatra*. Popularized by two saints, an Egyptian hermit of the 4th century and St Antony of Padua (1195–1231), the name has been in regular use in the English-speaking world since the 12th century.
Variants: **Antoine, Anton, Antonio**.
Diminutive: **Tony**.
Feminine forms: **Antoinette, Antonia, Antonina**.

**Antoine** the French form of **Anthony**, occasionally used in the USA.

**Antoinette** a feminine form of **Anthony**, of French origin. The name is generally associated with the French queen Marie Antoinette, wife of King Louis XVI, who was guillotined during the French Revolution. It has been in regular use in the English-speaking world since the mid-19th century.
Diminutive: **Toni**.

**Anton** the German or Russian form of **Anthony**, borne by thé Russian dramatist Anton Chekhov (1860–1904). The name is occasionally found in English-speaking countries.

**Antonia, Antonina** feminine forms of **Anthony**, borne by two saints of the 3rd century. *Antonia* is the more common form of the name in English-speaking countries, its most famous bearer in modern times being the British writer Lady Antonia Fraser.
Diminutive: **Toni, Tonia, Tonya**.

**Antonio** the Italian or Spanish form of **Anthony**, occasionally used in the USA.

**Antony** see **Anthony**.

**Anwen** (f) a Welsh name, meaning 'very beautiful'.

**Anya** a variant of **Anna**, borne by the British novelist Anya Seton.

**Aphra** (f) from Hebrew, meaning 'dust'. A reference in the Authorized Version of the Old Testament to 'the house of Aphrah', meaning 'the house of dust', led to a misinterpretation of the word as a first name. Aphra Behn, a British dramatist and novelist of the 17th century, is one of the earliest known bearers of the name. See also **Afra**.

**Apollonia** (f) from Greek, meaning 'of Apollo'. St Apollonia, a 3rd-century martyr whose various torments included that of having her teeth knocked out, has often been invoked against toothache. The name was in occasional use until the early 20th century.
Variants: **Appolina, Appoline**.

**Appoline, Appolina** variants of **Apollonia**.

**April** (f) from the name of the fourth month of the year; one of a number of month names that became fashionable in the 20th century.
Related name: **Avril**.

**Aquila** (m) from Latin, meaning 'eagle'. The name was borne by a number of Romans and early Christians and is mentioned in the New Testament; its use in English-speaking countries dates back to the 17th century.

**Arabella** probably a variant of **Annabel**, though some scholars believe the name to be derived from Latin *orabilis* 'yielding to prayer'. It was popular in Scotland during and after the Middle Ages, one of its most famous bearers being Lady Arabella Stuart, cousin of King James VI of Scotland. The name became fashionable in England at the end of the 18th century but is rarely found in other parts of the English-speaking world.
Diminutive: **Bella**.

**Araminta** (f) possibly a compound of **Arabella** and **Aminta**, invented by the Restoration dramatist Sir John Vanbrugh or one of his contemporaries.
Diminutive: **Minty**.

**Archelaus** [arki*lay*ŭs] (m) from Greek, meaning 'ruler of the people'. The name was borne by a Greek philosopher and a Macedonian king, both of

**Archer**

the 5th century BC, and by one of the sons of King Herod the Great, mentioned in the New Testament. It was revived in the 19th century and has been in occasional use since then.

**Archer** (m) from a surname originally borne by skilled archers of the Middle Ages; ultimately from Latin *arcus* 'bow'. It has been in occasional use as a first name since the 19th century.

**Archibald** (m) from the Old German name *Ercanbald*, a compound of *ercan* 'true' and *bald* 'bold'; probably influenced by Greek names beginning with *Archi-*, such as *Archimedes*. Introduced into Britain at the time of the Norman Conquest, *Archibald* replaced an Old English form of the name that had been in use since the 7th century. It was particularly popular in Scotland, where the second part of the name was sometimes interpreted as a reference to the shaven head of a monk, and remained in regular use in that country until the mid-20th century.

Diminutives: **Archie, Archy, Baldie**.

**Archie, Archy** diminutives of **Archibald**, sometimes used as independent names. *Archie*, the more common spelling of the name in Britain, was popularized by a ventriloquist's dummy in the radio programme 'Educating Archie'. The US poet and dramatist Don Marquis gave the alternative form of the name to a philosophical cockroach in *Archy and Mehitabel* (1927).

**Ariadne** [ariadni] (f) from Greek, meaning 'very holy'. The daughter of King Minos of Crete in Greek mythology, Ariadne helped Theseus to escape from the labyrinth after killing the Minotaur. The name and its variants are occasionally found in English-speaking countries.

Variants: **Ariane, Arianna**.

**Ariane** the French form of **Ariadne**.

**Arianna** the Italian form of **Ariadne**.

**Arlene, Arleen** see **Arline**.

**Arletta** the Latinized form of **Arlette**.

**Arlette** (f) a French name of uncertain origin; possibly derived from a feminine diminutive of **Charles**. It has been in use in the English-speaking world since the mid-19th century.

Variant: **Arletta**.

**Arline, Arlene, Arleen** probably variants of **Aline**; other possible derivations include a Celtic word meaning 'pledge' and a feminine form of **Charles**. The name has been in regular use since the early 20th century.

**Armand** the French form of **Herman**.

**Armin** a variant of **Herman**.

**Armine, Armina** feminine forms of **Herman**.

**Arnaud** the French form of **Arnold**.

**Arnold** (m) from Old German, meaning 'eagle power'. The name was introduced into Britain at the time of the Norman Conquest and remained in regular use until the end of the 13th century, giving rise to a number of surnames. Its revival in the late 19th century has been attributed to the popularity of the British poet and critic Matthew Arnold.
Variant: **Arnaud**.

**Art** a diminutive of **Arthur**.

**Artemas, Artemus** (m) a Greek name mentioned in the New Testament; probably connected with the goddess Artemis (see **Artemisia**). It was popularized by the US humorist Charles Farrar Browne, who adopted the pseudonym Artemus Ward in the mid-19th century.

**Artemisia** [artĕ*meezi*ă] (f) from Greek, meaning 'of Artemis' (Artemis was the Greek counterpart of the Roman goddess **Diana**). Artemisia, Queen of Caria, was responsible for the erection of the Mausoleum of Halicarnassus, one of the Seven Wonders of the World, in the 4th century BC. The name has been in occasional use in Britain since the mid-18th century.

**Artemus** see **Artemas**.

**Arthur** (m) a name of uncertain origin: it may be derived from Celtic *artos* 'bear', from Irish *art* 'stone', or from the Roman clan name *Artorius*. The earliest occurrence of the name in historical records refers to an Irish prince of the 6th century; the legend of King Arthur, undoubtedly the most famous bearer of the name, dates back to the early 9th century. Mentioned in various forms in the Domesday Book of 1086, the name was in regular use in Britain until the 14th century. Despite the publication in 1485 of Sir Thomas Malory's version of the Arthurian legend and the birth of King Henry VII's first son, Prince Arthur, in 1486, the name did not come back into fashion until the 19th century, when it was popularized by Arthur Wellesley, Duke of Wellington. In the early 20th century it was one of the most common masculine first names in the English-speaking world.
Diminutives: **Art, Artie, Arty**.
Feminine forms: **Arthuretta, Arthurina, Arthurine**.

**Arthurine, Arthurina, Arthuretta** feminine forms of **Arthur**.

**Artie, Arty** diminutives of **Arthur**.

**Asa** [*ayz*ă, *ays*ă] (m) from Hebrew, meaning 'physician'; borne in the Old Testament by a king of Judah. The name was revived by the Puritans in the 17th century and remains in occasional use, its most famous bearer in modern times being the historian Asa Briggs.

**Asher** (m) from Hebrew, meaning 'happy'. In the Old Testament Asher was one of the sons of Jacob by Zilpah, the maidservant of his wife Leah. The name has been in occasional use since its revival by the Puritans in the 17th century.

**Ashley** (m or f) from a surname and place name; ultimately from Old English, meaning 'ash wood'. Its popularity as a masculine first name has been attributed to a character in the immensely successful novel *Gone with the Wind* (1936), by the US writer Margaret Mitchell, which was filmed in 1939. *Ashley* is sometimes used as a feminine name, particularly in the USA.

**Aspasia** (f) from Greek, meaning 'welcome'. The name was borne in the 5th century BC by the mistress of the Athenian statesman Pericles; it also featured in a play by the 17th-century dramatists Beaumont and Fletcher, *The Maid's Tragedy*, and has been used occasionally since then.

**Astra** (f) from Latin *astralis* 'of the stars'; ultimately from Greek *astron* 'star'.

**Astrid** (f) a Scandinavian name, derived from one of two Germanic compounds, meaning 'divine strength' or 'divine beauty'. Borne by the mother of Olaf I, King of Norway, and by the Swedish wife of Olaf II (St Olaf), patron saint of Norway, the name has been in use in the royal families of Scandinavia for many hundreds of years. It is occasionally found in Britain and other parts of the English-speaking world.

**Athelstan** (m) from the Old English name *Aethelstan*, a compound of *aethel* 'noble' and *stan* 'stone', borne by an Anglo-Saxon king of the 10th century. It was revived in the early 19th century, when Sir Walter Scott used the name in his novel *Ivanhoe*, and has been in occasional use since then.

**Athene** [ătheenee] (f) the name of the Greek goddess of war and wisdom, after whom the city of Athens was named; sometimes used as a first name in English-speaking countries.

**Athol** (m) from a surname derived from the Scottish place name *Atholl*. It has been in occasional use as a first name since the late 19th century.

**Auberon** (m) probably a diminutive of the Old French name *Auberi* (see **Aubrey**), though some scholars believe the name to be derived from a compound of two Old German words meaning 'noble' and 'bear-like'. Auberon was the king of the fairies in medieval romance (Shakespeare altered the spelling to *Oberon* in *A Midsummer Night's Dream*); the most famous bearer of the name in modern times is the 20th-century British writer Auberon Waugh.

**Aubert** see **Albert**.

**Aubrey** (m) from Old French *Auberi*, a form of the Old German name *Alberich*, meaning 'elf ruler'. It was introduced into Britain by Aubrey de Vere, a companion of William the Conqueror whose grandson became the Earl of Oxford; both the name and the earldom remained in the family for many hundreds of years. A more recent bearer was the British actor C. Aubrey Smith (1863–1948). The name sometimes occurs in the form *Alberic*.
Variant: **Auberon**.

**Aud** a diminutive of **Audrey**.

**Audra** a variant of **Audrey**.

**Audrey** a variant of **Etheldreda**; originally a diminutive of the name, dating back to the 16th century. The word *tawdry*, meaning 'showy but worthless', derives from a reference to the cheap goods sold at St Audrey's fair in Ely (St Audrey was the name by which St Etheldreda had come to be known). *Audrey* was particularly popular in the first half of the 20th century: one of the most famous bearers of the name, the actress Audrey Hepburn, was born in 1929.
Variant: **Audra**.
Diminutive: **Aud**.

**August** [ow*goost*] the German form of **Augustus**, occasionally used in English-speaking countries. It is sometimes erroneously associated with the name of the eighth month of the year.

**Augusta** the feminine form of **Augustus**; originally borne by the female relatives of Roman emperors. The name was popularized in Britain by the mother of King George III, Augusta of Saxe-Gotha, and remained in regular use until the early 20th century.
Diminutives: **Gussie, Gusta**.
Related name: **Augustina**.

**Augustin** see **Augustine**.

**Augustina** the feminine form of **Augustine**.
Diminutive: **Gussie**.
Related name: **Augusta**.

**Augustine, Augustin** (m) from Latin *augustus* 'venerable'. The name was borne by two saints: Augustine of Hippo, who served as Bishop of Hippo until his death in 430, and the first Archbishop of Canterbury, sent to Britain as a missionary by Pope Gregory I in the late 6th century. During the Middle Ages *Augustine* was largely superseded by **Austin**; the original form of the name was revived in the 19th century and remains in occasional use.
Variants: **Austen, Austin**.
Diminutives: **Gus, Gussie**.

# Augustus

Feminine form: **Augustina**.
Related name: **Augustus**.

**Augustus** (m) from Latin, meaning 'venerable'; a title first bestowed on the
Roman emperor Octavian in 27 BC and subsequently borne by his suc-
cessors in that office. The name was given to a number of German princes
after the Renaissance; it was introduced into Britain by the Hanoverians
in the early 18th century and remained popular until the end of the 19th
century.
Variant: **August**.
Diminutives: **Gus, Gussie**.
Feminine form: **Augusta**.
Related name: **Augustine**.

**Aulay** a variant of **Olaf**; from *Amhblaibh*, the Scottish Gaelic form of the
name. It has given rise to a number of surnames, such as *Macaulay* and
*McAuliffe*, and remains in occasional use as a first name in Scotland.

**Aurea** (f) from Latin *aureus* 'golden'. The name is sometimes regarded as a
variant of **Aurora**.

**Aurelia** (f) the feminine form of the Roman clan name *Aurelius*; ultimately
from Latin *aurum* 'gold'. It has been in occasional use in Britain since the
17th century.
Variant: **Auriol**.

**Aurelian** (m) from the Latin name *Aurelianus*; ultimately from *aurum*
'gold'. Borne by a Roman emperor of the 3rd century, the name has been
in infrequent use in the English-speaking world since the Renaissance.

**Aureola, Aureole** see **Auriel**.

**Auriel** (f) a name of uncertain origin: it may be a variant of the 17th-century
names *Aureola* and *Aureole*, from Latin *aureolus* 'golden', or it may be
associated with **Oriel**. *Auriel* has been in regular use in Britain since the
19th century.
Variant: **Auriol**.

**Auriol** a variant of **Aurelia** or **Auriel**.

**Aurora** (f) the name of the Roman goddess of the dawn. It has been in
occasional use since the Renaissance, popularized by the heroine of
Charles Perrault's fairy tale 'The Sleeping Beauty' and by Elizabeth Barrett Browning's poem *Aurora Leigh* (1856). See also **Dawn**.
Variants: **Aurea, Aurore**.

**Aurore** the French form of **Aurora**.

**Austen** see **Austin**.

**Austin** a variant of **Augustine**; the usual form of the name in medieval
Britain. It fell from favour after the Reformation but survived as a surname, sometimes in the form *Austen*. Both spellings have been used as

first names in modern times, a famous example being the British statesman Sir Austen Chamberlain (1863–1937).

**Ava** probably a variant of **Eva**, from the European pronunciation of the
name. It was popularized in the mid-20th century by the US actress Ava
Gardner.

**Aveline** see **Evelina, Evelyn.**

**Averil** (f) from the Old English name *Everild*, derived from *eofor* 'boar' and
*hild* 'battle', borne by a 7th-century Yorkshire saint. *Averil*, the modern
form of the name, has been in use since the 17th century. See also **Avril.**

**Avery** a variant of **Alfred.**

**Avis, Avice** (f) a name of uncertain origin, probably introduced into Britain
at the time of the Norman Conquest. It may be from one of two Old
German names or from the feminine form of the Roman name *Avitius*;
*Avis*, the more common spelling of the name in modern times, has been
associated with Latin *avis* 'bird'.

**Avril** (f) from French *avril* 'April'. Sometimes regarded as a variant of **Averil**, the name has been in regular use in English-speaking countries since
the early 20th century.
Related name: **April.**

**Axel** (m) a Scandinavian name of uncertain origin, in occasional use in the
English-speaking world.

**Aylmer** (m) from the Old English name *Aethelmaer*, a compound of *aethel*
'noble' and *maer* 'famous'; probably influenced by an Old German name
introduced into Britain at the time of the Norman Conquest. In regular
use as a first name during the Middle Ages, *Aylmer* is more frequently
found as a surname in modern times.
Variant: **Elmer.**

**Aylwin** a variant of **Alvin.**

**Azariah** (m) from Hebrew, meaning 'whom God helps'; borne by a number
of Old Testament characters, including one of the kings of Judah. The
name has been in occasional use in English-speaking countries since the
17th century.

# B

**Bab** a diminutive of **Barbara**.

**Babette** a variant of **Elizabeth**; originally a French diminutive of the name.

**Babs** a diminutive of **Barbara**.

**Baldie** a diminutive of **Archibald**.

**Baldwin** (m) from the Old German name *Baldavin* or its Old English equivalent *Bealdwine*, meaning 'bold friend'. *Baldwin* was in frequent use in medieval Britain, giving rise to a number of surnames, but is rarely found as a first name today.

**Balthasar, Balthazar** (m) the Greek form of the Old Testament name *Belshazzar*, meaning 'Bel (a Babylonian god) protect the king'. According to legend, Balthasar was one of the Magi mentioned in the story of the Nativity (Matthew 2:1), whose cult was probably responsible for the popularity of the name in medieval Europe. It has been used only occasionally in English-speaking countries.

**Barbara** (f) from Greek *barbaros* 'foreign' or 'strange', a word originally used in imitation of the incomprehensible language of those who did not speak Greek. The popularity of the name in medieval Britain, where it often occurred in the form *Barbary*, has been attributed to the cult of the 3rd-century martyr St Barbara. Having fallen from favour after the Reformation, the name was rarely used until the early 20th century, when it became fashionable throughout the English-speaking world.
Variant: **Barbra**.
Diminutives: **Bab, Babs, Barbie, Baubie, Bobbie**.

**Barbary** see **Barbara**.

**Barbie** a diminutive of **Barbara**.

**Barbra** a variant of **Barbara**, popularized by the US singer Barbra Streisand (born 1942).

**Barclay** see **Berkeley**.

**Bardolph** (m) from the Old German name *Berhtolf*, meaning 'bright wolf'. Introduced into Britain at the time of the Norman Conquest, *Bardolph* replaced its Old English equivalent, *Beorhtwulf*, and gave rise to a number of surnames. It is rarely used as a first name today.

**Barnabas** (m) from Hebrew, meaning 'son of consolation' or 'son of exhortation'; borne by the New Testament apostle who accompanied St Paul on his early missionary journeys. The name has been in occasional use in Britain and other parts of the English-speaking world since the early 13th century.
Variant: **Barnaby**.
Diminutive: **Barney**.

**Barnaby** a variant of **Barnabas**; the usual form of the name in English-speaking countries. Popularized in the mid-19th century by Charles Dickens' novel *Barnaby Rudge*, it enjoyed a further revival in the 1960s.
Diminutive: **Barney**.

**Barnard** a variant of **Bernard**. A common form of the name in medieval Britain, it remains in occasional use today.
Diminutive: **Barney**.

**Barnet** (m) a name of uncertain origin: it may be from a surname and place name, ultimately from an Old English word meaning 'burning', or it may simply be a variant of **Bernard**.

**Barney** a diminutive of **Barnabas**, **Barnaby**, or **Barnard**.

**Baron, Barron** (m) either from a surname originally borne by members of a baron's family or household or from the title itself. The name is sometimes given to add distinction to a common surname, such as *Smith*.

**Barrett** (m) either from a surname of uncertain origin or from a form of the Old German name *Beroald*, meaning 'bear power', introduced into Britain at the time of the Norman Conquest. In regular use during the 19th century, *Barrett* is rarely found as a first name today.

**Barrie** see **Barry**.

**Barrington** (m) from a surname and place name of uncertain origin; occasionally used as a first name in Britain.

**Barron** see **Baron**.

**Barry** (m), **Barrie** (m *or* f) from the Irish name *Bearrach* or *Bearach*, ultimately from the word for 'spear'. Sometimes associated with the Welsh or Scottish place name, *Barry* has been in regular use throughout the English-speaking world since the early 20th century. The less common form *Barrie*, which is occasionally used as a feminine name, may have been inspired by Sir J. M. Barrie, creator of Peter Pan.

**Bart** a diminutive of **Bartholomew**. St Bartholomew's Hospital in London is often referred to as 'Bart's'.

**Bartholomew** (m) from Hebrew, meaning 'son of Talmai (or Tolmai)' (*Talmai* means 'abounding in furrows'). The popularity of the name in 12th-century Britain has been attributed to the cult of St Bartholomew, one of Jesus Christ's apostles (see also **Nathaniel**): St Bartholomew's Hospital in London and the annual Bartholomew Fair, abolished in 1855, date back to this period. The name was fairly common until the mid-19th century and remains in occasional use today.
Diminutives: **Bart, Bartle, Bartlet, Bartlett, Bat, Tolly**.

**Bartlett, Bartlet, Bartle** diminutives of **Bartholomew**, dating back to the 13th century; more frequently found as surnames than as first names in modern times.

**Bas, Baz, Basie** diminutives of **Basil**.

**Basil** (m) from Greek, meaning 'kingly'. One of the earliest bearers of the name was St Basil the Great, Bishop of Caesarea in the latter half of the 4th century. Introduced into Western Europe by the Crusaders, the name was little used in Britain until its revival in the 19th century. It is rarely found in other English-speaking countries. The only connection between the plant name *basil* and the first name is that both are ultimately derived from the same Greek word.
Diminutives: **Bas, Basie, Baz**.
Feminine forms: **Basilia, Basilie, Basilla**.

**Basilia, Basilie, Basilla** feminine forms of **Basil**.

**Bastian** a diminutive of **Sebastian**.

**Bat** a diminutive of **Bartholomew**.

**Bathsheba** (f) from Hebrew, meaning 'voluptuous'; borne by the wife of King David and mother of King Solomon in the Old Testament. Revived by the Puritans after the Reformation, the name remained in regular use until the late 19th century. Bathsheba Everdene is the heroine of Thomas Hardy's novel *Far from the Madding Crowd* (1874).
Diminutive: Sheba.

**Baubie** a Scottish diminutive of **Barbara**.

**Baz** see **Bas**.

**Bea, Bee, Beat** diminutives of **Beatrice** or **Beatrix**.

**Beata** (f) from Latin *beatus* 'happy'. In occasional use in Britain until the 18th century, the name is rarely found in the English-speaking world today.

**Beatrice** [*bee*ătris] a variant of **Beatrix**; the more common form of the name in English-speaking countries since the latter half of the Middle Ages. The character of Beatrice, Dante's guide through Paradise in the *Divina Commedia*, was probably inspired by Beatrice Portinari, the object of the poet's earliest and greatest love. Borne by the youngest daughter of Queen Victoria and Prince Albert, the name was very popular in the late 19th and early 20th centuries and remains in occasional use today.
Diminutives: **Bea, Beat, Beattie, Beatty, Bee, Tris, Trissie**.

**Beatrix** [*bee*ătrix] (f) from Latin, meaning 'bringer of joy'. The name was mentioned in the Domesday Book of 1086 and remained in regular use in Britain, often in the form **Beatrice**, throughout the Middle Ages. Revived in the latter half of the 19th century, it was borne by the children's writer and illustrator Beatrix Potter (1866–1943), creator of Peter Rabbit, Jemima Puddle-Duck, and a host of other animal characters.
Variants: **Beatrice, Bettrys**.
Diminutives: **Bea, Beat, Beattie, Beatty, Bee, Trix, Trixie**.

**Beattie, Beatty** diminutives of **Beatrice** or **Beatrix**. Their occasional use as independent names may be influenced by the surname *Beattie* (or *Beatty*), of uncertain origin.

**Beau** (m) from French, meaning 'handsome'; in occasional use since the mid-20th century, particularly in the USA. Earlier bearers of the name include the 19th-century British dandy Beau Brummell, whose real name was George Bryan Brummell, and Beau Geste, a fictional hero of the Foreign Legion.

**Becky** a diminutive of **Rebecca**, often used as a name in its own right. Its most famous bearer is the fictional character Becky Sharp, the unscrupulous heroine of Thackeray's novel *Vanity Fair* (1848).

**Bedelia** a variant of **Bridget**.
Diminutive: **Delia**.

**Bedford** (m) from an English place name, meaning 'Bede's ford'; in more frequent use as a surname than as a first name.

**Bee** see **Bea**.

**Bel** see **Belle**.

**Belinda** (f) from the Old German name *Betlindis*, the second part of which is derived from *lindi* 'snake'. The name features in plays by the Restoration dramatists William Congreve and Sir John Vanbrugh; it was further popularized in the early 18th century by the heroine of Alexander Pope's poem *The Rape of the Lock* and has been in regular use throughout the English-speaking world since then.
Diminutives: **Bel, Bell, Belle, Linda, Lindy**.

**Bell** see **Belle**.

**Bella** a diminutive of **Annabella, Arabella**, or **Isabella**, sometimes associated with Latin or Italian *bella* 'beautiful' and used as an independent name.

**Belle, Bell, Bel** diminutives of **Amabel, Annabel, Belinda**, or **Isabel**, sometimes associated with French *belle* 'beautiful' and used as independent names.

**Ben** a diminutive of **Benedict** or **Benjamin**, often used as a name in its own right. Famous bearers include the 17th-century dramatist Ben Jonson and Big Ben, the bell in the clock tower of the Houses of Parliament, which was named after the civil servant Sir Benjamin Hall.

**Benedick** a variant of **Benedict**, popularized by a character in Shakespeare's play *Much Ado About Nothing*.

**Benedict** (m) from Latin *benedictus* 'blessed'. One of the earliest known bearers of the name was the 6th-century Italian saint Benedict of Nursia, founder of the Benedictine order of monks and nuns (the famous liqueur was first made at a Benedictine monastery in France). The name was subsequently borne by a number of other saints, including the 7th-century English abbot St Benedict Biscop, and by fifteen popes. Largely superseded in medieval Britain by **Bennet** and its variants, *Benedict* remained in use in Roman Catholic families and was revived in the 20th century.

Variants: **Benedick, Benet, Benito, Bennet, Bennett.**
Diminutives: **Ben, Benny.**
Feminine forms: **Benedicta, Benita.**

**Benedicta** a feminine form of **Benedict**.

**Benet** see **Bennet**.

**Benita** a feminine form of **Benedict**, of Spanish origin; introduced into Britain from the USA in the early 20th century.

**Benito** a variant of **Benedict**; originally a Spanish diminutive of the name. Its most famous bearer, the Italian dictator Benito Mussolini (1883–1945), was named after the 19th-century Mexican president Benito Juárez.

**Benjamin** (m) from Hebrew, meaning 'son of my right hand'; often given to the youngest child of the family. The Benjamin of the Old Testament, Jacob's youngest and favourite son, was originally named *Ben-Oni*, meaning 'son of my sorrow', by his dying mother Rachel. The name became popular in the English-speaking world after the Reformation and remained in regular use until the 19th century, a famous bearer being the British statesman Benjamin Disraeli (1804–81). Its revival in the latter half of the 20th century has been attributed to the central character (played by the US actor Dustin Hoffman) of the immensely successful film *The Graduate* (1967).
Diminutives: **Ben, Benjy, Benny.**

**Benjy** a diminutive of **Benjamin**.

**Bennet, Bennett, Benet** variants of **Benedict**, from the Old French form of the name. After the Norman Conquest *Bennet* and its variants became more common in Britain than *Benedict* itself; they remained in regular use for several hundred years, giving rise to a number of surnames.

**Benny** a diminutive of **Benedict** or **Benjamin**, sometimes used as a name in its own right.

**Bentley** (m) from a surname and place name; ultimately from Old English, meaning 'clearing covered with coarse grass'.

**Berengaria** [berrĕn*gairi*ă] the feminine form of **Berenger**. The name was borne in the 12th century by the wife of Richard the Lionheart; its occasional use in the 20th century has been attributed to the transatlantic liner of the same name.

**Berenger** [*berr*ĕnjer] (m) from the Old German name *Beringer*, a compound of *berin* 'bear' and *ger* 'spear'. The name was fairly common in medieval Britain but is rarely used today.
Feminine form: **Berengaria**.

**Berenice** [berrĕ*nees*, berrĕ*nisee*] (f) from Greek, meaning 'bringer of victory'. The name was borne by the second wife of King Ptolemy I of Egypt and two of her granddaughters and by the sister of King Herod Agrippa II (see **Bernice**). It has been in occasional use in Britain and other parts of the English-speaking world since the Reformation.
Variant: **Bernice**.

**Berkeley** (m) from a surname and place name; ultimately from Old English, meaning 'birch wood'. The name also occurs in the form *Barclay*, from the Scottish spelling of the surname.

**Bernadette** a feminine form of **Bernard**, of French origin. The name became popular in the English-speaking world after the canonization of St Bernadette (Marie Bernarde Soubirous), a French peasant girl whose visions of the Virgin Mary in the mid-19th century led to the establishment of a Roman Catholic shrine at Lourdes.

**Bernadine, Bernadina** feminine forms of **Bernard**.

**Bernard** [*bern*ăd, (US) ber*nard*] (m) from the Old German name *Berinhard*, a compound of *berin* 'bear' and *hard* 'hard'; rendered in Old English as *Beornheard*. The name was borne by several saints: notably, the 11th-century priest St Bernard of Menthon, patron saint of mountaineers, who gave his name to two Alpine passes and a breed of dog used in mountain rescue work, and the 12th-century abbot and theologian St Bernard of Clairvaux. Introduced into Britain at the time of the Norman Conquest, the name was in frequent use until the 17th century; it was revived in the mid-19th century, a famous bearer being the Irish dramatist George Bernard Shaw (1856–1950), and has been regularly used throughout the English-speaking world since then.
Variants: **Barnard, Barnet, Bernhard**.
Diminutives: **Bernie, Berny**.
Feminine forms: **Bernadette, Bernadina, Bernadine, Bernardina, Bernardine**.

**Bernardine, Bernardina** feminine forms of **Bernard**.

**Bernhard** a variant of **Bernard**.

**Bernice** [*bern*is, ber*nees*] a variant of **Berenice**; the more common form of the name in English-speaking countries, especially the USA, in modern times. The Bernice of the New Testament, referred to elsewhere as Berenice, is believed to have had an incestuous relationship with her brother, King Herod Agrippa II.
Diminutives: **Bernie, Berny**.

**Bernie, Berny** diminutives of **Bernard** or **Bernice**.

**Berry** (m *or* f) probably from the name of the fruit; sometimes used as a diminutive of masculine or feminine names beginning with *Ber-*.

# Bert

**Bert** a diminutive of **Bertram**, **Bertrand**, or any name ending in *-bert*, notably **Albert**.

**Berta** a variant of **Bertha**.

**Bertha** (f) from Old German *berhta* or Old English *beorht* 'bright'. A variant form of the name was borne by the Teutonic goddess Berchta (or Perchta), whose feast day coincides with Epiphany; other early bearers include the mother of Charlemagne and the wife of King Ethelbert I. The name has been in regular use in the English-speaking world since the Norman Conquest and was particularly popular in the late 19th and early 20th centuries; its subsequent decline may have been caused by the nickname 'Big Bertha' given to a German howitzer used in World War I.
Variant: **Berta**.

**Berthold** (m) from two Old German words meaning 'bright' and 'power'; in occasional use in English-speaking countries.

**Bertie** a diminutive of **Bertram**, **Bertrand**, or any name ending in *-bert*, notably **Albert**.

**Bertram** (m) from an Old German name derived from *berhta* 'bright' and *hraben* 'raven'. It has been in regular use in Britain since the Norman Conquest but is rarely found in other parts of the English-speaking world.
Variant: **Bertrand**.
Diminutives: **Bert**, **Bertie**.

**Bertrand** the French form of **Bertram**, occasionally used in English-speaking countries, a famous bearer being the British philosopher and mathematician Bertrand Russell (1872–1970). Some scholars believe the second part of the name to be derived from a word meaning 'shield'.
Diminutives: **Bert**, **Bertie**.

**Beryl** (f) from the name of the precious stone; one of a number of jewel names that became fashionable in the 19th century. It was popular in Britain in the early 20th century; the British actress and comedienne Beryl Reid (born 1918) is a famous bearer of the name.

**Bess**, **Bessie**, **Bessy** diminutives of **Elizabeth**, dating back to the 16th century; sometimes used as independent names.

**Beta** a variant of **Elizabeth** in occasional use in the English-speaking world; originally a diminutive of the name found in a number of central and eastern European countries.

**Beth** a diminutive of **Elizabeth**, often used as an independent name; borne by one of the heroines of Louisa M. Alcott's novel *Little Women* (1868). It is also used as a diminutive of **Bethany** or **Bethia**.

**Bethan** (f) a name of uncertain origin: it may be derived from a compound of **Beth** and **Ann** or it may simply be a diminutive of **Bethany** or **Elizabeth**.

**Bethany** (f) from the name of a village near Jerusalem mentioned several times in the New Testament; occasionally used as a first name, particularly in the latter half of the 20th century.

Diminutives: **Beth**, **Bethan**.

**Bethel, Bethell** (m) either from a surname meaning 'son of **Ithel**' or from a biblical place name meaning 'house of God'; in occasional use as a first name.

**Bethia** [*beth*iă, be*thī*ă] (f) from Hebrew, meaning 'daughter (or worshipper) of God'. *Bithiah*, a variant form of the name, occurs in the Old Testament. The name *Bethia* came into regular use in English-speaking countries in the 17th century and was particularly popular in Scotland, where it was associated with Gaelic *beath* 'life'. It is rarely found in modern times.

Diminutive: **Beth**.

**Betsy** a diminutive of **Elizabeth**, often used as a name in its own right.

**Bette** [*beti*, bet] a diminutive of **Elizabeth**, of French origin; now regarded as a variant spelling of **Betty**. Its use by the US actress Bette Davis (born Ruth Elizabeth Davis) was influenced by the French writer Honoré de Balzac's novel *La Cousine Bette* (1846).

**Bettina** a variant of **Elizabeth**; originally an Italian or Spanish diminutive of the name.

**Bettrys** the Welsh form of **Beatrix**.

**Betty** a diminutive of **Elizabeth**, often used as a name in its own right. It was very popular in the 18th century and enjoyed a revival in the early 20th century: in the mid-1920s *Betty* was more common as an independent name than **Elizabeth** itself. The US actress Betty Grable (1916–73) was a famous bearer of the name. See also **Bette**.

**Beulah** [*bewlă*] (f) from Hebrew, meaning 'married'; an Old Testament place name. It was adopted as a first name in English-speaking countries after the Reformation and remains in occasional use, particularly in the USA.

**Beverley** (m *or* f), **Beverly** (f) from a surname and place name; ultimately from Old English, meaning 'beaver stream'. *Beverley* was adopted as a masculine first name in the late 19th century, a famous male bearer being the British novelist Beverley Nichols. It gradually came to be used in the USA as a feminine name, often in the form *Beverly* (as in the name of the US opera singer Beverly Sills); by 1960 both spellings were in frequent use as girls' names throughout the English-speaking world.

**Bevis** [*beevi*s, *bevi*s] (m) a name of uncertain origin: it may be from Old French, meaning 'handsome (or dear) son', or from the French place name *Beauvais*. Introduced into Britain at the time of the Norman Conquest, it enjoyed a slight revival in the late 19th century, after the publica-

# Bianca

tion of Richard Jefferies' novel *Bevis: the Story of a Boy* (1882), and remains in occasional use.

**Bianca** (f) from the feminine form of the Italian adjective *bianco* 'white'; a translation of the Latin name **Candida**. It was used by Shakespeare in two of his plays, *The Taming of the Shrew* and *Othello*, but is rarely found in the English-speaking world today.
Related name: **Blanche**.

**Biddy** a diminutive of **Bridget** or **Brigid**, occasionally used as a name in its own right.

**Bill, Billy, Billie** diminutives of **William**, dating back to the mid-19th century; often used as independent names. *Billie* is occasionally given to girls, sometimes in combination with another name, the US tennis player Billie-Jean King being a famous example.

**Bina** a diminutive of any name ending in *-bina*, such as **Albina**, **Columbina**, or **Robina**; often used as a name in its own right.

**Bing** (m) from the nickname of the US singer Bing Crosby (1901–77), whose real name was Harry Lillis Crosby; ultimately from *Bingo*, the name of a cartoon character. *Bing* is occasionally given as a first name in honour of the singer.

**Birdie** (f) from a colloquial word for 'bird'; in occasional use as a first name.

**Birgit** a diminutive of **Birgitta**, sometimes used as a name in its own right.

**Birgitta** (f) a Swedish name of uncertain origin: it may be from a Scandinavian word meaning 'protection' or it may simply be a variant of **Bridget**. Borne by a Swedish saint of the 14th century, known in the English-speaking world as St Bridget, the name is occasionally used by US families of Scandinavian descent.
Variant: **Brigitta**.
Diminutives: **Birgit**, **Brita**, **Britt**.

**Bjorn** (m) from a Scandinavian word meaning 'bear'; popularized in the English-speaking world in the late 1970s by the Swedish tennis player Bjorn Borg.

**Blaine** (m) from a surname of uncertain origin; possibly connected with the 6th-century Scottish bishop St Blane (or Blaan). *Blaine* has been in occasional use as a first name in Britain and the USA since the early 20th century.

**Blair** (m) from a surname and place name; ultimately from Scottish Gaelic, meaning 'a plain'. It was particularly popular as a first name in Canada in the mid-20th century.

**Blaise, Blase** (m) probably from Latin *blaesus* 'stammering'. One of the earliest known bearers of the name was St Blaise (or Blasius), the patron saint of wool combers, who was martyred in the early 4th century. The name was introduced into Britain in the Middle Ages and remains in occasional use. In 17th-century France it was borne by the philosopher and mathematician Blaise Pascal.

**Blake** (m) from a surname derived from one of two Old English words: *blac* 'pale' or *blaec* 'black'. It has been in occasional use as a first name since the early 20th century, a famous bearer being the US film director Blake Edwards (born William Blake McEdwards).

**Blanche, Blanch** (f) from the feminine form of the French adjective *blanc* 'white'; a translation of the Latin name **Candida**. An early bearer of the name was Blanche of Castile (1188–1252), wife of King Louis VIII of France and regent for her son Louis IX. The name was introduced into Britain in the 13th century and has remained in occasional use since then; it was particularly popular in the USA in the late 19th century.
Related name: **Bianca**.

**Blane** see **Blaine**.

**Blase** see **Blaise**.

**Blodwen** (f) from Welsh *blodyn* 'flower' and *gwen* 'white'; rarely used outside its country of origin.

**Blodyn** (f) a Welsh name, meaning 'flower'.

**Blossom** (f) from the English word *blossom*; one of a number of flower names that were fashionable in the late 19th and early 20th centuries.

**Blythe** (f) from a surname derived from the English word *blithe*; occasionally used as a first name.

**Boaz** [*bōaz*] (m) from Hebrew, meaning 'swiftness'; borne in the Old Testament by the husband of Ruth. The name was revived by the Puritans in the 17th century and remains in occasional use.

**Bob** a diminutive of **Robert**; sometimes used as a name in its own right.

**Bobbie** a diminutive of **Barbara, Roberta**, or **Robert**.

**Bobby** a diminutive of **Robert**. The word *bobby* is used as a colloquial term for a British policeman in honour of the statesman Sir Robert Peel, who founded the Metropolitan Police Force in 1829.

**Bonamy** (m) from a Guernsey surname; ultimately from French *bon ami* 'good friend'. It is in occasional use as a first name in the English-speaking world.

**Bonar** (m) from a surname ultimately derived from Old French, meaning 'courteous'. It is occasionally used as a first name in honour of the British statesman Andrew Bonar Law (1858–1923).

**Boniface** (m) from a Latin name meaning either 'good fate' or 'well-doer'. The name was borne by nine popes, by the English martyr St Boniface (or Winfrid), who went to Germany as a missionary in the early 8th century, and by an innkeeper in George Farquhar's play *The Beaux' Stratagem* (1707). It has rarely been used as a first name in English-speaking countries since the Reformation.

# Bonita

**Bonita** (f) from Spanish, meaning 'pretty'. The name has been in occasional use throughout the English-speaking world since the mid-20th century. Diminutives: **Bonnie, Bonny**.

**Bonnie, Bonny** (f) from the Scottish dialect word *bonny*, meaning 'beautiful'; ultimately from Latin *bonus* 'good'. The name was popularized by a character in Margaret Mitchell's *Gone with the Wind* (see **Ashley**), to whom it was originally given as a nickname, and by the heroine of the film *Bonnie and Clyde* (1967). It is sometimes used as a diminutive of **Bonita**.

**Boris** (m) a Russian name, meaning 'fight'; occasionally used in the English-speaking world. Famous bearers include Boris Godunov, Tsar of Russia from 1598 to 1605, immortalized in Mussorgsky's opera of the same name; the Russian writer Boris Pasternak (1890–1960), author of *Dr Zhivago*; and the British film actor Boris Karloff (born William Pratt), who made his name as Frankenstein's monster in 1931.

**Botolph, Botolf, Botulf** (m) a name of uncertain origin, possibly connected with the Old German word for 'wolf'; borne by the 7th-century saint after whom the Lincolnshire town of Boston (Botulf's stone) was named. It is rarely used in modern times.

**Boyce** (m) from a surname derived from French *bois* 'wood'; in occasional use as a first name in English-speaking countries.

**Boyd** (m) from Scottish Gaelic *buidhe* 'yellow': generally interpreted as a reference to the colour of the bearer's hair. The name has been used in Scotland for many hundreds of years, both as a first name and as a surname (the latter is sometimes associated with the place name *Bute*). Its use as a first name in other parts of the English-speaking world dates back to the early 20th century.

**Brad** a diminutive of **Bradley**, often used as a name in its own right.

**Bradley** (m) from a surname and place name; ultimately from Old English, meaning 'broad clearing' or 'broad wood'. Rarely used as a first name in Britain, it has been fashionable in other parts of the English-speaking world since the mid-20th century.
Diminutive: **Brad**.

**Bram** a diminutive of **Abraham**. Of Dutch origin, this abbreviation was used by the 19th-century Irish writer Bram Stoker, author of *Dracula*.

**Brandon, Brandan** (m) from a surname and place name; ultimately from Old English, meaning 'hill covered with broom'. In Ireland the name is regarded as a variant of **Brendan**.

**Branwen** (f) from Welsh, meaning 'beautiful raven'; borne by the heroine of one of the tales of the *Mabinogion*. The name has been in regular use in Wales for several hundred years but is rarely found elsewhere.

**Brenda** (f) probably from the Norse masculine name *Brand*, meaning 'sword' or 'torch'; originally confined to the Shetland Islands of Scotland.

The use of the name gradually spread to other parts of the English-speaking world, possibly influenced by one of the heroines of Sir Walter Scott's novel *The Pirate* (1822); it was particularly popular in the mid-20th century. *Brenda* is sometimes erroneously associated with **Brendan** and used as a feminine form of that name.

**Brendan** (m) an Irish name, believed by some scholars to mean 'stinking hair'. St Brendan was a 6th-century Irish abbot, who founded a monastery at Clonfert in County Galway; according to legend, he sailed across the Atlantic on a voyage of discovery and adventure. Famous bearers of the name in modern times include the dramatist Brendan Behan and the athlete Brendan Foster. See also **Brenda**.

Variants: **Brandan, Brandon**.

**Brent** (m) from a surname and place name; ultimately from Old English, meaning 'high place', 'steep hill', or 'burnt'. It has been in occasional use as a first name, especially in the USA and Canada, since the 1930s.

**Brett, Bret** (m) from a surname meaning 'Breton' or 'Briton'; popularized as a first name by the 19th-century US writer Bret Harte (born Francis Brett Harte). In occasional use throughout the English-speaking world, *Brett* became particularly fashionable in Australia in the mid-20th century.

**Brian, Bryan** (m) a Celtic name of uncertain origin; possibly connected with the Irish word for 'hill'. Its most famous bearer in Ireland was Brian Boru, who became high king of that country in 1002; the introduction of the name into England, however, has been attributed to the Breton companions of William the Conqueror. In regular use in Britain since the Middle Ages, it became very popular throughout the English-speaking world in the mid-20th century.

**Brice** see **Bryce**.

**Bride** a variant of **Bridget**. Once a common form of the name in England and Scotland, it is rarely used today. See also **Brigid**.

Diminutive: **Bridie**.

**Bridget, Brigit** (f) from the Irish name *Brighid*, borne by a Celtic goddess; ultimately from one of two Celtic words meaning 'the high one' or 'strength'. Popularized by two saints (see **Birgitta, Brigid**), the name has been in regular use in the British Isles, especially Ireland, since the 17th century.

Variants: **Bedelia, Birgitta, Bride, Brigid, Brigitta, Brigitte**.

Diminutives: **Biddy, Bridie**.

**Bridie** a diminutive of **Bride** or **Bridget**, sometimes used as a name in its own right.

# Brighid

**Brighid** see **Bridget**.

**Brigid** a variant of **Bridget**. The name was borne by an Irish abbess, foundress of the first religious community for women in Ireland, who died in the early 6th century and was revered as one of the patron saints of her native country. Her cult gradually spread to Great Britain, where she was known as St Bridget or St Bride: the London prison that introduced the term *bridewell* into the English language originally stood near the site of St Bride's Well.
Diminutive: **Biddy**.

**Brigit** see **Bridget**.

**Brigitta** either a variant of **Birgitta** or the Latinized form of **Bridget**.

**Brigitte** the French form of **Bridget**, popularized in the latter half of the 20th century by the actress Brigitte Bardot.

**Briony** see **Bryony**.

**Brita** a diminutive of **Birgitta**, sometimes used as a name in its own right.

**Britannia** (f) from Latin, meaning 'Britain'. Its occasional use as a first name, dating back to the 18th century, may have been inspired by the patriotic song 'Rule Britannia', first performed in 1740.

**Britt** a diminutive of **Birgitta**, popularized as an independent name by the Swedish actress Britt Ekland (born 1942).

**Brock** (m) from a surname derived from the Old English word for 'badger'; occasionally used as a first name in English-speaking countries.

**Broderick** (m) probably from a surname meaning 'son of **Roderick**'; in occasional use as a first name. Its most famous bearer in modern times is the US actor Broderick Crawford.

**Bronwen, Bronwyn** (f) a Welsh name, meaning 'white breast'; in regular use since the early 20th century.

**Bruce** (m) from a surname introduced into Britain at the time of the Norman Conquest; ultimately from a French place name of uncertain origin. The surname is generally associated with Scotland, one of its most famous bearers being the Scottish king Robert the Bruce (1274–1329). It has been in regular use as a first name throughout the English-speaking world since the late 19th century.

**Brunetta** a feminine form of **Bruno**.

**Bruno** (m) from Old German *brun* 'brown'; borne by three German saints of the 10th and 11th centuries, including the founder of the Carthusian order of monks. The name has been in occasional use in English-speaking countries since the early Middle Ages.
Feminine form: **Brunetta**.

**Bryan** see **Brian**.

**Bryce, Brice** (m) a Celtic name of uncertain origin; borne by St Brice (or Britius), Bishop of Tours in the early 5th century. It remains in occasional use, both as a first name and as a surname.

**Bryn** (m) a Welsh name, meaning 'hill'; in regular use since the early 20th century. Its adoption as a first name may have been influenced by one of the many Welsh place names that begin with this word.

**Bryony, Briony** [*brīo*ni] (f) from the plant name; in regular use as a first name since the early 20th century.

**Bud** (m) from a colloquial term of address used in the USA; short for *buddy* 'friend'. It is more frequently given as a nickname than as a first name, a famous example being the US comedian Bud Abbott (of the Abbott and Costello duo), whose real name was William Abbott.

**Burt** (m) a name of uncertain origin: it may be from Old English *beorht* 'bright' or from the surname and place name *Burton*, meaning 'fortified enclosure'. It is rarely used in modern times, despite the popularity of the US actors Burt Lancaster and Burt Reynolds.

**Buster** (m) from a nickname or term of address used in the USA. It is occasionally given as a first name in honour of the US comic actor Buster Keaton (born Joseph Francis Keaton), who made his name in the silent films of the 1920s.

**Byron** (m) from a surname and place name; ultimately from Old English *byre* 'cowshed'. Its adoption as a first name in the mid-19th century has been attributed to the popularity of the poet Lord Byron. The name remains in occasional use, particularly in the USA.

# C

**Cadel, Cadell** (m) a Welsh name, meaning 'battle'.

**Cadwallader, Cadwaladr** [kad*wol*ăder] (m) a Welsh name, meaning 'battle leader', dating back to the 7th century. It is more frequently found as a surname than as a first name in modern times.

**Caesar** [*seezer*] (m) from the family name of the Roman dictator Gaius Julius Caesar, the origin of which is uncertain: possible Latin derivations include *caesaries* 'hair', *caesius* 'bluish-grey', or *caedere* 'to cut' (a reference to the dictator's birth by Caesarean section). *Caesar* has been in occasional use as a first name in English-speaking countries since the Renaissance but has never been common.

**Cai** [kī] a diminutive of **Caius**, often used in Wales as a name in its own right. See also **Kay** (m).

# Caitlin

**Caitlin** [*kayt*lin, *kat*lin] an Irish Gaelic variant of **Catherine**, ultimately from an Old French form of the name; occasionally used in other parts of the English-speaking world. See also **Kathleen**.

**Caius** [*kīus*] a variant of **Gaius**; the more common form of the name in Britain. Caius College in Cambridge is named after its founder, John Caius; the college name is pronounced [keez].
Diminutive: **Cai**.

**Caleb** [*kay*leb] (m) from Hebrew, meaning either 'dog' or 'bold'; borne in the Old Testament by one of the twelve leaders of the Israelites sent by Moses to explore the Promised Land (Numbers 13:6). The name was revived by the Puritans after the Reformation and remains in occasional use.

**Calum, Callum** variants of **Colum** or **Malcolm**.

**Calvin** (m) from the surname of the 16th-century Protestant reformer John Calvin; ultimately from Latin *calvus* 'bald'. The name was popularized in the USA in the early 20th century by President Calvin Coolidge (born John Calvin Coolidge).

**Cameron** (m) from a Scottish surname; ultimately from Gaelic, meaning 'crooked nose'. It was rarely used as a first name outside Scotland until the mid-20th century, when it became fashionable in Canadian and Australian families of Scottish descent.

**Camilla** the feminine form of **Camillus**; borne by a Volscian warrior queen in Roman mythology. The name was popularized in the late 18th century by Fanny Burney's novel *Camilla* and remains in regular use throughout the English-speaking world.
Variant: **Camille**.
Diminutives: **Millie, Milly**.

**Camille** the French form of **Camilla** or **Camillus**; borne by the heroine of Alexandre Dumas' *La Dame aux camélias* (1848) in a number of stage and screen versions of the story, notably the film *Camille* (1936) in which Greta Garbo played the title role. The name is occasionally given to girls in English-speaking countries but is not used as a masculine name outside France.

**Camillus** (m) a Latin name of unknown origin; borne by the young attendants of certain priests and priestesses in ancient Rome. The name is rarely used in the English-speaking world.
Variant: **Camille**.
Feminine form: **Camilla**.

**Campbell** (m) from a Scottish surname; ultimately from Gaelic, meaning 'crooked mouth'. It is occasionally used as a first name in Scotland and by families of Scottish descent in other parts of the English-speaking world.

**Candace, Candice** [*kan*dis] (f) from a title of unknown origin borne by a number of Ethiopian queens, one of whom is mentioned in the New Testament. The name has been in occasional use in English-speaking countries since the 17th century and was particularly popular in the USA and Canada in the mid-20th century. The US actress Candice Bergen (born 1946) is a famous bearer of the name.
Diminutive: **Candy**.

**Candida** [*kan*didă] (f) from the feminine form of the Latin adjective *candidus* 'white'; borne by a number of minor saints. George Bernard Shaw's play *Candida* (1898) does not appear to have popularized the name: it is rarely found in this form in English-speaking countries. See also **Bianca, Blanche**.
Diminutive: **Candy**.

**Candy** a diminutive of **Candace** or **Candida**, sometimes used as a name in its own right.

**Canice** see **Kenneth**.

**Cara, Kara** [*kar*ă] (f) from the feminine form of Italian *caro* or Latin *carus* 'dear'. The name has been in occasional use since the early 20th century and was particularly popular in the 1970s.
Variants: **Carina, Carita, Karina**.

**Caractacus** see **Caradoc**.

**Caradoc** [*kar*adŏk] (m) from Welsh, meaning 'amiable'; borne in the 1st century by a British king whose name is better known in its Latinized form, *Caractacus*. The name *Caradoc* is still used from time to time in Wales but is rarely found elsewhere.
Variant: **Caradog**.
Related names: **Carthach, Cerdic**.

**Caradog** a variant of **Caradoc**.

**Carey** [*kair*i] (m *or* f) a variant of **Cary**, reflecting the pronunciation of the surname and place name from which it is derived. *Carey* has been in occasional use as a first name since the 19th century.

**Carina, Karina, Carita** variants of **Cara**.

**Carl, Karl** variants of **Charles**, from the Germanic form of the name; introduced into the USA by German and Scandinavian immigrants in the 19th century. The name gradually spread to other parts of the English-speaking world during the first half of the 20th century; by the mid-1960s it was more common in Britain than *Charles* itself.
Feminine forms: **Carla, Carleen, Carlene, Carly**.

# Carla

**Carla** a feminine form of **Carl**.

**Carleen, Carlene** feminine forms of **Carl** or **Charles**.

**Carleton** see **Carlton**.

**Carlo, Carlos** the Italian and Spanish forms of **Charles**; occasionally used in English-speaking countries.

**Carlotta** a feminine form of **Charles**, of Italian origin.

**Carlton, Carleton** (m) from a surname and place name; ultimately from Old English, meaning 'peasants' settlement'. It has been in occasional use as a first name in Britain and the USA since the late 19th century. Variant: **Charlton**.

**Carly** a feminine form of **Carl**.

**Carmel** (f) from the name of a mountain in Israel; ultimately from Hebrew, meaning 'garden'. Its use as a first name is largely confined to Roman Catholic families (the Carmelite order of mendicant friars was founded on Mount Carmel in the 12th century).
Variants: **Carmela, Carmelita, Carmen**.

**Carmela, Carmelita** variants of **Carmel**, of Italian origin; in occasional use in the USA.

**Carmen** the Spanish form of **Carmel**; popularized in the English-speaking world by Bizet's opera of the same name, first performed in 1875. The name is sometimes associated with Latin *carmen* 'song'.

**Carol** (f) a feminine form of **Charles**; originally a diminutive of **Caroline**. The name has been in regular use in the USA, sometimes in the French form *Carole*, since the early 20th century; it gradually spread to other parts of the English-speaking world and was particularly popular in Britain in the 1950s. The English word *carol*, meaning 'song', has no connection with the first name.
Variants: **Carola, Caryl**.

**Carol** (m) a variant of **Charles**; from **Carolus**, the Latinized form of the name. One of its most famous bearers in modern times is Pope John Paul II, whose real name is Karol Wojtyla (*Karol* and *Karel* are variant spellings of the name used in a number of European countries). *Carol* is sometimes regarded as an anglicization of a common Irish name.

**Carola** a feminine form of **Charles**, dating back to the 17th century; sometimes regarded as a variant of **Carol** (f).

**Carole** see **Carol** (f).

**Carolina** [karrŏlīnă] the Latinized form of **Caroline**. The American states of North and South Carolina, named after the British king Charles I, may have influenced the use of *Carolina* as a feminine first name.
Diminutive: **Lina**.

**Caroline** [karrŏlīn, karrŏlin] a feminine form of **Charles**, of Italian origin. The name was popularized in Britain in the early 18th century by Caro-

line of Ansbach, the German-born wife of King George II, and has been in regular use throughout the English-speaking world since then. Lady Caroline Lamb, remembered for her liaison with the poet Lord Byron, was another famous bearer of the name.
Variants: **Carolina, Carolyn**.
Diminutive: **Carrie**.

**Carolyn** [*ka*rrŏlin] a variant of **Caroline**, dating back to the early 20th century.

**Carrie** a diminutive of **Caroline**, often used as a name in its own right. It was popular in the late 19th century and has recently been revived. See also **Cary**.

**Carter** (m) from a surname meaning 'cart driver (or maker)'; in occasional use as a first name.

**Carthach** the Irish equivalent of **Caradoc**. The name was borne by an Irish saint, also known as St Carthage, who founded a monastery at Lismore, County Waterford, in the early 7th century.
Variant: **Carthage**.

**Carthage** the anglicized form of **Carthach**.

**Cary** [*ka*rri] (m *or* f) from a surname and place name of uncertain origin; popularized as a masculine first name in the mid-20th century by the actor Cary Grant, whose real name was Archibald Leach. The feminine name is sometimes regarded as an alternative spelling of **Carrie**.
Variant: **Carey**.

**Caryl** a variant of **Carol** (f) or **Carys**.

**Carys** (f) a Welsh name, meaning 'love'.
Variants: **Caryl, Cerys, Cheryl**.

**Casey** (m *or* f) a name of uncertain origin; possibly a diminutive of **Casimir, Cassandra**, or **Catherine**. The masculine name was popularized by the US folk song 'Casey Jones'.

**Casimir** (m) from a Polish name meaning 'proclamation of peace'; occasionally used in Britain and the USA.
Diminutive: **Casey**.

**Caspar** see **Jasper**.

**Cass** a diminutive of **Cassandra**, sometimes used as a name in its own right.

**Cassandra** (f) from a Greek name of unknown origin, borne by a Trojan prophetess, the daughter of King Priam. The name was popular in medieval Britain and has remained in regular use since then; it became fashionable in the USA in the mid-20th century.
Diminutives: **Casey, Cass, Cassie, Sandra**.

**Cassie** a diminutive of **Cassandra**, sometimes used as a name in its own right.

**Cath, Kath** diminutives of **Catherine** or **Kathleen**.

**Catherine, Katherine, Katharine, Catharine** (f) from the Greek name *Aikaterina*, of unknown origin. *Katharina*, its Latinized form, was influenced by Greek *katharos* 'pure' or 'clear': this is the accepted meaning of the name today. It was borne by a number of saints, including St Catherine of Alexandria, who was martyred at the beginning of the 4th century after suffering torture on a spiked wheel (symbolized in modern times by the firework known as the Catherine wheel) and whose cult was introduced into Europe by the Crusaders in the early 12th century. The name became popular in Britain in a variety of forms and gradually spread to other parts of the English-speaking world; it remains one of the most common girls' names to this day. *Katharine*, the spelling used by the US actress Katharine Hepburn (born 1909), was largely superseded in the latter half of the 20th century by *Catherine*, the French form of the name.
Variants: **Caitlin, Cathleen, Catrin, Catriona, Karen, Karina, Kathleen, Kathryn**.
Diminutives: **Casey, Cath, Cathy, Kate, Kath, Kathy, Katie, Katy, Kay, Kit, Kitty**.

**Cathleen** see **Kathleen**.

**Cathy, Kathy** diminutives of **Catherine** or **Kathleen**, sometimes used as independent names.

**Catrin** a Welsh variant of **Catherine**.

**Catriona** [kătreeŏnă] a Scottish Gaelic variant of **Catherine**, popularized in the late 19th century by Robert Louis Stevenson's novel of the same name. It was rarely used outside Scotland until the mid-20th century.
Variants: **Katrina, Katrine**.
Diminutive: **Trina**.

**Cecil** [*ses*ĭl, (US) *sees*ĭl] (m) from the Roman clan name *Caecilius*; ultimately from Latin *caecus* 'blind'. The name has been in use in Britain since the Middle Ages; for several hundred years it was better known as the surname of the influential Cecil family, descendants of Queen Elizabeth I's adviser Lord Burghley, than as a first name. Its popularity in the late 19th and early 20th centuries has been attributed to the British statesman Cecil Rhodes (1853–1902), after whom the African state of Rhodesia (now Zimbabwe) was named. Other famous bearers of the name in modern times include the US film producer and director Cecil B. de Mille and the British photographer Sir Cecil Beaton.
Feminine forms: **Cecilia, Cecile**.

**Cecile** [*ses*eel] a feminine form of **Cecil**, of French origin.

**Cecilia** [si*seel*iă] a feminine form of **Cecil**; borne by the 2nd-century martyr St Cecilia, patron saint of music and musicians. The name was introduced into Britain by one of the daughters of William the Conqueror and was fairly common throughout the Middle Ages; it was gradually superseded by the anglicized form **Cicely** but was revived at the end of the 18th century after the publication of Fanny Burney's novel of the same name. *Cecilia* was particularly popular in the late 19th and early 20th centuries, when *Cecil* was a fashionable masculine name, and has remained in occasional use throughout the English-speaking world since then. See also **Celia**.

Variants: **Cecilie, Cecily, Cicely**.

Diminutives: **Cis, Ciss, Cissie, Cissy, Sissie, Sissy**.

**Cecily, Cecilie** [*se*sili, *si*sili] variants of **Cecilia**.

**Cedric** (m) the name of a character in Sir Walter Scott's novel *Ivanhoe* (1819); of uncertain origin. It may be a misspelling of *Cerdic*, the name of a 6th-century king of Wessex (*Cerdic* is probably derived from the same source as **Caradoc**); it may be from the Welsh name *Cedrych*, a compound of *ced* 'bounty' and *drych* 'pattern'; or it may simply be an invention. The name was further popularized in the late 19th century by the hero of Frances Hodgson Burnett's story *Little Lord Fauntleroy* (1886) and remains in occasional use today.

**Cedrych** see **Cedric**.

**Ceinwen** (f) a Welsh name, meaning 'beautiful gems'.

**Celeste** [si*lest*] (f) from the French name *Céleste*; ultimately from Latin *caelestis* 'heavenly'. Although *Céleste* is used as a masculine name in France, the anglicized form is given only to girls.

Variants: **Celestina, Celestine**.

**Celestine, Celestina** variants of **Celeste**. The name *Celestine* was borne by five popes, two of whom have been canonized, but is used almost exclusively as a feminine name in English-speaking countries.

**Celia** (f) from the Latin name *Caelia*, the feminine form of the Roman clan name *Caelius*; borne by one of the heroines of Shakespeare's play *As You Like It*. *Celia* has been in regular use since the 19th century, when it was generally regarded as a variant or diminutive of **Cecilia**, and was particularly popular in the mid-1950s. The British actress Dame Celia Johnson (1908–82) was a famous bearer of the name.

Variants: **Sheelagh, Sheila, Shelagh**.

**Celina** see **Selina**.

**Celine** [say*leen*, *say*leen] (f) from the French name *Céline*; probably from Latin *caelum* 'sky' or 'heaven', though some scholars believe the name to be etymologically associated with **Celia**. Its relatively frequent use in Canada is largely confined to French-Canadian families and it is rarely found in other parts of the English-speaking world.

Variants: **Celina, Selena, Selina**.

**Cerdic** see **Cedric**.

**Ceri** (m *or* f) a Welsh name, meaning 'loved one'.

**Ceridwen** [kĕ*rid*wĕn] (f) from Welsh *cerdd* 'poetry' and *gwen* 'fair' or 'white'; borne by the Welsh goddess of poetic inspiration. The name is rarely used outside its country of origin.

**Cerys** a variant of **Carys**.

**Chad** (m) from an Old English name of uncertain origin; possibly from Welsh, meaning 'battle'. Famous bearers of the name include the 7th-century bishop St Chad and the Rev Chad Varah (born 1911), founder of the Samaritans, a charitable organization that provides a telephone service for the suicidal and despairing. The name became fashionable in the USA in the 1970s but is rarely found in other English-speaking countries.

**Charis** [*ka*rris] (f) from Greek, meaning 'grace'. The name came into use in the English-speaking world after the Reformation but has never been common.
Variant: **Charissa**.

**Charissa** the Latinized form of **Charis**.

**Charity** (f) from Old French *charité* 'Christian love'; ultimately from Latin *caritas*. Charity, in the original sense of the word, is extolled in the New Testament (1 Corinthians 13:13) as the greatest of the three Christian virtues (see also **Faith, Hope**). Adopted as a first name by the Puritans, it remained in regular use for many years; its eventual fall from favour may have been brought about by the word's association with alms-giving.
Diminutives: **Chattie, Cherry**.

**Charlene** a feminine form of **Charles**.

**Charles** (m) from Old German *carl* or Old English *ceorl* 'man' (the English adjective *churlish* is ultimately derived from the same source). *Charles*, the French form of the name, was popularized in the early 9th century by Charles the Great (Charlemagne), the first ruler of the Holy Roman Empire, and was subsequently borne by a number of other European monarchs. Introduced into Britain at the time of the Norman Conquest, the name was little used until the 17th century, when it became fashionable among the royalist supporters of King Charles I and King Charles II. By the mid-19th century it had become one of the most common masculine names in the English-speaking world, a position it retained until the latter half of the 20th century; in 1948 it was chosen by Queen Elizabeth II (then Princess Elizabeth) for her first child, Prince Charles.
Variants: **Carl, Carlo, Carlos, Carol, Karl**.
Diminutives: **Charley, Charlie, Chas, Chay, Chuck**.
Feminine forms: **Carleen, Carlene, Carlotta, Carol, Carola, Carole, Caroline, Charlene, Charlotte**.

**Charlie, Charley** diminutives of **Charles** or **Charlotte**. *Charlie* was some-times used as an independent masculine name in 18th-century Scotland in honour of Charles Edward Stuart, better known as Bonnie Prince Charlie, the Young Pretender. The name was popularized throughout the English-speaking world in the early 20th century by the comic actor Charlie Chaplin, whose full name was Charles Spencer Chaplin.

**Charlotte** [*shar*löt] a feminine form of **Charles**, of French origin. The name was popularized in 18th-century Britain by the wife of King George III, Charlotte Sophia; it remained in regular use in the English-speaking world until the end of the 19th century and enjoyed a revival in the 1970s. Other famous bearers of the name include King George IV's daughter Princess Charlotte and the British writer Charlotte Brontë (1816–55).

Diminutives: **Charley, Charlie, Chattie, Lottie, Lotty, Totty**.

**Charlton** a variant of **Carlton**, publicized in the latter half of the 20th cen-tury by the US actor Charlton Heston (born John Charlton Carter).

**Charmaine** (f) a name of uncertain origin, made famous by a popular song of the mid-20th century. It is sometimes erroneously associated with **Charmian**.

**Charmian** [*char*miăn, *shar*miăn] (f) from Greek, meaning 'joy'. Borne by one of Cleopatra's attendants in Shakespeare's play *Antony and Cleopatra* and other versions of that story, the name remains in occasional use in modern times. See also **Charmaine**.

**Chas** [chaz] a diminutive of **Charles**, from the written abbreviation of the name.

**Chattie** a diminutive of **Charity** or **Charlotte**.

**Chauncey, Chauncy** (m) from a surname derived from a French place name. Its occasional use as a first name in the USA has been attributed to the popularity of Charles Chauncy (1592–1672), an early president of what is now Harvard University.

**Chay** a diminutive of **Charles**, made famous in the 1970s by the British long-distance yachtsman Chay Blyth and occasionally used as an inde-pendent name.

**Cherie, Sherry, Sherri** [*sher*ri] (f) from French *chérie* 'darling'; in occa-sional use as a first name in English-speaking countries, especially the USA.

**Cherry** originally a diminutive of **Charity**, borne by one of the daughters of Mr Pecksniff in Charles Dickens' novel *Martin Chuzzlewit* (1843–44). It is occasionally used in modern times as a name in its own right, some-times as a variant of **Cherie** or in association with the fruit name.

Variant: **Cheryl**.

# Cheryl

**Cheryl** [*cher*ril] a variant of **Cherry** (influenced by *Beryl*) or **Carys**; in regular use throughout the English-speaking world since the mid-20th century.
Variant: **Sheryl**.

**Chester** (m) from a surname and place name; ultimately from Latin *castra* 'camp'. Its use as a first name dates back at least to the early 19th century, a famous bearer being the US president Chester A. Arthur (1830–86).

**Chloe** [*klōi*] (f) from Greek, meaning 'green shoot'; a title borne by Demeter, the Greek goddess of agriculture. The name also occurs in the New Testament (1 Corinthians 1:11); in the Greek pastoral romance *Daphnis and Chloe*, on which Ravel's ballet of the same name (first performed in 1912) was based; and in the US writer Harriet Beecher Stowe's best-known work, *Uncle Tom's Cabin* (1852). It has been in occasional use in Britain and other parts of the English-speaking world since the 17th century.

**Chris** a diminutive of any masculine or feminine name beginning with *Chris-*, notably **Christian**, **Christina**, **Christine**, and **Christopher**.

**Chrissie, Chrissy** diminutives of **Christina**, **Christine**, or any other feminine name beginning with *Chris-*.

**Christabel** (f) from Latin *Christus* 'Christ' and *bella* 'beautiful'; generally interpreted as 'beautiful Christian'. The name has featured in a number of literary works, notably S. T. Coleridge's poem *Christabel* (1816); one of its most famous bearers in real life was the British suffragette Christabel Pankhurst (1880–1958). *Christabel* has been in occasional use in Britain since the 16th century but is rarely found in other parts of the English-speaking world.
Diminutives: **Christie, Christy**.

**Christian** (m *or* f) from Latin *Christianus* 'Christian'. In medieval Britain *Christian* was often used as a feminine name, sometimes in the Latinized form **Christiana**. Since the late 17th century, however, when the masculine name was popularized by the hero of John Bunyan's allegory *The Pilgrim's Progress* (1678; 1684), *Christian* has been given more frequently to boys than to girls. It remains in regular use throughout the English-speaking world today.
Variants: (f) **Christiana, Christiania, Kirsty**.
Diminutives: **Chris, Christie, Christy**.
Related name: **Christina**.

**Christiana, Christiania** variants of **Christian** (f), dating back to the Middle Ages; now regarded as feminine forms of the masculine name. Christiana, the wife of Christian, is the heroine of the second part of *The Pilgrim's Progress*. *Christiania* is also a former name of Oslo, the capital of Norway.

46

**Christie, Christy** diminutives of any masculine or feminine name beginning with *Christ-*, notably **Christabel**, **Christian**, and **Christopher**.

**Christina, Kristina** (f) from Old English *cristen* 'Christian'. Borne by an
early Christian martyr, *Christina* was little used until the 18th century,
when it began to replace **Christian** (f) and **Christiana**; the name was largely superseded by **Christine** in the mid-20th century but has recently enjoyed a revival in the USA. Famous bearers include Queen Christina of
Sweden (1626–89) and the 19th-century poet Christina Rossetti.

Variants: **Christine**, **Kristine**.

Diminutives: **Chris**, **Chrissie**, **Chrissy**, **Tina**.

Related name: **Christian**.

**Christine, Kristine** variants of **Christina**. *Christine* has been in regular use
throughout the 20th century and was particularly popular in the 1950s,
when it was one of the three most common feminine names in Britain.
The US tennis player Chris Lloyd (born Christine Evert) is a famous
bearer of the name.

Variants: **Kirsten**, **Kristen**, **Kristin**.

Diminutives: **Chris**, **Chrissie**, **Chrissy**.

**Christmas** (m *or* f) from the name of the Christian festival; occasionally
given to children born on Christmas Day. *Christmas* has been in use both
as a first name and as a surname since the Middle Ages; in modern times
the first name has been largely superseded by **Noel**, **Natalie**, and their
variants.

**Christopher** (m) from a Greek word meaning 'carrier of Christ', used figur-
atively by the early Christians to indicate that they bore Christ in their
hearts. A literal interpretation of this word gave rise to the legend of St
Christopher, patron saint of travellers, who is traditionally believed to
have carried the Christ-child across a river. The name has been in regular
use in Britain since the 15th century, a famous bearer being the English
dramatist Christopher Marlowe (1564–93); it was further popularized in
the early 20th century by Christopher Robin, the young son of the children's writer A. A. Milne, who featured in many of his father's stories and
poems (see also **Winnie**). At the beginning of the 1980s *Christopher* was
one of the most common masculine names in the English-speaking world.

Diminutives: **Chris**, **Christie**, **Christy**, **Chrystal**, **Crystal**, **Kester**, **Kit**, **Kris**.

**Christy** see **Christie**.

**Chrystal** see **Crystal** (m).

**Chuck** a diminutive of **Charles**, popularized in the late 1950s by the US
singer Chuck Berry (born Charles Edward Berry).

**Cicely** [*sisĕli*] a variant of **Cecilia**; the most common form of the name in the
English-speaking world until the late 19th century.

Variant: **Sisley**.

Diminutives: **Cis**, **Ciss**, **Cissie**, **Cissy**, **Sissie**, **Sissy**.

# Cilla

**Cilla** a diminutive of **Priscilla**, made famous in the 1960s by the British singer Cilla Black (born Priscilla White).

**Cinderella** (f) the name of a fairy-tale heroine, meaning 'little cinder girl'; one of the many unusual first names occasionally given to children born with a common surname, such as *Smith*.

Diminutive: **Cindy**.

**Cindy** a diminutive of **Cinderella** or **Lucinda**, often used as an independent name in the latter half of the 20th century.

**Cis, Ciss** diminutives of **Cecilia** or **Cicely**.

**Cissy, Cissie, Sissy, Sissie** diminutives of **Cecilia** or **Cicely**; regularly used as independent names until the early 20th century. Their subsequent fall from favour was probably brought about by the use of *sissy* as a slang term for an effeminate or cowardly male.

**Claire, Clare** variants of **Clara**. *Clare* was the usual spoken form of the name in Britain until the 19th century, when it was superseded by *Clara*; *Claire*, the French spelling, was popularized in the mid-20th century by the British actress Claire Bloom and has been in frequent use throughout the English-speaking world since then.

**Clara** [*klairă*] (f) from the feminine form of the Latin adjective *clarus* 'bright' or 'clear'. The name has been in use in the English-speaking world since the latter half of the Middle Ages, usually in the anglicized form *Clare*; St Clare (or Clara) of Assisi, who founded the order of nuns known as the Poor Clares in the early 12th century, was one of its most famous bearers. *Clara* became very fashionable in the 19th century and remains in occasional use; both *Clara* and *Clare* have been superseded in modern times by **Claire**, the French form of the name.

Variants: **Claire, Clare, Claribel, Clarice, Clarinda**.

Masculine equivalents: **Clarence, Sinclair**.

**Clare** see **Claire, Clara**.

**Clarence** [*klarrĕns*] (m) from the name of a dukedom created in the 14th century; ultimately from the surname and place name *Clare*, which may be derived from the same source as the feminine first name **Clara**. One of the most famous dukes of Clarence was George, the brother of King Edward IV and King Richard III, who is traditionally believed to have drowned in a butt of Malmsey wine. In the 19th century the title was borne by the future King William IV and by the elder son of King Edward VII; the first name *Clarence* came into fashion throughout the English-speaking world during this period and remains in occasional use today.

Related name: **Sinclair**.

**Claribel** probably a variant of **Clara**, influenced by other names ending in -*bel*; occasionally found in literary works but rarely given as a first name in modern times.

**Clarice** [*klar*ris] a variant of **Clara**, of French or Italian origin; in regular use in the English-speaking world since the 13th century.
Variant: **Clarissa**.

**Clarinda** a variant of **Clara**. The name occurs in Spenser's poem *The Faerie Queene* (1590; 1596) and a number of other literary works but is rarely used in modern times.

**Clarissa** the Latinized form of **Clarice**; popularized in the 18th century by Samuel Richardson's novel *Clarissa Harlowe*.

**Clark** (m) from a surname meaning 'cleric' or 'clerk'; popularized as a first name by the US actor Clark Gable (1901–60) and by the fictional character Clark Kent, alias Superman.

**Clarrie** a diminutive of any feminine name beginning with *Clar-*.

**Claud, Claude** [klawd] (m) from the Roman clan name *Claudius*; ultimately from Latin *claudus* 'lame'. *Claudius* was occasionally used as a first name in 1st- and 2nd-century Britain in honour of the Roman emperor Claudius I, who led the conquest of that country in 43 AD. The name *Claud*, from the French form *Claude*, was introduced into Scotland by the Hamilton family in the 16th century; it gradually spread to other parts of the English-speaking world but has never been common. The British actor Claude Rains (1889–1967) was one of the most famous bearers of the name outside France, where it has been in regular use for many hundreds of years.
Feminine forms: **Claudette, Claudia, Claudine**.

**Claudette** a feminine form of **Claud**, of French origin; popularized throughout the English-speaking world in the first half of the 20th century by the French-born US actress Claudette Colbert.

**Claudia** a feminine form of **Claud**. Mentioned in the New Testament (2 Timothy 4:21), the name has been in regular use in the English-speaking world since the 16th century.
Variant: **Gladys**.

**Claudine** a feminine form of **Claud**, of French origin; borne by the heroine of a series of novels by the 20th-century French writer Colette. The name is occasionally used in English-speaking countries.

**Claudius** see **Claud**.

**Clayton** (m) from a surname and place name; ultimately from a compound of Old English *claeg* 'clay' and *tun* 'settlement'. Its use as a first name dates back to the early 19th century.

**Cledwyn** (m) a Welsh name of uncertain origin; possibly from the name of a river.

# Clem

**Clem** a diminutive of **Clement**, dating back to the 13th century.

**Clemence, Clemency** variants of **Clementia**, favoured by the Puritans for their association with the abstract virtue of *clemency*.

**Clement** (m) from Latin *clemens* 'mild' or 'merciful'. A number of British churches, including the one referred to in the nursery rhyme 'Oranges and Lemons', are dedicated to St Clement, a disciple of St Paul who became pope in the late 1st century and whose name was adopted by thirteen of his successors in that office. A popular name in medieval Britain, *Clement* was partially revived in the 19th century but is rarely used today.
Diminutive: **Clem**.
Feminine forms: **Clementina, Clementine**.

**Clementia** (f) from Latin, meaning 'mildness'; borne by the Roman goddess of mercy. The name and its variants have been in occasional use in Britain since the Middle Ages but are rarely found in modern times.
Variants: **Clemence, Clemency**.

**Clementina** [klemĕn*teen*ă], **Clementine** [klemĕntīn] feminine forms of **Clement**, of German origin; in occasional use in English-speaking countries since the early 19th century. The name *Clementine* is generally associated with the heroine of a well-known folk song and the wife of Sir Winston Churchill.

**Cleo** [*klee*ō] originally a diminutive of **Cleopatra**; made famous in the latter half of the 20th century by the British jazz singer Cleo Laine, whose first name is actually *Clementina*.

**Cleopatra** (f) from Greek, meaning 'fame of her father'; borne by a number of Egyptian queens and princesses, the most famous of whom was the mistress of Julius Caesar and Mark Antony. *Cleopatra* has been used from time to time as a first name in the English-speaking world.
Diminutive: **Cleo**.

**Cliff** a diminutive of **Clifford** or **Clifton**; popularized as an independent name in the latter half of the 20th century by the British singer Cliff Richard (born Harry Webb).

**Clifford** (m) from a surname and place name; ultimately from Old English, meaning 'ford near a slope'. *Clifford* has been in regular use as a first name throughout the English-speaking world since the late 19th century; the pianist Sir Clifford Curzon was a famous bearer.
Diminutive: **Cliff**.

**Clifton** (m) from a surname and place name; ultimately from Old English, meaning 'settlement on a cliff'. *Clifton* is occasionally used as a first name in the USA but is rarely found in other English-speaking countries.
Diminutive: **Cliff**.

**Clint** a diminutive of **Clinton**, made famous by the US actor Clint Eastwood (born 1930).

**Clinton** (m) from a surname and place name; ultimately from Old English, meaning 'settlement on a hill'.
Diminutive: **Clint**.

**Clive** (m) from a surname and place name, meaning 'cliff'. Its adoption as a first name has been attributed to the fame of the British soldier and statesman Robert Clive (1725–74), known as 'Clive of India'. Further popularized by the hero of Thackeray's novel *The Newcomes* (1853–55), the name has been in regular use in Britain and other parts of the English-speaking world since the late 19th century.

**Clodagh** [klōdǎ] (f) from the name of an Irish river; in occasional use as a first name in Ireland but rarely found elsewhere.

**Clotilda** (f) from an Old German name derived from *hloda* 'loud' or 'famous' and *hildi* 'battle'; borne by a French saint of the 6th century, the wife of King Clovis, who played a major role in her husband's conversion to Christianity. The name is used from time to time in the English-speaking world but has never been common.

**Clyde** (m) from the name of a Scottish river; rarely used as a first name in Britain but occasionally found in other English-speaking countries, especially the USA.

**Colette** a feminine form of **Nicholas**; originally a diminutive of **Nicolette**, dating back to the Middle Ages. St Colette, a French nun of the 15th century, was an early bearer of the name; it was further popularized in the first half of the 20th century by the French writer Colette (born Sidonie Gabrielle Colette) and remains in regular use throughout the English-speaking world.

**Colin** either a variant of **Nicholas**, from a French diminutive of the name, or a translation of the Scottish Gaelic name *Cailean*, meaning 'young dog'. It has been in regular use in the British Isles, especially Scotland and Ireland, since the Middle Ages and was particularly popular in the mid-20th century.
Feminine form: **Colina**.

**Colina** a feminine form of **Colin**.

**Colleen** (f) from an Irish word for 'girl'. **Colleen** is rarely found as a first name in Ireland but has been in regular use in other English-speaking countries since the mid-20th century, a famous bearer being the Australian-born novelist Colleen McCullough.

**Colley** (m) from a surname meaning 'swarthy'; in occasional use as a first name. The 18th-century actor and dramatist Colley Cibber, whose mother's maiden name was *Colley*, is probably its best-known bearer.

**Colum, Colm** Irish variants of **Columba**; in regular use in Ireland but rarely found elsewhere.
Variants: **Callum, Calum**.

51

# Columba

**Columba** (m) from Latin, meaning 'dove'; borne by the Irish abbot and missionary St Columba, founder of the monastery on the Scottish island of Iona, who converted the inhabitants of Scotland and northern England to Christianity in the 6th century. The name survives only in its variant forms. See also **Malcolm**.
Variants: **Colm, Colum**.
Feminine forms: **Columbina, Columbine**.

**Columbina, Columbine** feminine forms of **Columba**.

**Conan** [*kōnăn*] (m) a Celtic name, meaning 'high'. Borne by a number of counts and dukes of Brittany, the name was introduced into Britain after the Norman Conquest; it remained in regular use until the 16th century but is rarely found outside Ireland in modern times. Sir Arthur Conan Doyle (1859–1930), creator of the detective Sherlock Holmes, was a famous bearer of the name.
Related name: **Conn**.

**Concepta** (f) from Latin, meaning 'conceived'; a reference to the Immaculate Conception.
Variant: **Concetta**.

**Concetta** the Italian form of **Concepta**; in occasional use in English-speaking countries.

**Conn** (m) an Irish name derived from the same source as **Conan**.

**Connie** a diminutive of **Constance**, sometimes used as a name in its own right.

**Connor, Conor** (m) from the Irish name *Conchubhar*, meaning 'high desire'. In Irish mythology the name was borne by an early king of Ulster; its most famous bearer in modern times is the Irish diplomat Conor Cruise O'Brien (born 1917). Outside Ireland, *Connor* is more frequently found as a surname than as a first name. See also **Cornelius**.

**Conrad** (m) from Old German *conja* 'bold' and *rad* 'counsel'; borne by four German kings of the Middle Ages. The name has been in occasional use in the English-speaking world since the 15th century.
Variants: **Curt, Kurt**.

**Constance** (f) from Latin *constantia* 'constancy'. The name has been in use in Britain since the time of the Norman Conquest; it was popular throughout the English-speaking world in the first half of the 20th century but is rarely used today.
Variants: **Constancy, Constantia**.
Diminutive: **Connie**.

**Constancy** a variant of **Constance** used by the Puritans in the 16th and 17th centuries.

**Constant** a variant of **Constantine**, favoured by the Puritans and revived in the 19th century.

**Constantia** the Latin form of **Constance**; fashionable in 19th-century Britain but rarely found in modern times.

**Constantine** (m) from Latin *constans* 'constant'. The name was borne by a number of Roman and Byzantine emperors, including Constantine the Great, the first Christian emperor, who gave his name to the city of Constantinople (now Istanbul), and in modern times by two 20th-century kings of Greece. It has been in occasional use in Britain since the Dark Ages but has never been common in the English-speaking world.
Variant: **Constant**.

**Cora** (f) from Greek *kore* 'girl' (*Kore* was a title borne by Persephone, the Greek goddess of the underworld). The name *Cora* was first used in the USA in the early 19th century, when it was chosen or invented by James Fenimore Cooper for the heroine of his novel *The Last of the Mohicans* (1826); it gradually spread to other parts of the English-speaking world and remains in occasional use today.
Variant: **Coralie**.
Related name: **Corinna**.

**Coral** (f) from the name of the pinkish substance used to make jewellery and ornaments; one of a number of jewel names that became fashionable in the 19th century.
Variant: **Coralie**.

**Coralie** probably a variant of **Cora** or **Coral**, of French origin. It has been in occasional use in English-speaking countries since the late 19th century.

**Cordelia** (f) a name of uncertain origin, borne by the youngest daughter of King Lear in Shakespeare's version of the tragedy. It may be ultimately derived from Latin *cor, cordis* 'heart'.
Diminutive: **Delia**.

**Corinna** (f) from Greek *kore* 'girl'; sometimes regarded as a variant or diminutive of **Cora**. Borne by a Greek poetess of the 5th century BC, the name was revived in the 17th century by the British poet Robert Herrick and his contemporaries.
Variant: **Corinne**.

**Corinne** the French form of **Corinna**. Popularized in the early 19th century by Mme de Staël's novel of the same name, *Corinne* is now the more common form of the name in the English-speaking world.

**Cormac** (m) from Gaelic, meaning 'charioteer'. According to legend, the name was borne by an Irish king of the 3rd century; it is still used from time to time as a first name in Ireland.

**Cornelia** the feminine form of **Cornelius**; borne in the 2nd century BC by the mother of the two Roman tribunes and reformers known as the Gracchi. The name is occasionally found in the English-speaking world but has never been common.

# Cornelius

**Cornelius** (m) from a Roman clan name probably derived from Latin *cornu* 'horn'. Early bearers of the name include a devout centurion converted to Christianity by St Peter (Acts 10) and a 3rd-century pope. The name was introduced into Britain from the Low Countries in the 15th century and gradually spread to other parts of the English-speaking world; in the USA it was borne by Cornelius Vanderbilt (1794–1877) and a number of his descendants. *Cornelius* is sometimes used in Ireland as a translation of the name *Conchubhar* (see **Connor**).
Diminutive: **Corney**.
Feminine form: **Cornelia**.

**Corney** a diminutive of **Cornelius**.

**Cosimo** the Italian form of **Cosmo**; borne by several members of the Medici family, including three grand dukes of Tuscany. Cosimo III, a close friend of the 2nd Duke of Gordon, was responsible for the introduction of the name *Cosmo* into the English-speaking world.

**Cosmo** (m) from Greek *kosmos* 'order'. An early form of the name was borne by St Cosmas, patron saint of physicians, who is believed to have been martyred in the early 4th century with his twin brother St Damian. The cult of St Cosmas popularized the name in Italy (see **Cosimo**); it was introduced into Scotland by the Gordon family in the 17th century and has been in occasional use in the English-speaking world since then.
Variant: **Cosimo**.

**Courtney, Courtenay** [*kort*ni] (m *or* f) from the surname of the aristocratic Courtenay family, of French origin; ultimately from Old French, meaning 'short nose', or from a French place name. Dating back at least to the 19th century as a masculine first name, it is now given to children of either sex.

**Craig** (m) from a Scottish surname; ultimately from a Celtic word meaning 'rock' or 'crag'. *Craig* came into general use as a first name in the USA in the mid-20th century and rapidly spread to other parts of the English-speaking world; it was particularly popular in Britain in the late 1970s.

**Cressida** (f) from a Greek name of uncertain origin; borne by the faithless mistress of Troilus in a number of versions of the medieval romance, notably Shakespeare's play *Troilus and Cressida* (earlier forms of the name include the original *Briseida* and Chaucer's *Criseyde*).

**Crispian** a variant of **Crispin**. The name occurs in a reference to St Crispin's Day (25th October) in Shakespeare's play *Henry V* (the Battle of Agincourt was fought on this date in 1415). It is rarely used in modern times.

**Crispin** (m) from the Roman family name *Crispinus*; ultimately from Latin *crispus* 'curled' or 'curly-haired'. The name was born by St Crispin and St Crispinian, patron saints of shoemakers, who are believed to have been martyred in the 3rd century. It has been in occasional use in the English-speaking world since the Middle Ages.

Variant: **Crispian**.

**Crystal** (f) from the English word *crystal*, with particular reference to crystal glass; ultimately from Greek *krustallos* 'ice'. Its use as a feminine first name was probably influenced by the fashion for jewel names that began in the late 19th century.

**Crystal, Chrystal** (m) Scottish diminutives of **Christopher**, rarely found in modern times.

**Cuddy, Cuddie** diminutives of **Cuthbert** that may have given rise to the Scottish dialect word *cuddy*, meaning 'donkey'.

**Curt** a diminutive of **Curtis** or an alternative spelling of **Kurt**.

**Curtis** (m) from a surname derived from Old French *curteis* 'courteous'; in regular use as a first name since the 19th century.
Diminutive: **Curt**.

**Cuthbert** (m) from Old English *cuth* 'famous' and *beorht* 'bright'. The name was popularized in northern Britain by the 7th-century monk St Cuthbert, Bishop of Lindisfarne, and remained in regular use until the 17th century. It was revived in the 19th century but is rarely used today.
Diminutives: **Cuddie, Cuddy**.

**Cy** [sī] a diminutive of **Cyril** or **Cyrus**.

**Cynthia** (f) from Greek, meaning 'of Cynthus' (a reference to Mount Cynthus on the island of Delos); a title borne by the goddess Artemis. The name features in a number of literary works, from the poems of Propertius in the 1st century BC to the 19th-century novel *Wives and Daughters*, by Mrs Gaskell. It has been in regular use as a first name in Britain since the early 20th century and was very popular in the USA in the 1950s.

**Cyprian** (m) from Latin *Cyprianus* 'of Cyprus'. The 3rd-century martyr St Cyprian, Bishop of Carthage, was an early bearer of the name. It has been in occasional use in Britain since the latter half of the Middle Ages but has never been common.

**Cyril** [sirrīl] (m) from Greek, meaning 'lord'; borne by a number of saints, including the 9th-century missionary who devised the Cyrillic alphabet used in Slavonic languages. The name has been in use in Britain since the 17th century and was particularly popular in the first half of the 20th century.
Diminutive: **Cy**.

**Cyrus** [syrŭs] (m) from the Persian name *Kurush*, meaning 'throne'; made famous by King Cyrus the Great, who founded the Persian empire in the 6th century BC and is mentioned in the Old Testament. *Cyrus* was adopted as a first name by the Puritans but has never been as popular in Britain as in the USA, its best-known bearer in modern times being the US statesman Cyrus Vance.

# Cytherea

Diminutive: **Cy**.

**Cytherea** [sith&#277;*ree*ă] (f) from *Cythera*, the name of a Greek island associated with the cult of Aphrodite; found in classical references to the goddess. Thomas Hardy gave the name to the two leading female characters of his first published novel, *Desperate Remedies* (1871).

# D

**Daff** see **Daph**.

**Dafydd** [*da*vidh] a Welsh form of **David**.

**Dagmar** (f) probably from a compound of two Germanic words meaning 'day' and 'famous'; introduced into the English-speaking world by Danish immigrants.

**Dai** [dī] a Welsh diminutive of **David**.

**Daisy** (f) from the flower name; ultimately from Old English, meaning 'day's eye'. *Daisy* became fashionable as a first name in the late 19th century, when it was sometimes regarded as a translation of the French name **Marguerite** and used as a pet form of **Margaret**; it was made famous by the popular song 'A Bicycle Built for Two', the chorus of which begins 'Daisy, Daisy, give me your answer, do'. Despite its use by the US writer Henry James for the heroine of his story *Daisy Miller* (1878), the name is rarely found outside Britain.

**Dale** (m *or* f) from a surname meaning 'valley'; in regular use as a first name since the early 20th century.

**Damaris** [*dam*ăris] (f) the name of an Athenian woman converted to Christianity by St Paul (Acts 17:34); probably from the Greek word for 'calf'. One of the many biblical names adopted by the Puritans in the 16th and 17th centuries, it is rarely used in modern times.

**Damian, Damien** (m) from the Greek name *Damianos*; ultimately from the verb 'to tame'. Borne by an early Christian martyr (see **Cosmo**), the name has been in occasional use in the English-speaking world since the Middle Ages and enjoyed a revival in the latter half of the 20th century. Variant: **Damon**.

**Damon** a variant of **Damian**; borne by the loyal friend of Pythias (or Phintias) in Greek legend. The best-known bearer of the name in modern times is the US writer Damon Runyon (1884–1946).

**Dan** (m) the name of one of the sons of Jacob in the Old Testament; now regarded as a diminutive of **Daniel** but sometimes used as a name in its own right.

**Dana** [*dah*nă, (US) *day*nă] (m *or* f) a name of uncertain origin; borne by the Celtic goddess of fertility. The boys' name may be from the English word or surname *Dane*, which also occurs from time to time as a masculine first name, or it may simply be a variant of **Daniel** (the girls' name is sometimes regarded as a feminine form of **Daniel**).

**Dane** see **Dana**.

**Danette** (f) a name of French origin used in English-speaking countries, especially the USA, as a feminine form of **Daniel**.

**Daniel** (m) from Hebrew, meaning 'God has judged' or 'God is judge'. Daniel was an Old Testament prophet of the 6th century BC, remembered for his miraculous survival in the den of lions (Daniel 6:16–23). The name has been in general use in Britain since the Middle Ages; having fallen from favour in the latter half of the 19th century, it was revived throughout the English-speaking world in the mid-20th century. Famous bearers of the name include the British writer Daniel Defoe, author of *Robinson Crusoe* (1719), and the 18th-century American pioneer Daniel Boone. *Daniel* is sometimes used in Ireland and Wales as a translation of the Gaelic name *Domhnall* (see **Donald**) or the Welsh name *Deiniol*, meaning 'attractive'.
Variant: **Dana**.
Diminutives: **Dan, Danny**.
Feminine forms: **Dana, Danette, Daniella, Danielle, Danita, Danuta**.

**Danielle, Daniella, Danita** feminine forms of **Daniel**. *Danielle*, the French feminine form of the name, has been in regular use in the English-speaking world since the mid-20th century.

**Danny** a diminutive of **Daniel**, often used as a name in its own right; popularized by the well-known folk song 'Danny Boy'.

**Dante** [*danti*] a diminutive of *Durante*, the Italian form of **Durand**; borne by the Italian poet Dante Alighieri (1265–1321), in whose honour the name is occasionally given in modern times. Its use in the English-speaking world is largely confined to families of Italian descent, a famous example being the 19th-century British poet and painter Dante Gabriel Rossetti.

**Danuta** a feminine form of **Daniel**.

**Daph, Daff** diminutives of **Daphne**.

**Daphne** [*dafni*] (f) from Greek, meaning 'laurel' (in Greek mythology the nymph Daphne was rescued from the unwanted attentions of the god Apollo by being turned into a laurel bush). The name was rarely used in English-speaking countries until the early 20th century, a famous bearer being the British novelist Daphne du Maurier (born 1907).
Diminutives: **Daff, Daph**.

**Darby, Derby** (m) a name of uncertain origin: it may be from the surname and place name *Derby*, meaning 'deer park', or from the Irish name *Diarmait* (see **Dermot**). In occasional use as a first name for several hundred years, it is generally associated in modern times with 'Darby and

Joan', the devoted elderly married couple originally depicted in a poem or ballad of the 18th century.

**Darcy, D'Arcy** (m *or* f) from a surname introduced into Britain at the time of the Norman Conquest; ultimately from the French place name *Arcy*.

**Darlene** (f) from the English word *darling*; in occasional use as a first name, especially in the USA and Canada, in the mid-20th century.

**Darrell, Darrel** see **Darryl**.

**Darren** (m) a name of uncertain origin, popularized throughout the English-speaking world in the 1960s by the husband of **Samantha** in the US television series *Bewitched*.

**Darryl, Darrell, Daryl, Darrel** (m) probably from a surname and French place name, though some scholars believe the name to be derived from Old English *deorling* 'darling'. It has been in occasional use as a first name since the 1860s and was particularly popular in the mid-20th century.

**Dave** a diminutive of **David**.

**David** (m) from Hebrew, meaning 'beloved' or 'friend'. The David of the Old Testament, remembered for his killing of the giant Goliath (1 Samuel 17), succeeded Saul as King of Israel in the 10th century BC. One of the earliest known bearers of the name in Britain was the 6th-century bishop St David (or Dewi), patron saint of Wales; the name was subsequently borne by three Welsh princes and two Scottish kings of the Middle Ages and has been in regular use, especially in Wales and Scotland, since then. By the 1950s it had become one of the five most popular masculine names in the English-speaking world, a position it still retains.
Variants: **Dafydd, Dewi**.
Diminutives: **Dai, Dave, Davy, Taffy**.
Feminine forms: **Davida, Davina, Davinia**.

**Davina, Davinia, Davida** feminine forms of **David**, of Scottish origin.
Diminutives: **Vida, Vina**.

**Davy** a diminutive of **David**, made famous by the US frontiersman Davy Crockett (1786–1836).

**Dawn** (f) from the English word *dawn*; a modern equivalent of **Aurora**. Adopted as a first name in the early 20th century, it remains in regular use throughout the English-speaking world.

**Dean** (m) from a surname derived either from Old English *denu* 'valley' or from Latin *decanus* 'leader of ten people'; in regular use as a first name since the mid-20th century. Famous bearers of the name include the US statesman Dean Acheson and the US actor and singer Dean Martin, whose real name is Dino Crocetti.

**Deanna** [dee*an*ă] a variant of **Diana**, made famous in the late 1930s by the young Canadian singer and film actress Deanna Durbin (born Edna Mae Durbin).

**Deanne** [dee*an*] a variant of **Diane**.

**Debbie, Deb** diminutives of **Deborah**. *Debbie* was popularized as an independent name in the 1950s by the US actress Debbie Reynolds, whose real name is Marie Frances Reynolds.

**Deborah** (f) from Hebrew, meaning 'bee'. The name was borne in the Old Testament by the devoted nurse of Isaac's wife Rebekah and by a prophetess and judge who led the Israelites in their struggle against the Canaanites (Judges 4). It came into general use in the English-speaking world in the 17th century, having been adopted as a first name by the Puritans, and was particularly popular in the mid-20th century. The British writer Mrs Gaskell gave the name to the formidable Miss Jenkyns in her novel *Cranford* (1853).
Variant: **Debra**.
Diminutives: **Deb, Debbie**.

**Debra** a variant of **Deborah**, dating back to the first half of the 20th century.

**Decima** the feminine form of **Decimus**.

**Decimus** (m) from Latin, meaning 'tenth'; formerly given by the parents of large families to their tenth child. The name is rarely required for this purpose in modern times but remains in occasional use.
Feminine form: **Decima**.

**Declan** [*dek*län] (m) an Irish name of unknown origin; borne by the 6th-century bishop St Declan. The name has been in regular use in Ireland since the mid-20th century but is rarely found elsewhere.

**Dee** (m *or* f) a diminutive of any name beginning with *D*, sometimes used as a name in its own right.

**Deirdre** [*deer*dri] (f) from an Irish name of uncertain derivation: possible interpretations include 'raging', 'broken-hearted', or 'fear'. The Deirdre of Irish and Scottish legend committed suicide after the treacherous killing of her lover; her tragic story was revived by the Irish dramatists W. B. Yeats (*Deirdre*; 1907) and J. M. Synge (*Deirdre of the Sorrows*; 1910) and the name soon became popular throughout the English-speaking world.

**Del** a diminutive of **Derek** or of any masculine or feminine name beginning with *Del-*.

**Delia** (f) from *Delos*, the name of the Greek island on which the god Apollo and the goddess Artemis are traditionally believed to have been born. The name is frequently found in pastoral poems of the 17th and 18th centuries and remains in occasional use today, sometimes as a diminutive of **Bedelia** or **Cordelia**.

**Delilah** (f) from Hebrew, meaning 'amorous' or 'delight'. The name is borne in the Old Testament by the mistress of Samson, who cajoled her lover into revealing the secret of his great strength and then betrayed him to the Philistines (Judges 16:4–21). *Delilah* has been in occasional use as a first name since its revival by the Puritans in the 16th century and has entered the English language as a synonym for 'temptress'.

**Della** a diminutive of **Adela**, in regular use as an independent name since the late 19th century.

**Delphine** (f) either from the Greek place name *Delphi*, the site of the oracle of Apollo, or from the plant name *delphinium*: both words are ultimately derived from Greek *delphis* 'dolphin'. Of French origin, *Delphine* was popularized in the early 19th century by Mme de Staël's novel of the same name; it is occasionally found in the English-speaking world but has never been common.

**Delwyn, Delwen** (f) a Welsh name, derived from the words for 'neat' and 'fair'; in occasional use in Wales since the early 20th century.

**Delyth** (f) a Welsh name, derived from the words for 'neat' and 'pretty'; rarely found outside its country of origin.

**Demelza** (f) from a Cornish place name; in occasional use as a first name since the early 20th century. It was popularized by the heroine of the British writer Winston Graham's *Poldark* novels, which were adapted for television in the mid-1970s.

**Denholm** [*den*ŏm] (m) from a surname and place name; ultimately from Old English *denu* 'valley' and *holm* 'island'. *Denholm* is occasionally used as a first name, the British actor Denholm Elliott being its best-known bearer in modern times.

**Denis** see **Dennis**.

**Denise** [dĕ*neez*, dĕ*nees*] the feminine form of **Dennis**; from the Latin name *Dionysia*. First used in Britain in the 12th century, the name was reintroduced into the English-speaking world from France in the early 20th century and was particularly popular in the 1950s.
Diminutive: **Dennie**.

**Dennie** a diminutive of **Denise**.

**Dennis, Denis, Denys** (m) from the Latin name *Dionysius*; ultimately from *Dionysos* or *Dionysus*, the name of the Greek god of wine (also known as Bacchus). The name was borne in its original form by Dionysius the Areopagite, an Athenian converted to Christianity by St Paul (Acts 17:34), and by the 3rd-century bishop St Dionysius of Alexandria. St Denys (or Denis), patron saint of France, was martyred in the 3rd century and is traditionally believed to have walked to his place of burial carrying his severed head in his hands. The name was introduced into Britain from France in the latter half of the Middle Ages; having fallen from favour in the 17th century, it came back into fashion in the 1920s and remains in regular use throughout the English-speaking world. See also **Duncan, Sidney**.
Diminutive: **Denny**.

Variant: **Dion**.
Feminine form: **Denise**.
Related name: **Dwight**.

**Denny** a diminutive of **Dennis**.

**Denys** see **Dennis**.

**Denzil** (m) from the Cornish surname and place name *Denzell*, of uncertain origin. It was adopted as a first name in the 16th century by the Holles family, the British statesman Denzil Holles (1599–1680) being one of its most famous bearers, and remains in occasional use today.

**Derby** see **Darby**.

**Derek, Derrick, Deryck, Deryk** [*d*errik] variants of **Theodoric**; introduced into Britain from the Low Countries in the 15th century. The spelling *Derrick* was used by a 17th-century hangman at Tyburn, whose name entered the English language as a synonym for 'gallows' and now denotes a type of crane. The name was revived in the early 20th century and has been in regular use throughout the English-speaking world since then.
Variant: **Dirk**.
Diminutives: **Del, Derry, Rick, Ricky**.

**Dermot** (m) from the Irish name *Diarmait* or *Diarmuid*, meaning 'free from envy', borne in Gaelic legend by the lover of Grainne (see **Grania**). Dermot MacMurrough, an Irish king of the 12th century, popularized the name in various parts of the country; it remains in regular use in Ireland to this day but is rarely found elsewhere. See also **Darby**.

**Derrick** see **Derek**.

**Derry** a diminutive of **Derek**, sometimes associated with the Irish place name and used as a name in its own right.

**Deryck, Deryk** see **Derek**.

**Deryn** (f) a Welsh name of uncertain origin; probably from *aderyn* 'bird'. It has been in regular use in Wales since the mid-20th century but is rarely found in other English-speaking countries.

**Des** a diminutive of **Desmond**.

**Desdemona** (f) from Greek, meaning 'misery'; borne by the heroine of Shakespeare's play *Othello*. It is rarely given as a first name in modern times.

**Desiree** [day*zee*ray] (f) from French *désirée* 'desired'. The name was borne by a mistress of Napoleon Bonaparte who married Jean Bernadotte, the future King Charles XIV John of Sweden, in 1798. It is occasionally found in the English-speaking world but has never been common.

**Desmond** (m) from a surname derived from Irish *Deas Mumhain* 'South Munster'. It came into use as a first name in 19th-century Ireland and gradually spread to other parts of the English-speaking world in the early 20th century.

# Dewi

Diminutive: **Des**.

**Dewi** a Welsh form of **David**.

**Dexter** (m) either from a surname, meaning 'dyer', or from Latin *dexter* 'right-handed'; in regular use as a first name since the early 20th century.

**Di** a diminutive of **Diana** or **Diane**, dating back to the 18th century.

**Diamond** (f) from the name of the precious stone; one of a number of jewel names that became fashionable in the 19th century. The name was also borne by Sir Isaac Newton's dog, traditionally believed to have destroyed the results of several years of its master's work by upsetting a lighted candle.

**Diana** (f) the name of the Roman counterpart of Artemis, goddess of fertility and childbirth, hunting, and the moon; probably from Latin *deus* 'god' or *divus* 'divine'. *Diana* has been in regular use in the English-speaking world since the 16th century; temporarily supplanted by the French form **Diane** in the mid-20th century, it was restored to favour in the early 1980s after the marriage of Prince Charles and Lady Diana Spencer.
Variants: **Deanna, Diane**.
Diminutive: **Di**.

**Diane** the French form of **Diana**, borne by Diane de Poitiers (1499–1566), mistress of King Henri II of France. The name was first used in the English-speaking world in the early 20th century and rapidly became more popular than *Diana* itself. *Dianne* is a frequent variant spelling of the name.
Variant: **Deanne**.
Diminutive: **Di**.

**Dianne** see **Diane**.

**Diarmuid, Diarmait** see **Dermot**.

**Dick, Dickie, Dicky** diminutives of **Richard**, which originated as rhyming variants of **Rick**. *Dick* is one of the oldest pet forms of the name, dating back at least to the 13th century.

**Dickon** a diminutive of **Richard**, rarely used for this purpose in modern times but occasionally given as a name in its own right.

**Dicky** see **Dick**.

**Digby** (m) from a surname and place name; ultimately from Old English, meaning 'farm by a ditch'. It has been in occasional use as a first name since the 19th century.

**Diggory** (m) a name of uncertain origin; possibly from French *égaré* 'astray'. It has been in occasional use in Britain since the 16th century but is rarely found in modern times.

**Dillon** (m) probably from an Irish surname derived from the Old German first name *Dillo*; sometimes used as a variant spelling of **Dylan**.

**Dilys** (f) from Welsh, meaning 'genuine'. The name was first used in Wales in the mid-19th century and gradually spread to other parts of Britain.

**Dinah** (f) from Hebrew, meaning 'judged' or 'lawsuit'. Borne in the Old Testament by the daughter of Jacob and Leah, the name was adopted by the Puritans in the 16th century and introduced by them into America, where it became very popular. The name remains in occasional use throughout the English-speaking world, a famous bearer being the British actress Dinah Sheridan (born 1920).

**Dion** [*deeŏn*] a variant of **Dennis**; originally a diminutive of *Dionysius*. Feminine forms: **Dione, Dionne**.

**Dionne, Dione** [*deeon*] feminine forms of **Dion**.

**Dionysia** see **Denise**.

**Dionysius** see **Dennis**.

**Dirk** a variant of **Derek**; originally a Dutch diminutive of the name. It is occasionally used in English-speaking countries in honour of the British actor Dirk Bogarde (born 1921).

**Dodie** a diminutive of **Dorothy**. The British writer Dodie Smith, author of the children's story on which Walt Disney's film *One Hundred and One Dalmatians* (1960) was based, is a famous bearer of the name.

**Doll, Dolly** diminutives of **Dorothy**, dating back to the 16th century. *Doll*, which has entered the English language as the name of a child's plaything and as a slang term for an attractive woman, is rarely used as a first name in modern times; *Dolly* remains in occasional use as an independent name, popularized in recent years by the long-running musical *Hello, Dolly!*

**Dolores** [*dolorĕz*] (f) from *Maria de los Dolores*, one of the titles of the Virgin Mary; ultimately from Spanish *dolor* 'sorrow'. The name has been in occasional use in the English-speaking world since the early 20th century.
Diminutives: **Lola, Lolita**.

**Dominic, Dominick** (m) from Latin *dominicus* 'of the Lord'; possibly a reference to the day on which the bearer was born (from Latin *dies dominica* 'day of the Lord'). St Dominic, founder of the Dominican order of preaching friars, popularized the name throughout the Christian world in the 13th century; its use was largely restricted to Roman Catholic families from the time of the Reformation to the mid-20th century, when it was revived by parents of all denominations.
Feminine forms: **Dominica, Dominique**.

**Dominica** a feminine form of **Dominic**.

**Dominick** see **Dominic**.

**Dominique** the French feminine form of **Dominic**, occasionally used in English-speaking countries in the latter half of the 20th century.

# Don

**Don** a diminutive of **Donald** or **Donovan**, sometimes used as a name in its own right.

**Donal** the Irish form of **Donald**.

**Donald** (m) from the Gaelic name *Domhnall*, derived from two Celtic words meaning 'world' and 'mighty'. Borne by a number of early Scottish kings, the name has been in regular use in that country for many hundreds of years; it gradually spread to other parts of Britain and was popular throughout the English-speaking world in the first half of the 20th century. The cartoon character Donald Duck, created by Walt Disney in the early 1930s, is a famous bearer of the name. See also **Daniel**.
Variant: **Donal**.
Diminutives: **Don, Donny**.
Feminine forms: **Donalda, Donaldina**.

**Donalda, Donaldina** feminine forms of **Donald**.

**Donna** (f) from Italian, meaning 'lady'. *Donna* has been in use as a first name in the English-speaking world since the early 20th century: it was very fashionable in the USA and Canada in the 1950s and gradually spread to Britain and Australia, reaching its peak of popularity there in the mid-1970s.

**Donny** a diminutive of **Donald** or **Donovan**, sometimes used as a name in its own right.

**Donovan** (m) from an Irish surname, meaning 'dark brown'; in occasional use as a first name throughout the English-speaking world since the beginning of the 20th century.
Diminutives: **Don, Donny**.

**Dora** originally a diminutive of **Dorothea, Dorothy**, or any name ending in *-dora*, notably **Theodora** (the daughter of William Wordsworth, named after the poet's sister Dorothy, was known in later life as Dora). It has been in regular use as an independent name since the mid-19th century, when it occurred in a number of literary works, including Charles Dickens' novel *David Copperfield*.
Variants: **Doreen, Dorette, Dorinda, Dorita**.

**Doran** (m) an Irish name, meaning 'stranger' or 'exile'.

**Dorcas** (f) from Greek, meaning 'gazelle'. The Dorcas of the New Testament, also known as **Tabitha**, was a charitable woman of Joppa raised from the dead by St Peter (Acts 9:36–41). The name was adopted by the Puritans in the 17th century but is rarely found in modern times.

**Doreen** (f) from the Irish name *Doirean*, of uncertain origin: it may be derived from a Celtic word meaning 'sullen' or it may simply be a variant of **Dora** or **Dorothy**. Borne by the heroine of a popular novel in the late 19th century, the name soon became fashionable throughout Britain and gradually spread to other parts of the English-speaking world.

**Dorette** a variant of **Dora**.

**Doria** the feminine form of **Dorian**.

**Dorian** [*dori*ăn] (m) from the name of an ancient Greek people, meaning either 'of Doris (a district of Greece)' or 'of Doros (a legendary Greek hero)'. The name has been in occasional use in English-speaking countries since the end of the 19th century, when it was popularized by Oscar Wilde's novel *The Picture of Dorian Gray* (1891). The showjumping commentator Dorian Williams was a more recent bearer of the name.
Feminine form: **Doria**.
Related name: **Doris**.

**Dorice** see **Doris**.

**Dorinda** (f) a literary invention of the 18th century, borne by a character in George Farquhar's play *The Beaux' Stratagem* (1707); generally regarded as a variant of **Dora** or **Dorothy**. The name enjoyed a slight revival in the mid-20th century and remains in occasional use today.

**Doris, Dorice** (f) a name borne in Greek mythology by the daughter of Oceanus and mother of the Nereids (sea nymphs); also the name of a district of Greece. The feminine first name may be derived from either or neither of these sources; it was rarely used in the English-speaking world until the late 19th century, when it suddenly became very fashionable (its adoption at this time may have been influenced by the popularity of other names beginning with *Dor-*, such as **Dora** and **Dorothy**). The US singer and actress Doris Day (born 1924) is a famous bearer of the name.
Variant: **Dorita**.
Related name: **Dorian**.

**Dorita** a variant of **Dora** or **Doris**.

**Dorothea** [dorrŏ*theeă*] (f) from Greek, meaning 'gift of God'. St Dorothea (or Dorothy), the earliest known bearer of the name, was martyred at the beginning of the 4th century. Introduced into Britain in the late 15th century, the name has always been more common in its variant form **Dorothy**, despite a temporary revival of *Dorothea* in the 19th century.
Variant: **Dorothy**.
Diminutives: **Dora**, **Thea**.
Related name: **Theodora**.

**Dorothy** a variant of **Dorothea**; the usual form of the name in English-speaking countries. It was particularly popular in the first half of the 20th century, a famous bearer being the young heroine (played by Judy Garland) of the film *The Wizard of Oz* (1939), based on a children's story written by the US novelist Frank Baum in 1900.
Variants: **Doreen**, **Dorinda**.
Diminutives: **Dodie**, **Doll**, **Dolly**, **Dora**, **Dot**, **Dottie**.

**Dorrie** a diminutive of any feminine name beginning with *Dor-*.

**Dot, Dottie** diminutives of **Dorothy**.

**Doug** a diminutive of **Douglas**.

**Dougal** [*doo*gäl] (m) from Irish Gaelic *dubhgall* 'dark stranger'; originally a nickname given by the Irish to the Vikings. The name has been in regular use in Scotland for several hundred years but is more readily associated in modern times with the canine hero of the children's television programme *The Magic Roundabout*.
Variant: **Dugald**.

**Dougie, Duggie** diminutives of **Douglas**.

**Douglas** (m) from a Scottish surname and place name (also the name of the capital of the Isle of Man); ultimately from Gaelic *dubhglas* 'dark water'. *Douglas* came into use as a first name in the late 16th century, when it was given to children of either sex; it gradually became established as a masculine name and was popularized throughout the English-speaking world in the first half of the 20th century by the actor Douglas Fairbanks and his son Douglas Fairbanks Jnr.
Diminutives: **Doug, Dougie, Duggie**.

**Dowsabel** see **Dulcie**.

**Dreda** a diminutive of **Eldreda** or **Etheldreda**, sometimes used as a name in its own right.

**Drew** a diminutive of **Andrew** or a variant of **Drogo**.

**Drogo** (m) an Old German name, possibly derived from *dragen* 'to bear (or carry)'. Introduced into Britain at the time of the Norman Conquest, the name remained in regular use, often in its variant form **Drew**, until the end of the 17th century. *Drogo* was partially revived in the 19th century but is rarely found in modern times.
Variant: **Drew**.

**Drusilla** (f) from the Roman family name *Drusus*; borne in the 1st century by a sister and mistress of the Roman emperor Caligula. Mentioned in the New Testament (Acts 24:24), the name was adopted by the Puritans in the 17th century and has been in occasional use throughout the English-speaking world since then.

**Duane, Dwayne** [dwayn] (m) a name of uncertain origin; probably from an Irish surname, meaning 'black'. It has been in regular use as a first name in various parts of the English-speaking world since the mid-20th century.

**Dud** a diminutive of **Dudley**.

**Dudley** (m) from a surname and place name; ultimately from Old English, meaning 'Dudda's clearing' (the identity of Dudda is uncertain). The surname was borne by an influential Tudor family and came into general use as a first name in the 19th century; the British comedian and musician

Dudley Moore (born 1935 is probably its best-known bearer in modern times.

Diminutive: **Dud**.

**Dugald** [*doo*gäld] a variant of **Dougal**.

**Duggie** see **Dougie**.

**Duke** (m) either from a surname originally borne by members of a duke's family or household or from the title itself. *Duke* is also used as a diminutive of **Marmaduke**. The US jazz musician Duke Ellington (born Edward Kennedy Ellington) was a famous bearer of the name.

**Dulce** a diminutive of **Dulcie**.

**Dulcibella** see **Dulcie**.

**Dulcie** (f) from Latin *dulcis* 'sweet'; sometimes regarded as a diminutive of the name *Dulcibella* (rendered in English as *Dowsabel*), which was first used in Britain in the Middle Ages but is now very rare. *Dulcie* has been in regular use since the 1880s and was particularly popular in the first half of the 20th century.

Diminutive: **Dulce**.

**Duncan** (m) from the Irish name *Donnchadh*, meaning 'brown warrior'. The name was borne by two Scottish kings of the 11th century, the more famous being Duncan I, who was killed by Macbeth in 1040; it has been in regular use in Scotland for several hundred years and is occasionally found in other parts of the English-speaking world. In Ireland, however, the name *Donnchadh* is usually translated as **Dennis**.

**Dunstan** (m) from Old English *dun* 'hill' and *stan* 'stone'; borne in the 10th century by St Dunstan, Archbishop of Canterbury. The name has been in occasional use in Britain since the Middle Ages but has never been common.

**Durand** [dew*rand*] (m) from Latin *durans* 'enduring'. Introduced into Britain from France at the time of the Norman Conquest, the name was in regular use during the Middle Ages but is rarely found in modern times. Variant: **Dante**.

**Dustin** (m) a name of uncertain origin, made famous in the late 1960s by the US actor Dustin Hoffman.

**Dwayne** see **Duane**.

**Dwight** (m) from a surname of uncertain origin; probably from *Diot*, a diminutive of *Dionysius* (see **Dennis**) or *Dionysia* (see **Denise**). Its use as a first name, which is largely confined to the USA, has been attributed to the popularity of Timothy Dwight (1752–1817), an early president of what is now Yale University. The 20th-century US president Dwight D. Eisenhower was a famous bearer of the name.

**Dylan** [*dil*än] (m) a Welsh name of uncertain derivation: possible interpretations include 'son of the wave' or 'influence'. Borne by a legendary

Welsh hero, *Dylan* is occasionally given in modern times in honour of the Welsh poet Dylan Thomas (1914–53) or the US folk singer Bob Dylan (born 1941). See also **Dillon**.

**Dymphna** [*dimf*nă] a variant of **Dympna**.

**Dympna** [*dimp*nă] (f) from the Irish name *Damhnait*, of uncertain origin; possibly derived from a word meaning 'fit' or 'eligible'. Borne by the martyr St Dympna, patron saint of the insane, the name is occasionally used by Roman Catholic families in Ireland but is rarely found elsewhere. Variant: **Dymphna**.

# E

**Eamon, Eamonn** [*ay*mŏn] the Irish form of **Edmund**. Famous bearers of the name in modern times include the Irish statesman Eamon De Valera and the media personality Eamonn Andrews, presenter of the long-running television programme *This Is Your Life*.

**Earl, Erle** (m) either from a surname originally borne by members of an earl's family or household or from the title itself; in occasional use as a first name, especially in the USA, since the 17th century. The jazz pianist Earl 'Fatha' Hines (1905–83) was a well-known bearer of the name and the variant spelling **Erle** was made famous by the US writer Erle Stanley Gardner (1889–1970), creator of the lawyer and detective Perry Mason. Variant: **Errol**.

**Earnest** see **Ernest**.

**Eartha** (f) from Old English *eorthe* 'earth'; made famous in the mid-20th century by the American creole singer Eartha Kitt.

**Easter** (m *or* f) from the name of the Christian festival; ultimately from *Eostre*, the name of a Germanic spring goddess. The feminine name is sometimes regarded as a variant of **Esther**.

**Eben** (m) from Hebrew, meaning 'stone'; sometimes used as a diminutive of **Ebenezer**.

**Ebenezer** [ebĕ*nee*zer] (m) from Hebrew, meaning 'stone of help'. In the Old Testament the name was given by Samuel to a stone set up in recognition of God's assistance in the defeat of the Philistines (1 Samuel 7:12). It was adopted as a first name by the Puritans in the 17th century and became very popular in the USA. The central character of Charles Dickens' novel *A Christmas Carol* (1843), the miser Ebenezer Scrooge, is a famous bearer of the name. Diminutive: **Eben**.

**Ed** a diminutive of **Edgar, Edmund, Edward,** or **Edwin**.

**Eda** see **Ada**. The name is sometimes used as a diminutive of **Edith**.

**Eddie, Eddy** diminutives of **Edgar, Edmund, Edward,** or **Edwin**, occasionally used as independent names.

**Eden** (m *or* f) from the biblical place name, with particular reference to the Garden of Eden; ultimately from Hebrew, meaning 'delight'. It was adopted as a first name by the Puritans in the 17th century and remains in occasional use today.

**Edgar** (m) from the Old English name *Eadgar*, a compound of *ead* 'rich' or 'happy' and *gar* 'spear'. The name was borne by a 10th-century king of England, a great grandson of Alfred the Great, and by a number of his descendants, including the 11th-century Anglo-Saxon prince Edgar the Aetheling. It remained in occasional use after the Norman Conquest and enjoyed a revival in the early 19th century, popularized by the hero of Sir Walter Scott's novel *The Bride of Lammermoor* (1819). The US writer Edgar Allen Poe was a famous bearer of the name.
Variant: **Adair**.
Diminutives: **Ed, Eddie, Eddy**.

**Edie** a diminutive of **Edith**, sometimes used as a name in its own right.

**Edith** (f) from the Old English name *Eadgyth*, a compound of *ead* 'rich' or 'happy' and *gyth* 'war'. The name was borne by the 10th-century nun St Edith (or Eadgyth), the illegitimate daughter of King Edgar, and by the first wife of King Henry I, who subsequently changed her name to Matilda; it has remained in regular use in Britain since the Middle Ages and was particularly popular in the late 19th and early 20th centuries. Famous bearers of the name include the poet Dame Edith Sitwell (1887–1964) and the actress Dame Edith Evans (1888–1976).
Diminutives: **Eda, Edie**.

**Edmund, Edmond** (m) from the Old English name *Eadmund*, a compound of *ead* 'rich' or 'happy' and *mund* 'protection'. The Suffolk town of Bury St Edmunds was named after the 9th-century martyr St Edmund, King of East Anglia; the name was also borne by two English kings of the 10th and early 11th centuries and by a second saint, Edmund Rich, who became Archbishop of Canterbury in 1234. The French spelling *Edmond* was introduced into Britain during the Middle Ages and remains in occasional use today, though it has never been as popular as the English form of the name. Famous bearers of the latter include the 16th-century poet Edmund Spenser and the New Zealand mountaineer Sir Edmund Hillary, who conquered Mount Everest in 1953.
Variants: **Eamon, Eamonn**.
Diminutives: **Ed, Eddie, Eddy, Ned, Neddie, Neddy, Ted, Teddie, Teddy**.

**Edna** (f) a name of uncertain origin: it may be from Hebrew, meaning 'rejuvenation', or it may simply be a variant of **Edwina**. The name occurs in the

Apocrypha but was rarely used as a first name in the English-speaking world before 1850; it came into fashion in the USA in the latter half of the 19th century and was particularly popular in Britain in the 1920s.

**Edom** a Scottish variant of **Adam**; an alternative name of the Old Testament character **Esau**.

**Edward** (m) from the Old English name *Eadweard*, a compound of *ead* 'rich' or 'happy' and *weard* 'guardian'. The name has been in fairly constant use at all levels of society since the early Middle Ages; its long association with the royal families of Britain dates back to the 9th century, when it was borne by King Edward the Elder, son of Alfred the Great. Subsequent royal bearers of the name include the 10th- and 11th-century monarchs St Edward the Martyr and St Edward the Confessor; a line of kings stretching from Edward I, who came to the throne in 1272, to Edward VIII, who abdicated in 1936; and the youngest son of Queen Elizabeth II, Prince Edward (born 1964). Despite the lasting popularity of the name, which has been translated into a number of other European languages, no feminine form or masculine variant of *Edward* has ever established itself in the English-speaking world.
Diminutives: **Ed, Eddie, Eddy, Ned, Neddie, Neddy, Ted, Teddie, Teddy**.

**Edwin, Edwyn** (m) from the Old English name *Eadwine*, a compound of *ead* 'rich' or 'happy' and *wine* 'friend'. The city of Edinburgh, capital of Scotland, is believed by some scholars to have been named after King Edwin of Northumbria, who was converted to Christianity in 627. The name was little used after the 12th century until its revival in the 19th century, when it was borne by the hero of Charles Dickens' last novel, *Edwin Drood*; it remained in regular use throughout the English-speaking world during the first half of the 20th century. The variant spelling *Edwyn* may have been influenced by the Anglo-Saxon name *Edwy*, which is now obsolete.
Diminutives: **Ed, Eddie, Eddy**.
Feminine form: **Edwina**.

**Edwina** the feminine form of **Edwin**.
Variant: **Edna**.

**Edwy, Edwyn** see **Edwin**.

**Effie** a diminutive of **Euphemia**, sometimes used as a name in its own right.

**Egbert** (m) from Old English *ecg* 'sword' and *beorht* 'bright'; borne in the 9th-century by King Egbert of Wessex, who held sway over all the kingdoms of England for a short part of his reign. The name enjoyed a slight revival in the 19th century but is rarely found in modern times.

**Egidia, Egidius** see **Giles**.

**Eileen** [īleen] (f) from the Irish name *Eibhlin*, probably derived from **Evelyn** or **Evelina** but sometimes regarded as a variant of **Helen**. Together with a

number of other Irish names, *Eileen* became fashionable in Great Britain in the late 19th century; it subsequently spread to the rest of the English-speaking world and remains in regular use today.
Variants: **Aileen, Eveleen.**
Diminutive: **Eily.**

**Eiluned** see **Eluned.**

**Eilwen** (f) a Welsh name, meaning 'fair brow'.

**Eily** a diminutive of **Eileen.**

**Eira** (f) a Welsh name, meaning 'snow'.

**Eirian** (f) a Welsh name, meaning 'silver'.

**Eithne** a variant of **Ethne.**

**Elain** (f) a Welsh name, meaning 'fawn'; sometimes erroneously associated with **Elaine.**

**Elaine** a variant of **Helen;** originally an Old French form of the name, borne in Arthurian legend by the mother of Sir Lancelot's son Galahad. The name was revived in the late 19th century, after the publication of Tennyson's version of the legend in his *Idylls of the King,* and was particularly popular in Britain in the latter half of the 20th century. See also **Elain.**

**Eldon** (m) from a surname and place name of uncertain origin; in occasional use as a first name since the 19th century.

**Eldred** a variant of **Aldred.**
Feminine form: **Eldreda.**

**Eldreda** the feminine form of **Eldred.**
Diminutive: **Dreda.**

**Eleanor, Elinor** [*e*ſinər] probably variants of **Helen,** of French origin; introduced into Britain in the 12th century by Eleanor of Aquitaine, wife of King Henry II. The name was further popularized by King Edward I's wife Eleanor of Castile (1246–90), in whose memory a series of 'Eleanor crosses' were erected at the twelve places where her funeral procession rested, the last of these being Charing Cross. The variant spelling *Elinor,* which first appeared in the 17th century, was used by Jane Austen for one of the heroines of her novel *Sense and Sensibility* (1811).
Variants: **Eleanora, Lenore, Leonora.**
Diminutives: **Ellie, Nell, Nellie, Nelly.**

**Eleanora** [eliănŏră] a variant of **Eleanor.**
Diminutives: **Nora, Norah.**

**Eleazar** [eli*a*yzer] (m) from Hebrew, meaning 'God is my help'; borne in the Old Testament by a son of Aaron and by one of King David's 'three mighty men' (2 Samuel 23:9). The name has been in occasional use in the English-speaking world since the 17th century.
Variant: **Lazarus.**

**Elena** a variant of **Helen**, dating back to the 12th century; now regarded as the Italian or Spanish form of the name.

**Eleonora** see **Leonora**.

**Elfreda, Elfrida** (f) from the Old English name *Aelfthryth*, a compound of *aelf* 'elf' and *thryth* 'strength'. Borne by the mother of Ethelred the Unready, the name was little used after the Norman Conquest until its revival in the 19th century.
Variant: **Alfreda**.
Diminutive: **Freda**.

**Eli** [*eelī*] (m) from Hebrew, meaning 'high'; borne by the Old Testament priest in whose care the prophet Samuel spent his early years. The name has been in occasional use in the English-speaking world since the 17th century.

**Elias** [*ilīãs*] the Greek form of **Elijah**. *Elias* and its variants were more common than *Elijah* in medieval Britain; since the Reformation both names have been in occasional use throughout the English-speaking world.
Variants: **Eliot, Elliot, Elliott, Ellis**.

**Elihu** [*ilīhew*] (m) from Hebrew, meaning 'God is he'; one of a number of Old Testament names adopted by the Puritans in the 16th and 17th centuries. It is rarely used in modern times.

**Elijah** [*ilījã*] (m) from Hebrew, meaning 'Jehovah is God'. Borne by an Old Testament prophet, the name was rarely used in this form in English-speaking countries until its revival by the Puritans in the 16th century.
Variant: **Elias**.

**Elined** see **Elumed**.

**Elinor** see **Eleanor**.

**Eliot** see **Elliott**.

**Elisabeth** the usual spelling of **Elizabeth** in Continental Europe; occasionally used in English-speaking countries.

**Elise** a variant of **Elizabeth**, from a French diminutive of the name; in occasional use in the English-speaking world since the late 19th century.

**Elisha** [*ilīshã*] (m) from Hebrew, meaning 'God is salvation'. Borne by an Old Testament prophet, the disciple and successor of Elijah, the name was adopted by the Puritans in the 17th century and remains in occasional use today.

**Elissa** (f) one of the names by which Dido, Queen of Carthage, was known; sometimes regarded as a variant of **Elizabeth**.

**Eliza** a diminutive of **Elizabeth**; often used as a name in its own right, particularly in the 18th and 19th centuries. One of its most famous bearers is Eliza Doolittle, the Cockney heroine of George Bernard Shaw's play *Pygmalion* (1913) and the musical *My Fair Lady*, derived from it.

# Ellis

**Elizabeth, Elisabeth** (f) from the Hebrew name *Elisheba*, meaning either 'oath of God' or 'God is satisfaction', borne in the Old Testament by the wife of Aaron; one of the earliest known bearers of the name in its Greek form, *Elizabeth*, was the mother of John the Baptist. The name was popularized in the 13th century by St Elizabeth of Hungary and went on to become one of the most common feminine names in Britain during the reign of Queen Elizabeth I in the latter half of the 16th century. It held this position until the end of the 19th century and has remained in regular use throughout the English-speaking world since then, thanks to the popularity of Elizabeth the Queen Mother (born Lady Elizabeth Bowes-Lyon) and her daughter Queen Elizabeth II.
Variants: **Babette, Beta, Bettina, Elise, Elissa, Elsa, Elsie, Elspeth, Ilse, Isabel, Isabella, Isabelle, Isobel, Liesel, Liesl, Lise, Lisette.**
Diminutives: **Bess, Bessie, Bessy, Beth, Bethan, Betsy, Bette, Betty, Eliza, Libby, Lili, Lilla, Lillah, Lisa, Lisbeth, Liz, Liza, Lizbeth, Lizzie, Lizzy, Tetty.**

**Elkanah** [elkahnă] (m) from Hebrew, meaning 'God has created'. Borne in the Old Testament by the father of the prophet Samuel, the name has been in occasional use in the English-speaking world since the 17th century.

**Ella** (f) from the Old German name *Alia*, meaning 'all'. Introduced into Britain at the time of the Norman Conquest, it was little used after the end of the Middle Ages until its revival in the 19th century, when it was sometimes regarded as a variant or diminutive of feminine names beginning with *El-* or ending in *-ella*. Famous bearers of the name in the USA include the poet Ella Wheeler Wilcox (1850–1919) and the jazz singer Ella Fitzgerald (born 1918).

**Ellen** a variant of **Helen**. The usual form of the name in the English-speaking world from the Middle Ages to the Renaissance, *Ellen* remained in regular use in Britain until the mid-20th century, by which time it had become very fashionable in the USA. The British actress Dame Ellen Terry (1847–1928) was a famous bearer of the name.
Diminutives: **Ellie, Nell, Nellie, Nelly.**

**Ellery** (m) from a surname of uncertain origin; possibly derived from **Eulalia** or **Hilary**. The best-known bearer of the name in modern times is Ellery Queen, the hero of a series of detective stories written by Frederic Dannay and Manfred B. Lee.

**Ellie** a diminutive of **Eleanor** or **Ellen.**

**Elliott, Elliot, Eliot** (m) from a surname derived from a medieval diminutive of **Elias**; revived as a first name in modern times.

**Ellis** (m) from a surname derived from a medieval variant of **Elias**; revived as a first name in modern times.

73

**Elma** (f) either a diminutive of a feminine name ending in *-elma* or a compound of the first two letters of **Elizabeth** and **Mary**.

**Elmer** a variant of **Aylmer**. The name is generally associated with the USA, where its popularity has been attributed to the prominent role played by two brothers, Ebenezer and Jonathan Elmer, in the War of American Independence. The US writer Sinclair Lewis gave the name to the central character of his satirical novel *Elmer Gantry* (1927).

**Eloisa** the Latinized or Italian form of **Eloise**.

**Eloise** [elōeez] (f) probably from the Old German name *Helewidis*, derived from two words meaning 'hale' and 'wide', which developed into the English name *Helewise*. This was eventually replaced by *Eloise*, from the French form *Héloïse*, popularized by the love letters of Abelard and Héloïse. Some scholars believe the name to be a variant of *Aloysia*, ultimately a feminine form of **Louis**.

Variants: **Eloisa, Lois**.

**Elroy** a variant of **Leroy**.

**Elsa** a variant of **Elizabeth**; originally a German diminutive of the name. (Some scholars favour an alternative derivation, ultimately from Old German *athal* 'noble'.) Famous bearers of the name include the heroine of Wagner's opera *Lohengrin* and the tame lioness featured in Joy Adamson's book *Born Free* (1960).

Variant: **Ailsa**.

**Elsie** a variant of **Elizabeth**; originally a diminutive of the Scottish form **Elspeth**. Popular throughout the English-speaking world in the late 19th and early 20th centuries, it remains in occasional use today.

**Elspeth** a Scottish variant of **Elizabeth**, rarely found outside its country of origin.

Diminutives: **Elsie, Elspie**.

**Elspie** a diminutive of **Elspeth**.

**Elton** (m) from a surname and place name of uncertain origin; popularized as a first name in the 1970s by the British singer Elton John (born Reginald Kenneth Dwight).

**Eluned, Elined, Eiluned** [elinĕd] (f) from Welsh *eilun* 'idol'; rarely used outside Wales until the 20th century.

Variants: **Linette, Linnet, Lynette, Lynnette**.

**Elvie** a diminutive of **Elvina**.

**Elvin** a variant of **Alvin**.

Feminine form: **Elvina**.

**Elvina** the feminine form of **Elvin**.

Diminutive: **Elvie**.

**Elvira** [elveerǎ, elvyrǎ] (f) a Spanish name of uncertain origin; possibly a variant of **Albreda**. It occurs in the legend of Don Juan, on which a number of literary and musical works, notably Mozart's opera *Don Gio-vanni* (1787), have been based. The name is occasionally found in English-speaking countries and was used by Noel Coward for the heroine of his play *Blithe Spirit* (1941).

**Elvis** probably a variant of **Alvis**. The name has been in use in the English-speaking world since the early 20th century but has never been common, despite the immense success of its most famous bearer, the US popular singer Elvis Presley.

**Elwyn** (m) a name of uncertain origin: it may be from Welsh, meaning 'fair brow', or it may simply be a variant of **Alvin**.

**Em** a variant of **Emma**; the usual form of the name in Britain from the Middle Ages until the 18th century. It is now regarded as a diminutive of any feminine name beginning with *Em-*.

**Emanuel, Emmanuel** (m) from Hebrew, meaning 'God with us'; an Old Testament name for the Messiah. It has been in occasional use in the English-speaking world since the 15th century but has never been common.
Variant: **Manuel**.
Diminutive: **Manny**.
Feminine forms: **Emanuela, Emmanuela**.

**Emanuela, Emmanuela** feminine forms of **Emanuel**.

**Emeline, Emelyn, Emblyn, Emblem** see **Emmeline**.

**Emerald** (f) from the name of the precious stone.
Related name: **Esmeralda**.

**Emery** (m) from the Old German name *Emmerich*, possibly derived from *amal* 'labour' and *ric* 'ruler'. Introduced into Britain after the Norman Conquest, *Emery* is more familiar as a surname than as a first name in modern times.

**Emil** (m) a German name, ultimately from the Roman clan name *Aemilius*, occasionally used in English-speaking countries. The name also occurs in the French form, *Emile*, popularized in the latter half of the 19th century by the French writer Emile Zola.
Feminine equivalent: **Emily**.

**Emile** see **Emil**.

**Emilia** see **Emily**.

**Emily** (f) from the Latin name *Aemilia*, the feminine form of the Roman clan name *Aemilius*. It was introduced into Britain in the Middle Ages: the 14th-century Italian poet Boccaccio gave the name *Emilia* to the heroine of the *Teseida*, which Chaucer used as a source for *The Knight's Tale*, anglicizing the name as *Emelye*. *Emily* became fashionable in the 18th century, when it was generally regarded as a variant of **Amelia**, and re-

# Emlyn

mained in regular use until the early 20th century. It enjoyed a further revival in the 1970s. See also **Emmeline**.

Diminutives: **Millie, Milly**.

Masculine equivalent: **Emil**.

**Emlyn** (f) see **Emmeline**.

**Emlyn** (m) a Welsh name of uncertain origin: it may be derived from the Latin name *Aemilianus* or from the Welsh place name *Newcastle Emlyn*. Famous bearers of the name in the 20th century include the Welsh actor and dramatist Emlyn Williams and the English footballer Emlyn Hughes.

**Emma** (f) from Old German *ermin* or *irmin* 'universal'. The name was introduced into Britain in the 11th century by Emma of Normandy, wife of King Ethelred the Unready and King Canute, and soon became familiar in a number of variant forms, notably **Em**. The original form of the name came back into fashion in the 18th century and remained in regular use until the early 20th century; it enjoyed a further revival in the late 1960s, when it was popularized by the character of Emma Peel (played by the actress Diana Rigg) in the British television series *The Avengers*. Other famous bearers of the name include Lady Emma Hamilton, mistress of Lord Horatio Nelson, and the heroine of Jane Austen's novel *Emma* (1815).

Variant: **Em**.

Related name: **Irma**.

**Emmanuel** see **Emanuel**.

**Emmanuela** see **Emanuela**.

**Emmeline** (f) from the Old French name *Ameline*, ultimately from Old German *amal* 'labour'; sometimes erroneously associated with **Emily**. The name was introduced into Britain at the time of the Norman Conquest and has existed in a variety of forms, including *Emeline, Emelyn, Emlyn, Emblyn*, and *Emblem*, most of which are now obsolete. The British suffragette Emmeline Pankhurst (1858–1928) was a famous bearer of the name.

Related name: **Amelia**.

**Emmie** a diminutive of any feminine name beginning with *Em-*.

**Emrys** the Welsh form of **Ambrose**; more frequently used in modern times than its English equivalent.

**Ena** (f) a name of uncertain origin: it may be a diminutive of **Eugenia**, a diminutive of any name ending in *-ena*, or a variant of **Ethne**. It was popularized as an independent name by Queen Victoria's granddaughter Victoria Eugénie Julia Ena, known as Princess Ena, who became Queen of Spain in 1906.

Related name: **Ina**.

**Enid** [eenid] (f) probably from Welsh *enaid* 'soul' or 'life'. The name occurs in Arthurian legend: it came into general use in Britain after the publication of Tennyson's version of the story of Geraint and Enid in his *Idylls of the King* (1859). The children's writer Enid Blyton (1897–1968), creator of such characters as Noddy, was one of the best-known bearers of the name.

**Enoch** [eenok] (m) from Hebrew, meaning 'dedicated' or 'trained'; borne in the Old Testament by the father of Methuselah. Adopted by the Puritans in the 17th century, the name was popularized by Tennyson in his poem *Enoch Arden* (1864); its most famous bearer in modern times is the British politician Enoch Powell (born 1912).

**Enos** (m) from Hebrew, meaning 'man'; borne in the Old Testament by a grandson of Adam and Eve. The name has been in occasional use in the English-speaking world since the 19th century.

**Eoghan** (m) an Irish name of uncertain origin: it may be related to a Gaelic word meaning 'youth' or it may simply be a variant of **Eugene**.
Variants: **Ewan**, **Ewen**.

**Ephraim** [eefrayim, eefraym, eefrăm] (m) from Hebrew, meaning 'fruitful'. Borne in the Old Testament by one of the sons of Joseph, the name was adopted by the Puritans in the 17th century and remained in regular use until the early 20th century. It is still found from time to time in the USA.

**Eppie** a diminutive of **Euphemia** or **Hephzibah**, sometimes used as a name in its own right.

**Erasmus** (m) from Greek, meaning 'desired' or 'beloved'. The martyr St Erasmus (or Elmo), patron saint of sailors, gave his name to the phenomenon known as St Elmo's fire. Other famous bearers of the name include the Dutch humanist Desiderius Erasmus (1466–1536) and the British physician and poet Erasmus Darwin (1731–1802), grandfather of Charles Darwin. *Erasmus* has been in occasional use as a first name in the English-speaking world since the 17th century but is rarely found in modern times.

**Eric** (m) from Norse, meaning 'ever ruler' or 'island ruler'; borne by the 10th-century Norwegian explorer Eric the Red. The name was introduced into Britain by the Vikings but was little used until the latter half of the 19th century, when it was popularized by Frederic Farrar's story *Eric: or, Little by Little* (1858). It was particularly fashionable in Britain in the 1920s and subsequently spread to the USA, where the Scandinavian spelling *Erik* is sometimes found.
Diminutives: **Rick**, **Ricky**.
Feminine forms: **Erica**, **Erika**.

**Erica, Erika** feminine forms of **Eric**; sometimes associated with the plant name *erica*. The name has been in regular use throughout the English-speaking world since the late 19th century.

# Erik

Diminutives: **Rica, Ricki, Rika, Rikki**.

**Erik** see **Eric**.

**Erika** see **Erica**.

**Erin** (f) from an ancient or poetic name for Ireland. Borne by a character in the US television series *The Waltons*, *Erin* came into fashion as a first name in the USA and Canada in the 1970s.

**Erle** see **Earl**.

**Ermintrude, Ermyntrude** (f) from Old German *ermin* 'universal' and *drudi* 'strength'. Popularized by the writers of romantic fiction, *Ermintrude* was occasionally given as a first name in the 18th and 19th centuries but is rarely found in modern times.
Diminutives: **Trudi, Trudie, Trudy**.

**Ern** a diminutive of **Ernest**.

**Ernest** (m) from the Old German name *Ernust*, meaning 'earnestness' or 'vigour'. The name was introduced into Britain by the Hanoverians but was little used until the latter half of the 19th century, when it became popular throughout the English-speaking world. The occasional use of the alternative spelling *Earnest* may have been influenced by the play on words in the title of Oscar Wilde's comedy *The Importance of Being Earnest* (1895).
Diminutives: **Ern, Ernie**.
Feminine form: **Ernestine**.

**Ernestine** the feminine form of **Ernest**.

**Ernie** a diminutive of **Ernest**, sometimes used as a name in its own right. In Britain it may also be associated with the Electronic Random Number Indicator Equipment used to select winning Premium Bond numbers.

**Errol** (m) a name of uncertain origin: it may be from a Scottish surname and place name or it may simply be a variant of **Earl** or **Harold**. Made famous in the first half of the 20th century by the Australian actor Errol Flynn, the name remains in occasional use in various parts of the English-speaking world.

**Erwin** see **Irwin**.

**Esau** [*eesaw*] (m) from Hebrew, meaning 'hairy'; borne in the Old Testament by the elder son of Isaac, who sold his birthright to his twin brother Jacob (Genesis 25:29–34). The name has been in occasional use in English-speaking countries since the Reformation. See also **Edom**.

**Esme** [*ezmi*] (m *or* f) from Old French, ultimately from Latin *aestimatus* 'esteemed' or *amatus* 'loved' (see **Amy, Amyas**). Popularized in Scotland by Esmé Stuart, a cousin of King James VI of Scotland who became Duke of Lennox in 1581, the name eventually spread to England and was given to children of either sex. Its use as a feminine name, sometimes in the form *Esmee*, may have been influenced by **Ismay**.

**Esmee** see **Esme**.

**Esmeralda** (f) from Spanish, meaning 'emerald'; borne by the heroine of Victor Hugo's novel *The Hunchback of Notre Dame* (1831). It has been in occasional use in English-speaking countries since the 19th century.
Related name: **Emerald**.

**Esmond** (m) from the Old English name *Estmund*, a compound of *est* 'grace' and *mund* 'protection'. *Esmond* was rarely used as a first name after the end of the Middle Ages but survived as a surname; it enjoyed a temporary revival in the latter half of the 19th century, after the publication of Thackeray's novel *Henry Esmond* (1852).

**Essie** a diminutive of **Estella**, **Estelle**, or **Esther**.

**Estella** (f) from the Old French form of the Latin word *stella*, meaning 'star'. Popularized by the beautiful heroine of Charles Dickens' novel *Great Expectations* (1860–61), the name remained in occasional use until the mid-20th century, when it was largely superseded by the modern French form **Estelle**.
Variant: **Estelle**.
Diminutive: **Essie**.
Related name: **Stella**.

**Estelle** a variant of **Estella**, of French origin; the more common form of the name in the English-speaking world in modern times.
Diminutive: **Essie**.

**Esther** [*ester*] (f) from a Persian word for 'star', with particular reference to the planet Venus (*Esther* may be a variant of *Ishtar*, the name of the Babylonian goddess of love). The Esther of the Old Testament, a Jewish orphan who became Queen of Persia in the 5th century BC, also bore the name *Hadassah*, meaning 'myrtle' or 'bride'. Both names were adopted by the Puritans in the 17th century; *Hadassah* soon fell from favour but *Esther* remained in regular use in various parts of the English-speaking world until the mid-20th century. See also **Stella**, **Vanessa**.
Variants: **Easter**, **Hester**.
Diminutives: **Essie**, **Ettie**, **Etty**.

**Eth** a diminutive of **Ethel**.

**Ethan** (m) from Hebrew, meaning 'constancy'; mentioned in the Old Testament (1 Kings 4:31). The name is generally associated with the USA, where it was popularized in the latter half of the 18th century by the soldier Ethan Allen, who played a prominent role in the War of American Independence.

**Ethel** (f) from Old English *aethel* 'noble'; originally a diminutive of **Etheldreda**, **Ethelinda**, or any other feminine name beginning with *Ethel-*. Popularized by a character in Thackeray's novel *The Newcomes*, *Ethel* came into general use as an independent name in the 1850s and was particularly fashionable around the turn of the century. Famous bearers of the name include the US actresses Ethel Barrymore (1879–1959) and Ethel Merman (born 1908).

Diminutive: **Eth**.

Related names: **Adela, Adeline**.

**Ethelbert** (m) from the Old English name *Aethelbeorht*, a compound of *aethel* 'noble' and *beorht* 'bright'. Borne by two English kings of the 6th and 9th centuries, the name was largely superseded by the various forms of **Albert** after the Norman Conquest. It was revived in the 19th century and has been used occasionally since then.

**Etheldreda** (f) from the Old English name *Aethelthryth*, a compound of *aethel* 'noble' and *thryth* 'strength'. St Etheldreda, later known as St Audrey, was the wife of a 7th-century Northumbrian king and the foundress of a monastery at Ely. The name was largely superseded in the 16th century by **Audrey** and in the 19th century by **Ethel**, but remains in occasional use.

Variant: **Audrey**.

Diminutives: **Dreda, Ethel**.

**Ethelinda** (f) from *Aethelind*, the Old English equivalent of an Old German name derived from *athal* 'noble' and *lindi* 'snake'. The name was revived in the 19th century but is rarely found in modern times.

Diminutive: **Ethel**.

**Ethelred** (m) from Old English *aethel* 'noble' and *raed* 'counsel'; borne by two Anglo-Saxon kings, the second of whom was nicknamed Ethelred the Unready. The name was revived in the 19th century but is rarely found in modern times.

**Ethne** (f) from Irish Gaelic, meaning 'little fire'. The name and its variants have been popular in Ireland for many hundreds of years.

Variants: **Aine, Aithne, Eithne, Ena**.

Masculine equivalent: **Aidan**.

**Etta** see **Ada**. The name is sometimes used as a diminutive of **Henrietta**.

**Ettie, Etty** diminutives of **Esther** or **Henrietta**, sometimes used as independent names.

**Eugene** [*yoo*jeen, yoo*jeen*] (m) from Greek, meaning 'well-born'. The name was borne by four popes, including St Eugenius (died 657); it was popularized in Europe by Prince Eugene of Savoy (1663–1736) and gradually spread to Britain and other parts of the English-speaking world. *Eugene* was particularly fashionable in the USA in the late 19th century, the US dramatist Eugene O'Neill (1888–1953) being a famous bearer of the name.

Variants: **Eoghan, Ewan, Ewen, Owain, Owen**.

Diminutive: **Gene**.

Feminine forms: **Eugenia, Eugenie**.

**Eugenia** [yoo*jee*niä] (f) from a Greek name meaning 'nobility'; generally regarded as a feminine form of **Eugene**. Borne by an early Roman martyr, the name has been in occasional use in the English-speaking world since the Middle Ages.
Variant: **Eugenie**.
Diminutive: **Ena**.

**Eugenie** [yoo*zhay*ni] a variant of **Eugenia** or a feminine form of **Eugene**, of French origin. The name has been in occasional use in English-speaking countries since the 19th century, when it was popularized by the French empress Eugénie, wife of Napoleon III.

**Eulalia** [yoo*lay*liä] (f) from Greek, meaning 'sweetly speaking'; borne by the Spanish martyr St Eulalia, who died in the early 4th century. The name is occasionally found in the English-speaking world but has never been common. See also **Ellery**.
Variant: **Eulalie**.

**Eulalie** the French form of **Eulalia**.

**Eunice** [*yoo*nis] (f) from a Greek name meaning 'good victory'. Borne in the New Testament by the mother of Timothy, the name has been in occasional use in English-speaking countries since the early 17th century.

**Euphemia** [yoo*fee*miä] (f) from Greek, meaning 'auspicious speech' or 'good repute'. Borne by the 4th-century martyr St Euphemia, the name was introduced into Britain in the 12th century and became particularly popular in Scotland. It remains in occasional use in that country today but is rarely found elsewhere.
Diminutives: **Effie, Eppie, Phemie**.

**Eustace** [*yoo*stäs] (m) from Greek, meaning 'fruitful'. St Eustace (or Eustachius), a Roman soldier martyred in the 2nd century, was an early bearer of the name. Introduced into Britain at the time of the Norman Conquest, *Eustace* was fairly common in the latter half of the Middle Ages and remains in occasional use today.
Diminutives: **Stacey, Stacy**.
Feminine form: **Eustacia**.

**Eustacia** the feminine form of **Eustace**.

**Eva** [*ee*vä] the Latin form of **Eve**. Popularized by a character in Harriet Beecher Stowe's novel *Uncle Tom's Cabin* (1852), whose full name was **Evangeline**, *Eva* became fashionable throughout the English-speaking world in the late 19th century and remained in frequent use until the 1930s. Famous bearers of the name in other countries include Adolf Hitler's mistress Eva Braun and the Argentine actress and politician Eva Perón, better known by the pet form of her name, *Evita*.
Variant: **Ava**.
Diminutives: **Eveleen, Evie**.

# Evadne

**Evadne** [i*vad*ni] (f) from a Greek name of uncertain origin; borne in Greek mythology by the wife of Capaneus, one of the heroes of Aeschylus' play *Seven Against Thebes*. The name is used from time to time in the English-speaking world but has never been common.

**Evan** the Welsh form of **John**, rarely used outside its country of origin until the 19th century. *Evans*, meaning 'son of Evan', is one of the most common surnames in Britain.

**Evangelina** the Latinized form of **Evangeline**.

**Evangeline** (f) from Greek, meaning 'good news' (the English noun *evangelist* is derived from the same source). The name was first used in the English-speaking world by the US poet Longfellow, whose narrative poem *Evangeline* was published in 1847; it was further popularized by a character in *Uncle Tom's Cabin* (see **Eva**) and remains in occasional use today.

Variant: **Evangelina**.

**Eve** (f) from Hebrew, meaning 'life', 'living', or 'lively'; borne in the Old Testament by Adam's wife, the mother of the human race, whose tasting of the forbidden fruit led to the Fall of Man (Genesis 3). The name has been in occasional use in English-speaking countries since the Middle Ages.

Diminutives: **Eveleen, Evie**.

**Eveleen** [ev*ĕ*leen] an Irish variant of **Eileen, Evelina**, or **Evelyn** (f). The name is also used as a diminutive of **Eva** or **Eve**.

**Evelina** [ev*ĕleen*ă] (f) a name of uncertain origin: it may be from the Old German name *Avelina* or from Old French *aveline* 'hazel nut'. The name *Aveline* was introduced into Britain by the Normans; *Evelina* is the Latinized form, popularized in the late 18th century by Fanny Burney's novel of the same name.

Variants: **Eileen, Eveleen, Eveline, Evelyn**.

**Eveline** [ev*ĕ*leen, *eev*lin] a variant of **Evelina** or **Evelyn** (f).

**Evelyn** [*eev*lin, *ev*lin] (m *or* f) from a surname derived from *Aveline* (see **Evelina**). The existence of *Evelyn* as a masculine first name dates from the 17th century, the novelist Evelyn Waugh being a famous 20th-century bearer; its use as a feminine name was a later development, influenced by **Evelina**.

Variants: (f) **Eileen, Eveleen, Evelina, Eveline**.

**Everard** (m) from the Old German name *Eburhard*, derived from *ebur* 'boar' and *hardu* 'hard'. Introduced into Britain at the time of the Norman Conquest, *Everard* was fairly common in the latter half of the Middle Ages and enjoyed a partial revival in the 19th century.

**Everild** see Averil.

**Evie** a diminutive of **Eva, Eve,** or any other feminine name beginning with *Ev-*.

**Evita** see Eva.

**Evonne** see Yvonne.

**Ewan, Ewen** variants of **Eoghan** or **Eugene.** Formerly popular in England, where it gave rise to a number of surnames, *Ewan* is now regarded as a Scottish name.
Variants: **Owain, Owen.**

**Ezekiel** [izeekiĕl] (m) from Hebrew, meaning 'God strengthens' or 'may God strengthen'. Ezekiel was an Old Testament prophet of the 6th century BC; the name was adopted by the Puritans in the 17th century but is rarely found in modern times.
Diminutive: **Zeke.**

**Ezra** (m) from Hebrew, meaning 'help'; borne in the Old Testament by a religious reformer of the 5th century BC. The name was adopted by the Puritans and remained in regular use in Britain and the USA until the end of the 19th century, the US poet Ezra Pound (1885–1972) being one of its best-known bearers in modern times.

# F

**Fabian** (m) from the Latin name *Fabianus*, derived from the Roman clan name *Fabius*, possibly meaning 'bean-grower' or 'bean-seller'. (The socialist Fabian Society, founded in the late 19th century, was named after one of the members of this clan, the Roman general Fabius Cunctator.) Borne by the 3rd-century pope and martyr St Fabian, the name has been in occasional use in Britain since the Middle Ages but is rarely found in modern times.
Feminine form: **Fabiana.**

**Fabiana** the feminine form of **Fabian.**

**Faith** (f) from the name of one of the three Christian virtues (see **Charity, Hope**); borne by two legendary saints. It was adopted as a first name by the Puritans in the 16th century, together with a number of other names of abstract qualities, and is one of the few names of this type that have survived into the latter half of the 20th century.
Variants: **Fay, Faye.**

**Fanny, Fan** diminutives of **Frances.** *Fanny* was regularly given as an independent name from the end of the 17th century until the early 20th century, when its use as a slang term accelerated its fall from favour. Famous bearers of the name include Fanny Hill, the heroine of John Cleland's novel *Memoirs of a Woman of Pleasure* (1748–49), which was banned soon after publication, and the 19th-century murder victim Fanny Adams, whose name is used euphemistically in the expression *sweet Fanny Adams*, meaning 'nothing'.

**Faron** see **Farran**.

**Farquhar** [*far*ker] (m) from the Scottish Gaelic name *Fearchar*, meaning either 'friendly man' or 'very dear one'; more common as a surname than as a first name. Borne by an early king of Scotland, the name remains in occasional use in that country but is rarely found elsewhere.

**Farran, Farren, Faron** (m *or* f) from a surname of uncertain origin: it may be from Old French, meaning 'pilferer' or 'ferret', or from a medieval form of **Ferdinand**.

**Faustina** (f) from Latin *faustus* 'fortunate'. The name has never been common in the English-speaking world.

**Fay, Faye** (f) a name of uncertain origin: it may be from the English word *fay*, meaning 'fairy', or it may simply be a variant of **Faith**. Famous bearers of the name, which was first used in the late 19th century, include the British actress Fay Compton and the US actress Faye Dunaway.

**Feargus** see **Fergus**.

**Fedora** a variant of **Feodora**.

**Felice** a variant of **Felicia**; often confused with **Phyllis**.

**Felicia** the feminine form of **Felix**. The name was in regular use in Britain, often in the variant form **Felice**, from the 12th century until the 19th century; it is rarely found in modern times. The British poet Felicia Hemans (1793–1835), remembered for the opening line of her poem 'Casabianca' ('The boy stood on the burning deck...'), was a famous bearer of the name.

Variant: **Felice**.

**Felicity** (f) from the Latin name *Felicitas*, meaning 'happiness' or 'good luck', which was borne by the Roman goddess of good luck and by two early martyrs (both of whom are also known as St Felicity). *Felicity* was one of the many names of abstract qualities adopted by the Puritans in the 16th and 17th centuries; it remains in regular use in modern times, a famous bearer being the British actress Felicity Kendal.

**Felix** (m) from Latin, meaning 'happy' or 'lucky'; borne by several saints, including the 7th-century missionary who gave his name to the Suffolk town of Felixstowe. It has been in occasional use in the English-speaking world since the Middle Ages but has never been common. Famous bearers of the name in modern times include the British actor Felix Aylmer and the cartoon character Felix the Cat.

Feminine form: **Felicia**.

**Fenella** (f) from the Gaelic name *Fionnghuala* or *Fionnuala*, meaning 'white shoulder'. The actress Fenella Fielding is a famous bearer of the name. See also **Penelope**.
Variants: **Finola, Nuala.**

**Feodora** the Russian form of **Theodora.**
Variant: **Fedora.**

**Ferdinand** (m) from Old German *fardi* 'journey' and *nanthi* 'venture'; borne by three Holy Roman emperors and by a number of Spanish and Italian kings. The name was introduced into Britain in the Old French form *Ferrand* or *Ferrant* at the time of the Norman Conquest; *Ferdinand* developed at a later date from the Italian form *Ferdinando*. It has been in occasional use in English-speaking countries since the 16th century but has never been common.
Variants: **Faron, Farran, Farren, Fernando.**

**Fergie** a diminutive of **Fergus.**

**Fergus, Feargus** (m) from the Gaelic name *Fearghas*, derived from two Celtic words meaning 'man' or 'supreme' and 'choice'. The name is generally associated with Scotland, although it remains in occasional use in Ireland; it is also used by families of Scottish descent in other parts of Britain and the English-speaking world.
Diminutive: **Fergie.**

**Fern** (f) from the plant name; in occasional use as a first name, especially in the USA, since the early 20th century.

**Fernando** the Spanish form of **Ferdinand**; occasionally found in the USA.

**Fidel** (m) from Latin *fidelis* 'faithful'. Borne by the Cuban revolutionary leader Fidel Castro (born 1926), the name occurs from time to time in the English-speaking world.
Feminine form: **Fidelia.**

**Fidelia** the feminine form of **Fidel.**

**Fifi** [*fee*fee] a diminutive of **Josephine**, of French origin, sometimes used as a name in its own right.

**Finlay** (m) from a Scottish Gaelic name meaning 'fair hero', borne by the father of Macbeth. *Finlay* has been in regular use in Scotland, both as a first name and as a surname, for many hundreds of years, the Scottish actor Finlay Currie being one of its best-known bearers in modern times.

**Finola** the Irish form of **Fenella.**
Diminutive: **Nola.**

**Fiona** [fiŏnă] (f) from Gaelic *fionn* 'white' or 'fair'; invented by the Scottish writer William Sharp (1855–1905) for his pseudonym Fiona MacLeod. The name was rarely used outside Scotland until the latter half of the 20th century, when it became very popular in other parts of Britain and in Australia and Canada.

# Fionnuala

**Fionnuala, Fionnghuala** see Fenella, Nuala, Penelope.

**Fitzroy** (m) from a surname meaning 'son of the king' (originally a nickname borne by a monarch's illegitimate offspring). It has been in occasional use as a first name since the mid-19th century.

**Flavia** (f) from the Roman clan name *Flavius*, probably derived from Latin
*flavus* 'yellow' or 'golden' (a reference to the colour of the bearer's hair).
The name is occasionally found in the English-speaking world but has
never been common.

**Fletcher** (m) from a surname meaning 'maker (or seller) of arrows'; in occasional use as a first name. It was borne by the naval officer Fletcher
Christian, who led the famous mutiny on the 'Bounty' in 1789.

**Fleur** [fler] (f) from French, meaning 'flower'. The British writer John Galsworthy gave the name to one of the heroines of *The Forsyte Saga* (1922),
played by the actress Susan Hampshire in the television adaptation of the
novels in the late 1960s.
Related names: **Flora, Flower**.

**Flo** a diminutive of **Flora** or **Florence** (f).

**Flora** (f) from Latin *flos, floris* 'flower'; borne by the Roman goddess of
flowers and by the 9th-century martyr St Flora. Probably introduced into
Scotland from France, the name was further popularized in that country
by the Scottish heroine Flora MacDonald (1722–90), who helped Bonnie
Prince Charlie to escape from Scotland after his defeat at the Battle of
Culloden. It gradually spread to other parts of Britain and the English-
speaking world, one of the best-known bearers of the name in modern
times being the British actress Dame Flora Robson.
Variants: **Floretta, Florette, Florinda**.
Diminutives: **Flo, Florrie, Floss, Flossie**.
Related names: **Fleur, Flower**.

**Florence** (m *or* f) from the Latin names *Florentius* (m) and *Florentia* (f),
derived from *florens* 'flowering' or 'flourishing'. Formerly given to children of either sex, *Florence* was rarely used as a masculine name outside
Ireland after the 17th century. The feminine name was popularized in the
1850s by the British nurse Florence Nightingale (named after the Italian
city of her birth), whose work in the military hospitals of the Crimean
War made her a national heroine: by the end of the 19th century *Florence*
was one of the most common girls' names in the English-speaking world.
It gradually fell from favour during the 20th century but remains in occasional use today.
Diminutives: (f) **Flo, Florrie, Floss, Flossie, Floy**; (m) **Flurry**.

**Floretta, Florette** variants of **Flora**.

**Florian** (m) from Latin, meaning 'flowery' or 'flourishing'. St Florian, a Roman soldier martyred at the beginning of the 4th century, was an early bearer of the name.

**Florinda** a variant of **Flora**.

**Florrie, Flossie, Floss** diminutives of **Flora** or **Florence** (f).

**Flower** (f) from the English word *flower*; rarely used as a first name in modern times.
Related names: **Fleur, Flora**.

**Floy** a diminutive of **Florence** (f).

**Floyd** a variant of **Lloyd**, based on an attempt to anglicize the Welsh pronunciation of the name. (*Fluellen*, the name of a character in Shakespeare's play *Henry V*, is derived from a similar corruption of the Welsh name **Llewellyn**). The boxer Floyd Patterson, world heavyweight champion 1956–58 and 1961–62, is one of the best-known bearers of the name.

**Fluellen** see **Floyd**.

**Flurry** a diminutive of **Florence** (m), made famous by a character in *Some Experiences of an Irish RM* (1899), by Edith Somerville and Martin Ross, which was adapted for television in the early 1980s.

**Fortunatus** (m) from Latin, meaning 'lucky' or 'prosperous'. It has been in occasional use in English-speaking countries since the 17th century.

**Fortune** (f) from Latin *fortuna* 'good luck'; adopted by the Puritans in the 17th century but rarely used in modern times.

**Foster** (m) from a surname meaning 'forester', 'foster child (or parent)', or 'cutler'; in occasional use as a first name. The US statesman John Foster Dulles (1888–1959) was named after his maternal grandfather John W. Foster.

**Fran** a diminutive of **Frances** or **Francis**.

**Franca** a diminutive of **Francesca** or **Francisca**.

**Frances** the feminine form of **Francis**. It has been in regular use throughout the English-speaking world since the 17th century and was particularly popular in the late 19th and early 20th centuries. Famous bearers of the name in Britain include the novelist Frances Burney (1752–1840) and the actress Frances Kemble (1809–93), both of whom are better known by the diminutive **Fanny**.
Variants: **Francesca, Francine, Francisca**.
Diminutives: **Fan, Fanny, Fran, Francie, Frankie, Frannie, Franny**.

**Francesca** [fran*chesk*ă] the Italian form of **Frances**; borne in the 13th century by Francesca da Rimini, whose tragic story has inspired a number of literary and musical works, and in the 15th century by the Roman noblewoman St Francesca Romana, also known as St Frances of Rome. The

name is occasionally found in the English-speaking world in modern times, a famous bearer being the British actress Francesca Annis (born 1944).
Diminutive: **Franca**.

**Francesco** [fran*chesk*ō] the Italian form of **Francis**; in occasional use in English-speaking countries.
Diminutive: **Franco**.

**Francie** a diminutive of **Frances**.

**Francine** [fran*seen*] a variant of **Frances**; originally a French diminutive of the name.

**Francis** (m) from Latin *Franciscus* 'Frenchman'. One of the earliest and best-known bearers of the name was St Francis of Assisi (1182–1226), founder of the Franciscan order of friars; remembered for his love of nature, he was recently proclaimed patron saint of ecology by Pope John Paul II. The name was also borne by two famous Englishmen of the 16th century, the navigator Sir Francis Drake and the philosopher Francis Bacon; by the French bishop St Francis of Sales (1567–1622), patron saint of writers; and by two Holy Roman emperors. First used in Britain in the late 15th century, the name has been in regular use throughout the English-speaking world since the mid-19th century. Until the 17th century, when **Frances** was introduced, *Francis* was occasionally given as a feminine name.
Variants: **Francesco, Francisco**.
Diminutives: **Fran, Frank, Frankie**.
Feminine form: **Frances**.

**Francisca** the Spanish form of **Frances**.
Diminutive: **Franca**.

**Francisco** the Spanish form of **Francis**.
Diminutive: **Franco**.

**Franco** a medieval variant of **Frank** or a diminutive of **Francesco** or **Francisco**.

**Frank** (m) from the name of the Germanic people after whom the country of France was named; in regular use as a first name in medieval Britain. Subsequently regarded as a diminutive of **Francis**, it was frequently given as a name in its own right in the late 19th and early 20th centuries. The US singer Frank Sinatra (born Francis Albert Sinatra) is a famous bearer of the name.
Variant: **Franco**.

**Frankie** a diminutive of **Frances** or **Francis**, sometimes used as an independent name.

**Franklin** (m) from a surname derived from Middle English *francoleyn*, denoting a landowner of free birth. Popularized as a first name in the 1930s by the US president Franklin D. Roosevelt, it remains in occasional use in the USA and Canada but is rarely found in other English-speaking countries.

**Frannie, Franny** diminutives of **Frances**.

**Fraser, Frazer** (m) from a Scottish surname possibly derived from a French place name. Occasionally given as a first name in Scotland since the early 20th century, it is also used by families of Scottish descent in other parts of the English-speaking world. The British actor Frazer Hines (born 1944) is a famous bearer of the name.

**Fred** a diminutive of **Alfred** or **Frederick**, often used as a name in its own right.

**Freda** a diminutive of **Elfreda** or **Winifred**, often used as a name in its own right in the first half of the 20th century. It is sometimes regarded as a feminine form of **Frederick**. See also **Frieda**.

**Freddie, Freddy** diminutives of **Frederick**.

**Frederic** see **Frederick**.

**Frederica** a feminine form of **Frederick**.

**Frederick, Frederic, Fredrick, Fredric** (m) from the Old German name *Frithuric*, a compound of *frithu* 'peace' and *ric* 'ruler'. Its Old English equivalent, *Freodhoric*, was replaced after the Norman Conquest by a medieval French form of the name; *Frederick* was introduced into Britain by the Hanoverians in the 18th century and soon became fashionable throughout the English-speaking world, reaching its peak of popularity around 1900. Famous bearers of the name include the Holy Roman emperor Frederick Barbarossa, the Prussian king Frederick the Great (1712–1786), and the 20th-century US dancer and actor Frederick Austerlitz, better known as Fred Astaire.
Diminutives: **Fred, Freddie, Freddy**.
Feminine forms: **Freda, Frederica, Frederika, Fredrica, Fredrika, Frieda**.

**Frederika** a feminine form of **Frederick**.

**Fredric** see **Frederick**.

**Fredrica** a feminine form of **Frederick**.

**Fredrick** see **Frederick**.

**Fredrika** a feminine form of **Frederick**.

**Freya** [*fray*ä] (f) from *Freyja*, the name of the Norse goddess of love and fertility, meaning 'lady'. It has been in occasional use in English-speaking countries since the early 20th century.

**Frieda** [*freed*ä] a feminine form of **Frederick**, of German origin; borne in the early 20th century by the German wife of the British writer D. H. Lawrence. The name is occasionally found in the English-speaking world, where it is generally regarded as a variant spelling of **Freda**.

**Fulbert** (m) from the Old German name *Filibert*, meaning 'very bright'. Borne by the 7th century French abbot St Philibert, the name was introduced into Britain in the form *Filbert* or *Fulbert* at the time of the Norman Conquest; it remained in use for several hundred years but is rarely found in modern times.

# G

**Gabby, Gabbie, Gabi** see Gaby.

**Gabriel** [*gay*briĕl] (m) from Hebrew, meaning 'man of God'. The archangel Gabriel is mentioned several times in the Bible, notably in the New Testament account of the Annunciation (Luke 1:26–28). *Gabriel* has been in occasional use as a first name since the Middle Ages and has been borne by a number of fictional characters, including the farmer Gabriel Oak in Thomas Hardy's novel *Far from the Madding Crowd* (1874).
Feminine forms: **Gabriella, Gabrielle.**

**Gabriella** see Gabrielle.

**Gabrielle** [gabri*el*] a feminine form of **Gabriel**, of French origin. The Italian form *Gabriella* is also used from time to time in the English-speaking world.
Diminutives: **Gabbie, Gabby, Gabi, Gaby.**

**Gaby, Gabby, Gabbie, Gabi** diminutives of **Gabrielle.**

**Gaenor** see Gaynor.

**Gail, Gayle, Gale** diminutives of **Abigail,** frequently used as independent names since the early 20th century.

**Gaius** [*gī*ŭs] (m) from Latin *gaudere* 'to rejoice'; borne by the Roman dictator Gaius Julius Caesar. The name also occurs in the New Testament. *Gaius* and its variants have been in occasional use in Britain, especially Wales, for several hundred years. See also **Jay.**
Variants: **Caius, Kay.**

**Gale** see Gail.

**Gamaliel** [gă*may*liĕl, gă*mah*liĕl] (m) from Hebrew, meaning 'recompense of God'. Mentioned in the Bible, the name was adopted by the Puritans in the 16th century but is rarely used in modern times. *Gamaliel* was the middle name of the US president Warren G. Harding (1865–1923).

**Gareth** (m) probably from Welsh, meaning 'gentle'. Borne by one of King Arthur's knights of the Round Table in Sir Thomas Malory's *Morte d'Arthur* (1485), the name was further popularized by Tennyson's version of the legend in his *Idylls of the King* (1859) and has been in regular use in Britain, especially Wales, since the early 20th century. See also **Gary.**
Variant: **Garth.**

Diminutives: **Garry, Gary**.

**Garfield** (m) from a surname and place name; ultimately from Old English, meaning 'field of spears'. The most famous bearer of the name in modern times is the West Indian cricketer Sir Garfield St Aubrun Sobers, better known as Gary Sobers.

**Garnet** (m *or* f) from a surname of uncertain origin; in occasional use as a masculine first name since the 19th century, when it was borne by the British field marshal Lord Wolseley (Garnet Joseph Wolseley). Its subsequent adoption as a feminine name was probably influenced by the fashion for jewel names that began in the latter half of the century.

**Garret, Garrett** variants of **Gerard**, reflecting the medieval pronunciation of the name. *Garret* remains in use in Ireland, a famous bearer being the Irish statesman Garret FitzGerald (born 1926), but is rarely found in other parts of the English-speaking world.
Diminutives: **Garry, Gary**.

**Garrick** (m) from a surname derived from two Old English words meaning 'spear' and 'ruler'. Its adoption as a first name may have been influenced by the fame and popularity of the 18th-century British actor David Garrick, after whom a number of theatres were named. See also **Gary**.
Diminutives: **Garry, Gary**.

**Garry** see **Gary**.

**Garth** (m) a name of uncertain origin: it may be derived from a surname and place name, meaning 'garden', or it may simply be a variant of **Gareth**. *Garth* has been in occasional use since the 19th century, when it was borne by a number of fictional characters, but it has never been common.

**Gary, Garry** probably diminutives of **Garret**. *Gary* has been used as an independent name since its adoption by the US actor Gary Cooper (born Frank James Cooper) in the early 20th century. It rapidly became fashionable throughout the English-speaking world and may have contributed to the popularity of **Gareth** and **Garrick**, of which it is sometimes regarded as a diminutive form. See also **Garfield**.

**Gaspar** see **Jasper**.

**Gavin** [*gavin*] (m) a Scottish name of uncertain origin: it may be derived from the Old German name *Gawin*, meaning 'district of land', or it may simply be a variant of **Gawain**. The name was rarely used outside Scotland from the 17th century until the mid-20th century, when it began to spread to other parts of Britain and the English-speaking world.

**Gawain** [*gah*wayn] (m) from a Welsh name meaning 'little (or white) hawk'; borne in Arthurian legend by one of the knights of the Round Table, the nephew of King Arthur, whose exploits are recounted in the 14th-century poem *Sir Gawain and the Green Knight*. *Gawain* is rarely used as a first name in modern times.

# Gay

Variant: **Gavin**.

**Gay, Gaye** (f) from Old French *gai* 'merry'. The name has been in regular use throughout the English-speaking world since the early 20th century, although the use of the English word *gay* as a euphemism for 'homosexual' has caused a significant decline in its popularity in recent years. *Gay* is sometimes regarded as a diminutive of **Gaynor**.

**Gayle** see **Gail**.

**Gaylord** (m) probably from Old French, meaning 'high-spirited'; more frequently found as a surname than as a first name.

**Gaynor, Gaenor** variants of **Guinevere**. *Gaynor* has been in regular use in Britain since the mid-20th century but is rarely found in other English-speaking countries; the spelling *Gaenor* is largely confined to Wales. Diminutive: **Gay**.

**Gemma, Jemma** [*jem*ă] (f) from Italian, meaning 'gem'. Borne by a modern Italian saint, Gemma Galgani (1878–1903), the name has been in general use in English-speaking countries since the mid-20th century; it was further popularized by the actress Gemma Craven and by the heroine of the television series *Solo* and became very common in Britain in the early 1980s.

**Gene** [jeen] a diminutive of **Eugene**, often used as a name in its own right. It is particularly popular in the USA, the US actors Gene Kelly and Gene Hackman being two famous bearers of the name.

**Genevieve** [jenĕveev] (f) from a Celtic or Germanic name of uncertain origin; possibly derived from two words meaning 'race' and 'woman'. St Geneviève, patron saint of Paris, is traditionally believed to have protected the city against Attila and the Huns after their invasion of Gaul in 451. The name is occasionally used in English-speaking countries but has never been common, one of its best-known bearers being the vintage car that featured in the film *Genevieve* (1953).
Variant: **Ginette**.

**Genevra** see **Ginevra**.

**Geoff, Jeff** diminutives of **Geoffrey**. *Jeff* is sometimes used as a name in its own right.

**Geoffrey, Jeffrey, Jeffery** [*jef*ri] (m) from any of three Old German names, *Gaufrid*, *Walahfrid*, or *Gisfrid*, derived from the words for 'district', 'traveller', or 'pledge' and *frithu* 'peace'. The name was introduced into Britain from France in the 11th century; famous medieval bearers include Geoffrey Plantagenet, father of King Henry II; the 12th-century chronicler Geoffrey of Monmouth; and Geoffrey Chaucer, author of *The Canterbury Tales*. *Geoffrey* was little used after the 16th century until its revival in the late 19th century; by the mid-20th century it had become popular throughout the English-speaking world.

92

Diminutives: **Geoff, Jeff.**

**Geordie** a diminutive of **George** that originated in northern Britain; now used to denote a native of Tyneside. It is occasionally given as a name in its own right.

**George** [jorj] (m) from Greek *georgos* 'tiller of the soil' or 'farmer'. St George, patron saint of England since the 14th century, may have been a Roman soldier martyred in Palestine at the beginning of the 4th century; his cult was introduced into Europe by the Crusaders in the 12th century. The legend of St George and the dragon, which dates back to the Middle Ages, is of uncertain origin. The name became very common in Britain after the accession of King George I in 1714 and remained in favour for over two hundred years until the latter part of King George VI's reign; across the Atlantic it was popularized by George Washington (1732–99), first president of the USA.

Diminutives: **Geordie, Georgie.**

Feminine forms: **Georgette, Georgia, Georgiana, Georgina.**

**Georgette** a feminine form of **George**, of French origin. The 20th-century British novelist Georgette Heyer was a famous bearer of the name.

**Georgia** a feminine form of **George**; particularly popular in the USA (the American state of Georgia was named after the British king George II).

**Georgiana** a feminine form of **George**. It was fairly popular in the 18th and 19th centuries but is rarely used in modern times.

**Georgie** a diminutive of **George** or **Georgina**.

**Georgina** a feminine form of **George**; in regular use in Britain since the 18th century but rarely found in other English-speaking countries.

Diminutives: **Georgie, Gina.**

**Geraint** [gĕrīnt, gerrīnt] (m) a Welsh variant of the Latin name *Gerontius*, ultimately from Greek *geron* 'old'. Borne in Arthurian legend by the husband of **Enid**, the name was rarely used outside Wales until the mid-20th century, when it was popularized by the Welsh opera singer Sir Geraint Evans.

**Gerald** [jerrăld] (m) from an Old German name derived from *ger* 'spear' and *vald* 'rule'; introduced into Britain at the time of the Norman Conquest. The name was borne by a Welsh ancestor of the aristocratic Fitzgerald family of Ireland, grandfather of the medieval Welsh writer and clergyman Gerald of Wales (also known as Giraldus Cambrensis). Rarely used outside Ireland after the end of the Middle Ages, the name was revived in Great Britain in the 19th century and soon became popular throughout the English-speaking world.

Diminutives: **Gerry, Jerry.**

Feminine form: **Geraldine.**

# Geraldine

**Geraldine** the feminine form of **Gerald**; first used in the 16th century, when the poet Henry Howard, Earl of Surrey, addressed a number of love poems to 'the fair Geraldine' (Lady Elizabeth Fitzgerald). The name became fashionable in the 19th century, after the revival of *Gerald*, and remains in regular use today.

Diminutives: **Gerry, Jerry**.

**Gerard, Gerrard** [*jer*rard] (m) from an Old German name derived from *ger* 'spear' and *hardu* 'hard' or 'bold'. The name was introduced into Britain by the Normans and was very popular during the Middle Ages; it enjoyed a revival in the 19th century, when it was borne by the British poet Gerard Manley Hopkins, and remains in regular use today.

Variants: **Garret, Garrett**.

Diminutives: **Gerry, Jerry**.

**Gerda** [*gerd*ǎ] (f) a Norse name, meaning 'guardian', borne in Scandinavian mythology by the beautiful wife of Frey (or Freyr), the god of peace and fertility. The occasional use of the name in English-speaking countries since the 19th century has been attributed to a character in Hans Christian Anderson's story 'The Snow Queen'.

**Germain** see **Germaine**.

**Germaine** [jer*mayn*] (f) from the feminine form of the French name *Germain*, meaning 'German'; made famous in the English-speaking world in the early 1970s by the feminist writer Germaine Greer.

Masculine equivalent: **Jermaine**.

**Gerontius** see **Geraint**.

**Gerrard** see **Gerard**.

**Gerry, Jerry** diminutives of **Gerald, Gerard**, or **Geraldine**, sometimes used as independent names. *Jerry* is also a diminutive of **Jeremiah, Jeremy**, or **Jerome** and a slang term for a German soldier or a chamber pot. The US comic actor Jerry Lewis (born Joseph Levitch) is a famous bearer of the name.

**Gershom** [*gersh*ŏm] (m) from Hebrew, meaning 'alien' or 'bell'. Borne in the Old Testament by a son of Moses, the name was adopted by the Puritans in the 17th century but is rarely used in modern times.

**Gert, Gertie** diminutives of **Gertrude**.

**Gertrude** [*gert*rood] (f) from an Old German name derived from *ger* 'spear' and *drudi* 'strength'. The introduction of the name into Britain has been attributed to the cult of either of two saints, the 7th-century abbess St Gertrude of Nivelles or the 13th-century mystic St Gertrude the Great. In occasional use since the Middle Ages, the name was borne in the early 17th century by the mother of Hamlet in Shakespeare's famous tragedy but did not become popular until the late 19th century, one of its best-known bearers being the British actress Gertrude Lawrence (1898–1952).

Diminutives: **Gert, Gertie, Trudi, Trudie, Trudy**.

**Gervase, Gervais** [*jerv*ayz] (m) from an Old German name derived from *ger* 'spear' and a Celtic word meaning 'servant'; borne by the martyr St Gervase, whose remains were discovered in Milan in the late 4th century. The name was introduced into Britain at the time of the Norman Conquest and remains in occasional use today.

Variant: **Jarvis**.

**Gerwyn** (m) a Welsh name, meaning 'fair love'.

**Gethin** (m) a Welsh name, meaning 'dark-skinned'.

**Ghislaine** [*gil*ăn, gi*layn*] (f) from a French name possibly derived from Old German *gisil* 'pledge'. It is occasionally found in English-speaking countries.

**Gib** [gib] a diminutive of **Gilbert**, dating back to the Middle Ages. It gave rise to a number of surnames, notably **Gibbon**, **Gibbs**, and **Gibson**.

**Gideon** [*gidi*ŏn] (m) from Hebrew, meaning 'hewer' or 'having a stump (in place of a hand)'. The Gideons, members of a Christian organization that distributes Bibles to hotels, hospitals, and schools, took their name from the Old Testament story of Gideon's defeat of the Midianites (Judges 7). The name was adopted by the Puritans in the 17th century and remains in occasional use today.

**Gil** a diminutive of **Gilbert**.

**Gilbert** [*gil*bert] (m) from the Old German name *Gisilbert*, derived from *gisil* 'pledge' and *berhta* 'bright'; introduced into Britain at the time of the Norman Conquest. The name was borne in the 12th century by the English clergyman St Gilbert of Sempringham, founder of the religious order known as the Gilbertines. It was popular throughout the Middle Ages and has remained in regular use since then, both as a first name and as a surname, a famous example of the latter being the dramatist and humorist Sir W. S. Gilbert, who collaborated with Sir Arthur Sullivan in a series of comic operas. In Scotland *Gilbert* is sometimes used in place of the Gaelic name *Gilbride*, meaning 'servant of St Bridget'.

Diminutives: **Gib, Gil**.

Feminine forms: **Gilberta, Gilbertine**.

**Gilberta, Gilbertine** feminine forms of **Gilbert**.

**Gilda** (f) a name of uncertain origin; possibly derived from the Old English name *Eormengild*. It was popularized in the mid-20th century by the US film *Gilda* (1946), which starred Rita Hayworth.

**Giles, Gyles** [jīlz] (m) from the Latin name *Aegidius*; ultimately from Greek, meaning 'kid' or 'goatskin'. (Some scholars believe the name to be associated with Scottish Gaelic *gille* 'servant'). Borne by the 6th-century hermit St Giles, patron saint of cripples and beggars, the name first appeared in Britain in the 12th century; for many years it was given to children of either sex, sometimes in the Latin forms *Egidius* (m) or *Egidia* (f), but it is now used exclusively as a masculine name. Its association with farmers and other country folk has been attributed to the central character of Robert Bloomfield's popular poem 'The Farmer's Boy' (1800). The writer and broadcaster Gyles Brandreth (born 1948) is a famous bearer of the name.

**Gill, Jill** [jil] diminutives of **Gillian**, often used as independent names during the Middle Ages and in the 20th century. The name was so common in medieval times that it gradually came to be used as a colloquial word for 'girl' (see also **Jack**); the diminutive *Gillot* or *Jillet*, now obsolete, may have given rise to the verb 'to jilt'. *Jill* is the more frequent spelling of the name in modern times.

**Gillean, Gillian** [*gil*iăn] (m) from Scottish Gaelic, meaning 'servant of St John'; in occasional use in Scotland but rarely found elsewhere.

**Gillian, Jillian** [*ji*liăn] feminine forms of **Julian**. One of the most popular girls' names of the Middle Ages, *Gillian* eventually fell from favour in the 17th century but was revived throughout the English-speaking world in the 20th century. It was particularly popular in Britain in the 1950s and early 1960s. *Jillian* is a modern variant spelling of the name.
Diminutives: **Gill, Jill**.

**Gilroy** [*gil*roy] (m) from a surname derived from Gaelic, meaning 'servant of the red-haired man'. It has been in occasional use as a first name since the early 20th century.

**Gina** [*jee*nă] a diminutive of any name ending in *-gina*, notably *Georgina* and *Regina*; often used as a name in its own right. It was popularized in the mid-20th century by the Italian actress Gina Lollobrigida.

**Ginette** [ji*net*] a variant of **Genevieve**; originally a French diminutive of the name.

**Ginevra, Genevra** [ji*nev*ră] variants of **Guinevere**, of Italian origin.

**Ginger** [*jin*jer] a diminutive of **Virginia**. *Ginger* has been in occasional use as a name in its own right since the 1930s, when it was made famous by the US actress and dancer Ginger Rogers (born Virginia McMath), but it is more frequently found as a nickname for a person with red hair.

**Ginny** [*jin*i] a diminutive of **Virginia**.

**Gisela** [ji*zel*ă, *giz*elă] (f) from Old German *gisil* 'pledge'; in occasional use in the English-speaking world.
Variant: **Giselle**.

**Giselle** [ji*zel*] the French form of **Gisela**; made famous by Théophile Gautier's ballet of the same name, which was first performed in 1841.

**Glad** a diminutive of **Gladys**.

**Gladys** (f) from the Welsh name *Gwladys*, of uncertain origin. It is generally regarded as a variant of **Claudia**, though some scholars believe the name to be derived from Welsh *gwledig* 'ruler of a territory'. Popularized throughout the English-speaking world by a number of novels of the late 19th century, the name remained in frequent use until the 1930s. One of its most famous bearers was the British actress Dame Gladys Cooper (1888–1971).
Diminutive: **Glad**.

**Glen, Glenn** (m) from a surname derived from Gaelic *gleann* 'valley'; adopted as a first name in the 19th century. Famous bearers include the US band leader Glenn Miller, the Canadian-born actor Glenn Ford, and the US singer Glen Campbell, all of whom may have contributed to the popularity of the name in the 20th century.
Feminine form: **Glenna**.

**Glenda** (f) probably from a compound of two Welsh words meaning 'holy' and 'good'. The name has been in regular use since the early 20th century, its best-known bearer being the British actress Glenda Jackson (born 1936).

**Glenis** see **Glenys**.

**Glenn** see **Glen**.

**Glenna** the feminine form of **Glen**.

**Glenys, Glenis** (f) from Welsh, meaning 'holy'; used in various parts of the English-speaking world during the 20th century.

**Glinys** see **Glynis**.

**Gloria** (f) from Latin, meaning 'glory'. It came into general use in the late 19th century, when George Bernard Shaw gave the name to a character in his play *You Never Can Tell*. The US actress Gloria Swanson (born Josephine Swenson) publicized the name in the first half of the 20th century.

**Glyn** (m) from Welsh, meaning 'valley'; in regular use in England and Wales since the early 20th century but rarely found elsewhere.

**Glynis, Glinys** (f) from Welsh, meaning 'little valley'; popularized in the mid-20th century by the British actress Glynis Johns.

**Godfrey** (m) from the Old German name *Godafrid*, derived from *guda* 'god' and *frithu* 'peace'; introduced into Britain at the time of the Norman Conquest. It was fairly common during the Middle Ages and has remained in occasional use, both as a first name and as a surname, since then.

**Godwin** (m) from the Old English name *Godwine*, a compound of *god* 'god' and *wine* 'friend'. It was in frequent use throughout the Middle Ages, a

Goldie

famous bearer being the influential Earl of Wessex whose daughter married Edward the Confessor, but is rarely found in modern times.

**Goldie** (f) from the English word *gold*; in occasional use as a first name since the 19th century. The US actress Goldie Hawn (born 1945) is a famous bearer of the name.

**Goldwin, Goldwyn** (m) from the Old English name *Goldwine*, a compound of *gold* 'gold' and *wine* 'friend'; more familiar as a surname than as a first name in modern times.

**Gordon** (m) from a Scottish surname and place name of uncertain origin. Its use as a first name, which dates back to the 19th century, has been attributed to the popularity of the British general Charles George Gordon (1833–85).

**Grace** (f) from the English word *grace*, in the sense of 'God's favour'; ultimately from Latin *gratia*. *Grace* was one of the many names of abstract qualities adopted by the Puritans after the Reformation; having fallen from favour in the 18th century it enjoyed a revival in the latter half of the 19th century and has remained in regular use since then. Famous bearers of the name include the British heroine Grace Darling, who helped her father, a lighthouse keeper, to rescue the survivors of a shipwreck in 1838, and the US actress Grace Kelly (1928–82), who became Princess Grace of Monaco. In Ireland *Grace* is sometimes used as a translation of the Irish name *Grainne* (see **Grania**).
Diminutive: **Gracie**.

**Gracie** a diminutive of **Grace**, sometimes used as a name in its own right. It is generally associated with the British singer Dame Gracie Fields (1898–1979), whose real name was Grace Stansfield.

**Graham, Graeme, Grahame** [grayăm] (m) from a Scottish surname derived from the Lincolnshire place name *Grantham*; ultimately from Old English, meaning 'Granta's homestead'. It was rarely used as a first name outside Scotland until the mid-20th century, when it became very popular in other parts of Britain and the English-speaking world. The British writer Graham Greene (born 1904) is a famous bearer of the name.

**Grainne** see **Grania**.

**Grania** (f) from the Irish name *Grainne*, meaning 'love', borne by a heroine of Gaelic legend who eloped with Diarmuid (see **Dermot**). Both forms of the name remain in occasional use in Ireland but are rarely found elsewhere. See also **Grace**.

**Grant** (m) from a Scottish surname probably derived from French *grand* 'tall'. It was adopted as a first name in the USA in the 19th century, possibly in honour of President Ulysses S. Grant, and gradually spread to other English-speaking countries.

**Granville** (m) from a surname derived from a French place name; ultimately from Old French, meaning 'big town'. It has been in occasional use as a first name since the 18th century.

Variant: **Grenville**.

**Greg, Gregg** diminutives of **Gregory**, sometimes used as independent names.

**Gregor** a variant of **Gregory**, from a late medieval form of the name. It is still used in Scotland, where it has given rise to the surname *McGregor*, but is rarely found in other parts of the English-speaking world. *Gregor* is also the German form of *Gregory*.

**Gregory** (m) from Greek, meaning 'watchful'. The name was borne by several saints and by sixteen popes, notably St Gregory the Great (Pope Gregory I), who sent the missionary St Augustine to Britain in the late 6th century. *Gregory* was first used in the English-speaking world in the 12th century; having fallen from favour after the Reformation, it came back into use in the 19th century and was further popularized in the 1940s by the US actor Gregory Peck.

Variant: **Gregor**.

Diminutives: **Greg, Gregg**.

**Grenville** a variant of **Granville**.

**Greta** [*greet*ă] a variant of **Margaret**; originally a German or Swedish diminutive of the name. Rarely found in English-speaking countries until the late 1920s, when it was made famous by the Swedish actress Greta Garbo, the name remains in occasional use today.

**Gretchen, Gretel** German diminutives of **Margaret**, sometimes used as independent names in the English-speaking world. The name *Gretel* is generally associated with the young heroine of the German folk tale 'Hansel and Gretel'.

**Griffith** (m) from the Welsh name *Gruffudd* or *Gruffydd*, probably meaning 'strong warrior (or lord)', borne by a number of medieval Welsh monarchs. It remains in occasional use as a first name in Wales but is more familiar as a surname, usually in the form *Griffiths* or *Griffin*, in other parts of Britain.

**Griselda** [*griz*el*dă*] (f) probably from a compound of the Old German words for 'grey' or 'Christ' and *hildi* 'battle'; borne in the 14th century by the patient and obedient heroine of the final story of Boccaccio's *Decameron*, retold by Chaucer in his *Clerk's Tale*. The name remained in regular use in Scotland until the 19th century but is rarely found in modern times.

Variants: **Grizel, Grizzel**.

Diminutive: **Zelda**.

Grizel

**Grizel, Grizzel** [*griz*ĕl] variants of **Griselda**.

**Grover** (m) from a surname meaning 'grove dweller'; in occasional use as a first name in the USA since the late 19th century, when it was popularized by President Grover Cleveland. It is rarely found in other English-speaking countries.

**Guendolen** see **Gwendoline**.

**Guido** [*gwee*dō] a variant of **Guy**, dating back to the Middle Ages.

**Guinevere** [*gwin*iveer] (f) from the Welsh name *Gwenhwyfar*, meaning 'fair and yielding'; borne in Arthurian legend by the wife of King Arthur (see also **Lancelot**). *Guinevere* is rarely found in modern times but a number of its variant forms, especially **Jennifer**, remain in regular use.
Variants: **Gaenor, Gaynor, Genevra, Ginevra, Jenifer, Jennifer**.

**Gulielma** a feminine form of **William**, of Italian origin; in occasional use in English-speaking countries since the 17th century.

**Gunter, Gunther** (m) from either of two Old German names derived from *gundi* 'war' or 'battle'. Introduced into Britain at the time of the Norman Conquest, *Gunter* remained in regular use until the end of the 15th century. It is now regarded as a German name, a famous bearer being the 20th-century German writer Günter Grass.

**Gus** a diminutive of **Augustine** or **Augustus**, sometimes used as a name in its own right.

**Gussie** a diminutive of **Augusta, Augustina, Augustine,** or **Augustus**.

**Gusta** a diminutive of **Augusta**.

**Gustaf** see **Gustave**.

**Gustave, Gustav** (m) from the Swedish name *Gustaf*, probably meaning 'staff of the gods (or Goths)', borne by a number of kings of Sweden from the early 16th century to the latter half of the 20th century. The name has been in occasional use in English-speaking countries, often in the Latinized form *Gustavus*, since the 17th century. Its best-known bearer, the British composer Gustav Holst (1874–1934), was of Swedish parentage. *Gustave* is the French form of the name.

**Gustavus** see **Gustave**.

**Guy** [gī] (m) from the Old German name *Wido*, meaning 'wood' or 'wide'; introduced into Britain at the time of the Norman Conquest. St Guy (or Gui) is the French name for the early Christian martyr St Vitus, who gave his name to the disorder formerly known as St Vitus' dance. Borne by Guy of Warwick, the hero of a medieval romance on which a number of other literary works and ballads were based, the name was fairly common in Britain until the early 17th century, when the notoriety of Guy Fawkes caused it to fall rapidly from favour. It enjoyed a revival in the 19th century, popularized by such novels as Sir Walter Scott's *Guy Mannering* (1815), and has been in regular use throughout the English-speaking world since then. The slang term *guy*, meaning 'man', may be related to the first name, though some scholars believe the word to be derived from Hebrew *goy* 'Gentile'.

Variant: **Guido**.

**Gwen** (f) from Welsh, meaning 'white' or 'fair'; generally regarded as a diminutive of **Gwendoline** or any other feminine name beginning with *Gwen-*. It has been in regular use as an independent name since the late 19th century.

Masculine equivalent: **Gwyn**.

**Gwenda** (f) probably from a compound of two Welsh words meaning 'fair' and 'good'; sometimes regarded as a diminutive of **Gwendoline**.

**Gwendoline, Gwendolyn, Gwendolen, Guendolen** (f) from Welsh, meaning 'white circle' (possibly a reference to the moon); borne by a number of historical and legendary figures, including the wife of Merlin in Arthurian romance. The name has been in general use throughout the English-speaking world since the mid-19th century.

Diminutives: **Gwen, Gwenda**.

**Gwenllian** (f) from a compound of two Welsh words meaning 'fair' and 'flaxen'; rarely used outside its country of origin.

**Gwilym, Gwylim** [*gwil*im] Welsh variants of **William**, probably influenced by *Guillaume*, the French form of the name.

**Gwladys** see **Gladys**.

**Gwylim** see **Gwilym**.

**Gwyn** (f) a diminutive of **Gwyneth**.

**Gwyn** (m) from Welsh, meaning 'white' or 'fair'.

Feminine equivalent: **Gwen**.

**Gwynedd** [*gwin*ĕdh] see **Gwyneth**.

**Gwyneth, Gwynneth** [*gwin*ĕth] (f) from Welsh, meaning 'happiness' or 'blessed'. It also occurs in the form *Gwynedd*, which is the name of a county in North Wales (at the beginning of the Middle Ages Gwynedd was one of the principal divisions of the country). Largely confined to Wales until the early 20th century, *Gwyneth* is now used throughout Britain but is rarely found in other English-speaking countries. See also **Venetia**.

Diminutive: **Gwyn**.

**Gwynfor** (m) a Welsh name, meaning 'fair lord' or 'fair place'; in occasional use in Wales since the early 20th century but rarely found elsewhere.

Gwynneth see Gwyneth.
Gyles see Giles.

# H

Hadassah see Esther.

Hadrian a variant of Adrian.

Hagar [*hay*gă, *hay*gar] (f) from Hebrew, meaning 'forsaken'; borne in the Old Testament by the maidservant of Abraham's wife Sarah and the mother of his first son. The name was revived in the 19th century and remains in occasional use today.

Haidee (f) probably from Greek, meaning 'caressed' or 'modest'. Popularized in the early 19th century by a character in Byron's *Don Juan*, the name is still used from time to time in various parts of the English-speaking world.

Hal a diminutive of Harry or Henry.

Halcyon [*hal*siŏn] (f) from the name of a Greek mythological sea bird, also associated with the kingfisher; generally interpreted as 'calm' (from the expression *halcyon days*). It is occasionally used as a first name but has never been common.

Ham (m) from Hebrew, meaning 'hot'; borne in the Old Testament by one of the sons of Noah. In occasional use in English-speaking countries since the 17th century, the name is generally regarded in modern times as a diminutive of Abraham.

Hamilton (m) from a Scottish surname and place name; occasionally given as a first name in various parts of the English-speaking world since the early 19th century.

Hamish [*hay*mish] the Scottish form of James, from Gaelic *Seumas* (see also Seamus). The name has been in regular use in Scotland since the mid-19th century but is rarely found elsewhere.

Hamlet a variant of Hamo; originally a medieval diminutive of the name. Since the early 17th century it has been associated with Shakespeare's famous tragedy of the same name (the hero of the story on which the play is based actually bore the name *Amleth* or *Amlothi*, of uncertain origin). *Hamlet* remained in regular use in Britain until the end of the 18th century but is rarely found in modern times.

Hamlyn a variant of Hamo, from a medieval diminutive of the name; more frequently found as a surname than as a first name.

Hammond (m) a name of uncertain origin: it may be from the Old German name *Haimund*, meaning 'house (or home) protector', or it may simply be a variant of **Hamo**. It is more familiar as a surname than as a first name in modern times (Hammond Innes is actually the surname of the British writer known by that name).

**Hamnet** a variant of **Hamo**; borne by the son of William Shakespeare and Anne Hathaway.

**Hamo** [*haymō*] (m) from the Old German name *Haimo*, meaning 'house' or 'home'; introduced into Britain at the time of the Norman Conquest. The name was fairly common during the Middle Ages, giving rise to a number of surnames, but is rarely found in modern times.
Variants: **Hamlet, Hamlyn, Hammond, Hamnet, Hamon**.

**Hamon** a variant of **Hamo**.

**Hank** a diminutive of **Henry**, of Dutch origin, sometimes used as an independent name.

**Hannah** (f) from Hebrew, meaning 'God has favoured me'; generally interpreted as 'favour' or 'grace'. In the Old Testament Hannah was the mother of the prophet Samuel. The name became popular in Britain in the 17th century and remained in regular use until the latter half of the 19th century; it was revived in the mid-1970s.
Variants: **Ann, Anna, Anne**.

**Hannibal** (m) the name of a famous Carthaginian general of the 3rd century BC, remembered for his crossing of the Alps with some 30 000 men and 38 elephants at the beginning of the second Punic War. *Hannibal* has been in occasional use in English-speaking countries since the 16th century but is rarely found in modern times.

**Hans** a German variant of **John**; occasionally found in the English-speaking world.

**Hardy** (m) from a surname meaning 'bold' or 'hardy'; in occasional use as a first or middle name since the 19th century. One of its best-known bearers in modern times is the British couturier Hardy Amies (born 1909).

**Harley** (m) from a surname and place name; ultimately from Old English, meaning 'hare wood (or meadow)'. Harley Street in London was named after Edward Harley, 2nd Earl of Oxford (1689–1741).

**Harold** (m) from the Old English name *Hereweald*, a compound of *here* 'army' and *weald* 'power'; influenced by *Harivald* (or *Harald*), the Old Norse equivalent of the name. Although it had been borne in the 11th century by two kings of England, notably Harold II, who was killed at the Battle of Hastings in 1066, the name did not survive the Middle Ages; it enjoyed a revival in the mid-19th century, however, and soon became popular throughout the English-speaking world, falling from favour again in the 1930s. Famous 20th-century bearers of the name include the British statesmen Harold Macmillan, Earl of Stockton, and Sir Harold Wilson.

# Harriet

Variant: **Errol**.

Diminutive: **Harry**.

**Harriet** a variant of **Henrietta**; generally regarded as a feminine form of **Harry**. The derivation of *Harriet* from *Henrietta*, like that of *Harry* from **Henry**, reflects the anglicized pronunciation of the French form of the name. *Harriet* was particularly fashionable in the 18th and 19th centuries, when it sometimes occurred in the form *Harriot* or *Harriette*; its popularity declined during the first half of the 20th century but it remains in occasional use today. The US writer Harriet Beecher Stowe (1811–96), author of *Uncle Tom's Cabin*, was a famous bearer of the name.

Diminutives: **Hattie, Hatty**.

**Harriette, Harriot** see **Harriet**.

**Harrison** (m) from a surname meaning 'son of **Harry**'; in occasional use as a first name since the 19th century.

**Harry** originally a variant of **Henry**, from the medieval English pronunciation of the French form *Henri*. Since the Middle Ages *Harry* has been in regular use both as a name in its own right and as a diminutive of *Henry*: in 1984 the Prince and Princess of Wales announced that their second son, Prince Henry, would be known as Prince Harry. The name is also used as a diminutive of **Harold**.

Diminutive: **Hal**.

Feminine form: **Harriet**.

**Hartley** (m) from a surname and place name; ultimately from Old English, meaning 'stag wood (or meadow)'. It has been in regular use as a first name since the late 18th century, when it was borne by the British poet Hartley Coleridge, son of S. T. Coleridge.

**Harvey** (m) from the French name *Hervé*, derived from the Celtic words for 'battle' or 'strong' and 'worthy' or 'ardent'. Borne by a Breton saint of the 6th century, the name was introduced into Britain at the time of the Norman Conquest and was fairly common throughout the Middle Ages. It subsequently fell from favour, surviving only as a surname, but was revived as a first name in the 19th century and remains in occasional use today.

Variant: **Hervey**.

**Hattie, Hatty** diminutives of **Harriet**, sometimes used as independent names. The actress and comedienne Hattie Jacques was probably the best-known bearer of the name in Britain in the latter half of the 20th century.

**Haydn, Haydon, Hayden** [*hay*dŏn] (m) from a surname and place name of uncertain origin. Its adoption as a first name in Wales, where it remains in regular use today, may have been influenced by the Celtic name **Aidan**. There is no apparent connection between the first name and the 18th-century Austrian composer Joseph Haydn.

**Hayley** (f) from a surname and place name; ultimately from Old English, meaning 'hay field'. It was popularized as a first name in Britain by the actress Hayley Mills (named after her mother Mary Hayley Bell), who made her screen debut in 1959 at the age of thirteen.

**Hazel** (f) from the name of the nut-bearing shrub; in regular use since the late 19th century, when a number of flower and plant names came into fashion as first names.

**Heath** (m) from a surname derived from the English word *heath*; occasionally given as a first name in various parts of the English-speaking world. *Heath* was the middle name of the British cartoonist William Heath Robinson (1872–1944), remembered for his drawings of complex mechanical contrivances for performing simple tasks. The name is sometimes regarded as a masculine form of **Heather**.

**Heather** (f) from the plant name; in regular use as a first name since the late 19th century. It was particularly popular in the latter half of the 20th century.
Masculine form. **Heath**.

**Hebe** [*hee*bi] (f) from Greek, meaning 'youth'; borne in Greek mythology by the daughter of Zeus and Hera, goddess of youth and cupbearer to the gods. The name is occasionally found in the English-speaking world but has never been common.

**Heber** [*hee*ber] (m) from Hebrew, meaning 'associate' or 'fellowship'. Mentioned in the Old Testament, *Heber* was adopted as a first name by the Puritans after the Reformation and remained in occasional use until the early 20th century.

**Hector** (m) from Greek, meaning 'holding fast'; borne in Greek mythology by one of the chief warriors of the Trojan War, the eldest son of King Priam of Troy, whose name has entered the English language as a synonym for 'bully'. The name has been in occasional use in Britain, especially Scotland, since the Middle Ages; it enjoyed a partial revival in the late 19th century but is rarely found in modern times.

**Hedda** a diminutive of **Hedwig**, sometimes used as a name in its own right in the English-speaking world. It is generally associated with the heroine of the Norwegian dramatist Henrik Ibsen's play *Hedda Gabler* (1890).

**Hedley** (m) from a surname and place name; ultimately from Old English, meaning 'heathery clearing'. It has been in occasional use as a first name since the 19th century.

**Hedwig** (f) a German name, meaning either 'refuge in war' or 'struggle'. Its diminutives are sometimes given as independent names in English-speaking countries.
Diminutives: **Hedda, Hedy**.

# Hedy

**Hedy** a diminutive of **Hedwig**, sometimes used as a name in its own right in the English-speaking world. It was publicized in the 1940s by the Austrian actress Hedy Lamarr (born Hedwig Kiesler).

**Heidi** [*hīdi*] originally a diminutive of *Adelheid*, the German form of **Adelaide**. It was popularized as an independent name by the heroine of Johanna Spyri's novel *Heidi*, a children's classic first published in the late 19th century.
Related names: **Adelaide**, **Alice**.

**Helen** (f) from Greek, meaning 'the bright one'. The Helen of Greek mythology, whose elopement with Paris precipitated the Trojan War (inspiring Christopher Marlowe's reference to 'the face that launched a thousand ships'), was the beautiful daughter of Zeus and wife of Menelaus, King of Sparta. Popularized in medieval Britain by the cult of St Helen (see **Helena**), the name was more familiar for many years in the variant form **Ellen**; *Helen* came into general use after the Renaissance and was particularly popular in the latter half of the 20th century.
Variants: **Eileen**, **Elaine**, **Eleanor**, **Elena**, **Elinor**, **Ellen**, **Helena**, **Helene**, **Ilona**.
Diminutives: **Nell**, **Nellie**, **Nelly**.

**Helena** [*helēnă*, he*leenă*] a variant of **Helen**. St Helena (or Helen), mother of the Roman emperor Constantine the Great, was traditionally believed to have been a British princess; she is remembered for her alleged discovery of the cross of Jesus Christ on a visit to the Holy Land in the early 4th century. The name has been in regular use in the English-speaking world since the Renaissance but has never been as popular as **Ellen** or *Helen*.
Diminutive: **Lena**.

**Helene** a variant of **Helen**, from the French form of the name.

**Helewise** see **Eloise**.

**Helga** (f) a Scandinavian name, meaning 'holy', occasionally found in the English-speaking world.
Variant: **Olga**.

**Héloïse** see **Eloise**.

**Hen** a diminutive of **Henry**.

**Hennie, Henny** diminutives of **Henrietta**.

**Henri** see **Henry**.

**Henrietta** from *Henriette*, the French feminine form of **Henry**. The name was introduced into Britain in the 17th century by Henrietta Maria (Henriette Marie), the French-born wife of King Charles I, but was rapidly superseded by its variant form **Harriet**; *Henrietta* came back into fashion in the latter half of the 19th century and remains in occasional use today.
Variant: **Harriet**.
Diminutives: **Etta**, **Ettie**, **Etty**, **Hennie**, **Henny**, **Hetty**.

**Henriette** see **Henrietta**.

**Henry** (m) from the Old German name *Haimirich*, meaning 'home (or house) ruler'. *Henri*, the French form of the name, was introduced into Britain at the time of the Norman Conquest and soon became established as *Henry* or **Harry**. The name was borne by eight kings of England from the accession of King Henry I, the youngest son of William the Conqueror, in 1100 to the death of King Henry VIII in 1547. *Henry* remained in frequent use throughout the English-speaking world until the early 20th century, when it began to fall from favour; famous bearers of the name in the USA include the writer Henry James (1843–1916) and the actor Henry Fonda (1905–82).
Variant: **Harry**.
Diminutives: **Hal, Hank, Hen**.
Feminine form: **Henrietta**.

**Hephzibah** [*hef*sibă, *hep*sibă] (f) from Hebrew, meaning 'my delight is in her'. Mentioned in the Old Testament, the name was adopted by the Puritans in the 17th century and has been in occasional use in Britain and the USA since then. The pianist Hephzibah Menuhin (1920–80), sister of Yehudi Menuhin, was a well-known bearer of the name.
Variant: **Hepzibah**.
Diminutives: **Eppie, Hepsey, Hepsie, Hepsy**.

**Hepsie, Hepsey, Hepsy** diminutives of **Hephzibah**.

**Hepzibah** a variant of **Hephzibah**.

**Herb** a diminutive of **Herbert**.

**Herbert** (m) from an Old German name derived from *harja* 'army' and *berhta* 'bright'; rendered in Old English as *Herebeorht*. Introduced into Britain at the time of the Norman Conquest, *Herbert* remained in regular use until the 13th century; its revival in the early 19th century may have been an adoption of the aristocratic surname as a first name. Famous bearers include the British actor Sir Herbert Beerbohm Tree (1853–1917) and the US president Herbert C. Hoover (1874–1964).
Diminutives: **Herb, Herbie**.

**Herbie** a diminutive of **Herbert**.

**Hercules** [*her*kewleez] (m) the Latin form of the Greek name *Heracles*, possibly meaning 'glory (or glorious gift) of Hera (the Greek goddess of marriage)'. In classical mythology Hercules (or Heracles) was one of the sons of Zeus, remembered for the Twelve Labours he was obliged to perform after killing his wife and children in a fit of madness. The name has been in occasional use in parts of Britain since the 16th century; in the Shetland Islands it is sometimes used to translate the Scandinavian name *Hacon*, introduced by the Vikings in the Dark Ages.

**Hereward** [*herrĕwăd*] (m) from the Old English name *Hereweard*, a compound of *here* 'army' and *weard* 'protection'; generally associated with the Anglo-Saxon hero Hereward the Wake, who led a revolt against William the Conqueror in the 11th century. Charles Kingsley's last novel, *Hereward the Wake* (1866), does not appear to have popularized the name, which has never been common.

**Herman, Hermann** (m) from the Old German name *Hariman*, derived from *harja* 'army' and *mana* 'man'; introduced into Britain at the time of the Norman Conquest. It was revived in the mid-19th century and became particularly popular in the USA, one of its best-known bearers being the US writer Herman Melville, author of *Moby Dick* (1851).
Variants: **Armand, Armin**.
Feminine forms: **Armina, Armine**.

**Hermia** probably a feminine form of *Hermes* (see **Hermione**); made famous by a character in Shakespeare's play *A Midsummer Night's Dream*. The name is used only occasionally in modern times.

**Hermione** [*hermĭōni*] (f) from the Greek masculine name *Hermes*, possibly meaning 'stone'. In Greek mythology Hermes was the messenger of the gods and Hermione the daughter of King Menelaus of Sparta and Helen of Troy. Popularized by a number of fictional heroines, including one of the central characters of Shakespeare's play *The Winter's Tale*, the name has been in general use since the 17th century. Famous 20th-century bearers include the British actresses Hermione Gingold and Hermione Baddeley.

**Hervé** see **Harvey**.

**Hervey** a variant of **Harvey**.

**Hester** a Latinized form of **Esther**; in occasional use in the English-speaking world since the 17th century.
Diminutive: **Hetty**.

**Hetty** a diminutive of **Henrietta** or **Hester**, sometimes used as a name in its own right.

**Heulwen** (f) a Welsh name, meaning 'sunshine'.

**Hew** see **Hugh**.

**Hezekiah** [*hezĕkīă*] (m) from Hebrew, meaning 'God is strength' or 'God has strengthened'. Borne in the Old Testament by one of the kings of Judah, the name was adopted by the Puritans in the 17th century and remains in occasional use today.

**Hieronymus** [*hyronimŭs*] the Latin equivalent of **Jerome**; borne in the 15th century by the Dutch painter Hieronymus Bosch.

**Hilary, Hillary** (m *or* f) from the Latin name *Hilarius*, derived from *hilaris* 'cheerful'; borne in the 4th century by St Hilary, Bishop of Poitiers. The name was first used in Britain in the 12th century, when it was given to children of either sex; it gradually came to be regarded as a masculine name, surviving as such until the 17th century, but since its revival in the late 19th century it has been more popular in all parts of the English-speaking world as a feminine name. See also **Ellery**.

**Hilda** (f) from the Old English name *Hild*, meaning 'battle', which may have originated as a diminutive of any feminine name beginning or ending with this element. One of the earliest known bearers of the name was St Hilda (or Hild), who founded the abbey at Whitby in the mid-7th century. The name remained in regular use until the late Middle Ages and was revived throughout the English-speaking world in the latter half of the 19th century, falling from favour again in the 1940s. The variant spelling *Hylda* occurs from time to time, a notable example being the British actress and comedienne Hylda Baker.

**Hildebrand** (m) from an Old German name derived from *hildi* 'battle' and *branda* 'sword'; borne in the 11th century by St Hildebrand (Pope Gregory VII). The name became virtually obsolete after the end of the Middle Ages but enjoyed a partial revival in the 19th century.

**Hildegard, Hildegarde** (f) from an Old German name derived from *hildi* 'battle' (the second element is of uncertain origin); borne in the 12th century by the German abbess and mystic St Hildegard. The name is occasionally found in English-speaking countries; famous bearers include the actresses Hildegard Neff (born 1925) and Hildegarde Neil (born 1939).

**Hillary** see **Hilary**.

**Hippolyta** [hi*pol*ĭtă] the feminine form of **Hippolytus**. The name was borne in Greek mythology by a queen of the Amazons, the mother of Hippolytus; it was further popularized by a character in Shakespeare's play *A Midsummer Night's Dream* and remains in occasional use today.

**Hippolytus** [hi*pol*ĭtŭs] (m) from a Greek name probably derived from *hippos* 'horse' and the verb 'to let loose' (the Hippolytus of Greek legend, son of Theseus and Hippolyta, was dragged to his death by stampeding horses). Borne by the theologian St Hippolytus of Rome, who died in the 3rd century, the name was used from time to time in medieval Britain but is rarely found in modern times.

Feminine form: **Hippolyta**.

**Hiram** [*hyr*ăm] (m) from Hebrew, possibly meaning 'my brother is exalted'; borne in the Old Testament by a king of Tyre. The name has been in occasional use throughout the English-speaking world since the 17th century.

**Hob** a diminutive of **Robert** or **Robin**, from which the surnames *Hobson* and *Hopkins*, among others, and the noun *hobgoblin* are derived. It was fairly common in medieval Britain but is rarely used today.

# Hobart

**Hobart** a variant of **Hubert**.

**Holden** (m) from a surname and place name; ultimately from Old English, meaning 'hollow valley'. It has been in occasional use as a first name since the 19th century, a famous bearer being Holden Caulfield, the adolescent hero of J. D. Salinger's immensely successful novel *The Catcher in the Rye* (1951).

**Holly** (f) from the plant name; sometimes given to girls born during the Christmas season. In occasional use since the late 19th century, the name was popularized by one of the heroines of John Galsworthy's *The Forsyte Saga* (1922), which was adapted for television in the late 1960s.

**Homer** (m) either from the name of the Greek poet, author of the *Iliad* and the *Odyssey*, or from a surname meaning 'helmet maker' or 'pool in a hollow'. *Homer* has been in occasional use as a first name in English-speaking countries, especially the USA, since the 17th century.

**Honor** (f) from the Latin name *Honoria*, ultimately from *honor* 'honour'. Variants of the name have been in use in Britain since the time of the Norman Conquest. *Honor* was popular in the 16th and 17th centuries, when it was given to children of either sex; one of the many names of abstract virtues adopted by the Puritans, it often appeared in the anglicized form *Honour*. The name was revived in the 20th century, its most famous bearer being the British actress Honor Blackman.
Variants: **Annora, Honora, Nora, Norah**.
Related name: **Aneurin**.

**Honora** a variant of **Honor**.

**Honoria, Honour** see **Honor**.

**Hope** (f) from the name of one of the three Christian virtues (see **Charity, Faith**); adopted as a first name by the Puritans in the 16th century and formerly given to children of either sex. It remains in regular use in the USA but is rarely found in other parts of the English-speaking world in modern times.

**Horace** [*horrăs*] (m) from the Roman clan name *Horatius*; borne in the 1st century BC by the Roman poet Quintus Horatius Flaccus, now known as Horace. For many years *Horace* was used both as a name in its own right and as a spoken or diminutive form of **Horatio**; since the latter half of the 19th century *Horace* has been the more common of the two names. Famous bearers include the 18th-century British writer Horace Walpole and the 19th-century US journalist Horace Greeley.
Diminutive: **Horry**.
Feminine equivalent: **Horatia**.

**Horatia** (f) from the feminine form of the Roman clan name *Horatius*; borne in the 19th century by the daughter of Lord Horatio Nelson and Lady Emma Hamilton.

Masculine equivalents: **Horace, Horatio**.

**Horatio** [hŏrayshiō] (m) from the Roman clan name *Horatius*; in occasional use as a first name in English-speaking countries since the 16th century. The name was borne by the faithful friend of Hamlet in Shakespeare's famous tragedy; its best-known bearer, however, was the British admiral Lord Horatio Nelson, remembered for his victory over the French at the Battle of Trafalgar (1805), in which he was mortally wounded. See also **Horace**.
Diminutive: **Horry**.
Feminine equivalent: **Horatia**.

**Horry** a diminutive of **Horace** or **Horatio**.

**Hortense** the French form of **Hortensia**.

**Hortensia** (f) from the feminine form of the Roman clan name *Hortensius*, of uncertain origin; introduced into Britain via France in the 19th century.
Variant: **Hortense**.

**Howard** (m) from a surname of uncertain origin. Possible derivations include the Old German name *Huguard*, from *hugu* 'heart' and *vardu* 'protection' or *hardu* 'bold'; the Old English words for 'hog-warden' or 'ewe-herd'; and the surname *Hayward*, meaning 'fence guardian'. An aristocratic family name dating back many hundreds of years, *Howard* was adopted as a first name in the 19th century. Famous bearers include the US industrialist Howard Hughes (1905–76) and the US actor and singer Howard Keel (born 1917).

**Howell, Howel** see **Hywel**.

**Hubert** [hewbĕt] (m) from the Old German name *Hugubert*, derived from *hugu* 'heart' and *berhta* 'bright'; rendered in Old English as *Hygebeorht*. Popularized in the Middle Ages by the cult of the 8th-century bishop St Hubert, patron saint of hunters, the name remained in regular use until the end of the 14th century; it enjoyed a revival in the 19th century and is still found from time to time in the English-speaking world.
Variant: **Hobart**.

**Huey** see **Hughie**.

**Hugh, Huw, Hew** [hew] (m) from an Old German name derived from *hugu* 'heart' or 'mind', which may have originated as a diminutive of any masculine name containing this element, such as *Huguard* (**Howard**) or *Hugubert* (**Hubert**). The name was introduced into Britain at the time of the Norman Conquest and was further popularized by a number of medieval saints, notably the 12th-century bishop St Hugh of Lincoln and the nine-year-old martyr Little St Hugh (1246–55). It has remained in regular use since then. *Huw*, a Welsh spelling of the name, may be derived from a Celtic word for 'fire' or 'inspiration'.

# Hughie

Variant: **Hugo**.
Diminutives: **Huey, Hughie**.

**Hughie, Huey** diminutives of **Hugh**.

**Hugo** [*hewgō*] the Latin form of **Hugh**.

**Huldah, Hulda** (f) from Hebrew, meaning 'weasel'; borne by an Old Testament prophetess. Some scholars believe the variant spelling *Hulda* to be a separate name, derived from a Scandinavian word meaning 'muffled' or 'covered'. Both forms of the name occur from time to time in English-speaking countries.

**Humbert** (m) from an Old German name derived from *huni* 'giant' and *berhta* 'bright'; borne by Humbert Humbert, the antihero of Vladimir Nabokov's novel *Lolita* (1955). The name is occasionally found in the English-speaking world but has never been common.

**Humph** a diminutive of **Humphrey**.

**Humphrey** (m) from the Old English name *Hunfrith*, probably derived from the words for 'giant' and 'peace'. *Hunfrid*, the Old German equivalent of the name, was introduced into Britain at the time of the Norman Conquest; it gradually developed into *Humfridus*, *Humfrey* (from the Norman French form *Onfroi*), and, at a later date, *Humphrey*. (The change in spelling from *-f-* to *-ph-* may have been influenced by the Latin name *Onuphrius*, borne by an Egyptian saint.) *Humphrey* remains in regular use throughout the English-speaking world, the most famous 20th-century bearer of the name being the US actor Humphrey Bogart.
Diminutive: **Humph**.

**Huw** see **Hugh**.

**Hy** a diminutive of **Hyacinth** or **Hyman**.

**Hyacinth** (m *or* f) from the flower name; ultimately from the name of a flower that grew (according to Greek legend) out of the blood of the youth Hyacinthus, accidentally killed by Apollo. Borne by an early Roman martyr, *Hyacinth* has been in occasional use as a masculine name for several hundred years; its comparatively recent adoption as a feminine name was probably influenced by the fashion for flower names that began in the late 19th century.
Variant: (f) **Hyacintha**.
Diminutive: **Hy**.
Related name: **Jacinth**.

**Hyacintha** a variant of **Hyacinth** (f); originally a feminine form of the masculine name.

**Hylda** see **Hilda**.

**Hyman** (m) probably from a Hebrew word for 'life'. Its use in the English-speaking world is largely confined to Jewish families.
Diminutives: **Hy, Hymie**.

**Hymie** a diminutive of **Hyman**.

**Hypatia** [hīpayshiǎ] (f) from Greek *hypatos* 'highest'; borne by a philosopher and mathematician of Alexandria, the heroine of Charles Kingsley's novel *Hypatia* (1853), who was killed by a Christian mob in the early 5th century. The name has been in occasional use in Britain since the 19th century but has never been common.

**Hywel, Howell, Howel** [howĕl] (m) from Welsh *hywel* 'eminent'; borne in the 10th century by the Welsh king Hywel Dda (Howel the Good) and made famous in the latter half of the 20th century by the actor Hywel Bennett. *Howell* and *Howel* are anglicized spellings of the name.

# I

**Iago** [iahgō] a Welsh or Spanish form of **Jacob**. The name is generally associated with the wicked Iago of Shakespeare's play *Othello*.

**Ian, Iain** Scottish variants of **John**. *Iain*, the Gaelic form of the name, is rarely found outside Scotland; *Ian*, its anglicized spelling, has been in regular use throughout Britain and in Australia and Canada since the early 20th century. It was particularly popular in the 1950s and 1960s.

**Ianthe** [īanthi] (f) from Greek, meaning 'violet flower'. *Ianthe* was revived in the 19th century by a number of poets, notably Percy Bysshe Shelley, who used the name in his poem *Queen Mab* (1813) and also gave it to his first daughter. The name remains in occasional use today.
Related name: **Iolanthe**.

**Ib, Ibbie, Ibby** diminutives of **Isabel**.

**Ichabod** [ikăbod] (m) from Hebrew, meaning 'no glory' or 'the glory has departed'; mentioned in the Old Testament. The name was adopted by the Puritans in the 17th century but is rarely found in modern times.

**Ida** [īdǎ] (f) probably from an Old German name meaning 'labour'; introduced into Britain at the time of the Norman Conquest. The name was revived throughout the English-speaking world in the latter half of the 19th century, when it was borne by the heroine of Tennyson's poem *The Princess* and Gilbert and Sullivan's opera *Princess Ida*; it remains in occasional use today.

**Idonea** [idōniǎ] (f) a name of uncertain origin: it may be from Old Norse, meaning 'work', or from Latin *idoneus* 'suitable'. It has been in occasional use in Britain since the 13th century but has never been common.

**Idris** (m) from Welsh *iud* 'lord' and *ris* 'fiery'; borne by a Welsh mythological figure who gave his name to the mountain Cader Idris in Gwynedd. The name was revived in Wales in the 19th century but is rarely found elsewhere.

**Ifor** [*eevor*] (m) a Welsh name of uncertain origin: it may be from a Welsh word for 'lord' or it may simply be a variant of **Ivor**.
Variant: **Ivor**.

**Ignatius** (m) from a Greek name of unknown origin; sometimes associated with Latin *igneus* 'fiery'. Famous bearers of the name include St Ignatius of Antioch, who was martyred in the early 2nd century, and St Ignatius of Loyola (1491–1556), founder of the Jesuits. Its use in the English-speaking world is largely confined to Roman Catholic families.
Variant: **Inigo**.

**Igor** [*eegor*] (m) the Russian form of the Scandinavian name *Ingvar*, meaning 'Ing's warrior' (*Ing* was one of the names of the Norse god of peace and fertility). Borne by the 20th-century Russian composer Igor Stravinsky, who became a US citizen in 1945, the name is used from time to time in the English-speaking world.

**Ike** a diminutive of **Isaac**; also borne as a nickname by the US president Dwight D. Eisenhower (1890–1969).

**Ilma** a diminutive of **Wilhelmina**, sometimes used as a name in its own right.

**Ilona** the Hungarian form of **Helen**.

**Ilse** a variant of **Elizabeth**; originally a German diminutive of the name.

**Immy** a diminutive of **Imogen**.

**Imogen** [*imŏjĕn*] (f) the name of the heroine of Shakespeare's play *Cymbeline*. In Holinshed's *Chronicles*, the source used by Shakespeare for this and other plays, the name appears as *Innogen*; the misspelling *Imogen* was the result of a printing error in the Folio edition of the play. *Innogen* may be derived from Latin *innocens* 'innocent' or from an Irish word meaning 'daughter'; *Imogen* is generally interpreted as 'last born'.
Diminutive: **Immy**.

**Ina** [*eenă*] a diminutive of any name ending in *-ina*, such as **Georgina**, **Christina**, or **Edwina**; often used as a name in its own right.
Related name: **Ena**.

**Inez** [*eenez*] a variant of **Agnes**, of Spanish origin.

**Inga, Inge** diminutives of **Ingeborg**, often used as independent names.

**Ingeborg** (f) a Scandinavian name, meaning 'Ing's protection' (see **Igor**); occasionally used in the English-speaking world by families of Scandinavian descent.
Diminutives: **Inga, Inge**.

**Ingram** (m) from the Old German name *Ingilramnus*, probably meaning 'Ing's raven' (see **Igor**), introduced into Britain in the form *Ingelram* at the time of the Norman Conquest. *Ingram* was in regular use both as a first name and as a surname from the latter half of the Middle Ages until the 17th century; it was revived in the 19th century, when the surname was readopted as a first name.

**Ingrid** (f) a Scandinavian name, meaning 'Ing's ride' (see **Igor**), popularized in the English-speaking world by the Swedish actress Ingrid Bergman (1915–82).

**Ingvar** see **Igor**.

**Inigo** [*ini*gō] a variant of **Ignatius**, of Spanish origin (St Ignatius of Loyola was born Iñigo López de Recalde). Its best-known bearer in the English-speaking world was the architect Inigo Jones (1573–1652). The name remains in occasional use in modern times but has never been common.

**Iola** [īōlǎ] the feminine form of **Iolo**.

**Iolanthe** [īō*lan*thi] (f) from Greek, meaning 'violet flower'; made famous by Gilbert and Sullivan's opera of the same name, first performed in 1882.
Variants: **Yolanda, Yolande**.
Related name: **Ianthe**.

**Iolo** [īōlō] a diminutive of **Iorwerth**, often used as a name in its own right.
Feminine form: **Iola**.

**Iona** [īōnǎ] (f) either from the name of a Scottish island (see **Columba**) or from Greek *ion* 'violet'. It is occasionally given as a first name in Scotland but is rarely found elsewhere.

**Iorwerth** (m) a Welsh name, derived from *ior* 'lord' and *gwerth* 'worth'.
Variant: **Yorath**.
Diminutive: **Iolo**.

**Ira** (m) probably from a Hebrew word meaning 'watchful'; borne in the Old Testament by one of King David's men. It is occasionally found in English-speaking countries, especially the USA, a famous bearer being the US lyricist Ira Gershwin (1896–1983), brother of George Gershwin.

**Irene** [īreen, īreeni] (f) from Greek *eirene* 'peace'; borne by an early Christian martyr and by several Byzantine empresses but not used as a first name in the English-speaking world until the 19th century. It was particularly fashionable in the first half of the 20th century, reaching its peak of popularity in Britain in the 1920s, and has remained in occasional use since then. The trisyllabic Greek pronunciation [īreeni], favoured in Britain for many years, has been largely superseded by the US pronunciation [īreen].
Diminutives: **Rene, Renie**.

**Iris** (f) the name of the Greek goddess of the rainbow, which she used as a bridge when carrying messages from the gods to mankind. *Iris* is now regarded as a flower name, having come into fashion as such in the late 19th century (the plant is so named because of the variety of colours found amongst its flowers). The British novelist Iris Murdoch is one of the best-known bearers of the name in modern times.

**Irma** (f) a German name derived from Old German *irmin* or *ermin* 'universal', which may have originated as a diminutive of any feminine name beginning with this element. It has been in occasional use in English-speaking countries since the late 19th century.

Related name: **Emma**.

**Irvin, Irvine** (m) from a surname and Scottish place name; in occasional use as a first name since the 19th century. It is sometimes confused with **Irwin**.

Variant: **Irving**.

**Irving** a variant of **Irvin**, made famous by the 20th-century US songwriter Irving Berlin (born Israel Baline).

**Irwin, Erwin** (m) from Old English, meaning 'boar friend'. It survived the Middle Ages as a surname and was revived as a first name in the 19th century. See also **Irvin**.

**Isa** a diminutive of **Isabel**, sometimes used in Scotland as a name in its own right.

**Isaac, Izaak** [ĭzăk] (m) from Hebrew, meaning 'he laughs' or 'laughter'; given by the Old Testament patriarch Abraham and his wife Sarah to the son born in their old age. The name was used only occasionally in English-speaking countries until the Reformation, when it became very popular; it was still in regular use at the end of the 19th century but is rarely found in modern times. The alternative spelling *Izaak*, borne by Izaak Walton, author of *The Compleat Angler* (1653), dates back to the 17th century. The British scientist Sir Isaac Newton (1642–1727) is probably the best-known bearer of the name.

Diminutives: **Ike, Zack, Zak**.

**Isabel, Isobel, Isabelle, Isabella** variants of **Elizabeth**, of Spanish origin; more common in medieval Britain than *Elizabeth* itself. The name was in frequent use in the royal families of Europe and was popularized in Britain in the 13th and 14th centuries by the wives of King John, King Edward II, and King Richard II. It was revived in the 19th century, when the Latinized form *Isabella* was particularly popular and the spelling *Isobel* appeared; all forms of the name have been in regular use throughout the English-speaking world since then.

Variants: **Ishbel, Isla**.

Diminutives: **Bel, Bell, Bella, Belle, Ib, Ibbie, Ibby, Isa, Tibby**.

**Isadora** see **Isidora**.

**Isaiah** [ĭzīă] (m) from Hebrew, meaning 'the Lord is generous' or 'salvation of the Lord'. Borne by an Old Testament prophet of the 8th century BC, the name was adopted by the Puritans in the 17th century but is rarely found in modern times.

**Iseult** see **Isolde**.

**Ishbel** a Scottish variant of **Isabel**.

**Isidora, Isadora** feminine forms of **Isidore**. The US dancer Isadora Duncan (1878–1927) was a famous bearer of the name.

**Isidore** [*iz*idor] (m) from a Greek name of uncertain origin; generally interpreted as 'gift of Isis', although Isis was an Egyptian deity. The name was borne in the 7th century by the bishop and scholar St Isidore of Seville, who tried to convert Spanish Jews to Christianity; it was subsequently adopted as a Jewish name in Spain and, at a later date, in Britain and the USA.
Feminine forms: **Isadora, Isidora**.

**Isla** [*ī*lă] (f) a name of uncertain origin: it may be derived from the name of a Scottish river or it may simply be a variant of **Isabella**.

**Ismay** (f) a name of unknown origin, dating back at least to the 13th century. See also **Esme**.

**Isobel** see **Isabel**.

**Isolda, Isolde** [*iz*oldă] (f) either from Welsh, meaning 'beautiful', or from Old German *is* 'ice' and *vald* 'rule'. The name was popularized in the Middle Ages by the legend of **Tristan** and Isolde (or Iseult) and remained in regular use, in a variety of forms, for several hundred years. Its partial revival in the latter half of the 19th century has been attributed to the success of Wagner's opera *Tristan und Isolde* (1865), based on a German version of the medieval romance.

**Israel** [*iz*rayl] (m) from Hebrew, possibly meaning 'he struggles with God' or 'may God prevail'. The name of the Old Testament patriarch **Jacob** was changed to *Israel* (Genesis 35:10); it was subsequently applied to Jacob's descendants, the Jewish nation, and is now primarily associated with the Middle Eastern republic created in 1948. *Israel* came into general use as a first name after the Reformation but is rarely found in modern times. The 20th-century songwriter Israel Baline, better known as Irving Berlin, is a famous bearer of the name.

**Issy, Izzy** diminutives of a number of masculine and feminine names beginning with *Is-*, such as **Isaac**, **Isabel**, or **Isidore**.

**Ita** (f) an Irish name, meaning 'thirst'; borne by a 6th-century saint. The name remains in occasional use in Ireland but is rarely found elsewhere.

**Ithel** (m) a Welsh name, meaning 'generous lord'.

**Ivah** (f) from an Old Testament place name; in occasional use as a first name.

**Ivan** [*ī*văn] the Russian form of **John**; in occasional use throughout the English-speaking world since the late 19th century. The name was borne by a number of Russian princes and emperors, notably Ivan the Terrible (1530–84).

## Ives

**Ives** a variant of **Ivo**; borne by the patron saint of the Cambridgeshire town of St Ives (the Cornish place name *St Ives* is believed to be derived from the name of a different saint). *Ives* is more frequently found as a surname than as a first name in modern times.

**Ivo** (m) from Old German, meaning 'yew'. Introduced into Britain at the time of the Norman Conquest, the name was fairly common during the Middle Ages but is rarely used today. See also **Ivor**.
Variants: **Ives, Yves**.
Feminine forms: **Yvette, Yvonne**.

**Ivor** [īver] (m) a name of uncertain origin: it may be from the Old Norse name *Ivarr* or it may simply be an anglicized form of **Ifor**, influenced by **Ivo**. *Ivor* has been in general use in Britain for many hundreds of years but is rarely found in other English-speaking countries. Famous bearers of the name include the composer Ivor Novello (1893–1951), whose real name was David Ivor Davies, and the cartoon character Ivor the Engine.
Variant: **Ifor**.

**Ivy** (f) from the plant name, possibly intended to signify faithfulness. It came into use as a first name during the latter half of the 19th century and was particularly popular in the early 20th century.

**Izaak** see **Isaac**.

**Izzy** see **Issy**.

# J

**Jabez** (m) from Hebrew, possibly meaning 'pain' (the Jabez of the Old Testament was so named because his mother bore him in pain). The name was adopted by the Puritans in the 17th century and remained in regular use until the end of the 19th century; it is rarely found in modern times.

**Jacinta** a variant of **Jacinth**.

**Jacinth** (f) from the name of the precious stone; ultimately from the Greek flower name from which the word *hyacinth* is derived. *Jacinth* has been in occasional use as a first name since the 17th century, when it was given to children of either sex; the variant **Jacinta** is more popular in modern times.
Variant: **Jacinta**.
Related name: **Hyacinth**.

**Jack** a diminutive of **John**, dating back to the Middle Ages; sometimes erroneously associated with **Jacques** (*Jack* is ultimately derived from *Jankin*, a pet form of **Jan** (m)). The name was so common in medieval times that it gradually came to be used as a colloquial word for 'man' or 'boy' (see also **Gill**); it also featured in a number of nursery rhymes and

fairy tales, including 'Jack and Jill' and 'Jack and the Beanstalk', and entered the English language in such compounds as *jackass* and *jackpot*. *Jack* was rarely given as a name in its own right until the late 19th century; famous bearers of the name in modern times include the British actor Jack Hawkins and the US actor Jack Lemmon. See also **Jock**.
Diminutive: **Jackie**.

**Jackie** (m) a diminutive of **Jack**. The British motor-racing driver Jackie Stewart (born John Young Stewart) is a famous bearer of the name.

**Jackie, Jacky, Jacqui** (f) diminutives of **Jacqueline**, sometimes used as independent names.

**Jacob** [*jay*kŏb] (m) from a Hebrew name of uncertain origin; generally interpreted as 'he grasps the heel' or 'supplanter'. The Jacob of the Old Testament (see also **Israel**) was the younger son of Isaac and the twin brother of **Esau** (the name also occurs in the New Testament, where it is translated as **James**). *Jacob* has never been as common in the English-speaking world as its variant *James*; it enjoyed a partial revival after the Reformation but is rarely found in modern times. The sculptor Sir Jacob Epstein (1880–1959) was a famous bearer of the name.
Variants: **Iago, Jacques, Jago, James**.
Diminutive: **Jake**.
Feminine forms: **Jacoba, Jacobina**.

**Jacobina, Jacoba** feminine forms of **Jacob**. *Jacobina* remains in occasional use in Scotland but *Jacoba* is very rare.

**Jacqueline, Jacquelyn** [*jak*ĕlin] feminine forms of **Jacques**. Introduced into Britain from the Low Countries in the 13th century, the name was used only occasionally until the 20th century, when it became popular throughout the English-speaking world.
Diminutives: **Jackie, Jacky, Jacqui**.

**Jacques** [zhak, jayks] the French form of **Jacob**; occasionally found in English-speaking countries. See also **Jack, Jake**.
Feminine forms: **Jacqueline, Jacquelyn, Jacquetta**.

**Jacquetta** [ja*ket*ă] a feminine form of **Jacques**.

**Jade** (f) from the name of the precious stone; occasionally used as a first name in the latter half of the 20th century.

**Jael** [*jay*ĕl] (f) from Hebrew, meaning 'wild goat'. The Jael of the Old Testament murdered her guest Sisera by driving a tent peg through his head (Judges 4:21); this gruesome story did not deter the Puritans from adopting *Jael* as a first name after the Reformation. It has been used only occasionally since the 19th century.

**Jago** [*jay*gō] a Cornish variant of **Jacob**.

**Jake** a diminutive of **Jacob**, influenced by **Jacques**; sometimes used as a name in its own right.

# James

**James** a variant of **Jacob** derived from *Jacomus*, one of the Latin forms of the name (*Jacobus*, the other Latin form, gave rise to the adjective *Jacobean* 'of King James I' and the noun *Jacobite* 'supporter of King James II'). The name was borne in the New Testament by a brother or close relative of Jesus Christ, author of the Epistle of James, and by two of Jesus' apostles: St James the Great, son of Zebedee and brother of St John, and St James the Less. First used in Britain in the 13th century, the name was popularized in Scotland by five kings whose reigns ran consecutively from 1406 to 1542; it spread to England at the beginning of the 17th century, when King James VI of Scotland became King James I of England, and has been in frequent use throughout the English-speaking world since then.
Variants: **Hamish, Seamus, Shamus**.
Diminutives: **Jamie, Jem, Jemmy, Jim, Jimmy**.
Feminine forms: **Jamesina, Jamie**.

**Jamesina** a feminine form of **James**; in occasional use in Scotland but rarely found elsewhere.

**Jamie** a Scottish diminutive of **James**, sometimes used as a name in its own right. It also occurs as a feminine form of the name, especially in the USA.

**Jan** (f) a diminutive of **Janet**.

**Jan** (m) a variant of **John** found in a number of European countries; also a dialectal form of the name in England.

**Jane, Jayne** feminine forms of **John** derived from the Old French name *Jehane*. *Jane* was rarely found in Britain until the 16th century, when it was borne by King Henry VIII's third wife Jane Seymour, who died in 1537 after giving birth to the future King Edward VI. The name has been in frequent use throughout the English-speaking world since the latter half of the 18th century; famous bearers include the British novelist Jane Austen (1775–1817) and the US actress Jayne Mansfield (1932–67). See also **Janet, Janice**.
Variants: **Sheena, Sian, Sinead**.
Diminutives: **Janey, Janie, Jennie, Jenny**.

**Janet** a feminine form of **John**; originally a diminutive of **Jane**, influenced by **Jeanette**. It was generally regarded as a Scottish name until the early 20th century, when it began to spread to other parts of Britain and the English-speaking world, reaching its peak of popularity in the 1950s.
Variants: **Janetta, Janette**.
Diminutives: **Jan, Jennie, Jenny, Jessie**.

**Janetta** a Latinized form of **Janet**.

**Janette** a variant of **Janet**, popularized in the mid-20th century by the British actress Janette Scott.

**Janey** see **Janie**.

**Janice, Janis** feminine forms of **John**. Originally a diminutive of **Jane**, the name has been in regular use throughout the English-speaking world since the early 20th century; like **Janet**, it was particularly popular in the 1950s. The US singer Janis Joplin was a famous bearer of the name.

**Janie, Janey** diminutives of **Jane**, sometimes used as independent names.

**Janine** [jăneen] a variant of **Jeannine**; the more common form of the name in the English-speaking world.

**Janis** see **Janice**.

**Japheth** (m) from Hebrew, meaning 'may he expand' or 'enlargement'. Borne in the Old Testament by one of the sons of Noah, the name was adopted by the Puritans in the 17th century. It is rarely found in modern times.

**Jared** (m) from Hebrew, possibly meaning 'rose'; borne in the Old Testament by the father of Enoch. The name was adopted by the Puritans in the 17th century and enjoyed a further revival in the latter half of the 20th century. The modern variant spellings *Jarrod* and *Jarred* may be derived from surnames related to **Gerald** or **Gerard**.

**Jarrod, Jarred** see **Jared**.

**Jarvis** a variant of **Gervase**; more frequently found as a surname than as a first name in modern times.

**Jasmine** (f) from a flower name of Persian origin (see **Yasmin**); in regular use as a first name since the late 19th century.
Variants: **Jessamine, Jessamyn, Yasmin**.

**Jason** (m) from the Greek form of a Hebrew name (possibly **Joshua**); borne in Greek mythology by the leader of the Argonauts and in the New Testament by a relative of St Paul. *Jason* was one of the many biblical names adopted by the Puritans after the Reformation. It was popularized in the USA and Britain in the late 1960s and early 1970s by a number of television characters, including Jason King (played by Peter Wyngarde), who first appeared in the British television series *Department S*. Other famous bearers of the name include the US actor Jason Robards (1893–1963) and his son Jason Robards Jnr.

**Jasper** (m) from the name *Gaspar* or *Caspar*, traditionally borne by one of the Magi (see **Balthasar**); possibly from Persian, meaning 'bearer (or keeper) of treasure'. *Jasper*, the anglicized form of the name, has been in occasional use since the 14th century and occurs in a number of literary works. *Caspar* is also used from time to time in the English-speaking world.

**Jay** (m *or* f) from the bird name, which may be ultimately derived from the Latin name **Gaius**. *Jay* has been in occasional use since the Middle Ages, when it probably originated as a nickname for a talkative person; in modern times it is also used as a diminutive of any masculine or feminine name beginning with *J*.

**Jayne** see **Jane**.

**Jean** a feminine form of **John** derived from the Old French name *Jehane*. It was rarely found outside Scotland until the late 19th century, when it began to spread to other parts of Britain and the English-speaking world, reaching its peak of popularity in the 1930s. Famous bearers of the name include the British actress Jean Simmons (born 1929) and the heroine of Muriel Spark's novel *The Prime of Miss Jean Brodie* (1961), which was filmed in 1969 and adapted for television in 1978. See also **Jeanne**.
Diminutives: **Jeanette, Jeanie, Jeannette, Jeannie**.

**Jeanette, Jeannette** diminutives of **Jean**, often used as independent names. The 20th-century US actress and singer Jeanette MacDonald was a famous bearer of the name. See also **Janet**.

**Jeanie** see **Jeannie**.

**Jeanne** [zhan] the French feminine form of **John**, derived from Old French *Jehane*; the French equivalent of **Jane**, **Jean**, or **Joan**. (The name of the 15th-century French heroine Jeanne d'Arc (Joan of Arc) would probably have been translated as *Jane* if she had lived in the 18th century, when *Jane* was the most common feminine form of *John*.) *Jeanne* is sometimes used as a variant of *Jean* in English-speaking countries.
Diminutive: **Jeannine**.

**Jeannette** see **Jeanette**.

**Jeannie, Jeanie** diminutives of **Jean**, sometimes used as independent names; popularized by the song 'Jeanie with the Light Brown Hair', which was written by the 19th-century US composer Stephen Foster.

**Jeannine** [zha*neen*] a diminutive of **Jeanne**, occasionally used in English-speaking countries as a name in its own right.
Variant: **Janine**.

**Jed** a diminutive of **Jedidiah**, often used as a name in its own right.

**Jedidiah** (m) from Hebrew, meaning 'beloved (or friend) of the Lord'; an alternative name of the Old Testament king **Solomon**. The name was adopted by the Puritans in the 17th century but is rarely found in modern times.
Diminutive: **Jed**.

**Jeff** see **Geoff**.

**Jefferson** (m) from a surname meaning 'son of **Geoffrey**'. Its occasional use as a first name, which dates back to the early 19th century, has been attributed to the renown of the US president Thomas Jefferson (1743–1826).

**Jeffrey, Jellery** see **Geoffrey**.

**Jehane** see **Jane, Jean, Jeanne**.

**Jem** a diminutive of **James**.

**Jemima** [jĕmĩmă] (f) from Hebrew, meaning 'dove'. Borne in the Old Testament by one of the three beautiful daughters of Job, the name was adopted by the Puritans in the 17th century. It was particularly popular in the 19th century and has remained in occasional use since then, a famous bearer being Jemima Puddle-Duck, one of the animal characters created by Beatrix Potter in the early 20th century.
Diminutives: **Jemma, Mima**.

**Jemma** a diminutive of **Jemima** or an alternative spelling of **Gemma**.

**Jemmy** a diminutive of **James**. *Jemmy* has entered the English language as the name of a type of crowbar (known as a jimmy in the USA).

**Jen** a diminutive of **Jennifer** or **Jenny**.

**Jenifer** see **Jennifer**.

**Jenna** a variant of **Jenny**.

**Jennie** see **Jenny**.

**Jennifer, Jenifer** variants of **Guinevere**, of Cornish origin. The name was rarely used outside Cornwall until the early 20th century; by the 1950s it had become very popular throughout Britain and in other parts of the English-speaking world.
Diminutives: **Jen, Jennie, Jenny**.

**Jenny, Jennie** diminutives of **Jane, Janet** (in Scotland), or **Jennifer**; often used as independent names. The spinning jenny, patented in 1770, was named after the young daughter of its inventor, James Hargreaves.
Variants: **Jenna, Jinny**.
Diminutive: **Jen**.

**Jephthah** [*jef*thă] (m) from the Hebrew verb 'to open (or release)'. The Jephthah of the Old Testament, a leader of the Israelites, was obliged to sacrifice his only daughter in return for God's assistance in the defeat of the Ammonites (Judges 11:29–40). The name was adopted by the Puritans after the Reformation and has been in occasional use since then.

**Jeremiah** [jerrĕmĩă] (m) from Hebrew, meaning 'may Jehovah exalt'. The Jeremiah of the Old Testament, author of the book of Lamentations, was a prophet of the 7th century BC; the English word *jeremiad*, meaning 'lamentation', is derived from his name. Together with its Greek form *Jeremias*, the name was revived by the Puritans in the 17th century, when it was borne by Jeremiah Clarke, composer of what is now known as the *Trumpet Voluntary*. *Jeremiah* has remained in occasional use in various parts of the English-speaking world, especially Ireland, since then.
Variant: **Jeremy**.
Diminutive: **Jerry**.

# Jeremias

**Jeremias** see **Jeremiah**.

**Jeremy** [*jerrĕmi*] a variant of **Jeremiah**, dating back to the 13th century; the most common form of the name in English-speaking countries since its revival in the early 20th century. Famous bearers of the name in Britain include the philosopher Jeremy Bentham (1748–1832), who propounded the doctrine of utilitarianism, and the British politician Jeremy Thorpe (born 1929).

Diminutive: **Jerry**.

**Jermaine** (m) from the French name *Germain*, meaning 'German'; occasionally found in the USA and in other parts of the English-speaking world in the latter half of the 20th century.

Feminine equivalent: **Germaine**.

**Jerome** [*jĕrōm*] (m) from Greek, meaning 'holy name'; borne in the 4th century by the biblical scholar St Jerome (or Eusebius Hieronymus), who was responsible for the Latin translation of the Bible known as the Vulgate. The name has been in general use in Britain since the 12th century in a variety of forms, of which only *Jerome* appears to have survived. Famous bearers include the British writer Jerome K. Jerome (1859–1927) and the US composer and songwriter Jerome Kern (1885–1945).

Variant: **Hieronymus**.

Diminutive: **Jerry**.

**Jerry** see **Gerry**.

**Jess** a diminutive of **Jessamine**, **Jessica**, or **Jessie**.

**Jessamine, Jessamyn** variants of **Jasmine**.

Diminutives: **Jess, Jessie**.

**Jesse** [*jesi*] (m) from Hebrew, meaning 'Jehovah exists'. Borne in the Old Testament by the father of King David, the name was adopted by the Puritans after the Reformation and remains in occasional use. The US outlaw Jesse James (1847–82) is probably the best-known bearer of the name.

**Jessica** (f) from a Hebrew name meaning 'God beholds', which occurs in the Old Testament in the form *Iscah* (or *Jesca*). *Jessica* was popularized in the late 16th century, when Shakespeare gave the name to Shylock's daughter in his play *The Merchant of Venice*; it enjoyed a revival in the 1970s and remains in regular use in various parts of the English-speaking world.

Diminutives: **Jess, Jessie**.

**Jessie** a Scottish diminutive of **Janet**, dating back to the 18th century; often given as a name in its own right. It is also used throughout the English-speaking world as a diminutive of **Jessamine** or **Jessica**.

Diminutive: **Jess**.

**Jesus** (m) from a Hebrew name meaning 'Jehovah is generous' or 'Jehovah saves'. Borne in the New Testament by Jesus Christ, *Jesus* is generally considered too sacred to be given as a first name in many parts of the Christian world.
Related name: **Joshua**.

**Jethro** (m) from Hebrew, meaning 'pre-eminence', 'excellence', or 'abundance'. Borne in the Old Testament by the father of Moses' wife Zipporah, the name was adopted by the Puritans after the Reformation; the English agriculturalist Jethro Tull (1674–1741), inventor of the seed drill, was one of its most famous bearers. *Jethro* remained in regular use until the late 19th century and acquired some renewed popularity in the latter half of the 20th century as the name of an amiable character in the radio serial 'The Archers'.

**Jewel** (f) from the English word *jewel*; in occasional use as a first name since the early 20th century.

**Jill** see **Gill**.

**Jillian** see **Gillian**.

**Jim, Jimmy** diminutives of **James**, sometimes used as independent names. See also **Jemmy**.

**Jinny** a variant of **Jenny** or a diminutive of **Virginia**.

**Jo** a diminutive of **Joanna**, **Joanne**, or **Josephine**, sometimes used as a name in its own right.

**Joachim** [*jōākim*] (m) from Hebrew, meaning 'may Jehovah exalt'. The cult of St Joachim, who is traditionally believed to have been the father of the Virgin Mary, popularized the name in various parts of the world; it has been in occasional use in English-speaking countries since the 13th century.

**Joan** a feminine form of **John** derived from the Latin name *Johanna*. *Joan* was first used in Britain in the 12th century, when King Henry II and Eleanor of Aquitaine gave the name to their youngest daughter. It gradually became one of the most common girls' names in the country and consequently began to fall from favour; by the end of the 17th century it had been largely replaced by **Jane**. In the early 20th century *Joan* came back into fashion throughout the English-speaking world and remained in frequent use until the 1950s. Famous bearers of the name include a legendary female pope; the French heroine St Joan of Arc (**Jeanne d'Arc**), burned at the stake as a heretic in 1431; and a number of 20th-century actresses, such as Joan Crawford, Joan Fontaine, and Joan Collins.
Variant: **Siobhan**.

**Joanna** a feminine form of **John** derived from the Latin name *Johanna*. The Joanna of the New Testament was one of the women who bore the news

of Christ's resurrection to the apostles (Luke 24:10). The name was adopted by the Puritans after the Reformation and has been in regular use since then; the Latin form *Johanna* was revived in the 18th century and is still found from time to time as a variant spelling of the name.
Variant: **Joanne**.
Diminutive: **Jo**.

**Joanne** a feminine form of **John** derived from the Latin name *Johanna*; generally regarded as the French equivalent of **Joanna**. *Joanne* was rarely found in English-speaking countries until the early 20th century, when it came into fashion in the USA; in the 1970s it was one of the most popular girls' names in Britain.
Diminutive: **Jo**.

**Job** [jŏb] (m) from Hebrew, meaning 'persecuted'. The Job of the Old Testament is remembered for his great patience in the face of adversity; the name was adopted by the Puritans after the Reformation and remains in occasional use today.

**Jocasta** (f) from Greek, meaning 'shining moon'. In Greek mythology Jocasta was the mother and wife of Oedipus; on learning of the incestuous nature of their marriage Oedipus blinded himself and Jocasta committed suicide. The name is occasionally found in the English-speaking world but has never been common.

**Jocelyn, Joscelin** [*jos*lin] (m *or* f) probably from an Old German name meaning 'one of the Goths', though some scholars believe *Jocelyn* to be etymologically related to **Joyce** and many parents associate the name with the English words *jocose* or *jocund*. *Jocelyn* was introduced into Britain as a masculine name at the time of the Norman Conquest and was very popular during the Middle Ages; its adoption as a feminine first name in the early 20th century was probably influenced by the growing popularity of *Joyce* at that time.
Diminutive: **Joss**.

**Jock** a Scottish diminutive of **John**, influenced by **Jack**. It is rarely used as a first name in modern times, having degenerated into a nickname for a Scot or a slang term for a Scottish soldier. The English word *jockey* is derived from a diminutive of *Jock*.

**Jodie, Jodi, Jody** diminutives of **Judith**, in frequent use as independent names in the USA, Canada, and Australia since the mid-20th century.

**Joe** a diminutive of **Joseph**, often used as a name in its own right.

**Joel** [*jō*ĕl] (m) either from Hebrew, meaning 'Jehovah is God', or from the name of a Breton saint. The latter was introduced into Britain at the time of the Norman Conquest; the Hebrew name, borne by an Old Testament prophet of the 5th century BC, was adopted by the Puritans after the Reformation. *Joel* remains in occasional use in the USA but is rarely found in other parts of the English-speaking world in modern times.

**Joey** a diminutive of **Joseph**, sometimes used as a name in its own right. The Australian word *joey*, meaning 'young kangaroo', is not related to the first name.

**Johanna** see **Joan, Joanna, Joanne**.

**Johannes** see **John**.

**John, Jon** (m) from a Hebrew name meaning 'Jehovah is gracious' or 'Jehovah has favoured', rendered in Latin as *Johannes*. The immense popularity of the name throughout the Christian world is due to two New Testament bearers: St John the Baptist, who heralded the arrival of Jesus Christ, and the apostle and evangelist St John the Divine, author of the fourth Gospel, three epistles, and the book of Revelation. A number of variant forms of the name were introduced into Britain during the Middle Ages, giving rise to such surnames as *Hancock, Jackson, Jenkins, Jones*, and *Johnson*. By the end of the 16th century *John* had become one of the most common boys' names in the English-speaking world, a position it retained until the latter half of the 20th century. The name has been little used by the royal families of Britain since the reign of King John in the 13th century; it is, however, borne by the cartoon character John Bull, a personification of England or the typical Englishman created in the early 18th century by the Scottish physician and pamphleteer John Arbuthnot. See also **Jonathan**.
Variants: **Evan, Hans, Iain, Ian, Ivan, Jan, Juan, Sean, Shaun, Shawn**.
Diminutives: **Jack, Jock, Johnnie, Johnny**.
Feminine forms: **Jane, Janet, Janice, Janis, Jayne, Jean, Jeanne, Joan, Joanna, Joanne, Shona**.

**Johnny, Johnnie** diminutives of **John** or **Jonathan**, sometimes used as independent names.

**Jolene, Joleen** [*jō*leen] (f) a compound of **Jo** and the feminine name element *-lene*; in regular use in English-speaking countries, especially the USA, since the mid-20th century.

**Jolyon** [*jō*liŏn] a variant of **Julian**, popularized by a number of members of the Forsyte family in John Galsworthy's *The Forsyte Saga* (1922), which was adapted for television in the late 1960s.

**Jon** a variant spelling of **John** or a diminutive of **Jonathan**.

**Jonah** [*jō*nă] (m) from Hebrew, meaning 'dove'; borne by an Old Testament prophet of the 8th century BC. According to the book of Jonah (1:17–2:10) the prophet was swallowed by a 'great fish', possibly a whale, and disgorged onto dry land after three days and nights (the use of the name *Jonah* to denote a bringer of bad luck is derived from an earlier part of the same story). The variant form *Jonas* was fairly common in medieval Britain and *Jonah* was revived by the Puritans after the Reformation; both names are still used from time to time in English-speaking countries. Variant: **Jonas**.

**Jonas** [jōnăs] a variant of **Jonah**; the more common form of the name in the English-speaking world.

**Jonathan** [jonăthăn] (m) from Hebrew, meaning 'Jehovah has given' or 'Jehovah's gift'; sometimes erroneously associated with **John**. Borne in the Old Testament by a son of King Saul and close friend of David, the name was adopted by the Puritans after the Reformation and revived throughout the English-speaking world in the mid-20th century. Famous bearers include the Anglo-Irish writer Jonathan Swift (1667–1745), author of the political satire *Gulliver's Travels*, and an 18th-century governor of Connecticut, Jonathan Trumbull, who was the original 'Brother Jonathan' (an expression subsequently used to personify the USA or the typical American).
Diminutives: **Johnnie, Johnny, Jon**.

**Jonquil** (f) from the flower name; in occasional use as a first name since the mid-20th century.

**Jordan** (m) either from the name of the River Jordan in the Middle East, ultimately from the Hebrew verb 'to flow down', or from the Old German name *Jordanes*, of uncertain origin. *Jordan* was in frequent use as a first name during the latter half of the Middle Ages, when the children of returning Crusaders were often baptized with Jordan water brought back from the Holy Land; it is rarely found in modern times.
Diminutive: **Judd**.

**Joscelin** see **Jocelyn**.

**José** [hōzay] the Spanish form of **Joseph**; in occasional use in English-speaking countries, especially in US families of Spanish descent.

**Joseph** [jōzif] (m) from Hebrew, meaning 'may Jehovah add' or 'addition' (referring to an increase in the size of the family). The name was given by Rachel, wife of the Old Testament patriarch Jacob, to her elder son; in the New Testament it was borne by the husband of the Virgin Mary, now venerated as a saint, and by St Joseph of Arimathea, who assumed responsibility for the burial of Jesus Christ and is also associated with the legend of the Holy Grail. Largely confined to Jewish families during the Middle Ages, *Joseph* came into more general use in Britain after the Reformation, when it was one of the many biblical names revived by the Puritans; it was further popularized in the 17th century by the cult of St Joseph (of Nazareth) and has been in regular use throughout the English-speaking world since then.
Variant: **José**.
Diminutives: **Joe, Joey**.
Feminine forms: **Josepha, Josephine, Josette, Pepita**.

**Josepha** a feminine form of **Joseph**; from *Josephus*, the Latinized form of the name.

**Josephine** a feminine form of **Joseph**; from a diminutive of *Josèphe*, the French equivalent of **Josepha**. Popularized by the French empress Joséphine (1763–1814), wife of Napoleon Bonaparte, the name has been in regular use throughout the English-speaking world since the mid-19th century.
Diminutives: **Fifi, Jo, Josie**.

**Josette** a feminine form of **Joseph**, of French origin.

**Josh** a diminutive of **Joshua** or **Josiah**.

**Joshua** (m) from a Hebrew name meaning 'Jehovah is generous' or 'Jehovah saves'. The Joshua of the Old Testament was chosen to succeed Moses as leader of the Israelites on their journey into the Promised Land. The name was adopted by the Puritans after the Reformation and remained in regular use until the late 19th century, a famous bearer being the British painter Sir Joshua Reynolds (1723–92); it enjoyed a partial revival in the USA and Canada in the latter half of the 20th century.
Diminutive: **Josh**.
Related name: **Jesus**.

**Josiah** [jōsī́ā] (m) from Hebrew, meaning 'may Jehovah heal'; borne in the Old Testament by one of the kings of Judah. *Josiah* has been in general use as a first name in English-speaking countries since the Reformation, its best-known bearer being the British potter Josiah Wedgwood (1730–95). The name is still used from time to time in the Wedgwood family but is rarely found elsewhere.
Variant: **Josias**.
Diminutive: **Josh**.

**Josias** a variant of **Josiah**.

**Josie** a diminutive of **Josephine**.

**Joss** a diminutive of **Jocelyn**.

**Jotham** (m) from Hebrew, meaning 'Jehovah is perfect'. The name was borne in the Old Testament by Gideon's youngest son, who escaped the massacre in which his seventy brothers were killed (Judges 9:5), and by one of the kings of Judah. It is occasionally used in the English-speaking world but has never been common.

**Joy** (f) from the English word *joy*; in occasional use as a first name since the Middle Ages. One of the many names of abstract qualities favoured by the Puritans in the 17th century, it enjoyed a further revival in the late 19th century and is still fairly popular throughout the English-speaking world.

**Joyce** (f) from the name of the 7th-century hermit St Judoc (also known as St Judocus or St Josse), the son of a Breton king. In medieval Britain the name occurred in a variety of forms, such as *Josse* and *Jocea*, and was given to children of either sex; it survived the Middle Ages as a feminine name but was little used until the late 19th century, when it became fashionable throughout the English-speaking world. See also **Jocelyn**.

**Juan** [hwahn, *joo*ăn] the Spanish form of **John**; in occasional use in English-speaking countries, especially the USA.

Feminine form: **Juanita**.

**Juanita** [hwă*neetă*, jooă*neetă*] a feminine form of **Juan**.

**Judah** [*joo*dă] (m) from Hebrew, possibly meaning 'praise'. The Judah of the Old Testament was the fourth son of Jacob and Leah and a direct ancestor of Jesus Christ; the English nouns *Jew* and *Judaism* are ultimately derived from his name. *Judah* was one of the many biblical names adopted by the Puritans after the Reformation but is rarely found in this form in modern times.

Variants: **Judas, Jude, Yehudi**.

**Judas** the Greek form of **Judah**. The name is generally associated with the apostle Judas Iscariot, who betrayed Jesus Christ for thirty pieces of silver; it has entered the English language as a synonym for 'traitor' and is very rarely given as a first name. See also **Jude**.

**Judd** (m) either from an Old English name of uncertain origin or a diminutive of **Jordan**.

**Jude** a variant of **Judah**; the most familiar form of the name in the English-speaking world. St Jude, the author of the Epistle of Jude in the New Testament, was one of Jesus Christ's apostles, also known as Judas or Thaddaeus. The name was adopted by the Puritans after the Reformation and has been in occasional use since then; it was chosen by Thomas Hardy for the unfortunate hero of his novel *Jude the Obscure* (1895).

**Judi** see **Judy**.

**Judith** (f) from Hebrew, meaning 'Jewess'; borne by one of the wives of Esau in the Old Testament and by the heroine of the book of Judith in the Apocrypha. The name was introduced into Britain in the 9th century by the stepmother of King Alfred the Great, daughter of the French king Charles the Bald, but was rarely used until the 17th century; it was popular throughout the English-speaking world in the mid-20th century.

Diminutives: **Jodi, Jodie, Jody, Judi, Judy**.

**Judoc** see **Joyce**.

**Judy** a diminutive of **Judith**, often used as a name in its own right. The name is borne by the battered wife of Punch in the Punch and Judy puppet show, first performed in Britain in the 17th century; it is also used as a slang word for 'woman'. The variant spelling *Judi* was made famous by the British actress Judi Dench (born 1934).

**Jules** [zhool, joolz] the French form of **Julius**, made famous by the French science-fiction writer Jules Verne (1828–1905).

**Julia** the feminine form of **Julius**. Introduced into Britain from Italy in the late 16th century, when it was borne by a character in Shakespeare's play *Two Gentlemen of Verona*, the name was used only occasionally until the 18th century. It subsequently became fashionable throughout the English-speaking world and has remained in regular use since then.
Variants: **Julie, Juliet, Julitta**.

**Julian** (m) from the Latin name *Julianus*, derived from **Julius**; borne by a number of saints, notably St Julian the Hospitaller, patron saint of ferrymen, innkeepers, and travellers. *Julian* was first used in Britain in the latter half of the Middle Ages, when it was given to children of either sex; the feminine name was gradually superseded by **Gillian** but the masculine name remained in regular use, enjoying a revival in the 20th century. Famous bearers of the name include the British scientist Sir Julian Huxley (1887–1975) and the British guitarist Julian Bream (born 1933).
Variant: **Jolyon**.
Feminine forms: **Gillian, Jillian, Juliana, Julianne, Julienne**.

**Juliana** a feminine form of **Julian**; borne by the early Christian martyr St Juliana. The name has been in regular use in the Low Countries for many hundreds of years, the former Queen Juliana of the Netherlands being its best-known bearer in modern times. It was introduced into Britain in the late 12th century and was gradually superseded by **Gillian**; *Juliana* was revived in the 18th century but has never been common in English-speaking countries.
Diminutive: **Liana**.

**Julianne** a feminine form of **Julian**, probably derived from a compound of **Julie** and **Ann**. It has been in regular use in various parts of the English-speaking world since the mid-20th century.
Diminutive: **Lianne**.

**Julie** the French form of **Julia**; sometimes regarded as a diminutive of the name. It has been in frequent use throughout the English-speaking world since the mid-20th century. Famous bearers include the actresses Julie Andrews and Julie Christie, both of whom may have contributed to the immense popularity of the name in the 1960s and 1970s.

**Julienne** a feminine form of **Julian**, of French origin.

**Juliet** a variant of **Julia**, from an Italian diminutive of the name; generally associated with the young heroine of Shakespeare's play *Romeo and Juliet*. Its revival in the latter half of the 20th century has been attributed to the popularity of the related name **Julie**.
Variant: **Juliette**.

**Juliette** the French form of **Juliet**.

**Julitta** a variant of **Julia**; originally a diminutive of the name. Borne by the Christian martyr St Julitta, who died in the early 4th century, the name is

used from time to time in English-speaking countries but has never been
common.

**Julius** (m) from the clan name of the Roman dictator Gaius Julius Caesar;
possibly from Greek, meaning 'downy' or 'hairy'. The name has been in
occasional use in the English-speaking world since the 16th century but is
more frequently found in modern times in its derived form **Julian**.

Variant: **Jules**.

Feminine form: **Julia**.

**June** (f) from the name of the sixth month of the year; one of a number of
month names that became fashionable in the 20th century.

**Junior** (m) from Latin, meaning 'younger'. Generally used in the USA to
distinguish a son from his father, when both bear the same name, *Junior* is
occasionally given as a first name in its own right in various parts of the
English-speaking world.

**Juno** a variant of **Una**, made famous by the Irish dramatist Sean O'Casey's
play *Juno and the Paycock* (1924). The name of the Roman goddess Juno,
wife of Jupiter, is of uncertain origin.

**Justin** (m) from Latin *justus* 'just'. Early bearers of the name include the
2nd-century Christian apologist St Justin Martyr, a Roman historian of
the 3rd century, and two Byzantine emperors. *Justin* was rarely used
outside Ireland until the latter half of the 20th century, when it became
popular throughout the English-speaking world.

Feminine forms: **Justina, Justine**.

**Justina** [jus*teen*ă] a feminine form of **Justin**. Borne by two early Christian
martyrs, the name is occasionally found in English-speaking countries
but has never been common.

**Justine** [jus*teen*] a feminine form of **Justin**, of French origin. The name has
been popular throughout the English-speaking world since the mid-20th
century; it was used by the British writer Lawrence Durrell for *Justine*
(1957), the first novel of his *Alexandria Quartet*.

# K

**Kane** (m) from a surname of uncertain origin: it may be from Welsh, meaning 'beautiful'; from the French place name *Caen*, meaning 'field of com-
bat'; or from a Celtic word for 'warrior'. *Kane* is occasionally used as a
first name in various parts of the English-speaking world, especially Australia.

**Kara** see **Cara**.

**Karel** see **Carol** (m).

**Karen** [*ka*rrĕn] a variant of **Catherine**; originally a Danish diminutive of the name. Introduced into the USA by Danish immigrants in the early 20th century, the name subsequently spread to other parts of the English-speaking world; it was particularly popular in Britain in the 1960s. See also **Keren**.
Variant: **Karin**.

**Karin** a variant of **Karen**, of Swedish origin.

**Karina** an alternative spelling of **Carina** or a variant of **Catherine**.

**Karl** see **Carl**.

**Karol** see **Carol** (m).

**Kate** a diminutive of **Catherine** or **Kathleen**, often used as a name in its own right. It was particularly popular in the late 19th century and has recently enjoyed a further revival.

**Kath, Cath** diminutives of **Catherine** or **Kathleen**.

**Katherine, Katharine** see **Catherine**.

**Kathleen, Cathleen** variants of **Catherine**, from the Irish Gaelic form **Caitlin**. The name was rarely used outside Ireland until the 20th century, when it became popular throughout the English-speaking world.
Diminutives: **Cath, Cathy, Kate, Kath, Kathy, Katie, Katy, Kay, Kit, Kitty**.

**Kathryn** a variant of **Catherine**; in regular use since the mid-20th century.

**Kathy, Cathy** diminutives of **Catherine** or **Kathleen**, sometimes used as independent names.

**Katie, Katy** diminutives of **Catherine** or **Kathleen**, often used as independent names. Popularized by the young heroine of the US writer Susan Coolidge's *What Katy Did* trilogy, a series of children's books first published in the late 19th century, the name has recently enjoyed a further revival.

**Katrina, Katrine** variants of **Catriona**.

**Katy** see **Katie**.

**Kay** (f) a diminutive of **Katherine, Kathleen**, or any other feminine name beginning with *K*; often used as a name in its own right.

**Kay** [kay, kī] (m) a variant of **Gaius**; originally an alternative spelling of **Cai**. Sir Kay was one of the knights of the Round Table in Arthurian legend; the name was further popularized in the 19th century by a character in Hans Christian Andersen's story 'The Snow Queen'.

**Keeley** a variant of **Kelly**.

**Keir** [keer] (m) from a Scottish surname of uncertain origin; in occasional use as a first name since the late 19th century, when it was made famous by the British politician James Keir Hardie (1856–1915).

# Keith

**Keith** [keeth] (m) from a Scottish surname and place name possibly derived from a Gaelic word for 'wood'. *Keith* was rarely given as a first name outside Scotland until the late 19th century; by the mid-20th century it was in regular use throughout the English-speaking world.

**Kelda** (f) a name of uncertain origin; possibly from a Scandinavian word for 'spring' or 'fountain'.

**Kelly, Kellie** (f) either from an Irish surname meaning 'war' or from a Scottish surname and place name meaning 'wood'. *Kelly* was rarely used as a first name until the latter half of the 20th century; it was particularly popular in Britain in the 1980s.
Variant: **Keeley**.

**Kelvin** (m) a name of uncertain origin; possibly derived from two Old English words meaning 'ship' and 'friend' or from the name of a Scottish river. Its use in the 20th century may have been influenced by the British physicist Lord Kelvin (1824–1907).

**Ken** a diminutive of **Kenneth**.

**Kendal, Kendall** (m) from a surname and Cumbrian place name; ultimately from Old English, meaning 'valley of the River Kent'.

**Kendra** (f) a name of uncertain origin: it may be related to the English word *ken*, meaning 'knowledge', or it may be derived from a compound of **Ken** and **Sandra**.

**Kenelm** (m) from Old English *cene* 'brave' and *helm* 'helmet'. The sister of St Kenelm, son of King Coenwulf of Mercia, is traditionally believed to have had her brother murdered after the death of their father in the early 9th century. The name is rarely used in modern times.

**Kenneth** (m) from a Gaelic name meaning 'handsome'. The place name *Kilkenny* is derived from the Irish form of the name, borne by the 6th-century abbot St Canice; *Kenneth* is a translation of the Scottish form of the name, which gave rise to the surname *Mackenzie*. Popularized in Scotland by King Kenneth I MacAlpin, who reigned in the mid-9th century, the name has been used in that country for many hundreds of years; a more recent bearer was the Scottish-born writer Kenneth Grahame (1859–1932), author of *The Wind in the Willows*. In the late 19th century *Kenneth* began to spread to other parts of Britain; by the mid-20th century it was in regular use throughout the English-speaking world.
Diminutives: **Ken**, **Kenny**.

**Kenny** a diminutive of **Kenneth**.

**Kenrick** (m) either from the Old English name *Cynric*, derived from *cyne* 'royal' and *ric* 'ruler', or from a Welsh name meaning 'chief hero'. *Kenrick* was rarely used as a first name after the beginning of the 17th century but survived as a surname; since the 19th century the surname has occasionally been given as a first name.

**Kent** (m) from a surname derived from the name of an English county, ultimately from one of a number of Celtic words.

**Kentigern** (m) from a Celtic name meaning 'chief lord'. St Kentigern, who died in the early 7th century, is traditionally believed to have been the first bishop of Glasgow: the name was particularly popular in and around that city until the end of the 18th century but is rarely found in modern times. See also **Mungo**.

**Kenton** (m) from a surname and place name of uncertain origin; in occasional use as a first name in Britain and the USA.

**Keren** a diminutive of **Kerenhappuch** used as a name in its own right; the more common form of the name in modern times. It is sometimes erroneously associated with **Karen**.

**Kerenhappuch** [keeren*hap*uuk] (f) from Hebrew, meaning 'horn of antimony' (a reference to the former use of antimony as a cosmetic). Borne in the Old Testament by one of the three beautiful daughters of Job, the name was adopted by the Puritans in the 17th century; it is still used from time to time, especially in its diminutive form, in various parts of the English-speaking world.
Diminutive: **Keren**.

**Kerry, Kerrie, Kerri, Keri** (f) from the name of a county of Ireland; ultimately from Irish Gaelic, meaning 'descendants of Ciar'. It came into use as a masculine first name in Australia in the mid-20th century and was subsequently given to children of either sex; the feminine name rapidly spread to other English-speaking countries and was particularly popular in Britain in the 1970s.

**Kester** a diminutive of **Christopher**, rarely used in modern times.

**Keturah** [ke*tewr*ă] (f) from Hebrew, meaning 'fragrance'; borne in the Old Testament by Abraham's second wife. The name was adopted by the Puritans after the Reformation but is rarely found in modern times.

**Kevin** (m) from an Irish name meaning 'handsome at (or by) birth'. The 6th-century Irish hermit St Kevin, who founded a monastery at Glendalough in County Wicklow, popularized the name in his native country. *Kevin* was rarely found outside Ireland until the mid-20th century, when it became fashionable throughout the English-speaking world.

**Keziah, Kezia** [ke*zī*ă, ki*zī*ă] (f) from Hebrew, meaning 'cassia'. Borne in the Old Testament by one of the three beautiful daughters of Job, the name was adopted by the Puritans in the 12th century and remains in occasional use today.

**Kieran** [*keer*ăn] (m) from the Irish name *Ciaran*, meaning 'black' or 'dark', borne by two Irish saints of the 5th and 6th centuries. *Kieran* was rarely used outside Ireland until the mid-20th century, when it began to spread to other English-speaking countries.

# Kim

**Kim** (m *or* f) a diminutive of **Kimball** or **Kimberly**, often used as a name in its own right. The masculine name was borne by the hero of Rudyard Kipling's novel *Kim* (1901), whose full name was Kimball O'Hara. Popularized as a feminine name in the mid-20th century by the US actress Kim Novak (born Marilyn Novak), *Kim* is now given more frequently to girls than to boys.

**Kimball** (m) from a surname of uncertain origin; possibly derived from Old English *cynn* 'family' and *bald* 'bold' or from two Welsh words meaning 'chief' and 'war'. Despite its use in a novel by Rudyard Kipling (see **Kim**), *Kimball* is rarely given as a first name in this form.
Diminutive: **Kim**.

**Kimberly, Kimberley** (m *or* f) from a surname and place name meaning 'wood (or field) of Cyneburga (see **Kinborough**)'. Generally associated with a South African city and its famous diamond mines, *Kimberley* has been used as a masculine first name since the end of the 19th century. By the mid-20th century *Kimberly* and its diminutive **Kim** had established themselves as feminine names in the USA; both forms subsequently became fashionable throughout the English-speaking world.
Diminutive: **Kim**.

**Kinborough** (f) from an Old English name meaning 'royal fortress', borne in the 7th century by St Cyneburga, abbess of a convent in Northamptonshire. The name remained in regular use in England, especially the Midlands, until the 18th century but is rarely found in modern times. See also **Kimberly**.

**King** (m) from the English word *king*. Its use as a first name may be an adoption of the surname *King*, which was originally borne by members of a royal household or given as a nickname. One of the best-known bearers of the name is the 20th-century US film director King Vidor.

**Kingsley** (m) from a surname and place name; ultimately from Old English, meaning 'king's wood (or meadow)'. Adopted as a first name in the 19th century, it was popularized in the latter half of the 20th century by the British novelist Kingsley Amis.

**Kirby** (m *or* f) from a surname and place name; ultimately from Old Norse, meaning 'church farm (or village)'. It has been in occasional use as a first name since the 19th century.

**Kirk** (m) from a surname derived from Old Norse *kirkja* 'church'. It was popularized as a first name in the mid-20th century by the US actor Kirk Douglas.

**Kirsten** the Scandinavian form of **Christine**; sometimes regarded as a variant of **Kirsty**. It has been in occasional use throughout the English-speaking world since the mid-20th century.

**Kirsty** a variant of **Christian** (f) or **Christina**; originally a Scottish diminutive of either of these names or their variant forms. *Kirsty* was little used outside Scotland until the latter half of the 20th century, when it became popular in other parts of Britain and in Australia and Canada.
Variant: **Kirsten**.

**Kit** a diminutive of **Catherine, Kathleen**, or **Christopher**. The Italian navigator and explorer Christopher Columbus gave this pet form of his name to the Caribbean island of St Kitts, which he discovered in 1493.

**Kitty** a diminutive of **Catherine** or **Kathleen**; the oldest known pet form of these names. It was in regular use as an independent name until the early 20th century.

**Kris** a diminutive of **Christopher**, from the Scandinavian form of the name; popularized in the 1970s by the US actor and singer Kris Kristofferson.

**Kristen, Kristin** variants of **Christine**.

**Kristina, Kristine** variant spellings of **Christina** and **Christine**, of Scandinavian origin; rarely used in Britain but occasionally found in other parts of the English-speaking world.

**Kurt, Curt** variants of **Conrad**. *Kurt* was originally a German diminutive of the name.

**Kyle** (m *or* f) from a surname derived from a Scottish word for 'strait' or 'channel'; ultimately from Gaelic *caol* 'narrow'. It has been in occasional use as a first name since the mid-20th century.

**Kylie** (f) an Australian name, possibly from an Aboriginal word meaning 'boomerang'.

# L

**Laban** [*lay*băn] (m) from Hebrew, meaning 'white'. In the Old Testament Laban was the brother of Isaac's wife Rebekah and the father of Jacob's wives Leah and Rachel. The name was adopted by the Puritans in the 17th century but is rarely found in modern times.

**Lachlan** [*lok*lăn, *lak*lăn] (m) from Scottish Gaelic, meaning either 'warlike' or 'land of fjords' (a reference to Scandinavia or the Vikings). The name has been in regular use in Scotland for many hundreds of years but is rarely found elsewhere.

**Laetitia** see **Letitia**.

**Lalage** [*lal*ăji] (f) from Greek, meaning 'babble'. The name occurs in the works of the Roman poet Horace and other writers; it is occasionally given as a first name but has never been common.

137

# Lambert

**Lambert** (m) from an Old German name derived from *landa* 'land' and *berhta* 'bright'. The 7th-century bishop and martyr St Lambert of Maastricht popularized the name throughout the Low Countries; it was introduced into Britain during the Middle Ages and was still in occasional use in the early 20th century. One of the best-known bearers of the name was the impostor Lambert Simnel, who was involved in a conspiracy to oust King Henry VII from the English throne in 1487.

**Lana** [*lah*nă] probably a diminutive of **Alana**. It was popularized as an independent name in the mid-20th century by the US actress Lana Turner (born Julia Turner).

**Lance** (m) a name of French origin, ultimately from Old German *landa* 'land'. The name was in use in Britain as early as the 13th century; it was gradually superseded by the diminutive form **Lancelot**, which in turn was reduced to *Lance*. As a result, the name is now regarded as a short form of its own diminutive.
Variant: **Launce**.
Diminutives: **Lancelot, Launcelot**.

**Lancelot** probably a diminutive of **Lance**, though some scholars believe *Lancelot* to be derived from the Norman name *Ancel*, meaning 'servant' or 'godlike'. The name is generally associated with Sir Lancelot, probably the most famous of King Arthur's knights of the Round Table, whose adulterous love for Queen Guinevere forms a central theme of later versions of the legend. *Lancelot* was in regular use in English-speaking countries until the early 20th century.
Variant: **Launcelot**.
Diminutives: **Lance, Launce**.

**Lanty** an Irish diminutive of **Laurence**.

**Laraine, Larraine** variants of **Lorraine**.

**Larissa** (f) a name of uncertain derivation: it may be from Latin *hilaris* 'cheerful', from a Greek place name meaning 'citadel', or of Russian origin.

**Larraine** see **Laraine**.

**Larry** a diminutive of **Laurence**, sometimes used as a name in its own right.

**Lars** a Scandinavian form of **Laurence**.

**Launce** a variant of **Lance**.

**Launcelot** a variant of **Lancelot**.

**Laura** [*lor*ă] (f) probably from Latin *laurus* 'laurel' or 'bay' (as symbols of victory or triumph). The name was first used in Britain during the Middle Ages; it became fashionable throughout the English-speaking world in the mid-19th century and remains in frequent use today. The variant spelling *Lora*, of Provençal origin, was popular in Britain for several hundred years but is rarely found outside the USA in modern times. The

14th-century Italian poet Petrarch addressed most of his sonnets to a lady called Laura, whose identity has been the subject of much speculation; a more recent bearer of the name was the fashion designer Laura Ashley (1925–85).

Variants: **Lauraine, Laureen, Lauren, Lauretta, Laurette, Laurina, Laurinda, Loreen, Loren, Loretta, Lorette, Lorinda**.

Diminutives: **Lauri, Laurie, Lolly, Lori**.

Related name: **Laurel**.

**Lauraine** a variant of **Laura** or **Lorraine**.

**Laureen, Loreen** variants or diminutives of **Laura**.

**Laurel** [*lorrĕl*] (f) from the name of the evergreen shrub; sometimes regarded as a variant of **Laura**. It was particularly popular in the USA and Canada in the mid-20th century.

**Lauren** (m) see **Loren**.

**Lauren, Loren** (f) variants or diminutives of **Laura**. Popularized in the mid-20th century by the US actress Lauren Bacall (born Betty Joan Perske), wife of Humphrey Bogart, the name remains in occasional use throughout the English-speaking world. The variant spelling *Loren* is more frequently found as a masculine name.

**Laurence, Lawrence** [*lorrĕns*] (m) from Latin *Laurentius* 'of Laurentum' (Laurentum was an ancient Italian town named after its laurel groves). One of the earliest bearers of the name was the Roman deacon St Lawrence (or Laurence), who is traditionally believed to have been martyred on a gridiron in the mid-3rd century. (The St Lawrence River in North America was discovered by the French navigator Jacques Cartier on the feast day of St Lawrence, 10th August 1535). The name became very common in Britain during the Middle Ages and has been in regular use since then; in the 20th century it was popularized by Lawrence of Arabia (the soldier and writer T. E. Lawrence) and by the British actor Lord Olivier (Laurence Olivier). The Irish name *Lorcan*, meaning 'fierce', is sometimes translated as *Laurence*, a famous example being the 12th-century monk St Laurence O'Toole (Lorcan ua Tuathail), Archbishop of Dublin.

Variants: **Lars, Lauren, Loren, Lorenzo, Lorin**.

Diminutives: **Lanty, Larry, Laurie, Lawrie**.

Feminine forms: **Laurencia, Laurentia**.

# Laurentia

**Laurentia, Laurencia** feminine forms of **Laurence**.

**Lauretta** see **Loretta**.

**Laurette, Lorette** variants or diminutives of **Laura**, of French origin.

**Lauri** see **Laurie** (f).

**Laurie** (m) a Scottish diminutive of **Laurence**, often used as a name in its own right. The English writer Laurie Lee, author of *Cider with Rosie* (1959), is a famous bearer of the name.

**Laurie, Lauri, Lori** (f) diminutives of **Laura**, often used as independent names since the mid-20th century.

**Laurina** a variant or diminutive of **Laura**.

**Laurinda** see **Lorinda**.

**Lavena** see **Lavina**.

**Laverne** (f) a name of uncertain origin: it may be from the Californian place name *La Verne* or from *Laverna*, the name of an ancient Italian deity regarded as the goddess of thieves.

**Lavina, Lavena** variants of **Lavinia**, dating back to the latter half of the Middle Ages.

**Lavinia** (f) the name of the daughter of King Latinus and wife of the Trojan hero Aeneas in classical mythology; the ancient Italian city of Lavinium was founded by Aeneas after their marriage and named in her honour. The name came into general use after the Renaissance and was particularly popular in the 18th century; it is still found from time to time in various parts of the English-speaking world.
Variants: **Lavena, Lavina**.
Diminutives: **Vinnie, Vinny**.

**Lawrence** see **Laurence**.

**Lawrie** a Scottish diminutive of **Laurence**.

**Layton** see **Leighton**.

**Lazarus** the Greek form of **Eleazar**; borne by the beggar Lazarus in one of the New Testament parables (Luke 16:19–31) and by the brother of Mary and Martha, miraculously raised from the dead after four days (John 11:1–44). The name has been in occasional use in the English-speaking world since the 17th century.

**Leah** (f) from Hebrew, meaning 'cow'; borne in the Old Testament by Jacob's first wife, the elder daughter of Laban. Jacob was tricked into marrying Leah instead of her younger and more attractive sister Rachel, his chosen bride, who subsequently became his second and favourite wife. The name was adopted by the Puritans after the Reformation and remains in occasional use today.

**Leander** [lee*an*der] (m) from Greek, meaning 'lion man'. In Greek mythology Leander was the lover of the priestess Hero, to whom he swam across the Hellespont each night. The name was borne in the 6th century by St

Leander, Bishop of Seville; it is occasionally found in English-speaking countries but has never been common.

**Leanne, Lianne** (f) possibly from a compound of **Lee** and **Anne**; in occasional use in Britain and the USA since the mid-20th century. The variant spelling *Lianne* is sometimes regarded as a diminutive of **Julianne**.

**Lee, Leigh** [lee] (m *or* f) from a surname derived from Old English *leah* 'meadow' or 'wood'. The adoption of *Lee* as a first name has been attributed to the renown of the 19th-century US general Robert E. Lee; the US actor Lee Marvin (born 1924) is a famous bearer. Both spellings of the name may be given to children of either sex, but in many parts of the English-speaking world *Leigh* is generally regarded as the feminine form and *Lee* the masculine form.

**Leighton, Layton** [*laytŏn*] (m) from a surname and place name; ultimately from Old English, meaning 'herb garden'. It has been in occasional use as a first name since the 19th century.

**Leila, Leilah, Lela, Lila** [*leelă, līlă*] (f) a Persian name, meaning 'dark'. Popularized by the heroine of Byron's Oriental tale *The Giaour* (1813), the name came into general use in English-speaking countries in the 19th century but has never been common.

**Lela** an alternative spelling of **Leila** or a variant of **Lelia**.

**Lelia** (f) from the feminine form of the Roman family name *Laelius*. The name has been in occasional use in the English-speaking world since the 19th century, when it was popularized by the French writer George Sand's novel *Lélia* (1833).
Variant: **Lela**.

**Lemmy** a diminutive of **Lemuel**.

**Lemuel** (m) from Hebrew, meaning 'devoted to God'. Borne by an Old Testament king and by Lemuel Gulliver, the hero of Jonathan Swift's famous satire, the name has been in occasional use in English-speaking countries since the 17th century.
Diminutive: **Lemmy**.

**Len** a diminutive of **Leonard**.

**Lena** [*leenă*] a diminutive of **Helena**, often used as a name in its own right.

**Lennie** see **Lenny**.

**Lennox** (m) from a Scottish surname and place name; occasionally used as a first name in Scotland but rarely found elsewhere.

**Lenny, Lennie** diminutives of **Leonard**.

**Lenore** [*lĕnor*] a variant of **Eleanor**, of German origin.

**Leo** [*leeō*] (m) from Latin *leo* 'lion'. Borne by the 5th-century pope St Leo the Great and by twelve of his successors in that office, four of whom are also venerated as saints, the name has been in regular use in English-speaking countries since the Middle Ages. It has been publicized in the

20th century by a number of famous bearers, such as the Australian-born actor Leo McKern. The name may be given to boys born under the zodiac sign of Leo, from 23rd July to 22nd August.
Related name: **Leon**.

**Leofric** (m) from Old English *leof* 'dear' and *ric* 'ruler'; borne in the 11th century by the husband of Lady Godiva. Unlike many other Anglo-Saxon names, *Leofric* remained in regular use after the Norman Conquest and is still found from time to time in various parts of Britain.

**Leoline** an anglicized form of **Llewellyn**, dating back to the 13th century.

**Leon** [*lee*ŏn, *lay*on] (m) from Greek *leon* 'lion'; generally regarded as a variant of **Leo** (*Léon* and *León* are the French and Spanish forms of *Leo*). The name was first used in Britain in the Middle Ages and was revived throughout the English-speaking world in the 19th century. It is particularly popular with Jewish families. See also **Lionel**.
Feminine forms: **Leona**, **Leonie**.
Related name: **Leo**.

**Leona** a feminine form of **Leon**.

**Leonard** [*len*ăd] (m) from the Old German name *Leonhard*, derived from *levon* 'lion' and *hardu* 'hardy'. One of the earliest bearers of the name was the hermit St Leonard, patron saint of prisoners, who is traditionally believed to have founded a monastery near the French city of Limoges in the 5th or 6th century. The name has been in general use in Britain since . the Middle Ages; it was revived throughout the English-speaking world in the 19th century and was particularly popular in the first half of the 20th century. The Italian form of the name was made famous by the Renaissance artist and scientist Leonardo da Vinci; the US conductor and composer Leonard Bernstein is one of the best-known bearers of the name in modern times.
Diminutives: **Len**, **Lennie**, **Lenny**.

**Leonie** [leeŏni, layŏni, *lee*ŏni, *lay*ŏni] a feminine form of **Leon**, of French origin.

**Leonora** [leeŏ*nor*ă] a variant of **Eleanor**; originally a diminutive of *Eleonora*, the Italian form of the name. Borne by the heroine of Beethoven's opera *Fidelio* (1814), for which the composer's three *Leonora* overtures were originally written, the name has been in occasional use in English-speaking countries since the early 19th century.
Diminutives: **Nora**, **Norah**.

**Leopold** [*lee*ŏpŏld] (m) from an Old German name derived from *leudi* 'people' and *balda* 'bold'. The name was borne by St Leopold of Austria (1073–1136), two Holy Roman emperors, and three kings of Belgium; it was popularized in Britain in the 19th century by the Belgian king Leopold I, uncle of Queen Victoria and Prince Albert, who gave the name to their youngest son.

Diminutive: **Poldie**.

**Leroy** [*lee*roy] (m) from a surname derived from Old French, meaning 'the king'. It has been in regular use as a first name, especially in the USA, since the latter half of the 19th century.
Variant: **Elroy**.

**Les** a diminutive of **Lesley** or **Leslie**.

**Leslie** (m *or* f), **Lesley** (f) from a Scottish surname and place name of uncertain origin. It was rarely used as a first name before the late 19th century, two notable exceptions being the heroine of Robert Burns' poem 'Bonnie Lesley' and Sir Leslie Stephen (1832–1906), father of the British novelist Virginia Woolf. The spelling *Lesley* is used almost exclusively as a feminine name; *Leslie* is generally regarded as the masculine form of the name but is sometimes given to girls, especially in the USA. Famous bearers of the name in the 20th century include the British actor Leslie Howard and the French actress Leslie Caron.
Diminutive: **Les**.

**Lester** (m) from a surname possibly derived from the English place name *Leicester*; in regular use as a first name since the 19th century. Famous bearers include the Canadian statesman Lester B. Pearson (1897–1972) and the British jockey Lester Piggott (born 1935).

**Leta** (f) from Latin *letus* 'glad'.

**Letitia, Laetitia** [lĕ*tish*ă] (f) from Latin *laetitia* 'joy'. The name was most frequently found in the variant form **Lettice** until the 18th century, when *Laetitia* came into fashion; the simplified spelling *Letitia* remains in occasional use today.
Variant: **Lettice**.
Diminutives: **Lettice, Letty, Tisha**.

**Lettice** [*let*is] a variant of **Letitia**. *Lettice* was the most common form of the name in medieval Britain; it remained in regular use for several hundred years but is rarely found in modern times.

**Letty, Lettie** diminutives of **Letitia**, sometimes used as independent names.

**Levi** [*lee*vī] (m) from Hebrew, meaning 'attached' or 'pledged'. Borne in the Old Testament by one of the sons of Jacob and Leah and in the New Testament by the apostle Matthew, the name has been in occasional use in English-speaking countries since the 17th century.

**Lew** a diminutive of **Lewis**.

**Lewis** an anglicized form of **Louis** that developed after the introduction of the name into Britain by the Normans and remained in regular use until the revival of the French form in the 19th century. *Lewis* was particularly popular in Wales, where it was sometimes used in place of **Llewellyn**. Its most famous bearer was the 19th-century British writer Lewis Carroll, whose real name was Charles Lutwidge Dodgson (*Lutwidge* is a rare variant of *Louis*).

Diminutive: **Lew**.

**Lex** a diminutive of **Alexander**.

**Liam** [*lee*ăm] an Irish variant or diminutive of **William**, sometimes found in other parts of the English-speaking world.

**Liana** [li*ah*nă] a diminutive of **Juliana** or any other name ending in *-liana*. Its adoption as a name in its own right may have been influenced by the name of the climbing plant.

**Lianne** see **Leanne**.

**Libby** a diminutive of **Elizabeth**, sometimes used as a name in its own right.

**Liddy** a diminutive of **Lydia**.

**Liesl, Liesel** [*leez*ĕl] variants of **Elizabeth**. Originally a German diminutive of the name, *Liesl* has been in occasional use in English-speaking countries since the 1960s, when it was popularized by the eldest daughter of the Trapp family in the immensely successful film *The Sound of Music* (1965).

**Lil** a diminutive of **Lilian** or **Lily**.

**Lila** see **Leila**.

**Lilac** (f) from the name of the flowering shrub. *Lilac* is less common than many of the other plant and flower names that came into fashion in the late 19th and early 20th centuries.

**Lili** a German diminutive of **Elizabeth**, popularized in the English-speaking world by the song 'Lili Marlene'. See also **Lilian, Lily**.

**Lilian, Lillian** (f) either from Latin *lilium* 'lily' or from a diminutive of **Elizabeth** (see **Lili**). The name has been in use in Britain since the 16th century and was particularly popular in the late 19th and early 20th centuries. The US actress Lillian Gish, who starred in a number of silent films, is a famous bearer of the name.

Variants: **Lilias, Lillias, Lillie, Lily**.

Diminutive: **Lil**.

**Lilias, Lillias** Scottish variants of **Lilian**, from the Gaelic form of the name; occasionally used in other parts of the English-speaking world.

**Lilith** (f) a name borne in Jewish folklore by a female demon traditionally believed to have been the first wife of Adam; it is sometimes interpreted as 'night monster' or 'storm goddess'. The name is occasionally used in English-speaking countries but has never been common.

**Lilla, Lillah** (f) a name of uncertain origin: it may be a variant of **Lily**, possibly influenced by **Leila**, or it may simply be a diminutive of **Elizabeth**.

Lionel

**Lillian** see **Lilian**.

**Lillias** see **Lilias**.

**Lily, Lillie** variants of **Lilian**, influenced by the flower name (the lily is a symbol of purity). It has been in regular use in the English-speaking world since the 19th century, a famous bearer being the British actress Lillie Langtry (born Emilie Charlotte Le Breton), known as the 'Jersey Lily', whose many admirers included the future King Edward VII.
Variants: **Lilla, Lillah**.
Diminutive: **Lil**.

**Lina** [*lĩnă, leenă*] a diminutive of **Carolina** or any other name ending in *-lina*; sometimes used as a name in its own right.

**Lincoln** [*lincŏn*] (m) from the surname of the US president Abraham Lincoln (1809–65); ultimately from the English place name *Lincoln*, meaning 'Roman colony at the pool'. It has been in occasional use as a first name in Britain and the USA since the 19th century.

**Linda, Lynda** (f) from the Old German word *lindi*, meaning 'snake', found in a number of feminine names; sometimes regarded as a diminutive of **Belinda** or any other name ending in *-linda*. The name is also associated with the feminine form of the Spanish adjective *lindo* 'pretty'. It has been in regular use in the English-speaking world since the late 19th century and was particularly popular in the mid-20th century.
Variants: **Lyn, Lynn, Lynne**.
Diminutive: **Lindy**.

**Lindsay** (m *or* f), **Lindsey, Lynsey** (f) [*linzi*] from a Scottish surname and English place name. In the early 20th century *Lindsay* was generally regarded as a masculine name; it gradually came to be used for children of either sex and is now given more frequently to girls than to boys. *Lindsey* and *Lynsey* are just two of the many variant spellings of the feminine name.

**Lindy** a diminutive of **Linda**, often found as a name in its own right. It is also used as a diminutive of **Belinda** or any other name ending in *-linda* or *-lind*.

**Linette** see **Lynette**.

**Linnet** originally a variant of **Eluned**, from the medieval French form of the name; now associated with the name of a songbird, ultimately derived from Latin *linum* 'flax'.

**Lionel** [*lĩŏnĕl*] originally a diminutive of **Leon** or its medieval variant *Lyon*; borne by one of King Arthur's knights of the Round Table and generally interpreted as 'young lion'. *Lionel* has been in regular use as an independent name since the Middle Ages, when it was popularized by the third son of King Edward III; more recent bearers of the name include the US

145

# Lisa

actor Lionel Barrymore (1878–1954) and the British actor Lionel Jeffries (born 1926).

**Lisa** [*lee*să, *lee*ză] a diminutive of **Elizabeth**, often used as a name in its own right. Despite the fame of Leonardo da Vinci's *Mona Lisa*, the name was little used in English-speaking countries until the 1970s, when it suddenly became very popular. See also **Liza**.

**Lisbeth** see **Lizbeth**.

**Lise** a variant of **Elizabeth**; originally a German diminutive of the name.

**Lisette** a variant of **Elizabeth**; originally a French diminutive of the name.

**Lita** [*lee*tă] a diminutive of **Lolita** or any other name ending in *-lita*, often used as a name in its own right.

**Liz** a diminutive of **Elizabeth**; possibly the only diminutive of the name that has yet to become established in its own right.

**Liza** [*lee*ză, *lī*ză] a diminutive of **Elizabeth**, often used as a name in its own right. It has been in regular use since the mid-20th century, a famous bearer being the US singer and actress Liza Minnelli (born 1946), but has never been as popular as **Lisa**.

**Lizanne** a compound of **Liz** and **Anne**.

**Lizbeth, Lisbeth** diminutives of **Elizabeth**, sometimes used as independent names.

**Lizzie, Lizzy** diminutives of **Elizabeth**, sometimes used as independent names in the late 19th and early 20th centuries.

**Llewellyn, Llewelyn** [loo*eff*in] (m) from the Welsh name *Llywelyn*, derived either from *llyw* 'leader' or from two words meaning 'lion' and 'likeness'. Borne by two Welsh princes of the 13th century, the name has been in regular use in Wales for several hundred years but is rarely found elsewhere. See also **Floyd, Lewis**.
Variant: **Leoline**.
Diminutive: **Lyn**.

**Llinos** (f) a Welsh name, meaning 'linnet'.

**Lloyd** [loid] (m) from Welsh *llwyd* 'grey'; in regular use both as a first name and as a surname in various parts of the English-speaking world, especially Wales.
Variant: **Floyd**.

**Llywelyn** see **Llewellyn**.

**Lo** a diminutive of **Lola**.

**Lois** [*lō*is] (f) a biblical name, probably of Greek origin, borne by the grandmother of Timothy in the New Testament. Adopted by the Puritans in the 16th century, the name was subsequently introduced into North America and has been in regular use in various parts of the English-speaking world since then. *Lois* is sometimes regarded as a variant of **Louise** or **Eloise**.

146

**Lola** a diminutive of **Dolores**, often used as a name in its own right. The 19th-century British dancer Lola Montez, mistress of King Louis I of Bavaria, was a famous bearer of the name.
Diminutive: **Lo**.

**Lolita** a diminutive of **Dolores**, often used as a name in its own right. It is generally associated with the monstrous young heroine of Vladimir Nabokov's novel *Lolita* (1955).
Diminutive: **Lita**.

**Lolly** a diminutive of **Laura**.

**Lonnie** a diminutive of **Alonso**, made famous in the 1950s by the British popular singer Lonnie Donegan.

**Lora** see **Laura**.

**Loraine** see **Lorraine**.

**Loreen** see **Laureen**.

**Loren** (f) see **Lauren** (f).

**Loren, Lauren, Lorin** (m) variants of **Laurence**. The US conductor Lorin Maazel (born 1930) is a famous bearer of the name. The variant spelling *Lauren* is more frequently found as a feminine name.

**Lorenzo** the Spanish or Italian form of **Laurence**; occasionally found in English-speaking countries, especially the USA. Shakespeare gave the name to **Jessica**'s lover in his play *The Merchant of Venice*.

**Loretta, Lauretta** variants or diminutives of **Laura**, dating back to the Middle Ages. In the mid-20th century *Loretta* was the more popular form of the name, especially in the USA and Canada; it is sometimes associated with *Loreto*, the name of an Italian town to which the Holy House of the Virgin Mary is traditionally believed to have been transported in the 13th century.

**Lorette** see **Laurette**.

**Lori** see **Laurie** (f).

**Lorin** see **Loren** (m).

**Lorinda, Laurinda** variants or diminutives of **Laura**.

**Lorn** see **Lorne**.

**Lorna** (f) invented by the British novelist R. D. Blackmore for the heroine of *Lorna Doone* (1869). Blackmore is believed by some scholars to have derived the name from the title of the Marquesses of **Lorne**; others favour an association with the English word *lorn*, meaning 'forsaken'. *Lorna* has been in regular use throughout the English-speaking world since the late 19th century; it is particularly popular in Scotland.

**Lorne, Lorn** (m *or* f) from the name of an early Scottish chieftain, which subsequently became a place name; a 19th-century Marquess of Lorne married Princess Louise, daughter of Queen Victoria and Prince Albert. The name is now regarded as a masculine form or variant of **Lorna**; the

# Lorraine

Canadian actor Lorne Greene, who played a leading role in the television series *Bonanza* (1959–71), is a famous bearer.

**Lorraine, Loraine** (f) from the name of a region of France originally known as Lotharingia, from Latin *Lotharii regnum* 'Lothair's kingdom' (Lothair was a 9th-century ruler of the region). The name was rarely used in English-speaking countries until the 19th century; it was particularly popular in Britain in the latter half of the 20th century.
Variants: **Laraine, Larraine, Lauraine**.

**Lottie, Lotty** diminutives of **Charlotte**, sometimes used as independent names.

**Lou** a diminutive of **Louis, Louisa,** or **Louise**.

**Louella, Luella** (f) a compound of **Lou** and **Ella**. The name was publicized by the Hollywood gossip columnist Louella Parsons (1880–1972).

**Louie** a variant or diminutive of **Louis**, probably influenced by the French pronunciation of the name.

**Louis** [*loo*i, *loo*is] (m) from the Old German name *Chlodovech*, the meaning of which is generally interpreted as 'famous warrior'. The 5th-century Frankish king Chlodowig, later known as Clovis, was an early bearer of the name; in the form *Louis* it was used by the French royal family for over a thousand years and was borne by eighteen kings. On its introduction into Britain at the time of the Norman Conquest the name underwent a further transformation (see **Lewis**); the French form was revived in English-speaking countries in the 19th century and has remained in use since then. The US jazz musician Louis Armstrong (1900–71) was a famous bearer of the name.
Variants: **Aloysius, Lewis, Louie, Ludovic**.
Diminutives: **Lou, Louie**.
Feminine forms: **Louisa, Louise**.

**Louisa** a feminine form of **Louis**; the Latinized form of **Louise**. It was popular in the 18th and 19th centuries, its most famous bearer being the US novelist Louisa M. Alcott, author of *Little Women* (1868).
Diminutives: **Lou, Lulu**.

**Louise** a feminine form of **Louis**, of French origin. The name was first used in the English-speaking world in the 17th century, when it was popularized by Louise de Kéroualle, one of King Charles II's mistresses. It was largely replaced by **Louisa** in the 18th century but returned to fashion, particularly in the USA, at the end of the 19th century. *Louise* has been very popular in Britain since the late 1950s.
Variants: **Lois, Louisa**.
Diminutives: **Lou, Lulu**.

**Loveday** (f) a name originally given to children born on a loveday (a day set aside for reconciliation and settlement of disputes). First used in the 12th century, *Loveday* is still found from time to time as a girls' name and as a surname.

**Lovell** (m) from Old French, meaning 'wolf cub'; introduced into Britain in the 11th century. The name is more frequently found as a surname than as a first name in modern times.
Variant: **Lowell**.

**Lowell** a variant of **Lovell**.

**Lucas** the Latinized form of **Luke**; in frequent use in medieval Britain. *Lucas* survived the Middle Ages as a surname and was readopted as a first name in the 20th century.

**Lucasta** (f) invented by the 17th-century British poet Richard Lovelace, whose poem of that name (published in 1649) was probably addressed to a bearer of the first name **Lucy** or the surname **Lucas**.

**Luce** see **Lucia**.

**Lucetta, Lucette** variants or diminutives of **Lucia** or **Lucy**.

**Lucia** [*loo*siă] the feminine form of **Lucius**; now regarded as the Italian equivalent of **Lucy**. The virgin martyr St Lucia (or Lucy), who died in the early 4th century, is traditionally believed to have had her eyes torn out; for this reason (or because her name means 'light') she is invoked against eye disease. The cult of St Lucia popularized the name, together with its anglicized forms *Lucy* and *Luce*, in medieval Britain; *Lucia* was still in regular use in the 17th century but is rarely found in modern times.
Variants: **Lucetta, Lucette, Lucie, Lucilla, Lucina, Lucinda, Lucy**.

**Lucian, Lucien** [*loo*siăn] (m) from the Latin name *Lucianus*, of uncertain origin. The name was borne by a Syrian satirist of the 2nd century and by the theologian St Lucian of Antioch, who was martyred in the early 4th century; it is occasionally found in English-speaking countries but has never been common. *Lucien* is the French form of the name.
Feminine forms: **Luciana, Lucienne**.

**Luciana** a feminine form of **Lucian**.

**Lucie** the French form of **Lucia**; sometimes used in English-speaking countries as a variant spelling of **Lucy**.

**Lucien** see **Lucian**.

**Lucienne** a feminine form of **Lucian**.

**Lucilla** a variant of **Lucia**; originally a Latin diminutive of the name. Borne by a Roman martyr of the 3rd century, the name *Lucilla* is occasionally found in English-speaking countries but is more familiar in the French form **Lucille**.
Variant: **Lucille**.

**Lucille** [*looseel*] the French form of **Lucilla**. The name has been in occasional use in the English-speaking world since the 19th century; it was popularized in the latter half of the 20th century by the US comedienne Lucille Ball (see also **Lucy**).

**Lucina** (f) the name of the Roman goddess of childbirth (a title applied to Juno and Diana); generally regarded as a variant of **Lucia**. *Lucina* is occasionally found in English-speaking countries but has never been common.

**Lucinda** a variant of **Lucia** or **Lucy**, dating back to the 17th century.
Diminutive: **Cindy**.

**Lucius** [*loo*siŭs] (m) from Latin *lux, lucis* 'light'; a common first name in ancient Rome. The name was borne by the 3rd-century pope St Lucius I and by two of his successors in that office; it has been in occasional use in the English-speaking world since the Renaissance.
Feminine form: **Lucia**.

**Lucky** (f) from the English word *lucky*; sometimes used as a diminutive of any feminine name beginning with *Luc-*.

**Lucrece** [loo*krees*] a variant of **Lucretia**, of French origin.

**Lucretia** [loo*kree*shă] (f) from the Roman clan name *Lucretius*, of uncertain origin. The story of the rape of Lucretia by a son of Tarquinius Superbus, King of Rome, has been retold in a number of literary and musical works, notably Shakespeare's poem *The Rape of Lucrece* (1594) and an opera by Benjamin Britten, first performed in 1946. *Lucrezia*, the Italian form of the name, is generally associated with the unjustly maligned daughter of Pope Alexander VI, Lucrezia Borgia. *Lucretia* has been in occasional use in the English-speaking world since the 16th century but has never been common.
Variant: **Lucrece**.

**Lucrezia** see **Lucretia**.

**Lucy** a variant of **Lucia**, dating back to the Middle Ages; the usual form of the name in English-speaking countries. The name *Lucy* featured in a number of literary and musical works of the 18th and 19th centuries and became very popular in Britain and the USA; it enjoyed a revival in the latter half of the 20th century, having been publicized by *The Lucy Show* and two other television series starring the US comedienne Lucille Ball. See also **Lucie**.
Variants: **Lucetta, Lucette, Lucinda**.
Diminutive: **Lulu**.

**Ludo** a diminutive of **Ludovic**.

**Ludovic** a variant of **Louis**, from the Latinized form of the name, sometimes used in Scotland.
Diminutive: **Ludo**.

**Luella** see **Louella**.

**Luke** (m) from the Greek name *Loukas*, derived from Latin *Lucanus* 'of Lucania (a district of ancient Italy)'. St Luke, author of the third Gospel and the Acts of the Apostles in the New Testament, is venerated as a patron saint of doctors and artists (he was a physician by profession and is traditionally believed to have been a talented painter). The name was introduced into Britain after the Norman Conquest and has been in regular use since then; it enjoyed a slight revival in various parts of the English-speaking world in the latter half of the 20th century.
Variant: **Lucas**.

**Lulu** a diminutive of **Louisa**, **Louise**, or **Lucy**.

**Luther** (m) from the surname of the German religious reformer Martin Luther (1483–1546), the meaning of which is generally interpreted as 'famous people' (the English surname *Luther* is derived from an Old French word for 'lute player'). The name was publicized in the 20th century by the black civil-rights leader Martin Luther King, a prominent figure in the struggle for racial equality in the USA.

**Lydia** [*lidiă*] (f) from Greek, meaning 'woman of Lydia (a region of Asia Minor)'. The Lydia of the New Testament was converted to Christianity by St Paul at Philippi (Acts 16:14–15). The name has been in regular use in English-speaking countries since the 17th century; famous bearers in literature include Lydia Languish, a character in Sheridan's play *The Rivals* (1775), and the heroine of H. E. Bates' novel *Love for Lydia* (1952).
Diminutive: **Liddy**.

**Lyle** (m) from a surname and place name; ultimately from Old French, meaning 'the island'. It has been in occasional use as a first name since the 19th century.

**Lyn** (f) see **Lynn**.

**Lyn** (m) a diminutive of **Llewellyn**, often used as a name in its own right.

**Lynda** see **Linda**.

**Lyndon** (m) from a surname and place name; ultimately from Old English *lind* 'lime tree' and *dun* 'hill'. In regular use as a first name since the mid-19th century, *Lyndon* was further popularized in the 1960s by the US president Lyndon Baines Johnson.

**Lynette, Lynnette, Linette** variants of **Eluned**; from the medieval French form of the name, which occurs in Arthurian legend. The modern form first appeared in Tennyson's version of the story of Sir Gareth and Lynette, one of his *Idylls of the King* (1859); it was particularly popular in Australia in the mid-20th century.
Variants: **Lyn, Lynn, Lynne**.

# Lynn

**Lynn, Lynne, Lyn** variants or diminutives of **Linda** or **Lynette**; in frequent use throughout the English-speaking world in the latter half of the 20th century.

**Lynnette** see **Lynette**.

**Lynsey** see **Lindsay**.

**Lyra** (f) from Greek, meaning 'lyre'.

**Lyulf, Lyulph** (m) from the Old English name *Ligulf*, derived from *lig* 'flame' and *wulf* 'wolf'. It is rarely found in modern times.

# M

**Mabel, Mable** [*may*bĕl] originally diminutives of **Amabel**. The use of *Mabel* as an independent name dates back to the 12th century; it was revived in the latter half of the 19th century and remained popular throughout the English-speaking world until the 1920s.
Variants: **Mabella, Mabelle**.

**Mabella** the Latinized form of **Mabel**.

**Mabelle** a variant of **Mabel**, sometimes associated with French *ma belle* 'my beautiful one'.

**Mable** see **Mabel**.

**Maddie, Maddy** diminutives of **Madeleine**.

**Madeleine, Madeline** [*mad*ĕlin] variants of **Magdalene**, introduced into Britain from France during the Middle Ages. *Madeline* was the more common spelling of the name in English-speaking countries until the early 20th century, when the French form *Madeleine* came into fashion.
Variant: **Madelina**.
Diminutives: **Maddie, Maddy**.

**Madelina** a variant of **Madeleine**.

**Madeline** see **Madeleine**.

**Madge** a diminutive of **Margaret**, often used as a name in its own right. It was particularly popular in the early 20th century.

**Madoc** [*mad*ŏk] (m) a Welsh name, meaning 'fortunate'. It has been in occasional use in various parts of Britain, especially Wales, since the 11th century.

**Mae** see **May**.

**Maeve, Meave** [mayv] (f) from the Irish name *Meadhbh*; borne in Irish legend by an early queen of Connaught. The name is occasionally found outside its country of origin in modern times.

**Magda** a German diminutive of **Magdalene**, sometimes used in English-speaking countries as a name in its own right.

152

**Magdalen** see **Magdalene**.

**Magdalena** a variant of **Magdalene**.

**Magdalene, Magdalen** [*mag*dălin] (f) from the name of the New Testament character St Mary Magdalene; ultimately from Hebrew, meaning 'woman of Magdala'. The French form of the name (see **Madeleine**) was introduced into Britain during the Middle Ages and gave rise to the variant *Maudlin*, reflecting an early pronunciation that has survived in the names of Magdalen College in Oxford and Magdalene College in Cambridge. *Maudlin* is no longer used as a first name but has entered the English language as an adjective meaning 'tearfully sentimental' (from the portrayal in art of St Mary Magdalene as a weeping penitent). The names *Magdalene* and *Magdalen* were revived throughout the English-speaking world after the Reformation and remain in occasional use today.
Variants: **Madeleine, Madeline, Magdalena**.
Diminutive: **Magda**.

**Maggie** a diminutive of **Margaret**.

**Magnolia** (f) from the name of the flowering shrub. *Magnolia* is less common than many of the other plant and flower names that came into fashion in the late 19th and early 20th centuries.

**Magnus** (m) from Latin *magnus* 'great'. The name was borne by a number of Scandinavian kings: Magnus I (1024–47), son of St Olaf, was named after the Holy Roman emperor Charles the Great (Carolus Magnus), better known as Charlemagne. *Magnus* was subsequently introduced into Scotland and Ireland, where it remains in occasional use today; the television personality Magnus Magnusson (born 1929) has publicized the name in other parts of the British Isles.
Variant: **Manus**.

**Mahala, Mahalah** (f) from Hebrew, possibly meaning 'tenderness' or 'barren'. It has been in occasional use in the English-speaking world since the 17th century.
Variants: **Mahalia, Mehala, Mehalah, Mehalia**.

**Mahalia** a variant of **Mahala**.

**Maidie** (f) a name of uncertain origin: it may be from the English word *maid*, meaning 'girl', or it may be a Scottish diminutive of **Margaret** or **Mary**.

**Mair** [myr] the Welsh form of **Mary**.

**Maire** see **Moira**.

**Mairin** see **Maureen**.

**Maisie** a Scottish diminutive of **Margaret**, used in various parts of the English-speaking world as a name in its own right.
Variant: **Mysie**.

# Malachi

**Malachi** [*mal*ākī] (m) from Hebrew, meaning 'my messenger'. *Malachi* is the title of the last book of the Old Testament; it was adopted as a first name after the Reformation but is rarely found in modern times.
Variant: **Malachy.**

**Malachy** an Irish variant of **Malachi.** It was popularized in the 12th century by St Malachy, Archbishop of Armagh, whose real name was Mael Maedoc ua Morgair (see **Marmaduke**).

**Malcolm** [*mal*kŏm] (m) from Gaelic, meaning 'servant (or disciple) of **Columba**'; borne by four Scottish kings, the best-known being Malcolm III, who succeeded to the throne after the death of Macbeth in 1057. The name was rarely found outside Scotland from the end of the Middle Ages until the early 20th century, when it came into general use throughout Britain and in other parts of the English-speaking world. It was particularly popular in the 1950s. Famous bearers of the name in modern times include the British conductor Sir Malcolm Sargent and the US black militant Malcolm X (born Malcolm Little).
Variants: **Callum, Calum.**

**Malise** [ma*leez*] (m) from Gaelic, meaning 'servant of **Jesus**'.

**Mallory, Malory** (m) from a surname derived from Old French, meaning 'unfortunate'. It is occasionally used as a first name in modern times.

**Malvin** the masculine form of **Malvina.**
Variants: **Melvin, Melvyn.**

**Malvina** (f) invented by the 18th-century Scottish poet James Macpherson, who may have derived the name from the Gaelic words for 'smooth brow'.
Variant: **Melvina.**
Masculine form: **Malvin.**

**Mamie** [*may*mi] a diminutive of **Mary** or any other feminine name beginning with *M*; sometimes used as an independent name, especially in the USA.

**Manasseh** [mă*nase*] (m) from the Hebrew verb 'to forget'; borne in the Old Testament by Joseph's elder son. The name has been in occasional use in Britain since the Middle Ages; it was revived by the Puritans after the Reformation but is rarely found in modern times.
Variant: **Manasses.**

**Manasses** [mă*nase*z] a variant of **Manasseh.**

**Mandy** a diminutive of **Amanda.** It was popularized as a name in its own right by the moving film *Mandy* (1952), in which a young deaf girl, played by the child actress Mandy Miller, was taught to speak.

**Manfred** (m) from an Old German name derived from *mana* 'man' and *frithu* 'peace'. It was introduced into Britain at the time of the Norman

154

Conquest but has never been common, despite the publication of Byron's poem of the same name in 1817.

**Manley** (m) from a surname derived from the English word *manly*. It has been in occasional use as a first name since the 19th century, especially by admirers of the British poet Gerard Manley Hopkins (1844–89).

**Manny** a diminutive of **Emanuel** or **Manuel**.

**Mansel, Mansell** (m) from a surname possibly derived from the French place name *Le Mans*.

**Manuel** a variant of **Emanuel**; now regarded as the Spanish form of the name.
Diminutive: **Manny**.
Feminine form: **Manuela**.

**Manuela** the feminine form of **Manuel**.

**Manus** a Gaelic variant of **Magnus**, which gave rise to the Irish surname *McManus*.

**Mara, Marah** [*mar*ă] (f) from Hebrew, meaning 'bitter'; a name adopted by **Naomi** after the death of her husband and her two sons (Ruth 1:20). It has been in occasional use in the English-speaking world since the 17th century.

**Marc** the French form of **Marcus**, sometimes used in English-speaking countries as a diminutive of the name or as an alternative spelling of **Mark**.

**Marcel** [mar*sel*] the French form of **Marcellus**; in occasional use in the English-speaking world since the 19th century. The French mime artist Marcel Marceau (born 1923) is a famous bearer of the name.
Feminine form: **Marcelle**.

**Marcella** the feminine form of **Marcellus**; borne by the Roman widow St Marcella (325–410), a disciple of St Jerome, and by a character in Cervantes' novel *Don Quixote* (1605; 1615). The name is occasionally found in the English-speaking world but has never been common.

**Marcelle** the feminine form of **Marcel**.

**Marcellus** a Latin diminutive of **Marcus**, used as a family name in ancient Rome. Borne by two popes of the 4th and 16th centuries and by a number of minor saints, the name is rarely found in this form in English-speaking countries.
Variant: **Marcel**.
Feminine form: **Marcella**.

**Marcia** [*mar*siă] (f) from the Roman clan name *Marcius*; ultimately from *Mars*, the name of the Roman god of war. *Marcia* came into general use throughout the English-speaking world during the 19th century and was particularly popular in the mid-20th century.
Variant: **Marsha**.

# Marcie

Diminutives: **Marcie, Marcy**.
Related names: **Marcus, Marius**.

**Marcie, Marcy** diminutives of **Marcia**, sometimes used as independent names.

**Marco** the Italian form of **Marcus**; borne by the Venetian traveller Marco Polo (1254–1324). The name is occasionally found in English-speaking countries, especially the USA.

**Marcus** (m) a Latin name, probably derived from *Mars* (see **Marcia**). *Marcus* was a common first name in ancient Rome, a famous bearer being the Roman triumvir Marcus Antonius, better known as Mark **Antony**. Rarely used in the English-speaking world until the mid-19th century, it enjoyed a further revival in the 1970s, when the variant **Mark** was at its peak of popularity.
Variants: **Marc, Marco, Mark**.
Diminutive: **Marcellus**.
Related names: **Marcia, Marius**.

**Marcy** see **Marcie**.

**Margaret** (f) from Latin *margarita* and Greek *margaron* 'pearl' (some scholars believe the name to be ultimately derived from a Persian word meaning 'child of light'). One of the earliest bearers of the name was the legendary martyr St Margaret of Antioch, who is traditionally believed to have been beheaded in the 3rd century. The name was introduced into Britain in the 11th century by St Margaret of Scotland, sister of Edgar the Aetheling and wife of the Scottish king Malcolm III; it went on to become one of the most popular girls' names of the Middle Ages and remained in frequent use throughout the English-speaking world until the 1960s. In the 20th century the name was borne by a number of famous actresses, such as Dame Margaret Rutherford; by Princess Margaret, sister of Queen Elizabeth II; and by Margaret Thatcher, the first woman to be prime minister of the United Kingdom. See also **Daisy**.
Variants: **Greta, Gretchen, Gretel, Margareta, Margaretta, Margarita, Margery, Margo, Margot, Marguerita, Marguerite, Marjorie, Megan, Meta, Rita**.
Diminutives: **Madge, Maggie, Maidie, Maisie, May, Meg, Meggie, Meggy, Peg, Peggy**.

**Margarita, Marguerita, Margareta, Margaretta** variants of **Margaret**.

**Marge** a diminutive of **Marjorie**.

**Margery** see **Marjorie**.

**Margie** a diminutive of **Marjorie**.

**Margot, Margo** [*margō*] variants of **Margaret**, of French origin. The British ballerina Dame Margot Fonteyn (born Margaret Hookham) is probably the best-known bearer of the name in modern times.

**Marguerita** see **Margarita**.

**Marguerite** [marg*ĕreet*] the French form of **Margaret**. As a flower name (from French *marguerite* 'daisy') it came into general use in English-speaking countries in the late 19th century.

**Maria** [mă*reeă*, mă*rīă*] the Latin form of **Mary**. *Maria* is the usual form of that name in Germany, Italy, Spain, and a number of other European countries; in the English-speaking world it has been in regular use as a variant of *Mary* since the 18th century. The name was popularized in the latter half of the 20th century by the heroine of Leonard Bernstein's musical *West Side Story* (1957), filmed in 1961.
Variants: **Mia**, **Mitzi**.

**Mariabella** a compound of **Maria** and **Bella**; generally interpreted as 'beautiful Mary'. It has been in occasional use in Britain and other parts of the English-speaking world since the 17th century.

**Mariam, Mariamne** see **Mary**.

**Marian** see **Marianne, Marion**.

**Marianne** [marri*an*] (f) a French name derived from a compound of **Marie** and *Anne* (see **Ann**); generally regarded as a variant of *Marian* (see **Marion**). It has been in occasional use in English-speaking countries since the 18th century, when the double name *Mary-Ann* was popular (*Mary-Ann* had developed from the erroneous interpretation of *Marian* as a compound of these two names). Jane Austen gave the name *Marianne* to one of the heroines of her novel *Sense and Sensibility* (1811); in France it is a nickname for the French Republic.

**Marie** [mă*ree*, *mari*] the French form of **Mary**. In regular use in medieval Britain, the name was revived throughout the English-speaking world in the latter half of the 19th century and eventually became more popular than *Mary* itself. Famous British bearers of the name include the music-hall artiste Marie Lloyd (1870–1922) and the birth-control pioneer Marie Stopes (1880–1958).

**Mariel** a variant of **Mary**; originally a German diminutive of the name.

**Marietta, Mariette** variants of **Mary** (*Mariette* is a French diminutive of the name). *Marietta* has been in occasional use as a first name in English-speaking countries, especially the USA, since the 19th century; it is also a place name in the American states of Ohio and Georgia (the Ohio town, founded in 1788, was named after the French queen Marie Antoinette).

**Marigold** (f) from the flower name; in occasional use as a first name since the late 19th century.

**Marilyn** a variant of **Mary**, influenced by other names ending in *-lyn*. Adopted as a stage name by a number of US actresses in the first half of the 20th century, it is generally associated with the film star and sex symbol Marilyn Monroe (1926–62), whose real name was Norma Jean Baker

# Marina

(or Mortenson). *Marilyn* was in frequent use as a first name throughout the English-speaking world in the 1940s and 1950s.

Variants: **Merilyn, Merrilyn**.

**Marina** [mă*reenă*] (f) a name of uncertain origin; possibly from Latin *marinus* 'of the sea'. It was borne by an early saint who is believed to have spent most of her life in a monastery in Bithynia, disguised as a monk. First used in Britain in the late Middle Ages, the name was revived throughout the English-speaking world after the marriage of Prince George, Duke of Kent, to Princess Marina of Greece in 1934. See also **Marnie**.

**Mario** the Italian form of **Marius**. Publicized in the mid-20th century by the US singer Mario Lanza (born Alfredo Cocozza), the name is occasionally found in the English-speaking world.

**Marion, Marian** [*marriŏn*] variants of **Mary**. Originally a diminutive of **Marie**, *Marion* was introduced into Britain from France during the Middle Ages and soon established itself as an independent name, with the alternative spelling *Marian*, a famous bearer being Robin Hood's sweetheart Maid Marion (or Marian). The word *marionette*, meaning 'puppet', is derived from the name. *Marion* is occasionally given as a masculine name: the US actor John Wayne (1907–79) was born Marion Michael Morrison.

Variant: **Marianne**.

**Marisa, Marissa, Marita** variants or diminutives of **Mary**.

**Marius** (m) from a Roman clan name probably derived from *Mars* (the name of the Roman god of war). It is occasionally found in English-speaking countries, a famous bearer being the 20th-century British actor Marius Goring.

Variant: **Mario**.

Related names: **Marcia, Marcus**.

**Marjorie, Margery** [*marjŏri*] variants of **Margaret**; from *Margerie*, a French diminutive of **Marguerite**. Both spellings date back to the 12th century, when the name was first used in the English-speaking world; since its revival in the late 19th century *Marjorie* has been the more popular form.

Diminutives: **Marge, Margie**.

**Mark** the English form of **Marcus**. The name was borne in the New Testament by St Mark, author of the second Gospel, and in medieval romance by **Tristan**'s uncle King Mark of Cornwall; however, it was used only occasionally until the latter half of the 20th century, when it became very popular throughout the English-speaking world. The US writer Mark Twain (1835–1910), whose real name was Samuel Langhorne Clemens, derived his pseudonym from a Mississippi boatmen's expression meaning 'two fathoms deep'. See also **Marc**.

**Marla** a variant of **Marlene**.

**Marlene** [*mar*leen, mar*layn*ă] (f) from a compound of **Maria** and **Magdalene**, the first names of the German actress and singer Marlene Dietrich (Maria Magdalene von Losch). Further popularized during World War II by the song 'Lili Marlene', the name has been in regular use throughout the English-speaking world since the 1930s.
Variants: **Marla, Marlin, Marlyn**.

**Marlin, Marlyn** variants of **Marlene**.

**Marmaduke** (m) possibly from the Irish name *Maelmaedoc*, meaning 'servant of **Madoc**'. It has been in occasional use in Britain, especially Yorkshire, since the Middle Ages.
Diminutive: **Duke**.

**Marnie, Marni** (f) a name of uncertain origin; possibly derived from a variant of **Marina**.

**Marsha** a variant of **Marcia**.

**Marshall, Marshal** (m) from a surname derived from Old French *mareschal* 'marshal'; ultimately from Old German, meaning 'horse servant'. It has been in occasional use as a first name since the 19th century.

**Marta** a variant of **Martha**.

**Martha** (f) from Aramaic, meaning 'lady'. The Martha of the New Testament, sister of Lazarus and Mary of Bethany, is remembered for her preoccupation with housework (Luke 10:38–42). Adopted as a first name in Britain after the Reformation, *Martha* was popularized in 18th-century America by the wife of George Washington and remained in regular use throughout the English-speaking world until the mid-20th century.
Variant: **Marta**.
Diminutives: **Marti, Martie, Marty, Mattie, Matty, Pattie, Patty**.

**Marti, Martie** diminutives of **Martha**.

**Martin, Martyn** (m) from the Latin name *Martinus*, derived from *Martius* 'of Mars (the Roman god of war)' or 'warlike'. St Martin, Bishop of Tours, was a 4th-century soldier who was converted to Christianity after sharing his cloak with a naked beggar; a number of English churches, such as St Martin-in-the-Fields in London, are dedicated to this early bearer of the name. The cult of St Martin popularized the name in medieval Britain; it remained in regular use after the Reformation (Martin **Luther** was one of the leaders of the movement) and enjoyed a further revival in the latter half of the 20th century. The bird name *martin* may be associated with Martinmas, the feast day of St Martin (11th November).
Diminutive: **Marty**.
Feminine forms: **Martina, Martine**.

**Martina** a feminine form of **Martin**. The US tennis player Martina Navratilova, born in Czechoslovakia, is a famous bearer of the name.

# Martine

**Martine** the French feminine form of **Martin**; occasionally used in English-speaking countries.

**Marty** a diminutive of **Martha** or **Martin**.

**Martyn** see **Martin**.

**Marvin, Marvyn** (m) a name of uncertain origin: it may be from the Old English name *Maerwine*, meaning 'famous friend', or it may simply be a variant of **Mervyn**. *Marvin* was revived as a first name in the USA in the 19th century; in other English-speaking countries it is more familiar as a surname.
Variants: **Mervin, Mervyn**.

**Mary** [*mairi*] (f) from a name that occurs in the Bible in a variety of forms; possibly from Hebrew, meaning 'wished-for child' or 'rebellion'. In the Old Testament the name is translated as **Miriam**; in early Greek and Latin versions of the New Testament it appears in the form *Mariam* or **Maria**. *Mariamne*, another variant, was the name of one of the ten wives of King Herod the Great. The name was borne by a number of New Testament characters, such as Mary of Bethany, sister of Martha and Lazarus, and Mary Magdalene. It is generally associated, however, with the Virgin Mary, mother of Jesus Christ; for several hundred years it was considered too sacred to be given as a first name. *Mary* came into general use in Britain during the Middle Ages, fell from favour after the Reformation, and was revived in the 17th century; it went on to become one of the most common feminine names in the English-speaking world, a position it retained until the mid-20th century. Famous royal bearers of the name include Queen Mary I (1516–58), whose persecution of the Protestants earned her the nickname 'Bloody Mary'; Mary, Queen of Scots (1542–87); and Queen Mary II (1662–94), wife of William of Orange. See also **May**.
Variants: **Mair, Maire, Maria, Marian, Marie, Mariel, Marietta, Mariette, Marilyn, Marion, Marisa, Marissa, Maura, Maureen, Moira, Moyra**.
Diminutives: **Maidie, Maisie, Mamie, May, Mimi, Minnie, Moll, Molly, Poll, Polly**.

**Mat** see **Matt**.

**Matilda** (f) from the Old German name *Mahthildis*, derived from *mahti* 'strength' and *hildi* 'battle'. Introduced into Britain by Queen Matilda, wife of William the Conqueror, the name was popularized in the 12th century by the wife and daughter of King Henry I (see also **Maud**) but fell from favour towards the end of the Middle Ages. It was revived in the 18th century and remains in occasional use throughout the English-speaking world today. In Australia (and in the well-known Australian folk song 'Waltzing Matilda') the name is used as a slang term for a bushman's pack.
Variants: **Maud, Maude**.

160

Diminutives: **Mattie, Matty, Pattie, Patty, Tilda, Tilly**.

**Matt, Mat** diminutives of **Matthew**, made famous in the 1960s by the British popular singer Matt Monro.

**Matthew** (m) from the Hebrew name *Mattathiah*, meaning 'gift of the Lord'; borne in the New Testament by St Matthew, author of the first Gospel. The name was introduced into Britain by the Normans in a variety of forms, such as *Matheu* or *Mathiu* (the modern French spelling of the name is *Mathieu* or *Matthieu*); it remained in regular use for several hundred years and was revived throughout the English-speaking world in the latter half of the 20th century. The 19th-century British writer Matthew Arnold was a famous bearer of the name.
Variant: **Matthias**.
Diminutives: **Mat, Matt**.

**Matthias** [măthīăs] a variant of **Matthew**, of Greek origin. In the New Testament St Matthias was the disciple chosen to replace Judas Iscariot as an apostle of Jesus Christ (Acts 1:23–26). The name has been in occasional use in English-speaking countries since the 17th century but has never been common.

**Mattie, Matty** diminutives of **Martha** or **Matilda**, sometimes used as independent names.

**Maud, Maude** variants of **Matilda**, dating back to the Middle Ages. King Henry I's daughter Matilda, wife of the Holy Roman emperor Henry V and Geoffrey of Anjou, was also known as Empress Maud. The name was revived throughout the English-speaking world in the latter half of the 19th century, after the publication of Tennyson's poem *Maud* (1855), but is rarely found in modern times.
Diminutive: **Maudie**.

**Maudie** a diminutive of **Maud**.

**Maura** see **Moira**.

**Maureen** a variant of **Mary**; from the Irish name *Mairin*, a diminutive of *Maire* (see **Moira**). Popularized by the Irish-born actresses Maureen O'Sullivan and Maureen O'Hara, the name has been in regular use throughout the English-speaking world since the early 20th century.

**Maurice, Morris** [*m*orris] (m) from the Latin name *Mauritius*, meaning 'Moorish' or 'swarthy'. St Maurice, after whom the Swiss resort of St Moritz is named, was a commanding officer of the Theban Legion of Christian soldiers, who were martyred in Switzerland in the late 3rd century. The name was introduced into Britain at the time of the Norman Conquest and soon became popular in the anglicized form *Morris* (the name of the traditional English folk dance is ultimately derived from the same source as the first name). Since its revival in the mid-19th century *Maurice* has been the more common spelling of the name: *Morris* remains in occasional use but is more familiar as a surname than as a first name in modern times. The French singer and actor Maurice Chevalier popularized the name throughout the English-speaking world in the 20th century.

**Mavis** [*may*vis] (f) from the English word *mavis*, meaning 'song thrush'; ultimately from Old French *mauvis*. The adoption of *Mavis* as a first name in the late 19th century has been attributed to the British writer Marie Corelli, who used the name in one of her novels; it was popular in Britain during the first half of the 20th century and remains in occasional use today.

**Max** a diminutive of **Maximilian** or **Maxwell**, often used as a name in its own right. Famous bearers include the British writer Sir Max Beerbohm (1872–1956), whose full name was Henry Maximilian Beerbohm, and the British entertainer Max Bygraves (born 1922).
Feminine form: **Maxine**.

**Maximilian** (m) from Latin *maximus* 'greatest'; borne by the 3rd-century martyr St Maximilian. (Some scholars believe the name to have been invented for the Holy Roman emperor Maximilian I (1459–1519) from the Latin names *Maximus* and *Aemilianus*.) The name is rarely found in this form in English-speaking countries.
Diminutive: **Max**.

**Maxine** [*mak*seen] the feminine form of **Max**; in regular use throughout the English-speaking world since the early 20th century.

**Maxwell** (m) from a Scottish surname and place name, possibly meaning '**Magnus**' spring'. *Maxwell* has been in regular use as a first name in Scotland and other parts of the English-speaking world since the 19th century.
Diminutive: **Max**.

**May** a 19th-century diminutive of **Margaret** or **Mary**, often used as a name in its own right; now regarded as one of the month names that became fashionable in the 20th century. Queen Mary, wife of King George V, was known to the royal family as May (coincidentally, her date of birth was 26th May, 1867). The variant spelling *Mae* was popularized by the US actress and sex symbol Mae West (1892–1980).

**Maynard** (m) from the Old German name *Maganhard*, derived from *magan* 'strength' and *hardu* 'hardy'. The name was introduced into Britain at the time of the Norman Conquest, replacing its Old English equivalent *Maegenheard*; in modern times it is more frequently found as a surname than as a first name.

**Meave** see **Maeve**.

**Meg** a diminutive of **Margaret**.

**Megan** [*meg*ăn] a Welsh variant of **Margaret**, probably derived from the diminutive form **Meg**. Megan Lloyd George (1902–66), daughter of the

British statesman David Lloyd George, publicized the name outside its country of origin through her involvement with the Liberal and Labour parties. The variant spelling *Meghan* occurs from time to time, especially in the USA.

Diminutives: **Meggie, Meggy**.

**Meggie, Meggy** diminutives of **Margaret** or **Megan**.

**Meghan** see **Megan**.

**Mehala, Mehalah, Mehalia** variants of **Mahala**.

**Mehetabel** [mĕhetăbel] (f) a biblical name, meaning 'God benefits'. It was adopted by the Puritans after the Reformation but is rarely found in modern times.

Variant: **Mehitabel**.

**Mehitabel** [mĕhităbel] a variant of **Mehetabel**, borne by the feline heroine of Don Marquis' *Archy and Mehitabel* (1927).

**Meirion, Merrion** [merriŏn] (m *or* f) from the Welsh name for the former county of Merionethshire; in occasional use as a first name.

**Mel** a diminutive of **Melanie, Melvin**, or any other name beginning with *Mel-*. The US film director Mel Brooks (born Melvin Kaminsky) is a famous bearer of the name.

**Melania** see **Melanie**.

**Melanie, Melloney** [melăni] (f) from *Melania*, the name of two Roman saints of the 4th and 5th centuries; ultimately from Greek *melas* 'black' or 'dark' (*Melaina*, meaning 'the black one', was one of the titles of the Greek goddess Demeter). Introduced into Britain from France in the mid-17th century, the name was rarely found outside Devon and Cornwall until the 20th century, when it was popularized throughout the English-speaking world by one of the heroines of Margaret Mitchell's *Gone with the Wind* (see **Ashley**).

Diminutive: **Mel**.

**Melba** (f) from the surname of the Australian opera singer Dame Nellie Melba (1861–1931); ultimately from the Australian place name *Melbourne*. It has been in occasional use as a first name since the early 20th century.

**Melicent** a variant of **Millicent**.

**Melinda** (f) from Latin *mel* 'honey', influenced by other names ending in *-inda*.

**Meliora** (f) possibly from Latin *melior* 'better'. The name has been in occasional use in Britain, especially Cornwall, since the Middle Ages.

**Mélisande, Melisent** see **Millicent**.

**Melissa** (f) from Greek, meaning 'bee'. Rarely used in the English-speaking world until the 18th century, the name enjoyed a further revival, especially in the USA, in the latter half of the 20th century.

# Melloney

**Melloney** see **Melanie**.

**Melody, Melodie** (f) from the English word *melody*; in occasional use as a lyrical first name since the 18th century.

**Melva** (f) a name of uncertain origin: it may be from a Celtic word for 'chief' or it may simply be a variant of **Melvina**.
Diminutive: **Melvina**.

**Melville** (m) from a Scottish surname ultimately derived from a French place name; in occasional use as a first name since the 19th century.
Variants: **Melvin, Melvyn**.

**Melvin, Melvyn** (m) a name of uncertain origin: it may be from an Old English name ending in *-wine* 'friend' or it may simply be a variant of **Malvin** or **Melville**. The US actor Melvyn Douglas popularized the name in the 1930s.
Diminutive: **Mel**.
Feminine form: **Melvina**.

**Melvina** a variant of **Malvina**, diminutive of **Melva**, or feminine form of **Melvin**.
Variant: **Melva**.

**Melvyn** see **Melvin**.

**Mercedes** [mer*say*deez] (f) from *Maria de las Mercedes*, one of the titles of the Virgin Mary; ultimately from Spanish *merced* 'mercy'. Since the early 20th century the name has been associated with the Mercedes motor car (named after the daughter of the company's business executive); *Mercedes* is rarely given as a first name in modern times.
Diminutives: **Mercy, Sadie**.

**Mercia** [*mer*siǎ] (f) from the name of the Anglo-Saxon kingdom of Mercia, ultimately from Old English *Merce* 'people of the borderland'. Its adoption as a first name may have been influenced by **Mercy**.

**Mercy** (f) from the English word *mercy*. One of the many names of abstract qualities adopted by the Puritans after the Reformation, it is rarely found in modern times. The name is also used as a diminutive of **Mercedes**.
Diminutive: **Merry**.

**Meredith** [*mer*rĕdith, mĕ*red*ith] (m *or* f) from the Welsh name *Maredudd*, meaning 'great chief'. Until the 20th century *Meredith* was rarely found outside Wales, except as a surname, and was given only to boys as a first name. It is now used as a masculine or feminine name throughout the English-speaking world.
Diminutive: **Merry**.

**Meriel** [*mer*riĕl] a variant of **Muriel**, dating back to the Middle Ages. It was revived in the late 19th century and remains in occasional use today.

**Merilyn, Merrilyn** variants of **Marilyn** or **Meryl**.

**Merle** (f) from French *merle* 'blackbird'. Popularized in the first half of the 20th century by the actress Merle Oberon, the name remains in occasional use today.

**Merlin** (m) from the Welsh name *Myrddin*, possibly derived from the place name *Carmarthen*. The name was borne in Arthurian legend by the wizard Merlin Ambrosius (Myrddin Emrys), adviser to King Arthur and his father Uther Pendragon; it is occasionally used as a first name in modern times but has never been common.

**Merrilyn** see **Merilyn**.

**Merrion** see **Meirion**.

**Merry** a diminutive of **Mercy** or **Meredith**. Influenced by the English word *merry*, it is sometimes given as a name in its own right.

**Merton** (m) from a surname and place name; ultimately from Old English, meaning 'settlement by a lake'.

**Merv** a diminutive of **Mervyn**.

**Mervyn, Mervin** (m) a name of uncertain origin: it may be from the Welsh name *Myrddin* (see **Merlin**) or it may simply be a variant of **Marvin**. Rarely found outside Wales, except as a surname, until the early 20th century, *Mervyn* is now used as a first name in most parts of the English-speaking world. It was borne by the British writer Mervyn Peake (1911–68).
Variants: **Marvin, Marvyn**.
Diminutive: **Merv**.
Related name: **Merlin**.

**Meryl** a variant of **Muriel**, of Welsh origin. The US actress Meryl Streep (born Mary Louise Streep) publicized the name in the 1980s.
Variants: **Merilyn, Merrilyn**.

**Meta** [*meetă*] a variant or diminutive of **Margaret**.

**Mia** (f) a name of uncertain origin: it may be from the feminine form of the Italian or Spanish word for 'my' or it may simply be a variant or diminutive of **Maria**. The US actress Mia Farrow (born 1945) is a famous bearer of the name.

**Micah** [*mīkă*] a variant of **Michael**. Borne by an Old Testament prophet of the 8th century BC, the name was adopted by the Puritans in the 17th century but is rarely found in modern times.

**Michael** [*mīkl*] (m) from Hebrew, meaning 'Who is like God?'; borne in the Bible by the archangel St Michael, conqueror of Satan and patron saint of soldiers. The name was very popular in medieval Britain and gave rise to a number of surnames: some of these, such as *Mitchell* and *Myall*, reflect early variant pronunciations of the name. *Michael* remained in regular use after the end of the Middle Ages; in the latter half of the 20th century it was one of the most common masculine names in the English-speaking world.

Variants: **Micah, Miles, Myles.**

Diminutives: **Mick, Mickey, Micky, Mike, Mitch.**

Feminine forms: **Michaela, Michele, Michelle.**

**Michaela** [mi*kay*lă, mi*kī*lă] a feminine form of **Michael**; in regular use since the mid-20th century.

**Michelle, Michele** [mee*shel*, mi*shel*] feminine forms of **Michael**, of French origin. The name was in frequent use throughout the English-speaking world during the latter half of the 20th century.

**Mick** a diminutive of **Michael**, now used as a slang term for an Irishman (the name *Michael* was formerly more common in Ireland than in other English-speaking countries).

**Mickey, Micky** diminutives of **Michael**, sometimes used as independent names in the USA. Famous bearers include the US writer Mickey Spillane (born Frank Morrison Spillane) and the cartoon character Mickey Mouse.

**Mignon** [*mee*nyon, *min*yŏn] (f) from French *mignon* 'darling'. The name was borne by the heroine of Goethe's novel *Wilhelm Meisters Lehrjahre* (1795–96), on which the 19th-century French composer Ambroise Thomas based his opera *Mignon*; it is occasionally found in English-speaking countries but has never been common.

**Mike** a diminutive of **Michael**.

**Milborough** (f) from the Old English name *Mildburh* or *Mildburga*, derived from *milde* 'mild' and *burg* 'borough' or 'fortress'. The name was borne in its original form by the 7th-century abbess St Mildburh (or Mildburga), sister of St **Mildred**; *Milborough* has been in occasional use as a first name since the Middle Ages.

**Milburn** (m) from a surname and place name; ultimately from Old English, meaning 'mill stream'.

**Mildred** (f) from the Old English name *Mildthryth*, derived from *milde* 'mild' and *thryth* 'strength'. The abbess St Mildred (or Mildthryth), daughter of a 7th-century king of Mercia, was an early bearer of the name. *Mildred* was popular throughout the English-speaking world, especially in the USA, in the late 19th and early 20th centuries but is rarely found in modern times.

Diminutives: **Millie, Milly.**

**Miles, Myles** (m) a name of uncertain origin; probably a variant of **Michael** or **Milo** (the surname *Miles*, which influenced the revival of the first name in the 19th century, may be derived from Latin *miles* 'soldier'). The name has been in occasional use throughout the English-speaking world since the Middle Ages; in Ireland *Miles* and *Milo* are sometimes used to translate *Maolmuire*, meaning 'servant of Mary', and other Irish names beginning with *Maol-* or *Mael-*.

**Millicent** [*mil*isĕnt] (f) from an Old German name derived from *amal* 'work' and *swintha* 'strong'. It was introduced into medieval Britain from France in the form *Melisent* (the name *Mélisande*, borne by the heroine of Maeterlinck's play *Pelléas et Mélisande* (1892) and Debussy's opera of the same name, is another French variant). The spelling and pronunciation of the name gradually developed into the more familiar form *Millicent*, which was fairly popular in the late 19th and early 20th centuries and remains in occasional use today.
Variant: **Melicent**.
Diminutives: **Millie, Milly**.

**Millie, Milly** diminutives of **Amelia, Camilla, Emily, Mildred**, or **Millicent**, occasionally used as independent names.

**Milo** [*mīlō*] (m) an Old German name, possibly meaning 'merciful', introduced into Britain at the time of the Norman Conquest. It remains in occasional use in Ireland (see **Miles**) but is rarely found in this form in other English-speaking countries.
Variants: **Miles, Myles**.

**Milton** (m) from a surname and place name; ultimately from Old English, meaning 'middle (or mill) settlement'. The US economist Milton Friedman (born 1912) is a famous bearer of the first name; the surname is generally associated with the 17th-century British poet John Milton.

**Mima** a diminutive of **Jemima**.

**Mimi** [*mee*mee] a diminutive of **Mary** or any other feminine name beginning with *M*. *Mimi* has been in occasional use as an independent name since the late 19th century, when it was popularized by the heroine of Puccini's opera *La Bohème* (1896).

**Mina** [*mī*nă, *mee*nă] a diminutive of **Wilhelmina** or any other name ending in *-mina*, sometimes used as a name in its own right.

**Minerva** (f) the name of the Roman goddess of wisdom, arts and crafts, and war; possibly from Latin *mens* 'mind' or *memini* 'remember'. It is occasionally given as a first name in English-speaking countries.

**Minna** probably a diminutive of **Wilhelmina**, of Scottish origin, though some scholars believe the name to be derived from an Old German word for 'love'. *Minna* has been in occasional use as an independent name since the 19th century, when it was popularized by one of the heroines of Sir Walter Scott's novel *The Pirate* (1822).

**Minnie** a diminutive of **Mary** or **Wilhelmina**, often used as an independent name in the late 19th and early 20th centuries. Walt Disney gave the name to the cartoon character Minnie Mouse, girlfriend of the more famous Mickey Mouse.

# Minty

**Minty** a diminutive of **Aminta** or **Araminta**.

**Mira** [*myră*, *mirră*] a variant spelling of **Myra** or a diminutive of **Mirabel** or **Miranda**.

**Mirabel, Mirabelle** [*mirrăbel*] (f) from Latin *mirabilis* 'wonderful'. The name was fairly popular in medieval Britain and occurs, sometimes as a masculine name, in a number of literary works of the 17th and 18th centuries. It is rarely given as a first name in modern times.
Variant: **Mirabella**.
Diminutive: **Mira**.

**Mirabella** a variant of **Mirabel**.

**Mirabelle** see **Mirabel**.

**Miranda** [*mirandă*] (f) from a Latin word meaning 'worthy of admiration' or 'wonderful'; adopted as a first name by Shakespeare for the heroine of his play *The Tempest*. It has been in occasional use throughout the English-speaking world since the 17th century.
Diminutives: **Mira, Randy**.

**Miriam** [*mirriăm*] (f) from a biblical name (see **Mary**); borne in the Old Testament by the sister of Moses and Aaron. *Miriam* was adopted as a first name by the Puritans after the Reformation and remains in regular use throughout the English-speaking world.

**Mitch** a diminutive of **Michael** or **Mitchell**.

**Mitchell** (m) from a surname derived from **Michael**; in occasional use as a first name since the 19th century.
Diminutive: **Mitch**.

**Mitzi** a variant of **Maria**; originally a German diminutive of the name. The US actress Mitzi Gaynor (born 1930) is a famous bearer.

**Modesty** (f) from the English word *modesty*. As a first name it is generally associated with the British comic-strip heroine Modesty Blaise, created by Jim Holdaway and Peter O'Donnell.

**Moira, Moyra, Maura, Maire** variants of **Mary** (*Maire* is the Irish form of the name; *Maura, Moira* and *Moyra* are its anglicized spellings). *Moira* has been in regular use throughout the English-speaking world since the early 20th century and is particularly popular in Scotland; the Scottish-born ballerina Moira Shearer is a well-known bearer of the name. See also **Maureen**.

**Molly, Moll** diminutives of **Mary**. *Molly* was in regular use as an independent name in the first half of the 20th century. *Moll* has entered the English language as a slang term for a gangster's companion or a prostitute.

**Mona** (f) from the Irish name *Muadhnait*, derived from *muadh* 'noble' (*Mona* is also an ancient name for the Isle of Man and the Welsh island of Anglesey). The name was rarely used outside Ireland until the latter half of the 19th century, when it began to spread to Great Britain and other

parts of the English-speaking world. It is sometimes associated with Leonardo da Vinci's famous portrait of the *Mona Lisa*, wife of Francesco del Giocondo, (the painting is known on the Continent as *La Gioconda*).
Variant: **Moyna**.

**Monica** [*moni*kă] (f) a name of uncertain origin: possible derivations include Greek *monos* 'alone' and Latin *monere* 'to advise'. Borne in the 4th century by St Monica, mother of St Augustine of Hippo, the name did not come into regular use in English-speaking countries until the 20th century. It is not known whether *moniker* (or *monicker*), a slang word for 'name', is related to the first name.
Variant: **Monique**.

**Monique** [mo*neek*] the French form of **Monica**; occasionally found in the English-speaking world in the latter half of the 20th century.

**Montague, Montagu** [*mont*ăgew] (m) from an aristocratic surname derived from a French place name; ultimately from Old French, meaning 'pointed hill'. It has been in occasional use as a first name since the 19th century.
Diminutives: **Monte, Monty**.

**Monte** see **Monty**.

**Montgomery** (m) from a surname derived from a French place name (the former Welsh county of Montgomeryshire was named after a Norman bearer of the name). The surname *Montgomery* is generally associated with the British field marshal Lord Montgomery of Alamein (1887–1976); it was publicized as a first name by the US actor Montgomery Clift (1920–66).
Diminutives: **Monte, Monty**.

**Monty, Monte** diminutives of **Montague** or **Montgomery**, often used as independent names. *Monty* was the nickname of Lord Montgomery of Alamein.

**Morag** [*mora*g] (f) from Gaelic, meaning either 'great' or 'sun'. The name is popular in Scotland; its use in other English-speaking countries is largely confined to families of Scottish descent.

**Moray** see **Murray**.

**Mordecai** [mor*dĕkī*] (m) a biblical name, possibly meaning 'follower (or worshipper) of Marduk (a Babylonian god)'. Borne in the Old Testament by the cousin and guardian of Esther, the name was adopted by the Puritans in the 17th century and remained in regular use until the late 19th century. It is rarely found in modern times.

**Morgan** (m) a Welsh name, derived from the words for 'sea' or 'great' and 'bright'. *Morgan* has been in regular use in Wales for many hundreds of years: the Welsh county of Glamorgan is named after a 10th-century bearer of the name. In other parts of the English-speaking world it is more familiar as a surname than as a first name. Borne in Arthurian legend by the sorceress Morgan le Fay, sister of King Arthur, *Morgan* is occasionally found as a feminine name.

**Morna** (f) from Gaelic *muirne* 'beloved'; more frequently found in its variant form in most parts of the English-speaking world.
Variant: **Myrna**.

**Morris** see **Maurice**.

**Mort** a diminutive of **Mortimer**.

**Mortimer** (m) from the surname of an influential Anglo-Norman family; ultimately from the French place name *Mortemer*, meaning 'dead sea' (referring to a stagnant lake, not the Dead Sea of the Holy Land). It was adopted as a first name in the 19th century, a famous bearer being the British archaeologist Sir Mortimer Wheeler (1890–1976).
Diminutives: **Mort, Morty**.

**Morty** a diminutive of **Mortimer**. In Ireland *Morty* is sometimes used to translate the Irish name *Murtagh* (see **Murdoch**).

**Morwenna** (f) probably from Welsh *morwyn* 'maiden', though some scholars believe the name to be derived from Welsh *mor* 'sea' and *gwaneg* 'wave'. Borne by a Celtic saint of the 5th century, after whom the Cornish village of Morwenstow was named, *Morwenna* remains in occasional use in Wales and Cornwall but is rarely found elsewhere.

**Moses** [*mōziz*] (m) a biblical name of Hebrew or Egyptian origin, possibly meaning 'son' (an alternative interpretation is given in Exodus 2:10). The story of Moses, called by God to lead the Israelites out of Egypt, fills four books of the Old Testament, from his mother's concealment of her infant son amongst the bulrushes of the River Nile to his death outside the Promised Land at the age of 120. The name has been used by Jewish families since the Babylonian exile of the 6th century BC; it came into more general use in Britain during the Middle Ages and was one of the many biblical names adopted by the Puritans after the Reformation.
Variants: **Moshe, Moss**.

**Moshe** [*moshĕ*] a variant of **Moses**. The Israeli general Moshe Dayan (1915–81) was a famous bearer of the name.

**Moss** a variant or diminutive of **Moses**, dating back to the Middle Ages; more frequently found as a surname than as a first name in modern times.

**Moyna** probably a variant of **Mona**.

**Moyra** see **Moira**.

**Muir** [mewr] (m) from a Scottish surname meaning 'moor'; in occasional use as a first name.

**Mungo** (m) possibly from a Gaelic word meaning 'amiable' or 'beloved'; the nickname of St **Kentigern**. The name is occasionally found in Scot-

# Myrtle

land, its best-known bearer being the Scottish explorer Mungo Park (1771–1806), who led two expeditions along the River Niger in Africa.

**Murdoch** [*merdō, mer*dok] (m) from a Gaelic name meaning 'mariner'. *Murdoch* is the Scottish form of the name; *Murtagh* (see **Morty**) is its Irish equivalent. The name remains in occasional use in Scotland; in other parts of the English-speaking world it is more familiar as a surname than as a first name.

**Muriel** [*mewri*ĕl] (f) from a Celtic name rendered in Irish Gaelic as *Muirgheal*, from *muir* 'sea' and *geal* 'bright'. *Muriel*, which is probably derived from the Breton equivalent of the Irish name, was introduced into Britain at the time of the Norman Conquest; it remained in frequent use until the end of the Middle Ages and was revived throughout the English-speaking world in the late 19th century. The British writer Muriel Spark, author of *The Prime of Miss Jean Brodie* (1961), is a famous bearer of the name.

Variants: **Meriel, Meryl.**

**Murray, Moray** [*mu*rri] (m) from a Scottish surname and place name; ultimately from a Gaelic word meaning 'sea'. *Murray* is the more common spelling of the first name: it has been in regular use throughout the English-speaking world, especially in families of Scottish descent, since the 19th century.

**Murtagh** see **Morty, Murdoch.**

**Myfanwy** [*mĭvan*wi] (f) a Welsh name, meaning 'my fine (or rare) one'.

**Myles** see **Miles.**

**Myra** (f) invented by the Elizabethan writer Fulke Greville, Lord Brooke, for his love poem of the same name. *Myra* subsequently occurred in a number of of other literary works but was rarely given as a first name until the 19th century. The British pianist Dame Myra Hess (1890–1965) was a famous bearer of the name. See also **Mira.**

**Myrna** [*mern*ă] a variant of **Morna**; the more common form of the name in most parts of the English-speaking world. It was popularized in the first half of the 20th century by the US actress Myrna Loy.

**Myron** (m) from Greek, meaning 'perfumed oil'; borne by a Greek sculptor of the 5th century BC. The name is occasionally used in the USA and Canada but is rarely found in other English-speaking countries.

**Myrtilla** a variant of **Myrtle.**

**Myrtle** [*mert*l] (f) from the name of the flowering shrub; one of the many plant names that came into fashion in the 19th century.

Variant: **Myrtilla.**

Mysie a variant of **Maisie**.

# N

**Nada** [*nah*dă] a variant of **Nadia**.

**Nadia** [*nah*diă] (f) from the Russian name *Nadezhda*, meaning 'hope'. *Nadia* and its variants have been in occasional use throughout the English-speaking world since the beginning of the 20th century. In the world of music the name is generally associated with the French teacher, conductor, and composer Nadia Boulanger (1887–1979).
Variants: **Nada**, **Nadine**.

**Nadine** [*nah*deen] a variant of **Nadia**, of French origin.

**Nahum** [*nay*hŭm] (m) from Hebrew, meaning 'comforting'. Borne by an Old Testament prophet of the 7th century BC, the name was adopted by the Puritans after the Reformation but is rarely found in modern times.

**Nan** a diminutive of **Ann**, often used as a name in its own right.

**Nance** a variant of **Nancy**.

**Nancy** a variant of **Ann**; originally a diminutive of the name, dating back to the 18th century. In the early 20th century *Nancy* began to be used as a slang term for an effeminate male and gradually fell from favour as a first name in Britain; it remained popular in the USA and Canada, however, until the end of the 1950s.
Variant: **Nance**.

**Nanette** a variant of **Ann**. Originally a diminutive of **Nan**, it was popularized as an independent name in the 20th century by the musical *No, No, Nanette* (1925), starring Binnie Hale, and by the British actress Nanette Newman.

**Nanny** a diminutive of **Ann**. By the beginning of the 20th century the name had acquired a number of additional meanings, including those of 'female goat' and 'nursemaid', which may have contributed to its obsolescence.

**Naomi** [*nay*ŏmi] (f) from Hebrew, meaning 'pleasant'. The name was borne in the Old Testament by the mother-in-law of Ruth (see also **Mara**); it was adopted by the Puritans in the 17th century and enjoyed a further revival in the latter half of the 20th century.

**Napoleon** (m) a name of uncertain origin: possibly from *Neapolis*, the ancient name of the Italian city of Naples, influenced by Italian *leone* 'lion'. It is occasionally given as a first name in English-speaking countries in honour of the French emperor Napoleon Bonaparte (1769–1821).

**Narcissus** (m) the name of a character in Greek mythology: a beautiful youth who fell in love with his own reflection and was ultimately transformed into the flower that bears his name. *Narcissus* is occasionally given as a first name in English-speaking countries but has never been common; the introduction of the term *narcissism* into the English language probably contributed to its lack of popularity.

**Nat** a diminutive of **Nathan** or **Nathaniel**.

**Natalia** [na*tah*liă] (f) from Latin *natalis* 'birthday' (a reference to Christmas Day). The name was borne in the 4th century by St Natalia, wife of the Christian martyr St Adrian; it has been in occasional use in English-speaking countries for several hundred years but is more frequently found in its variant forms. See also **Christmas**.
Variants: **Natalie, Natasha**.

**Natalie** [*nat*ăli] a variant of **Natalia**, of French origin. It was popularized throughout the English-speaking world in the latter half of the 20th century by the US actress Natalie Wood (born Natasha Gurdin).

**Natasha** a variant of **Natalia**, of Russian origin. Borne by the heroine of Leo Tolstoy's epic *War and Peace* (1865–69), the name was popularized in the 1960s by a British television adaptation of the novel; it remains in regular use throughout the English-speaking world today.

**Nathan** [*nay*thăn] (m) from Hebrew, meaning 'gift'. Borne in the Old Testament by a prophet at the court of King David, the name came into general use in English-speaking countries in the 17th century and enjoyed a partial revival in the latter half of the 20th century.
Diminutive: **Nat**.

**Nathanael** see **Nathaniel**.

**Nathaniel** [nă*than*yĕl] (m) from Hebrew, meaning 'gift of God'. The variant form *Nathanael* was borne in St John's Gospel by an apostle of Jesus Christ, generally identified with **Bartholomew**. Both forms of the name, *Nathaniel* being the more popular, have been in occasional use in English-speaking countries, especially the USA, since the Reformation. Famous bearers include the 19th- and 20th-century US writers Nathaniel Hawthorne and Nathanael West (born Nathan Weinstein).
Diminutive: **Nat**.

**Neal** see **Neil**.

**Ned** a diminutive of **Edmund** or **Edward**, dating back to the 14th century.

**Neddie, Neddy** diminutives of **Edmund** or **Edward**. *Neddy* has entered the English language as a child's word for 'donkey'.

**Nehemiah** [neei*mī*ă] (m) from Hebrew, meaning 'comfort of the Lord'; borne in the 5th century BC by a governor of Jerusalem, author of the Old Testament book of Nehemiah. The name was adopted by the Puritans in the 17th century but is rarely found in modern times.

**Neil, Neill, Neal, Niall** (m) from Irish *niadh* 'champion'. One of the earliest bearers of the name was the Irish king Niall of the Nine Hostages, who

died at the beginning of the 5th century. *Neil* was introduced into Great Britain, possibly via Scandinavia and France, during the Middle Ages; the name has been in general use in various parts of the English-speaking world, especially Scotland, since then. It was particularly popular in the latter half of the 20th century.
Variant: **Nigel**.

**Nell, Nellie, Nelly** diminutives of **Eleanor**, **Ellen**, or **Helen**, sometimes used as independent names. Famous bearers include King Charles II's mistress Nell Gwyn, whose real name was Eleanor or Elinor, and the Australian opera singer Dame Nellie **Melba** (born Helen Mitchell).

**Nelson** (m) from a surname meaning 'son of **Neil**'. It was adopted as a first name, possibly in honour of the British admiral **Horatio** Nelson, in the 19th century; famous bearers include the US politician Nelson Rockefeller (1908–79) and the South African black activist Nelson Mandela (born 1918).

**Nerina** a variant of **Nerissa**.

**Nerissa** (f) probably from Greek *Nereid* 'sea nymph'. Borne by a character in Shakespeare's play *The Merchant of Venice*, the name is occasionally found in various parts of the English-speaking world.
Variant: **Nerina**.

**Nerys** [*nerris*] (f) from Welsh *ner* 'lord'; made famous by the British television actress Nerys Hughes (born 1940).

**Nessie, Nessa** diminutives of **Agnes**. *Nessie* is also used as a nickname for the Loch Ness monster.

**Nesta, Nest** Welsh diminutives of **Agnes**. *Nesta* is sometimes used as a name in its own right.

**Netta, Nettie** diminutives of any name ending in *-nette*, such as **Annette**, **Antoinette**, **Janette**, or **Jeanette**.

**Neva** (f) probably from Spanish *nevar* 'to snow'.

**Neville, Nevil** (m) from a surname introduced into Britain at the time of the Norman Conquest; ultimately from the French place name *Neuville*, meaning 'new town'. The Nevilles played an important role in the politics of the Wars of the Roses, one of the most influential members of the family being Richard Neville, Earl of Warwick (1428–71), nicknamed 'Warwick the Kingmaker'. *Neville* was rarely used as a first name until the latter half of the 19th century; famous 20th-century bearers include Neville Chamberlain, prime minister of the United Kingdom at the beginning of World War II, and the British-born novelist Nevil Shute.

**Newton** (m) from a surname and place name; ultimately from Old English, meaning 'new settlement'. *Newton* has been in occasional use as a first name since the 19th century; the surname is generally associated with the great 17th-century scientist Sir Isaac Newton.

**Niall** see **Neil**.

**Nichola** see **Nicola**.

**Nicholas, Nicolas** (m) from the Greek name *Nikolaos*, a compound of *nike* 'victory' and *laos* 'people'. One of the earliest and most famous bearers of the name was the 4th-century bishop St Nicholas, patron saint of children, sailors, and pawnbrokers, on whom the jovial and benevolent figure of Father Christmas or Santa Claus is based (*Santa Claus* is derived from the Dutch form of his name). Mentioned in the New Testament (Acts 6:5), the name was also borne by five popes, two Russian emperors, and the hero of Charles Dickens' novel *Nicholas Nickleby* (1838–39). It was very popular in Britain in the latter half of the Middle Ages and has remained in regular use since then, enjoying a revival in the mid-20th century, when it became fashionable throughout the English-speaking world.
Variants: **Colin, Nicol**.
Diminutives: **Nick, Nicky**.
Feminine forms: **Colette, Nichola, Nicola, Nicole, Nicolette**.

**Nick** a diminutive of **Nicholas**. 'Old Nick' is a colloquial name for the Devil.

**Nicky** a diminutive of **Nicholas, Nicola**, or any other name beginning with *Nic*-; sometimes used as a name in its own right. *Nikki* is one of several variant spellings of the feminine name.

**Nicodemus** [nikŏdeemŭs] (m) from Greek *nike* 'victory' and *demos* 'people'. The Nicodemus of the New Testament, a member of the Jewish ruling council, assisted Joseph of Arimathea with the burial of Jesus Christ (John 19:39–40). The name has been in occasional use in English-speaking countries since the 17th century.

**Nicol** a variant of **Nicholas**, dating back to the Middle Ages. The British actor Nicol Williamson (born 1939) is probably the best-known bearer of the name in modern times.

**Nicola, Nichola** feminine forms of **Nicholas**, of Italian origin. *Nicola* has been in regular use in the English-speaking world since the mid-20th century and was particularly popular in Britain in the 1970s. Its French equivalent, *Nicole*, is preferred in the USA, Canada, and Australia.
Diminutives: **Nicky, Nikki**.

**Nicolas** see **Nicholas**.

**Nicole** see **Nicola, Nicolette**.

**Nicolette** a feminine form of **Nicholas**; originally a diminutive of *Nicole* (see **Nicola**). Its own diminutive, **Colette**, is the more common form of the name in English-speaking countries.
Diminutive: **Colette**.

**Nigel** [nījĕl] from *Nigellus*, the Latinized form of **Neil**; sometimes erroneously associated with Latin *niger* 'black'. The name has been in general use in Britain for several hundred years and was particularly popular in the mid-20th century; it is used only occasionally, however, in other English-speaking countries.

**Nikki** see **Nicky**.

**Nina** [*neenă, nīnă*] a variant of **Ann** (originally a Russian pet form of the name) or a diminutive of any name ending in *-nina*, such as **Antonina**. It has been in regular use throughout the English-speaking world since the 19th century.
Variant: **Ninette**.

**Ninette** [nee*net*] a variant of **Nina**. The British ballerina and choreographer Dame Ninette de Valois (born Edris Stannus) is probably the best-known bearer of the name.

**Ninian** (m) a name of uncertain origin; possibly related to *Nennius*, the name of an early Welsh historian, or to **Vivian**. St Ninian was a bishop and missionary sent to Scotland in the early 5th century to convert the southern Picts to Christianity. The name has been in occasional use in Scotland and northern England for several hundred years but is rarely found elsewhere.

**Nita** a diminutive of any name ending in *-nita*, such as **Anita** or **Juanita**; sometimes used as a name in its own right.

**Noah** [*nōă*] (m) from Hebrew, meaning 'long-lived' or 'repose'. The name is generally associated with the story of Noah's Ark, in which the Old Testament patriarch Noah and his family, together with a pair of every species of animal, survived the Flood (Genesis 6–8). *Noah* was adopted as a first name by the Puritans in the 17th century and remains in occasional use throughout the English-speaking world.

**Noel** [*nōël*] (m) from French *Noël* 'Christmas'; ultimately from Latin *natalis* (see **Natalia**). The name was in regular use in medieval Britain, sometimes in the form *Nowell* (which has survived as a surname); it was originally given to children of either sex but is now regarded as a masculine name, with a variety of feminine forms. Famous bearers of the name include the British dramatist and actor Sir Noel (or Noël) Coward (1899–1973) and the British media personality Noel Edmonds (born 1948). See also **Christmas**.
Feminine forms: **Noele, Noeleen, Noeline, Noelle**.

**Noelle, Noele, Noeleen, Noeline** feminine forms of **Noel**.

**Nola** (f) from the name of an Italian town near Naples; also regarded as a diminutive of **Finola** or the feminine form of **Nolan**.

**Nolan** (m) from an Irish surname meaning 'famous' or 'noble'; occasionally used as a first name in the 20th century.
Feminine form: **Nola**.

**Nona** (f) from Latin *nonus* 'ninth'; formerly given by the parents of large families to their ninth child. The name is rarely required for this purpose in modern times but remains in occasional use.

**Nora, Norah** variants of **Honor**. Originally a diminutive of the name (from **Honora** or **Annora**), *Nora* was introduced into Ireland after the Norman Conquest and has remained in regular use since then. It is sometimes regarded as a diminutive of **Eleanora** or **Leonora**.
Diminutive: **Noreen**.

**Norbert** (m) probably from an Old German name derived from *nord* 'north' and *berhta* 'bright'; borne in the 12th century by St Norbert, Archbishop of Magdeburg. The name remains in occasional use in the USA and Canada but is rarely found in other parts of the English-speaking world in modern times.

**Noreen** a diminutive of **Nora**, often used as a name in its own right.

**Norm** a diminutive of **Norman**.

**Norma** (f) probably from Latin *norma* 'rule' or 'pattern'; sometimes regarded as a feminine form of **Norman**. Borne by the heroine of Bellini's opera *Norma* (1831), a Druidess who falls in love with a Roman proconsul, the name has been in regular use throughout the English-speaking world since the 19th century. It was further popularized in the first half of the 20th century by the US actress Norma Shearer.

**Norman** (m) from an Old English or Old German name meaning 'man from the north' (referring to Scandinavia); a term subsequently applied to the Viking settlers of the region of France now known as Normandy. *Norman* was a fairly common name in medieval Britain before and after the arrival of William the Conqueror; it survived the Middle Ages as a first name in Scotland but was rarely found in England, except as a surname, for several hundred years. Revived throughout the English-speaking world in the mid-19th century, the name was particularly popular in the first half of the 20th century and remains in occasional use today.
Diminutive: **Norm**.
Feminine form: **Norma**.

**Norris** (m) from Old French, meaning 'northerner' or 'nurse'. It is more familiar as a surname than as a first name in modern times.

**Norton** (m) from a surname and place name; ultimately from Old English, meaning 'northern settlement'. It has been in occasional use as a first name since the 19th century.

**Nova** (f) from Latin *novus* 'new'. Its adoption as a first name may have been influenced by the use of the term *nova* (from Latin *nova stella*) to denote a type of star.

# Nowell

**Nowell** see **Noel**.

**Nuala** [*noo*lă] a diminutive of *Fionnuala* (see **Fenella**), often used as a name in its own right.

**Nye** a diminutive of **Aneurin**.

**Nyree** (f) a name of Maori origin, popularized in the 1960s and 1970s by the New Zealand actress Nyree Dawn Porter.

# O

**Obadiah** [ōbă*dī*ă] (m) from Hebrew, meaning 'servant (or worshipper) of the Lord'; borne by the prophet Obadiah, author of the shortest book in the Old Testament. The name was adopted by the Puritans in the 17th century but is rarely found in modern times.

**Oberon** see **Auberon**.

**Octavia** the feminine form of **Octavius**; borne in ancient Rome by Octavian's sister, whose political marriage to Mark Antony ended in divorce in 32 BC. The name is occasionally found in English-speaking countries but has never been common.

**Octavian** see **Augustus, Octavius**.

**Octavius** (m) from a Roman clan name derived from Latin *octavus* 'eighth'. Gaius Octavius was the original name of the Roman emperor Augustus (63 BC–14 AD), also known as Octavian. The name *Octavius* (or its feminine form **Octavia**) was formerly given by the parents of large families to their eighth child; it is rarely required for this purpose in modern times but remains in occasional use.
Feminine form: **Octavia**.

**Odette, Odile** feminine forms of **Odo** or variants of **Ottilia**. Of French origin, both names are occasionally used in English-speaking countries, *Odette* being the more common of the two. The French-born war heroine Odette Churchill, a British agent who was captured and tortured by the Gestapo and subsequently escaped from concentration camp, was a famous bearer of the name.

**Odilia** see **Ottilia**.

**Odo** [ōdō] (m) from the Old German name *Audo* or *Odo*, meaning 'wealth'. The French abbot St Odo of Cluny (879–942) was an early bearer of the name. Introduced into Britain at the time of the Norman Conquest, the name occurs in the Domesday Book of 1086 in a variety of forms, including *Odo*, *Otho*, and **Otto**; subsequent medieval variants gave rise to such surnames as *Oates*, *Oddie*, and *Otis*. The first names *Odo* and *Otho* are rarely found in modern times.
Variant: **Otto**.

Feminine forms: **Odette, Odile**.

**Ogden** (m) from a surname and place name; ultimately from Old English, meaning 'oak valley'. It has been in occasional use as a first name since the 19th century, a famous bearer being the US humorist Ogden Nash (1902–71).

**Olaf** (m) from the Old Norse name *Anleifr*, a compound of two words meaning 'ancestor' and 'relics'. Borne by a number of Scandinavian kings, including St Olaf, patron saint of Norway, the name was introduced into Britain by the Vikings. It has rarely been used in this form in the English-speaking world since the Norman Conquest.
Variants: **Aulay, Olav, Olave, Oliver**.

**Olave, Olav** variants of **Olaf**. *Olave* is the usual form of the name in English-speaking countries.

**Olga** the Russian form of **Helga**. One of the earliest bearers of the name was St Olga, regent of Kiev, whose conversion to Christianity in the mid-10th century paved the way for the establishment of the Russian Orthodox Church. The name has been in regular use throughout the English-speaking world since the late 19th century; in the 1970s it was publicized by the Russian gymnast Olga Korbut.

**Oliff, Oliva** see **Olive**.

**Olive** (f) from Latin *oliva* 'olive' (a symbol of peace). In medieval Britain the name occurred in a variety of forms, notably *Oliva*, *Oliff*, and the diminutive *Olivet*. *Olive* itself has been in general use since the 16th century; it was temporarily superseded by **Olivia** but enjoyed a revival in the late 19th century, when a number of other plant names came into fashion, and was particularly popular in the 1920s.
Variant: **Olivia**.
Diminutive: **Ollie**.
Masculine equivalent: **Oliver**.

**Oliver** (m) a name of uncertain origin: it may be ultimately derived from Latin *oliva* (see **Olive**), via Old French *olivier* (or *oliver*) 'olive tree'; it may be from the Old German name *Alfihar*, meaning 'elf army'; or it may simply be a variant of **Olaf**. Borne in the *Chanson de Roland* by one of Charlemagne's paladins, **Roland**'s companion in arms, the name was fairly popular in Britain during and after the Middle Ages; its subsequent association with Oliver Cromwell, however, caused it to fall rapidly from favour in the latter half of the 17th century, following the Restoration. The name was revived in the 19th century and remains in regular use throughout the English-speaking world. Other famous bearers include the 18th-century Irish writer Oliver Goldsmith; the hero of one of Charles Dickens' best-known novels, *Oliver Twist* (1838); and the British actor Oliver Reed (born 1938).
Variant: **Olivier**.

# Olivet

Diminutive: **Ollie**.

Feminine equivalent: **Olive**.

**Olivet** see **Olive**.

**Olivia** the Italian form of **Olive**; borne by one of the heroines of Shakespeare's play *Twelfth Night*. *Olivia* became fashionable throughout the English-speaking world in the 18th century, when Oliver Goldsmith used the name in his novel *The Vicar of Wakefield*. Famous 20th-century bearers include the actresses Olivia de Havilland and Olivia Hussey.

**Olivier** [*oliv*iay] the French form of **Oliver**. It is occasionally given as a first name in English-speaking countries but is more familiar as the surname of the British actor **Laurence** Olivier.

**Ollie** a diminutive of **Olive**, **Oliver**, or any other name beginning with *Ol-*. Perhaps it is most commonly associated with the comedian Ollie Hardy, the fatter half of the Laurel and Hardy duo.

**Olwen, Olwyn** (f) from Welsh, meaning 'white track' (referring to the white flowers that grew from the footprints of the heroine of 'Culhwch and Olwen', one of the medieval Welsh tales of the *Mabinogion*). The name was rarely used outside Wales until the late 19th century, when it began to spread to other parts of Britain and the English-speaking world.

**Olympia** (f) from Greek, meaning 'of Olympus (the home of the gods)' or 'of Olympia (the original site of the Olympic Games)'. In the form *Olympias* the name was borne by a 4th-century saint and by the mother of Alexander the Great; *Olympia* is occasionally found in English-speaking countries but has never been common.

**Omar** [*ō*mar] (m) a biblical name, meaning 'eloquent'; borne in the Old Testament by a grandson of Esau. The name is occasionally found in English-speaking countries, publicized in the 19th century by a translation of the *Rubaiyat of Omar Khayyam* and in the 20th century by the international film actor of Egyptian origin, Omar Sharif.

**Ona** a variant of **Una** or a diminutive of any name ending in *-ona*.

**Onuphrius** see **Humphrey**.

**Oonagh, Oona** [*oon*ă] variants of **Una**, reflecting the Irish pronunciation of the name. Largely confined to Ireland or to families of Irish descent in other parts of the English-speaking world, it was made famous by the marriage of Oona O'Neill, daughter of the dramatist Eugene O'Neill, to Charlie Chaplin in 1943.

**Opal** (f) from the name of the precious stone; one of a number of jewel names that became fashionable in the 19th century.

**Ophelia** [*o*feeliă] (f) from Greek, meaning 'help'. The name is generally associated with the Shakespearean heroine who is driven to insanity by the irrational behaviour of her lover Hamlet. *Ophelia* is occasionally given as a first name in various parts of the English-speaking world but has never been common.

**Oriana** [ŏrri*ahn*ă, ori*ahn*ă] (f) from Latin *oriri* 'to rise'; sometimes interpreted as 'sunrise' or 'dawn'. *Oriana* occurs in a number of literary works, from the 14th-century romance *Amadis de Gaul* to Tennyson's ballad 'Oriana' (1830), but is rarely given as a first name in modern times.

**Oriel** [*ori*ĕl] (f) from the Old German name *Aurildis* or *Orieldis*, derived from *aus* 'fire' and *hildi* 'strife'; introduced into Britain by the Normans. It is sometimes associated with the English word *oriel* (from Old French *oriol* 'gallery'), denoting a type of bay window, or with the name of Oriel College in Oxford. The name was revived in the early 20th century and remains in occasional use. See also **Auriel**.

**Orlando** the Italian form of **Roland**. It has been in occasional use outside its country of origin since the 16th century, a famous bearer being the English composer Orlando Gibbons (1583–1625). The name occurs in a number of literary works, notably Ariosto's poem *Orlando Furioso* (see **Angelica**), Shakespeare's play *As You Like It*, and, more recently, Virginia Woolf's biographical fantasy *Orlando* (1928).

**Orrell** (m) from a surname and place name; ultimately from Old English, meaning 'ore hill'.

**Orson** (m) from French *ourson* 'bear cub'. The name occurs in the medieval tale of Valentine and Orson, twin brothers who are separated at an early age (Orson is carried off by a bear and reared in the forest). In modern times, however, the name is generally associated with the US actor and director Orson Welles; it remains in occasional use in the USA but is rarely found elsewhere.

**Orval** a variant of **Orville**.

**Orville** (m) probably from a French place name. A famous bearer was the US aviator Orville Wright (1871–1948), who designed and built (with his brother Wilbur) the first aircraft capable of controlled powered flight. Variant: **Orval**.

**Osbert** (m) from the Old English name *Osbeorht* (or its Old German equivalent), a compound of *os* 'god' and *beorht* 'bright'. The name remained in regular use in Britain until the end of the Middle Ages and enjoyed a partial revival in the 19th century. Famous bearers include the British writer Sir Osbert Sitwell (1892–1969) and the British cartoonist Sir Osbert Lancaster (born 1908).

**Osborn, Osborne** (m) from the Old English name *Osbeorn* (or its Old Norse equivalent), a compound of *os* 'god' and *beorn* 'man' (the second element of the Old Norse name means 'bear'). The name survived the Middle Ages as a surname, which was readopted as a first name in the 19th century and remains in occasional use today.

# Oscar

**Oscar** (m) from the Old English name *Osgar*, a compound of *os* 'god' and *gar* 'spear'. *Oscar* was little used in Britain from the time of the Norman Conquest until its revival in the 18th century, when the Scottish poet James Macpherson gave the name to the son of the Gaelic hero Ossian. It was subsequently borne by two 19th-century kings of Sweden and by the Irish poet and dramatist Oscar Wilde (1854–1900), whose trial and imprisonment for homosexuality caused the name to fall from favour towards the end of the century. The statuettes awarded annually by the Academy of Motion Picture Arts and Sciences are said to have been named after an Academy employee's Uncle Oscar.
Diminutives: **Ossie, Ossy**.

**Osmond** (m) from the Old English name *Osmund*, a compound of *os* 'god' and *mund* 'protection'. Borne in the 11th century by St Osmond (or Osmund), Bishop of Salisbury, the name remained in regular use in Britain until the end of the Middle Ages and enjoyed a partial revival in the 19th century. It is more familiar as a surname than as a first name in modern times.

**Osmund** see **Osmond**.

**Ossy, Ossie** diminutives of **Oscar** or any other name beginning with *Os-*.

**Oswald** (m) from the Old English name *Osweald*, a compound of *os* 'god' and *weald* 'power'. The name was borne by two saints: a 7th-century king of Northumbria, who may have given his name to the Shropshire town of Oswestry, and St Oswald of Worcester, Archbishop of York in the 10th century. *Oswald* remained in regular use after the end of the Middle Ages and is still found from time to time; the British fascist politician Sir Oswald Mosley (1896–1980) was a notorious bearer of the name.
Diminutives: **Ozzie, Ozzy**.

**Oswin** (m) an Old English name derived from *os* 'god' and *wine* 'friend'. The name was little used from the end of the Middle Ages until its partial revival in the 19th century; it is rarely found in modern times.

**Otho** [ōthō] see **Odo**.

**Otis** [ōtis] (m) from a surname derived from a medieval variant of **Odo**. It is in regular use as a first name in the USA but is rarely found in other parts of the English-speaking world.

**Ottilia** (f) from an Old German name meaning 'of the fatherland'; borne by the abbess St Ottilia (or Odilia), patron saint of Alsace, who died in the early 8th century.
Variants: **Odette, Odile, Ottilie**.

**Ottilie** a variant of **Ottilia**.

**Otto** a variant of **Odo**, borne by four Holy Roman emperors of the 10th and 13th centuries; in regular use in Britain during the Middle Ages. Now regarded as the modern German form of the name, *Otto* was revived throughout the English-speaking world in the 19th century in honour of the German statesman Prince Otto von Bismarck (1815–98), the Iron Chancellor. Its popularity declined during the 20th century, especially after World War II, but it remains in occasional use.

**Owen, Owain** variants of **Eugene** or **Ewan**, of Welsh origin. The name is frequently found in Welsh history and legend, two of its most famous bearers being the 12th-century prince Owen Gwynedd and the national hero Owen Glendower, who led a revolt against King Henry IV in the early 15th century. *Owen* has been in regular use in other parts of Britain and the English-speaking world since the 18th century.
Feminine form: **Owena**.

**Owena** the feminine form of **Owen**.

**Ozzy, Ozzie** diminutives of **Oswald** or any other name beginning with *Os-*.

# P

**Pablo** the Spanish form of **Paul**; in occasional use in English-speaking countries, especially the USA. The Spanish artist Pablo Picasso (1881–1973) was a famous bearer of the name.

**Paddy** a diminutive of **Patrick** or **Patricia**. *Paddy* is also used as a colloquial term for an Irishman or a term for a fit of temper.

**Padraig** an Irish variant of **Patrick**; rarely found outside its country of origin.

**Palmer** [*pah*mer] (m) from a surname meaning 'pilgrim'; in occasional use as a first name.

**Pam** a diminutive of **Pamela**.

**Pamela** [*pam*ĕlă] (f) invented by Sir Philip Sidney for one of the heroines of his prose romance *Arcadia*, first published in 1590. Some scholars believe the name to be derived from the Greek words for 'all' and 'honey'. Popularized by Samuel Richardson's immensely successful novel *Pamela* (1740), the name came into general use throughout the English-speaking world in the latter half of the 18th century; it was particularly fashionable in the mid-20th century.
Variant: **Pamelia**.
Diminutive: **Pam**.

**Pamelia** [pa*mee*liă] a variant of **Pamela**, influenced by an early pronunciation of the name [pa*mee*lă] and by the first name **Amelia**.

**Pandora** (f) from the Greek words for 'all' and 'gift'. The Pandora of Greek legend is said to have released all the evils of the world by opening 'Pandora's box'; hope, alone, remained inside when the lid was closed. The name is occasionally found in English-speaking countries but has never been common.

**Pansy** (f) from the flower name; in occasional use as a first name during the late 19th and early 20th centuries. Its lack of popularity in modern times may reflect its slang use for an effeminate male.

**Paolo** the Italian form of **Paul**; sometimes used in English-speaking countries, especially the USA.

**Parker** (m) from a surname meaning 'park keeper'; in occasional use as a first name since the 19th century.

**Parnel, Parnell** see **Petronilla**.

**Parry** (m) from a Welsh surname meaning 'son of **Harry**'.

**Parthenia** [par*thee*niă] (f) from Greek *parthenos* 'virgin'. The name is occasionally found in English-speaking countries but has never been common.

**Pascal** (m) from Old French, meaning 'of Easter'; ultimately from the Hebrew word for 'Passover'. The name has been in general use in Britain since the Middle Ages and enjoyed a slight revival in the latter half of the 20th century.
Variant: **Pascoe**.
Feminine form: **Pascale**.

**Pascale** the feminine form of **Pascal**.

**Pascoe** a variant of **Pascal**. The name has been in occasional use in Cornwall since the 16th century but is rarely found elsewhere.

**Pat** a diminutive of **Patrick** or **Patricia**.

**Patience** [*pay*shĕns] (f) from the English word *patience*; one of the many names of abstract qualities adopted by the Puritans after the Reformation. Borne by the heroine of Gilbert and Sullivan's opera of the same name, first performed in 1881, *Patience* is still given from time to time as a first name in Britain and other parts of the English-speaking world.

**Patricia** [pă*trish*ă] (f) from Latin *patricius* 'noble'; borne in the 7th century by St Patricia, one of the patron saints of Naples. The name was used only occasionally until the end of the 19th century, when it was popularized throughout the English-speaking world by Princess Patricia (born Victoria Patricia Helena Elizabeth), granddaughter of Queen Victoria. It was particularly fashionable in the mid-20th century.
Diminutives: **Paddy, Pat, Patsy, Patti, Pattie, Patty, Tricia, Trisha**.
Masculine equivalent: **Patrick**.

**Patrick** (m) from Latin *patricius* 'noble'. One of the earliest known bearers of the name was the British-born missionary St Patrick, patron saint of Ireland, who converted the inhabitants of that country to Christianity in the 5th century. *Patrick* was rarely used as a first name by the Irish, however, until the 17th century; it went on to become one of the most common masculine names in Ireland. The name was popular in Scotland and northern England during the Middle Ages and gradually spread to other parts of Britain; by the early 20th century it was in regular use throughout the English-speaking world.

Variant: **Padraig**.

Diminutives: **Paddy, Pat, Patsy**.

Feminine equivalent: **Patricia**.

**Patsy** a diminutive of **Patricia** or (rarely) **Patrick**, sometimes used as a name in its own right. It is not known whether the US slang term *patsy*, denoting a dupe, scapegoat, or butt of ridicule, is related to the first name.

**Patti, Patty, Pattie** diminutives of **Patricia** (*Pattie* and *Patty* are also diminutives of **Martha** or **Matilda**, having originated as rhyming variants of **Mattie**). *Patti* is often used as a name in its own right, especially in the USA and Canada.

**Paul** [pawl] (m) from Latin *paulus* 'small'. The apostle St Paul (formerly known as **Saul** of Tarsus), author of at least ten books of the New Testament, had been actively involved in the persecution of the Christians before his conversion at Damascus (Acts 9:3–19). The name was subsequently borne by a number of other saints, including the 6th-century Celtic monk St Paul Aurelian (or St Pol de Léon), who gave his name to a village in Cornwall and a town in Brittany. *Paul* was occasionally given as a first name during the Middle Ages, with the variant pronunciations [pōl] and [powl], but did not come into general use until the 17th century. It went on to become one of the most common masculine names in the English-speaking world, popularized in the latter half of the 20th century by the US actor Paul Newman, the British pop musician Paul McCartney, and other famous bearers from the world of entertainment.

Variants: **Pablo, Paolo**.

Feminine forms: **Paula, Paulette, Pauline**.

**Paula** a feminine form of **Paul**; borne by the Roman widow St Paula (347–404), a disciple of St Jerome, and by the heroine of Pinero's play *The Second Mrs Tanqueray* (1893). The name has been in regular use throughout the English-speaking world since the mid-20th century.

**Paulette** a feminine form of **Paul**, of French origin. The name was popularized in the English-speaking world by the US actress Paulette Goddard (born Marion Levy), whose screen career began in 1931.

**Pauline** [*paw*leen] a feminine form of **Paul**, of French origin. The name has been in regular use in English-speaking countries since the 19th century; it was particularly popular in Britain in the mid-20th century.

**Peace** (f) from the English word *peace*; one of the many names of abstract qualities adopted by the Puritans after the Reformation. It is rarely found in modern times.

# Pearl

**Pearl** (f) from the jewel name; in regular use as a first name since the latter half of the 19th century. The US novelist Pearl Buck (1892–1973) was a famous bearer of the name.
Diminutive: **Pearlie**.

**Pearlie** a diminutive of **Pearl**.

**Pedro** the Spanish form of **Peter**; in occasional use in English-speaking countries, especially the USA.

**Peggy, Peg** diminutives of **Margaret**, which originated as rhyming variants of **Meg**. *Peggy* was in frequent use as a name in its own right during the first half of the 20th century, a famous bearer being the British actress Dame Peggy Ashcroft.

**Pelham** [*pel*ăm] (m) from an aristocratic surname derived from a Hertfordshire place name. *Pelham* was the first name of the British-born writer P. G. Wodehouse (1881–1975), known to his friends as 'Plum'.

**Pen** a diminutive of **Penelope**.

**Penelope** [pĕ*nel*ŏpi] (f) a name of uncertain origin: possibly from Greek *pene* 'bobbin', though some scholars believe the name to be associated with a type of bird. In Homer's *Odyssey* Penelope was the faithful wife of Odysseus (see **Ulysses**), who rejected the advances of numerous suitors during her husband's long absence. The name has been in general use in English-speaking countries since the 16th century and enjoyed a slight revival in the latter half of the 20th century. The British actress Penelope Keith is a famous bearer of the name. In Ireland *Penelope* is sometimes used to translate the Gaelic name *Fionnghuala* (see **Fenella**).
Diminutives: **Pen, Penny**.

**Penny** a diminutive of **Penelope**, often used as a name in its own right in the latter half of the 20th century.

**Pepita** a feminine form of **Joseph**; from *Pepito*, a Spanish diminutive of the name.

**Perce** a diminutive of **Percival** or **Percy**.

**Percival, Perceval** [*pers*ivăl] (m) the name of one of King Arthur's knights of the Round Table, a participant in the quest for the Holy Grail; probably invented by the 12th-century French poet Chrétien de Troyes for his version of the Arthurian legend. *Parsifal*, a German variant of the name, is the title of Wagner's operatic account of the exploits of Sir Perceval (or Percival). The first name is generally interpreted as a compound of French *perce* 'pierce' and *val* 'valley'; the aristocratic surname may be derived from a French place name. First used in Britain in the 14th century, the name was fairly popular in the late 19th and early 20th centuries but is rarely found in modern times. See also **Percy**.
Diminutive: **Perçe**.

**Percy** (m) from an aristocratic surname introduced into Britain by William de Percy (or Perci), a companion of William the Conqueror; ultimately from the name of a village in Normandy. Originally confined to relatives of the Percy family, the first name was popularized by the poet Percy Bysshe Shelley (1792–1822) and subsequently came into more general use; it was particularly fashionable in the late 19th and early 20th centuries, when it was sometimes regarded as a diminutive of **Percival**.
Diminutive: **Perce**.

**Perdita** [*per*dită] (f) from the feminine form of Latin *perditus* 'lost'; adopted as a first name by Shakespeare for the heroine of his play *The Winter's Tale*. It is occasionally found in various parts of the English-speaking world but has never been common.

**Peregrine** [*per*rĕgrin] (m) from Latin *peregrinus* 'foreigner' or 'stranger'; generally interpreted as 'pilgrim' or 'traveller'. The name was borne by a Greek philosopher of the 2nd century and by a number of saints; it has been in occasional use in Britain since the 13th century but is rarely found in modern times.
Diminutive: **Perry**.

**Peronel** a variant of **Petronilla**, dating back to the Middle Ages.

**Perpetua** (f) from Latin *perpetuus* 'perpetual'. The name is used from time to time in Roman Catholic families, in honour of St Perpetua, who was martyred at Carthage in the early 3rd century.

**Perry** (m) either from a surname meaning 'pear tree' or from a medieval or foreign variant of **Peter**; also used as a diminutive of **Peregrine**. It was popularized in the 20th century by the fictional lawyer and detective Perry Mason (see also **Earl**) and by the US singer Perry Como.

**Peta** [*pee*tă] a feminine form of **Peter**.

**Pete** a diminutive of **Peter**.

**Peter** (m) from Greek *petros* 'stone' or *petra* 'rock'; a translation of the Aramaic name *Cephas*, which Jesus gave to his disciple Simon (John 1:42; Matthew 16:18). St Peter went on to become the leader of Christ's apostles and the first Bishop of Rome; more than a thousand English churches are dedicated to this early bearer of the name. In frequent use throughout the Christian world during the Middle Ages, the name was introduced into Britain by the Normans in the French form **Piers**, which gave rise to such surnames as *Pierce* and *Pearson*, and appeared in the Domesday Book of 1086 in the Latinized form *Petrus*. By the 16th century *Peter* had established itself as the usual form of the name in English-speaking countries. Having fallen temporarily from favour after the Reformation, through its association with the Roman Catholic Church, the name came back into fashion during the 20th century, reaching its peak of popularity in the 1950s. This sudden but sustained revival has been attributed to the lasting success of J. M. Barrie's play *Peter Pan*, first performed in 1904.

Variants: **Pedro, Pierre, Piers.**

Diminutive: **Pete.**

Feminine forms: **Peta, Petra, Petrina.**

**Petra, Petrina** feminine forms of **Peter.**

**Petronella** a variant of **Petronilla,** dating back to the Middle Ages.

**Petronilla** (f) from the Roman clan name *Petronius*; ultimately from Greek *petra* 'rock'. Borne in the 1st century by St Petronilla, who was traditionally believed to have been a daughter of St Peter, the name was fairly popular in Britain during the Middle Ages. Of its many medieval variants only **Peronel** and **Petronella** have survived; *Parnel* remained in occasional use as a first name until the 17th century but is more familiar as the surname *Parnell* in modern times.

Variants: **Peronel, Petronella.**

**Petula** [pĕ*tew*lǎ] (f) a name of uncertain origin; possibly from Latin *petere* 'to seek' or 'to attack' (the English word *petulant* is ultimately derived from this verb). The name was popularized in the latter half of the 20th century by the British singer and actress Petula Clark.

**Phebe** see **Phoebe.**

**Phemie** a diminutive of **Euphemia.**

**Phil** a diminutive of **Philip, Philippa,** or any other name beginning with *Phil-.*

**Philadelphia** (f) from Greek, meaning 'brotherly love'. *Philadelphia* was the name of an ancient city of Asia Minor, mentioned in the New Testament (Revelation 3:7); it was adopted as a first name by the Puritans and revived as a place name by William Penn, founder of the US city of Philadelphia.

**Philemon** [fi*lee*mon, fi*lee*mon] (m) from Greek, meaning 'kiss'. *Philemon* was adopted as a first name by the Puritans from the New Testament book of that name, one of the epistles of St Paul; it is rarely found in modern times.

**Philibert** see **Fulbert.**

**Philip, Phillip** (m) from Greek, meaning 'fond of horses'. The name was borne in the 4th century BC by King Philip of Macedon, father of Alexander the Great, and in the 1st century AD by St Philip, one of Jesus Christ's apostles. It was in frequent use in Britain during and after the Middle Ages but fell temporarily from favour in the latter half of the 16th century, when it was associated with King Philip II of Spain, who launched the Spanish Armada against England in 1588. The name was popularized in the mid-20th century by Queen Elizabeth II's husband

Prince Philip, Duke of Edinburgh, and remains in regular use throughout the English-speaking world.

Diminutives: **Phil, Pip.**

Feminine forms: **Philippa, Phillipa, Phillippa.**

**Philippa, Phillipa, Phillippa** feminine forms of **Philip**. Borne by Philippa of Hainault, wife of King Edward III, the name has been in regular use in Britain and other English-speaking countries for several hundred years, although its bearers were generally known by the masculine form of the name until the 19th century.

Diminutives: **Phil, Pippa.**

**Phillida** see **Phyllida**.

**Phillip** see **Philip**.

**Phillipa, Phillippa** see **Philippa**.

**Phillis** see **Phyllis**.

**Philomena** [filŏmeenă] (f) from Greek, meaning 'loved'. The name came into general use in the 19th century, when the supposed relics of an early Christian martyr, St Philomena, were discovered in Rome.

**Phineas, Phinehas** [finiăs] (m) a biblical name of uncertain origin; borne by one of the two sons of the Old Testament priest **Eli**. It was adopted as a first name in the 16th century and remained in regular use until the late 19th century; well-known bearers include the English poet Phineas Fletcher (1582–1650) and the US showman Phineas T. Barnum (1810–91).

**Phoebe, Phebe** [feebi] (f) from Greek, meaning 'the shining one'; one of the names by which the Greek goddess of the moon was known. Mentioned in the New Testament (Romans 16:1), *Phoebe* was adopted as a first name by the Puritans after the Reformation; it was fairly popular in the latter half of the 19th century and remains in occasional use today.

**Phyllida, Phillida** variants of **Phyllis**.

**Phyllis, Phillis** [filis] (f) from Greek, meaning 'leafy' or 'foliage' (the Phyllis of Greek legend was changed after her death into an almond tree, which bore no leaves until the return of her lover). The name was often given to country girls in classical poetry and in pastoral poems of the 17th century, such as Milton's *L'Allegro*; these rustic associations caused it to fall temporarily from favour as a first name. Revived in the late 19th century, *Phyllis* was popular throughout the English-speaking world during the first half of the 20th century. The British actress Phyllis Calvert is a famous bearer of the name. See also **Felice**.

Variants: **Phillida, Phyllida.**

**Pia** (f) from Latin *pius* 'pious'.

**Pierre** [pyair] the modern French form of **Peter**, in occasional use in English-speaking countries, especially the USA and Canada.

# Piers

**Piers** [peerz] a variant of **Peter**, of French origin. *Piers* was a common form of the name in medieval Britain; it was borne by the hero of William Langland's poem *Piers Plowman*, written in the 14th century. The name enjoyed a revival in the early 20th century and remains in regular use today.

**Pip** a diminutive of **Philip**; borne by the hero of Charles Dickens' novel *Great Expectations* (1860–61), whose full name was Philip Pirrip.

**Pippa** a diminutive of **Philippa**, made famous by Robert Browning's verse drama *Pippa Passes* (1841). It is sometimes given as a name in its own right.

**Piran** (m) a name of uncertain origin. The Celtic abbot St Piran was venerated in Cornwall as the patron saint of miners; *Perran*, a variant of his name, survives in a number of Cornish place names.

**Pleasance** (f) from an archaic word for 'pleasure'; ultimately from Old French *plaisance*. It has been in occasional use as a first name since the Middle Ages but is rarely found in modern times.

**Poldie** a diminutive of **Leopold**.

**Polly, Poll** diminutives of **Mary**, which originated as rhyming variants of **Molly**. *Polly* has been used as an independent name since the 18th century, when it was borne by the heroine of John Gay's *The Beggar's Opera* (1728); its frequent use as a name for parrots is of uncertain origin.

**Pollyanna** a compound of **Polly** and **Anna**, invented by the US writer Eleanor Porter for the optimistic young heroine of her novel *Pollyanna* (1913).

**Poppy** (f) from the flower name; in occasional use as a first name since the late 19th century.

**Portia** [*por*shǎ] (f) from *Porcia*, the feminine form of the Roman clan name *Porcius*, borne in the 1st century BC by the second wife of Marcus Junius Brutus. The name is generally associated with one of the heroines of Shakespeare's play *The Merchant of Venice*; it is sometimes given as a first name in various parts of the English-speaking world but has never been common.

**Preston** (m) from a surname and place name; ultimately from Old English, meaning 'priest's settlement'. It has been in occasional use as a first name since the 19th century.

**Primrose** (f) either from the flower name or from a Scottish surname. The latter was adopted as a first name in the 18th century and came into more frequent use in the late 19th century, when flower and plant names became fashionable.

**Prince** (m) from the English word *prince*. Its occasional use as a first name may be an adoption of the surname *Prince*, which was originally borne by members of a prince's household or given as a nickname to a person with princely airs.

Prisca see **Priscilla**.

**Priscilla** [prisi*lă*] (f) from Latin *priscus* 'former' or 'ancient'. Borne by a New Testament character (whose name sometimes appears in the form *Prisca*) and by the early Christian martyr St Priscilla (or Prisca), the name was adopted by the Puritans in the 17th century and remained in regular use until the latter half of the 20th century.
Diminutives: **Cilla, Prissy**.

**Prissy** a diminutive of **Priscilla**.

**Pru** see **Prue**.

**Prudence** [*proo*dĕns] (f) from the English word *prudence*. First used in the 13th century, *Prudence* was one of the many names of abstract qualities adopted or revived by the Puritans after the Reformation. It remains in occasional use in Britain and other parts of the English-speaking world.
Diminutives: **Pru, Prue**.

**Prue, Pru** diminutives of **Prudence**.

**Prunella** [proo*nelă*] (f) from Latin, meaning 'little plum'; made famous in the latter half of the 20th century by the British actress Prunella Scales.

# Q

**Queena** a variant of **Queenie**.

**Queenie, Queeny** (f) from the English word *queen*; used as a name in its own right or as a pet form of **Regina**. In the 19th century *Queenie* was sometimes given as a nickname to bearers of the name **Victoria**.
Variant: **Queena**.

**Quentin** a variant of **Quintin**; the usual form of the name in most English-speaking countries. The 3rd-century martyr St Quentin (or Quintinus) gave his name to a town in northern France, the scene of a decisive battle of World War I. The name was popularized in the 19th century by the hero of Sir Walter Scott's novel *Quentin Durward* (1823); its best-known bearer in modern times is the writer and self-publicist Quentin Crisp.

**Quincy** (m) from a surname derived from a French place name; ultimately from Latin *quintus* 'fifth'. The US president John Quincy Adams (1767–1848) was named after his mother's grandfather, John Quincy, who died in the year of Adams' birth.

**Quinn** (m) from an Irish surname, possibly meaning 'counsel'; in occasional use as a first name.

**Quintin** (m) from the Latin name *Quintinus*, derived from *quintus* 'fifth'; introduced into Britain at the time of the Norman Conquest. *Quintin* remains in occasional use in Scotland; in other parts of the English-speaking world **Quentin** is the more common form of the name. Famous

bearers include the 19th-century philanthropist Quintin Hogg and his grandson, the Conservative politician Lord Hailsham.
Variant: **Quentin**.

# R

**Rabbie, Rab** Scottish diminutives of **Robert**. *Rabbie* is the pet name of Scotland's best-known poet, Robert Burns (1759–96).

**Rachel, Rachael** [*ray*chĕl] (f) from Hebrew, meaning 'ewe'; borne in the Old Testament by Jacob's second and favourite wife (see **Leah**), the mother of Joseph and Benjamin. The use of *Rachel* as a first name was largely confined to Jewish families until the Reformation, when it was one of the many biblical names adopted by the Puritans; it enjoyed a further revival in the latter half of the 20th century.
Diminutive: **Rae**.

**Radcliff, Radcliffe** (m) from a surname and place name; ultimately from Old English, meaning 'red cliff'.

**Rae** a diminutive of **Rachel**, sometimes used as a name in its own right.

**Raelene** [*ray*leen] (f) a compound of **Rae** and the feminine name element *-lene*. It has been in regular use in Australia since the mid-20th century but is rarely found in other English-speaking countries.

**Rafael** see **Raphael**.

**Rafaela** see **Raphaela**.

**Rafe** a variant of **Ralph** that was in regular use in 17th-century Britain and is still found from time to time. The spelling of the name reflects the alternative pronunciation of *Ralph*, which may date back to the Middle Ages.

**Raina, Raine** [*ray*nă] (f) a name of uncertain origin: it may be from the French name *Reine*, meaning 'queen', or it may simply be a feminine form of **Rayner**. The name has been in occasional use in various parts of the English-speaking world since the mid-20th century.

**Rainer** see **Rayner**.

**Ralph** [ralf, rayf] (m) from the Old English name *Raedwulf* (or its Old Norse equivalent), a compound of *raed* 'counsel' and *wulf* 'wolf'. *Radulf* and *Rauf* were two of the many medieval forms of the name; the variant *Ralf* appeared in the 16th century and the modern spelling *Ralph* in the 18th century. The name remains in regular use throughout the English-speaking world; famous bearers include the US philosopher Ralph Waldo Emerson (1803–82) and the British actor Sir Ralph Richardson (1902–83).
Variants: **Rafe, Raoul**.

**Ramon** a variant of **Raymond**, of Spanish origin; in occasional use in English-speaking countries, especially the USA.
Feminine form: **Ramona**.

**Ramona** [rămōnă] the feminine form of **Ramon**; made famous by the US writer Helen Hunt Jackson's novel *Ramona* (1884), which dealt with the plight of the American Indians.

**Ramsay, Ramsey** [*ram*zi] (m) from a surname and place name; ultimately from the Old English words for 'wild garlic' or 'ram' and 'island'. The name was popularized in the early 20th century by the British statesman Ramsay MacDonald (1866–1937), the first Labour prime minister, and remains in occasional use today.

**Ranald** (m) a Scottish form of the Old Norse equivalent of **Reginald** (see also **Ronald**); rarely found outside its country of origin.
Related names: **Reginald, Reynold, Ronald**.

**Randall, Randal** (m) from the Old English name *Randwulf*, a compound of *rand* 'shield' and *wulf* 'wolf'. *Randal*, one of the most common forms of the name in medieval Britain, gave rise to such surnames as *Rankin* and *Ransom*; it was readopted as a first name in the 19th century, together with the variant spelling *Randall*, and became particularly popular in the USA and Canada.
Variant: **Randolph**.
Diminutive: **Randy**.

**Randolph** from *Randulfus*, a Latinized form of *Randal* (see **Randall**) that occurred in the Domesday Book of 1086 and other medieval documents. *Randolph* has been in general use since the 18th century; famous bearers of the name include the two Randolph Churchills, father and son of Sir Winston Churchill, and the US actor Randolph Scott.
Diminutive: **Randy**.

**Randy** a diminutive of **Miranda, Randall**, or **Randolph**. *Randy* is rarely found as a name in its own right outside the USA; in Britain its slang use to describe someone who is sexually aroused precludes its use as a first name, although it may be given as a nickname.

**Raoul** [rowl] the French form of **Ralph**. First used in Britain during the Middle Ages, the name was reintroduced into the English-speaking world in the 20th century.

**Raphael, Rafael** [*ra*fayĕl] (m) from Hebrew, meaning 'God heals'; the name of one of the archangels, mentioned in the Apocrypha. The use of *Raphael* as a first name was largely confined to Jewish families until the 16th century; it has never been common in the English-speaking world. The Italian painter Raphael (born Raffaello Santi or Sanzio), one of the greatest artists of the Renaissance, was a famous bearer of the name.
Feminine forms: **Raphaela, Rafaela**.

**Raphaela, Rafaela** feminine forms of **Raphael**.

**Ray** a diminutive of **Raymond**, often used as a name in its own right.

**Raymond, Raymund** (m) from an Old German name derived from *ragan* 'counsel' or 'might' and *mund* 'protection'; introduced into Britain at the time of the Norman Conquest. The name was borne by the 13th-century Spanish friar St Raymond and by a number of counts of Barcelona and Toulouse but was rarely used in the English-speaking world until the 19th century. It became very popular during the first half of the 20th century and remains in regular use today.
Variant: **Ramon**.
Diminutive: **Ray**.
Feminine form: **Raymonde**.

**Raymonde** the feminine form of **Raymond**.

**Raymund** see **Raymond**.

**Rayner, Raynor** (m) from an Old German name derived from *ragan* 'counsel' or 'might' and *harja* 'army'. The name was introduced into Britain at the time of the Norman Conquest and remained in regular use until the 14th century; it survived the Middle Ages as a surname, which was re-adopted as a first name in the 19th century. The German poet Rainer Rilke (1875–1926) was a famous bearer of the name in its modern German form.
Feminine forms: **Raina, Raine**.

**Rebecca, Rebekah** [rĕbekǎ] (f) from Hebrew, possibly meaning 'knotted cord'. Borne in the Old Testament by Isaac's wife, the mother of Esau and Jacob, the name was adopted by the Puritans after the Reformation and was very popular in the 17th century. Its revival in the latter half of the 20th century has been attributed to the immense success of Daphne du Maurier's novel *Rebecca* (1938), filmed (under the direction of Alfred Hitchcock) in 1940. Other famous bearers of the name in the literary world include the heroine of Thackeray's *Vanity Fair* (see **Becky**) and the 20th-century British writer Dame Rebecca West (born Cicily Isabel Fairfield).
Diminutive: **Becky**.

**Redvers** (m) from an aristocratic surname; popularized as a first name in the late 19th century by the British general Sir Redvers Buller (1839–1908).

**Reg** [rej], **Reggie** [*rej*i] diminutives of **Reginald**.

**Regina** [rĕjīnǎ] (f) from Latin, meaning 'queen'; adopted as a first name during the Middle Ages. The name was revived in the 19th century, during the reign of Queen Victoria, and remains in occasional use today. See also **Queenie**.
Masculine equivalent: **Rex**.

**Reginald** [*rej*inăld] (m) from the Old English name *Regenweald*, a compound of *regen* 'counsel' or 'might' and *weald* 'power', which was largely superseded in medieval Britain by **Reynold** (in official documents *Reynold* sometimes appeared in the Latinized form *Reginaldus*). *Reginald* came into general use in the 15th century and enjoyed a revival in the 19th century; it was particularly popular in Britain in the first half of the 20th century.
Diminutives: **Reg, Reggie, Rex**.
Related names: **Ranald, Reynold, Ronald**.

**Reine** see **Raina**.

**Rena, Rina** diminutives of any name ending in *-rena* or *-rina*, such as **Serena** or **Marina**; often used as independent names.

**Renata** [rĕ*nah*tă] (f) from Latin *renatus* 'reborn'; in occasional use throughout the English-speaking world since the 17th century.
Related names: **René, Renée**.

**Rene** [*ree*ni] see **Renie**.

**René** [*ren*ay] (m) a French name, meaning 'reborn'; ultimately from Latin *renatus*. The name was borne in the 17th century by the French missionary St René Goupil, who was martyred in North America by the Iroquois; it is sometimes found in English-speaking countries but has never been common.
Feminine form: **Renée**.
Related name: **Renata**.

**Renée** [*ren*ay] the feminine form of **René**; sometimes confused with **Renie**. It has been in regular use in various parts of the English-speaking world since the early 20th century.
Related name: **Renata**.

**Renie, Rene** [*ree*ni] diminutives of **Irene**, sometimes used as independent names. See also **Renée**.

**Reuben** [*roo*bĕn] (m) from Hebrew, meaning 'behold, a son'; borne in the Old Testament by the eldest son of Jacob. The name has been in general use in English-speaking countries since the 17th century.

**Rex** (m) from Latin *rex* 'king'; adopted as a first name at the end of the 19th century. It is sometimes used as a diminutive of **Reginald**, the British actor Rex Harrison (born Reginald Carey Harrison) being a famous example.
Feminine equivalent: **Regina**.

**Reynard** [*ren*ard, *ray*nard] (m) from an Old German name derived from *ragan* 'counsel' or 'might' and *hardu* 'hard'; introduced into Britain by the Normans. It is generally associated with the medieval stories of Reynard the Fox and is rarely given as a first name.

**Reynold** [*ren*ŏld] (m) from *Reinald* or *Reynaud*, French forms of the Old German equivalent of **Reginald**, which were introduced into Britain at the time of the Norman Conquest. *Reynold* remained in frequent use until the end of the 15th century but is more familiar in modern times as the surname *Reynolds* (meaning 'son of Reynold').
Related names: **Ranald, Reginald, Ronald.**

**Rhea** [*reeă*] (f) the name of the mother of Zeus in Greek mythology; occasionally given as a first name in English-speaking countries. See also **Ria**.

**Rhiannon** [ri*an*ŏn] (f) a Welsh name, meaning 'nymph' or 'goddess'.

**Rhoda** (f) from Greek *rhodon* 'rose'. Mentioned in the New Testament (Acts 12:13), *Rhoda* has been in general use as a first name throughout the English-speaking world since the 17th century.

**Rhona** (f) a name of uncertain origin; possibly a variant of **Rhonwen** or an alternative spelling of **Rona**. It has been in regular use in Britain, especially Scotland, since the late 19th century.

**Rhonda** (f) a name of uncertain origin; possibly from the Welsh place name *Rhondda*. It was popularized throughout the English-speaking world in the mid-20th century by the US actress Rhonda Fleming.

**Rhonwen** (f) from two Welsh words meaning 'lance' (generally interpreted as 'slender') and 'fair'. This form of the name is rarely found outside Wales.
Variants: **Rhona, Rowena.**

**Rhys** [rees] (m) a Welsh name, possibly meaning 'ardour' or 'rashness'. The name was borne by two medieval Welsh lords, Rhys ap Tewdwr and his grandson Rhys ap Gruffudd; it gave rise to a number of surnames, such as *Rees*, *Reece*, *Rice*, and *Price* (from Welsh *ap Rhys* 'son of Rhys'). *Rhys* remains in regular use as a first name in Wales but is rarely found in other parts of the English-speaking world.

**Ria** [*reeă*] a diminutive of any name ending in *-ria*, such as **Maria** or **Victoria**. Its adoption as an independent name may have been influenced by **Rhea**.

**Rica, Rika** [*reekă*] Scandinavian diminutives of **Erica**, sometimes used as independent names in the English-speaking world.

**Ricarda** a feminine form of **Richard**.

**Ricardo** the Spanish form of **Richard**; in occasional use in English-speaking countries, especially the USA.

**Rich** a diminutive of **Richard**, dating back to the Middle Ages.

**Richard** (m) from the Old German name *Ricohard*, derived from *ric* 'ruler' and *hardu* 'hard'; introduced into Britain at the time of the Norman Conquest. *Richard* and its variant *Ricard* were very popular during the Middle Ages; their many diminutives gave rise to a wide range of surnames, such as *Dixon* (from **Dick**) and *Hitchcock* (from *Hitch*, an obsolete rhym-

ing variant of **Rich**). Famous medieval bearers of the name include King Richard I (1157–99), better known as Richard the Lionheart, and St Richard of Wyche, Bishop of Chichester in the 13th century. The name was subsequently borne by two other kings of England, whose notoriety does not appear to have affected its popularity: in the 20th century *Richard* was still one of the most common masculine names in the English-speaking world.
Variant: **Ricardo**.
Diminutives: **Dick, Dickie, Dicky, Dickon, Rich, Richie, Rick, Ricky**.
Feminine forms: **Ricarda, Richenda, Richmal**.

**Richenda** a feminine form of **Richard**.

**Richie** a diminutive of **Richard**.

**Richmal** (f) a name of uncertain origin; generally regarded as a feminine form of **Richard**. Its best-known bearer is the British children's writer Richmal Crompton (1890–1969), author of *Just William* and its many sequels.

**Rick** a diminutive of **Derek, Eric,** or **Richard**, sometimes used as a name in its own right.

**Ricki, Rikki** diminutives of **Erica, Ricarda,** or any other feminine name beginning with *Ric-* or ending in *-rica*; sometimes used as independent names.

**Ricky** a diminutive of **Derek, Eric,** or **Richard**, sometimes used as a name in its own right.

**Rika** see **Rica**.

**Rikki** see **Ricki**.

**Rina** see **Rena**.

**Rita** [*reetă*] a variant of **Margaret**; originally an Italian or Spanish diminutive of the name. In regular use in English-speaking countries since the early 20th century, it was further popularized in the 1940s by the US actress Rita Hayworth.

**Roald** [*rŏăld*] (m) a Scandinavian name, publicized in the English-speaking world by the British writer Roald Dahl (born in 1916 of Norwegian parents). Another famous bearer of the name was the Norwegian explorer Roald Amundsen (1872–1928).

**Rob, Robbie** diminutives of **Robert** or **Robin**, sometimes used as independent names. The Scottish outlaw Rob **Roy** (1671–1734), hero of Sir Walter Scott's novel of that name, was born Robert Macgregor.

**Robert** (m) from the Old German name *Hrodebert*, derived from *hrothi* 'fame' and *berhta* 'bright'. The name was introduced into Britain at the time of the Norman Conquest, replacing its Old English equivalent *Hreodbeorht*, and was popularized in Scotland by the national hero Robert the **Bruce**. Its many medieval diminutives gave rise to such surnames as

# Roberta

*Dobson* (from *Dob*, an obsolete rhyming variant of **Rob**), *Hopkins* (see **Hob**), and *Robinson*. *Robert* remains one of the most common masculine names in the English-speaking world, a position it has held for several hundred years.

Variant: **Robin**.

Diminutives: **Bob, Bobbie, Bobby, Hob, Rab, Rabbie, Rob, Robbie**.

Feminine form: **Roberta**.

Related name: **Rupert**.

**Roberta** the feminine form of **Robert**.

Diminutive: **Bobbie**.

**Robin** a variant of **Robert**; originally a medieval diminutive of the name. The two most famous bearers of the name are both legendary characters: the mischievous sprite Robin Goodfellow, also known as Puck, and the outlaw Robin Hood. The use of *robin* as a bird name dates back at least to the 16th century.

Diminutives: **Hob, Rob, Robbie**.

Feminine forms: **Robina, Robyn**.

**Robina, Robyn** feminine forms of **Robin**.

**Rochelle** (f) possibly from *La Rochelle*, the name of a port on the west coast of France; ultimately from French *roche* 'rock'. It has been in occasional use as a first name, especially in the USA, since the mid-20th century.

**Rod, Roddy** diminutives of **Roderick** or **Rodney**, sometimes used as independent names. Famous bearers include the US actor Rod Steiger and the British actor and former child star Roddy McDowall.

**Roderick** (m) from the Old German name *Hrodric*, derived from *hrothi* 'fame' and *ricja* 'rule'. *Roderick* was formerly regarded as a Scottish name: it was borne by the hero of the Scottish writer Tobias Smollett's novel *Roderick Random* (1748) and was used in Scotland to translate the Gaelic name from which **Rory** is derived. The name is now found throughout the English-speaking world but has never been common.

Variant: **Rodrigo**.

Diminutives: **Rod, Roddy**.

**Rodge** a diminutive of **Roger**.

**Rodger** see **Roger**.

**Rodney** (m) from a surname and Somerset place name; adopted as a first name in honour of the British admiral Lord Rodney (1719–92). It has been in regular use throughout the English-speaking world since the mid-19th century.

Diminutives: **Rod, Roddy**.

**Rodolph** a variant of **Rudolph**.

**Rodrigo** the Spanish form of **Roderick**; occasionally found in English-speaking countries. The 11th-century Spanish hero Rodrigo Diaz, better known as El Cid or El Campeador, was a famous bearer of the name.

**Roger, Rodger** [*roj*er] (m) from the Old English name *Hrothgar* or its Old German equivalent *Hrodgar*, derived from the words for 'fame' and 'spear'. The French form *Roger* was introduced into Britain at the time of the Norman Conquest and soon became very common; its rhyming diminutives *Dodge* and *Hodge*, now obsolete, gave rise to such surnames as *Dodgson* and *Hodgkin*. The name began to fall from favour in the 16th century and did not come back into fashion until the late 19th century; it was particularly popular in the mid-20th century. From its use in signalling to represent the letter *R*, hence '(message) received', the name has entered the English language as a colloquial expression of agreement. It also occurs in the name of the traditional pirate flag, the Jolly Roger.

Diminutive: **Rodge**.

**Roisin** an Irish variant of **Rose**.

**Roland, Rowland** [*rō*länd] (m) from the Old German name *Hrodland*, derived from *hrothi* 'fame' and *landa* 'land'. The name was borne by one of Charlemagne's paladins, hero of the *Chanson de Roland*, an Old French epic poem of the Middle Ages; it was introduced into Britain at the time of the Norman Conquest. Until the 19th century *Rowland* was the usual spelling of the name; Sir Rowland Hill (1795–1879), who reformed the British postal service and invented the postage stamp, was a famous bearer. The French form *Roland* was readopted in the 18th century; by the 20th century it was in regular use throughout the English-speaking world.

Variant: **Orlando**.

Diminutives: **Rolly, Roly**.

**Rolf, Rolph** (m) from the Old German name *Hrodulf* or its Old Norse equivalent, derived from the words for 'fame' and 'wolf'. The name was introduced into Britain by the Normans and enjoyed a partial revival in the 19th century, but it has never been common in the English-speaking world. The best-known bearer of the name in modern times is the Australian entertainer Rolf Harris.

Variant: **Rollo**.

Related name: **Rudolph**.

**Rollo** [*rolō*] a variant of **Rolf**. The Viking founder of Normandy, who died in the 10th century, was an early bearer of the name.

# Rolly

**Rolly** a diminutive of **Roland**.

**Rolph** see **Rolf**.

**Roly** a diminutive of **Roland**.

**Roma** (f) from the Latin or Italian name for Rome, capital of Italy; in occasional use as a first name since the 19th century.

**Romaine** (f) from French, meaning 'woman of Rome'.

**Ron** a diminutive of **Ronald**.

**Rona** (f) a name of uncertain origin; it may be from a Scottish place name (Rona is an island near Skye) or it may simply be an alternative spelling of **Rhona**. The name has been in occasional use in Scotland and other parts of the English-speaking world since the late 19th century.

**Ronald** (m) a Scottish form of the Old Norse equivalent of **Reginald** (see also **Ranald**); in regular use throughout the English-speaking world since the late 19th century. Famous bearers of the name include the British actor Ronald Colman and the US president Ronald Reagan.
Diminutives: **Ron, Ronnie**.
Feminine forms: **Ronalda, Ronna, Ronnette**.
Related names: **Ranald, Reginald, Reynold**.

**Ronalda, Ronna, Ronnette** feminine forms of **Ronald**.

**Ronnie** a diminutive of **Ronald**, sometimes used as a name in its own right.

**Rory** (m) from a Gaelic name meaning 'red' (see also **Roderick**). The Irish king Rory O'Connor, who reigned in the latter half of the 12th century, was an early bearer of the name. *Rory* has been in regular use in Scotland and Ireland for several hundred years but is rarely found in other parts of the English-speaking world.

**Ros** [roz] a diminutive of **Rosalind, Rosamund**, or any other feminine name beginning with *Ros-* [roz].

**Rosa** the Latinized form of **Rose**. *Rosa* occurs in official documents of the Middle Ages, referring to bearers of the name *Rose*, but it was not used as an independent name until the 19th century.

**Rosabel, Rosabelle, Rosabella** variants of **Rose**, influenced by other names ending in *-bel*, *-belle*, or *-bella* (French and Italian words for 'beautiful').

**Rosaleen** a variant or diminutive of **Rose**, of Irish origin.

**Rosalia** [rōzayliă] (f) from Latin *rosa* 'rose'. The name was borne in the 12th century by St Rosalia, patron saint of Palermo; it is occasionally found in English-speaking countries but is more familiar in the French form **Rosalie**.
Variant: **Rosalie**.

**Rosalie** [rozăli, rōzăli] a variant of **Rosalia**, of French origin. It has been in regular use throughout the English-speaking world since the mid-19th

Rose

century and was popularized in the 1930s by the Hollywood musical of the same name, starring Nelson Eddy.

**Rosalind** [*roză*lind] (f) from the Old German name *Roslindis*, derived from *hros* 'horse' and *lindi* 'snake', or its Spanish form *Rosalinda*, meaning 'pretty rose' (the latter interpretation is preferred by most bearers of the name). *Rosalind* came into general use in the English-speaking world in the late 16th century; the name occurs in three literary works of that period: Edmund Spenser's *Shepheardes Calendar*, Thomas Lodge's prose romance *Rosalynde*, and Shakespeare's play *As You Like It* (based on Lodge's *Rosalynde*). It enjoyed a revival in the latter half of the 19th century and was further popularized in the 20th century by the US actress Rosalind Russell.
Variant: **Rosaline.**
Diminutive: **Ros.**

**Rosalinda** see **Rosalind.**

**Rosaline** [*roză*lin, *roză*līn] a variant of **Rosalind.** *Rosaline* occurs in two of Shakespeare's plays, *Love's Labour's Lost* and *Romeo and Juliet*; it is occasionally given as a first name in various parts of the English-speaking world.
Variants: **Rosalyn, Roseline, Roselyn, Roslyn.**

**Rosalyn** a variant of **Rosaline.**

**Rosamund, Rosamond** [*roză*mŭnd] (f) from Old German *hros* 'horse' and *munda* 'protection'; generally associated with Latin *rosa munda* 'pure rose' or *rosa mundi* 'rose of the world'. The name was introduced into Britain at the time of the Norman Conquest and has been in regular use throughout the English-speaking world since then; a famous medieval bearer was Henry II's mistress Rosamond Clifford, known as 'Fair Rosamond', who is traditionally believed to have been poisoned by the jealous Queen Eleanor of Aquitaine.
Diminutive: **Ros.**

**Rosanna, Roseanna** compounds of **Rose** and **Anna**; first used in the 18th century.

**Rosanne, Roseann, Roseanne** compounds of **Rose** and **Ann**; in occasional use since the 19th century.

**Rose** (f) from an Old German name derived from *hros* 'horse' or *hrothi* 'fame'; generally associated with the flower name (from Latin *rosa* 'rose'). It was introduced into Britain at the time of the Norman Conquest: the surname *Royce* is derived from one of the many medieval variants of the name. *Rose* was particularly popular in the late 19th and early 20th centuries, when the fashion for flower and plant names was at its height; it remains in occasional use throughout the English-speaking world.
Variants: **Roisin, Rosa, Rosabel, Rosabella, Rosabelle, Rosaleen, Rosetta, Rosina, Rosita.**

201

# Roseann

Diminutive: **Rosie**.

**Roseann** see **Rosanne**.

**Roseanna** see **Rosanna**.

**Roseanne** see **Rosanne**.

**Roseline, Roselyn** variants of **Rosaline**.

**Rosemarie** [rōzmă*ree*] the French form of **Rosemary**. It has been in occasional use in English-speaking countries since the 1920s, when it was popularized by the musical *Rose Marie*.

**Rosemary** [*rōz*mări] (f) from the plant name, derived from Latin *ros* 'dew' and *marinus* 'of the sea'; sometimes regarded as a compound of **Rose** and **Mary**. It came into general use as a first name in the late 19th century and was particularly popular in the mid-20th century.
Variant: **Rosemarie**.
Diminutive: **Rosie**.

**Rosetta** [rō*zet*ă] a variant of **Rose**; originally an Italian diminutive of the name. It has been in occasional use in English-speaking countries since the 18th century. The Rosetta Stone, which has assisted scholars in the interpretation of hieroglyphics, is named after the Egyptian town of Rosetta (or Rashid), near Alexandria.

**Rosie** [*rō*zi] a diminutive of **Rose**, **Rosemary**, or any other feminine name beginning with *Ros-* [rōz]; sometimes used as a name in its own right. The English writer Laurie Lee gave the name to the heroine of his novel *Cider with Rosie* (1959).

**Rosina** [rō*zeen*ă] a variant of **Rose**; originally an Italian diminutive of the name.

**Rosita** [rō*zeet*ă] a variant of **Rose**; originally a Spanish diminutive of the name.

**Roslyn** a variant of **Rosaline**.
Variant: **Rosslyn**.

**Ross** (m) from a surname and place name; ultimately from Scottish Gaelic, meaning 'promontory'. It has been in regular use as a first name since the 19th century.
Feminine form: **Rosslyn**.

**Rosslyn** (f) a name of uncertain origin; sometimes regarded as a variant of **Roslyn** or a feminine form of **Ross**. It has been in occasional use in Scotland since the early 20th century but is rarely found in other parts of the English-speaking world.

**Rowan** (m) either from the tree name (an alternative name for the mountain ash) or from Gaelic *ruadh* 'red'. It has been in occasional use as a first name since the mid-20th century and was popularized in the 1970s and 1980s by the comic actor Rowan Atkinson.

**Rowena** [rōeenă] probably a variant of **Rhonwen**, though some scholars believe the name to be of Old English origin. It was popularized in the 19th century by the heroine of Sir Walter Scott's novel *Ivanhoe* (1819) and remains in regular use today.

**Rowland** see **Roland**.

**Roxana** [roksahnă] (f) probably from Persian, meaning 'dawn'; borne in the 4th century BC by one of the wives of Alexander the Great. *Roxana* is also the title of a novel by Daniel Defoe, published in 1724; it is occasionally given as a first name in English-speaking countries, especially the USA.
Variants: **Roxane, Roxanna, Roxanne**.
Diminutive: **Roxy**.

**Roxane, Roxanne, Roxanna** variants of **Roxana**.
Diminutive: **Roxy**.

**Roxy** a diminutive of **Roxana** or any of its variant forms.

**Roy** (m) from Gaelic *ruadh* 'red' (a reference to the colour of the bearer's hair or complexion, the red-haired Scottish outlaw **Rob** Roy being a famous example). The frequent use of the name outside Scotland and Ireland has been attributed to its association with French *roi* 'king'; it was popular throughout the English-speaking world in the first half of the 20th century.

**Royal** (m) either from the English word *royal* or from a surname meaning 'rye hill'; in occasional use as a first name, especially in the USA.

**Royston** (m) from a surname and place name of uncertain origin; in regular use as a first name since the early 20th century.

**Rubina** a variant of **Ruby**, possibly influenced by **Reuben** or **Robina**.

**Ruby** (f) from the name of the precious stone; one of a number of jewel names that became fashionable in the 19th century. The US singer and dancer Ruby Keeler (born Ethel Keeler) publicized the name in the 1930s.
Variant: **Rubina**.

**Rudi** see **Rudy**.

**Rudolf** see **Rudolph**.

**Rudolph** [roodolf] (m) from *Rudolf*, the modern German form of *Hrodulf* (see **Rolf**). The name was rarely used in the English-speaking world until the 19th century, when it was borne by the central character of Anthony Hope's novel *The Prisoner of Zenda* (1894). It was further popularized in the early 20th century by the Italian-born US film star Rudolph (or Rudolf) Valentino (1895–1926) and remains in occasional use today. Other famous bearers of the name include the Russian-born ballet dancer Rudolf Nureyev and the hero of the children's Christmas song 'Rudolph, the Red-nosed Reindeer'.

# Rudy

Variant: **Rodolph**.
Diminutives: **Rudi**, **Rudy**.
Related name: **Rolf**.

**Rudy, Rudi** diminutives of **Rudolph**, sometimes used as independent names. The US singer and comedian Rudy Vallee (born Hubert Vallee) publicized the name in the first half of the 20th century.

**Rufus** [*roofŭs*] (m) from Latin, meaning 'red'. *Rufus* is the name by which King William II of England has been known throughout history: some scholars attribute the nickname to the colour of his complexion, others to the colour of his hair. The name is occasionally found in various parts of the English-speaking world but has never been common.

**Rupert** [*roopert*] (m) from *Rupprecht*, the modern German form of *Hrodebert* (see **Robert**); introduced into Britain in the 17th century by Prince Rupert of the Rhine, nephew of King Charles I. *Rupert* was further popularized by Anthony Hope's novel *Rupert of Hentzau* (1898) and, during World War I, by the British poet Rupert Brooke (1887–1915); it is probably more familiar to modern children as the name of a famous cartoon bear.

Feminine form: **Ruperta**.

**Ruperta** the feminine form of **Rupert**.

**Russ** a diminutive of **Russell**, sometimes used as a name in its own right. It was publicized in the 1950s and 1960s by the popular pianist Russ Conway (born Trevor Stanford).

**Russell, Russel** (m) from a surname derived from Old French *roux* 'red'; originally a nickname given to a person with red hair or a ruddy complexion. Adopted as a first name in the 19th century, *Russell* was particularly popular in the latter half of the 20th century.

Diminutive: **Russ**.

**Ruth** [*rooth*] (f) a biblical name of uncertain origin; possibly meaning 'companion' or 'vision of beauty'. (There is no etymological connection between the archaic English noun *ruth*, meaning 'compassion' or 'remorse', and the first name.) The Old Testament book of Ruth tells the story of Ruth the Moabitess, the faithful daughter-in-law of Naomi and great grandmother of King David. The name was adopted by the Puritans after the Reformation and has been in regular use throughout the English-speaking world since then.

Diminutive: **Ruthie**.

**Ruthie** a diminutive of **Ruth**.

**Ryan** [*rīăn*] (m) from an Irish surname of uncertain origin; in occasional use as a first name in Britain and the USA since the mid-20th century. The US actor Ryan O'Neal popularized the name in the 1970s.

# S

**Sabina** [săbeenă] (f) from Latin *Sabinus* 'Sabine' (the Sabines were members of a tribe living near ancient Rome). Borne by the early Roman martyr St Sabina, the name is occasionally found in English-speaking countries but has never been common.

**Sabrina** [săbreenă] (f) from the Roman name for the River Severn. According to legend, Sabrina was the illegitimate daughter of King Locrine of Britain, drowned in the River Severn by her father's ex-wife. Milton made use of this legend in his masque *Comus* (1634); *Sabrina Fair*, the title of a play by the 20th-century US dramatist Samuel Taylor, is a quotation from Milton's work. The name is used from time to time in various parts of the English-speaking world, especially the USA.

**Sacha** [*sash*ă] a variant of **Alexander**; originally a Russian diminutive of the name. It was popularized by the French film director and actor Sacha Guitry (1885–1957) and in the 1960s by the French singer Sacha Distel.

**Sacheverell** [săsheverěl] (m) from a surname of uncertain origin; possibly from a French place name or nickname. Its occasional use as a first name in the 18th century has been attributed to the renown of the political preacher Henry Sacheverell. The best-known bearer of the name in modern times is the British writer Sacheverell Sitwell (the Sitwell family are believed to have adopted the name in honour of the 17th-century Whig politician William Sacheverell).

**Sadie** [*say*di] a diminutive of **Mercedes** or **Sarah**, in regular use as an independent name since the 19th century.

**Saffron** (f) from the name of a type of crocus or the orange spice obtained from its flowers; in occasional use as a first name in the latter half of the 20th century.

**Sal** a diminutive of **Sally** or **Sarah**.

**Salamon** see **Solomon**.

**Salena, Salina** variants of **Sally** or **Selina**.

**Sally** a diminutive of **Sarah**, often given as a name in its own right. The phrase *Aunt Sally* (from the target of the fairground game) is used to denote a target of criticism or attack.
Variants: **Salena, Salina**.
Diminutive: **Sal**.

**Salome** [sălōmi] (f) from Hebrew *shalom* 'peace'. The name is generally associated with the granddaughter of Herod the Great; according to the New Testament story, in which her name is not mentioned, Salome danced for her stepfather Herod Antipas at his birthday feast and was prompted by her mother Herodias to ask for the head of John the Baptist

as a reward (Matthew 14:6–8). *Salome* has been in occasional use as a first name in the English-speaking world since the 17th century.
Related name: **Solomon**.

**Salvador** see **Salvatore**.

**Salvatore** (m) an Italian name, derived from Latin *salvator* 'saviour'; occasionally found in English-speaking countries, especially the USA. Its Spanish equivalent *Salvador*, borne by the surrealist painter Salvador Dali, is also used from time to time.

**Sam** a diminutive of **Samson**, **Samuel**, or **Samantha**, sometimes used as a name in its own right. *Uncle Sam*, a nickname for the USA, its government, or its people, is probably derived from the abbreviation *US*.

**Samantha** [săman̄thă] (f) a name of uncertain origin, possibly from a Hebrew word meaning 'hear' or 'listen'. The use of the name in the USA dates back at least to the 18th century. Its sudden increase in popularity throughout the English-speaking world in the latter half of the 20th century has been attributed to a number of possible sources, notably the US television series *Bewitched* (1964–71), the heroine of which was an attractive young witch called Samantha.
Diminutives: **Sam**, **Sammy**.

**Sammy** a diminutive of **Samson**, **Samuel**, or **Samantha**, sometimes used as a name in its own right.

**Samson, Sampson** (m) from Hebrew, meaning 'sun child'. The Samson of the Old Testament, leader of the Israelites, made use of his great strength to fight the Philistines and destroy their rulers (Judges 15–16). One of the earliest known bearers of the name in the English-speaking world was the 6th-century bishop St Samson, who travelled to Cornwall and Brittany from his native Wales; some scholars believe his name to be of Celtic origin and unrelated to that of the biblical hero. Reintroduced into Britain during the Middle Ages, the name was revived by the Puritans in the 17th century but is rarely found in modern times.
Diminutives: **Sam**, **Sammy**.

**Samuel** (m) from Hebrew, meaning 'name of God' or 'heard by God'. The Old Testament prophet Samuel anointed Saul and David as the first two kings of Israel; his name was revived by the Puritans after the Reformation and has been in regular use throughout the English-speaking world since then. Famous bearers include the 17th-century diarist Samuel Pepys and the 18th-century lexicographer Samuel Johnson. In Scotland and Ireland *Samuel* is sometimes used to translate a Gaelic name of Old Norse origin, meaning 'summer wanderer' or 'Viking'.
Diminutives: **Sam**, **Sammy**.

**Sanchia** (f) a Spanish name, derived from Latin *sanctus* 'holy'; in occasional use in English-speaking countries since the 13th century. *Sense, Saints,* and *Science*, all of which have been given as first names during the past 700 years, may be variants of *Sanchia*.

**Sandie** a diminutive of **Sandra**, sometimes used as a name in its own right.

**Sandra** a variant of **Alexandra**. Originally a diminutive of *Alessandra*, the Italian form of the name, *Sandra* became popular as an independent name in English-speaking countries in the mid-20th century. It is sometimes regarded as a diminutive of **Cassandra**.
Variant: **Zandra.**
Diminutives: **Sandie, Sandy.**

**Sandy** a diminutive of **Alexander** or **Sandra**, sometimes used as a name in its own right.

**Sapphira** (f) from Hebrew *sappir* 'sapphire'. Mentioned in the New Testament (Acts 5:1), the name is generally regarded in modern times as a variant of **Sapphire**.

**Sapphire** (f) from the name of the precious stone; ultimately from Hebrew *sappir*. *Sapphire* is less common than many of the other jewel names that came into fashion in the 19th century.
Variant: **Sapphira.**

**Sarah** [*sairă*], **Sara** [*sairă, sară*] (f) from Hebrew, meaning 'princess'. The Sarah of the Old Testament, wife of Abraham and mother of Isaac, was originally called *Sarai*, meaning 'quarrelsome'; her name was changed at God's command before the birth of her son (Genesis 17:15). In medieval Britain the usual form of the name was *Sarra*; the variant spelling *Sara*, of Greek origin, was also used at that time. *Sarah* was adopted as a first name by the Puritans after the Reformation and has been in regular use since then; in the early 1980s it was one of the most common girls' names in the English-speaking world. The name has been borne by a number of famous actresses, notably Sarah Siddons (1755–1831), Sarah Bernhardt (1844–1923), and Sarah Miles (born 1941). See also **Sorcha**.
Variants: **Sarina, Sarita, Zara.**
Diminutives: **Sadie, Sal, Sally.**

**Sarai** see **Sarah**.

**Saranna** from a compound of **Sarah** and **Anna**; in occasional use since the 18th century.

**Sarita, Sarina** variants of **Sarah**.

**Sarra** see **Sarah**.

**Saul** [sawl] (m) from Hebrew, meaning 'asked for'. The name was borne in the Old Testament by the first king of Israel and in the New Testament by Saul of Tarsus, better known as St **Paul** (*Saul* was the apostle's Jewish name; *Paul* was the name he adopted as a Roman citizen). *Saul* has been in occasional use in English-speaking countries since the 17th century, the US writer Saul Bellow being the best-known bearer of the name in modern times.

**Saxon** (m) from the name of a Germanic people that invaded Britain in the 5th century; ultimately from a word meaning 'dagger' or 'short sword'. *Saxon* has been in occasional use as a first name since the 19th century.

**Scarlett, Scarlet** (f) from a surname originally borne by wearers of scarlet clothing or dealers in scarlet cloth. *Scarlett* has been in occasional use as a first name since the publication of Margaret Mitchell's *Gone with the Wind* in 1936 (see also **Ashley**): Scarlett O'Hara is the name of the novel's self-willed heroine.

**Scott** (m) from a surname meaning 'Scot' or 'Scottish'. *Scott* has been in regular use as a first name throughout the English-speaking world since the early 20th century, when it was popularized by the US writer F. Scott Fitzgerald (1896–1940).

**Seamus, Shamus** [*shay*mŭs] the Irish form of **James**, from Gaelic *Seumas* (see also **Hamish**). The alternative spelling *Shamus* reflects the pronunciation of the name.

**Sean, Shaun, Shawn** [shawn] variants of **John** (*Sean* is the Irish form of the name; *Shaun* and *Shawn* are its anglicized spellings). Famous bearers include the Irish dramatist Sean O'Casey (1880–1964) and the Scottish actor Sean Connery (born Thomas Connery); the latter probably contributed to the popularity of the name in the 1960s and 1970s, when he played the part of the secret agent James Bond in such films as *Doctor No* and *Goldfinger*.
Variant: **Shane**.
Feminine form: **Shauna**.

**Seb** a diminutive of **Sebastian**.

**Sebastian** [sĕ*bast*iăn] (m) from Latin *Sebastianus*, meaning 'of Sebastia (a town in Asia Minor)'; ultimately from Greek *sebastos* 'venerable'. The early Christian martyr St Sebastian is usually depicted in art as a young man dying from arrow wounds; according to legend, Sebastian survived the archers' attempt to execute him and was subsequently battered to death. The name has been in occasional use in English-speaking countries since the Middle Ages but did not become fashionable until the latter half of the 20th century; the British athlete and Olympic medallist Sebastian Coe (born 1956) is probably its best-known bearer in modern times.
Diminutives: **Bastian, Seb**.

**Sefton** (m) from a surname and place name meaning 'settlement in the rushes'; in occasional use as a first name since the 19th century.

**Selby** (m) from a surname and place name meaning 'willow farm'; in occasional use as a first name since the 19th century.

**Selina, Selena, Celina** [sĕ*leen*ă] (f) a name of uncertain origin: it may be from *Selene*, the Greek name for the moon goddess, or it may simply be a variant of **Celine**. The name was first used in the English-speaking world in the Middle Ages; it was particularly popular in Britain in the 19th century and remains in occasional use today.

Variants: **Salena, Salina**.

**Selma** a diminutive of **Anselma**, often used as a name in its own right.

**Selwyn** (m) from a surname of uncertain origin: it may be from Old English *sele* 'house' and *wine* 'friend', from the Latin name **Silvanus**, or from two Welsh words meaning 'ardour' and 'fair'. Its adoption as a first name in the 19th century has been attributed to the renown of George Selwyn (1809–78), Bishop of New Zealand, after whom Selwyn College in Cambridge is named. The British statesman Selwyn Lloyd, raised to the peerage as Baron Selwyn-Lloyd in 1976, was a famous bearer of the name.

**Senga** (f) a Scottish name that may have originated as a reverse spelling of **Agnes**.

**Septima** the feminine form of **Septimus**.

**Septimus** (m) from Latin, meaning 'seventh'; formerly given by the parents of large families to their seventh child. The name is rarely required for this purpose in modern times but remains in occasional use.

Feminine form: **Septima**.

**Seraphina** [serră*feen*ă] (f) from the word *seraphim*, denoting the highest order of angels; ultimately from Hebrew, meaning 'fiery' or 'winged'. Borne by two saints of the 13th and 15th centuries, the name is occasionally found in English-speaking countries but has never been common.

**Serena** (f) from Latin *serenus* 'calm'; in occasional use in various parts of the English-speaking world since the 18th century.

**Serge, Sergei, Sergio** see **Sergius**.

**Sergius** (m) a Latin name of uncertain origin, borne by four popes and an early Christian martyr and popularized in Russia by the 14th-century abbot St Sergius. *Sergio*, the Italian form of the name, is occasionally found in English-speaking countries, especially the USA; *Serge* and *Sergei*, its French and Russian equivalents, are also used from time to time.

**Seth** (m) a biblical name of uncertain origin; borne in the Old Testament by the third son of Adam and Eve. Seth was regarded by his mother as a replacement for her dead son **Abel** (Genesis 4:25), which has led some scholars to interpret the meaning of the name as 'compensation'. The name came into general use in English-speaking countries in the 17th century and is still found from time to time, especially in the USA.

# Seumas

**Seumas** see **Hamish, Seamus**.

**Seward** (m) from a surname derived from an Anglo-Saxon or medieval name; ultimately from two Old English words meaning 'sea' or 'victory' and 'guard'. It was readopted as a first name in the 19th century.

**Sextus** (m) from Latin, meaning 'sixth', formerly given by the parents of large families to their sixth child.

**Seymour** (m) from an aristocratic surname derived from the French place name *Saint-Maur* (St Maur (or Maurus) was a Benedictine monk of the 6th century; *Maurus* is a Latin word for 'Moor' or 'Moorish'). *Seymour* has been in occasional use as a first name since the 19th century.

**Shamus** see **Seamus**.

**Shane** [shayn, shawn] a variant of **Sean**. Until the mid-20th century *Shane*, like *Shaun* and *Shawn*, was simply an anglicized spelling of the Irish name. The film *Shane* (1953), a classic western that was subsequently adapted for television, popularized the name throughout the English-speaking world and established [shayn] as its more common (and more logical) pronunciation.
Feminine form: **Shani**.

**Shani** (f) a name of uncertain derivation: it may be of African origin or it may simply be a feminine form of **Shane**.

**Shannon** (m *or* f) from a surname derived from the name of the River Shannon in Ireland; ultimately from Irish Gaelic, meaning 'old'. It has been in regular use as a first name in various parts of the English-speaking world, especially the USA, since the first half of the 20th century.

**Shari** a diminutive of **Sharon**, sometimes used as a name in its own right.

**Sharon, Sharron** [*sha*rrŏn] (f) from the name of the Plain of Sharon in the Holy Land: a biblical place name adopted as a first name by the Puritans. It spread to Britain from the USA during the first half of the 20th century and was particularly popular in the 1960s and 1970s.
Diminutive: **Shari**.

**Shaun** see **Sean**.

**Shauna** [*shaw*nă] a feminine form of **Sean**.

**Shaw** (m) from a surname derived from an Old English word for 'copse'; in occasional use as a first name since the 19th century.

**Shawn** see **Sean**.

**Sheba** a diminutive of **Bathsheba**, sometimes associated with the Queen of Sheba and used as a name in its own right.

**Sheelagh** see **Sheila**.

**Sheena, Shena** anglicized spellings of *Sìne*, the Scottish Gaelic form of **Jane**. The name was rarely used outside Scotland until the mid-20th century, when it spread to other parts of Britain and the English-speaking world.

**Sheila, Shelagh, Sheelagh, Sheilah** [*sheel*ă] variants of **Celia**; from *Sile*, the Irish Gaelic form of the name. *Sheila* has been in regular use in Britain and other parts of the English-speaking world since the early 20th century; in Australia the name is used as a slang word for 'girl' or 'woman'.

**Sheldon** (m) from a surname and place name; ultimately from Old English, meaning 'steep-sided valley' or 'flat-topped hill'. It has been in occasional use as a first name since the mid-20th century.

**Shelley, Shelly** (m *or* f) from a surname and place name; ultimately from Old English, meaning 'wood (or meadow) on a ledge'. *Shelley* was adopted as a masculine first name in the 19th century; in the latter half of the 20th century, having been popularized by the US actress Shelley Winters (born Shirley Schrift), it was used almost exclusively as a girl's name.

**Shem** (m) from Hebrew, meaning 'renown'; borne in the Old Testament by one of the sons of Noah. The name is occasionally found in English-speaking countries but has never been common.

**Shena** see **Sheena**.

**Sheridan** (m) from the surname of the Irish-born dramatist Richard Brinsley Sheridan (1751–1816); in occasional use as a first name since the 19th century. The British drama critic Sheridan Morley (born 1941) is a famous bearer of the name.

**Sherry, Sherri** see **Cherie**.

**Sheryl** a variant of **Cheryl**.

**Shirl** a diminutive of **Shirley**.

**Shirley** (f) from a surname and place name; ultimately from two Old English words meaning 'bright' or 'shire' and 'wood' or 'meadow'. *Shirley* came into general use as a feminine first name in the latter half of the 19th century, after the publication of Charlotte Brontë's novel *Shirley* (1849); it was further popularized in the 1930s by the US child star Shirley Temple.
Diminutive: **Shirl**.

**Sholto** (m) from Scottish Gaelic, meaning 'sower'.

**Shona** from a Gaelic feminine form of **John**; in regular use in Scotland and other parts of the English-speaking world.

**Shushana, Shushanna** variants of **Susannah**; in occasional use in English-speaking countries since the 17th century.

**Sian** [shahn] the Welsh form of **Jane**. The actress Sian Phillips is a famous bearer of the name.

# Sib

**Sib, Sibbie, Sibby** diminutives of Sybil.

**Sibella, Sibilla** variants of Sybil.

**Sibyl** see Sybil.

**Sibylla** a variant of Sybil.

**Sid, Syd** diminutives of Sidney (m), sometimes used as independent names.

**Sidney** (f) a variant of Sidony.

**Sidney, Sydney** (m) from a surname derived from any of a number of place names: it may be from Old English, meaning 'wide island' or 'south of the water', or from the French place name *Saint-Denis* (see **Dennis**). The Australian city of Sydney is named after the British statesman Thomas Townshend, 1st Viscount Sydney (1733–1800). *Sidney* was adopted as a first name in honour of the 17th-century British politician Algernon Sidney, who was executed for high treason in 1683; it was also used by descendants of the Elizabethan gentleman Sir Philip Sidney. The name was popular throughout the English-speaking world in the late 19th and early 20th centuries and remains in occasional use today. Famous bearers include Sydney Carton, a character in Charles Dickens' novel *A Tale of Two Cities* (1859), and the US actor Sidney Poitier (born 1924).
Diminutives: **Sid, Syd**.

**Sidonia, Sidonie** variants of Sidony. *Sidonie* is the French form of the name.

**Sidony** [*sidŏni*] (f) a name of uncertain origin: it may be from Greek *sindon* 'linen' (a reference to the shroud of Jesus Christ) or from Latin *Sidonia* 'woman of Sidon (an ancient Phoenician city)'. The name has never been common in any of its forms in the English-speaking world.
Variants: **Sidney, Sidonia, Sidonie**.

**Siegfried** [*seeg*freed] (m) a German name, derived from Old German *sigu* 'victory' and *frithu* 'peace'. Popularized by the hero of Wagner's operas *Siegfried* and *Götterdämmerung*, first performed in 1876, and by the British poet Siegfried Sassoon (1886–1967), the name has been in occasional use in English-speaking countries since the late 19th century.

**Sigismund** a variant of Sigmund, borne by a 15th-century Holy Roman emperor and by three kings of Poland. It has never been common in the English-speaking world.

**Sigmund** (m) from Old German *sigu* 'victory' and *mund* 'protection'. The name has been in occasional use in English-speaking countries since the latter half of the 19th century, when it was popularized by the Wagnerian character Siegmund, father of **Siegfried**, and by the Austrian psychoanalyst Sigmund Freud (1856–1939).
Variant: **Sigismund**.

**Silas** [*sīlăs*] a variant of Silvanus. The name was borne in the 1st century by the early Christian missionary St Silas, a companion of St Paul; it came into general use in English-speaking countries after the Reformation but is rarely found in modern times. The hero of George Eliot's novel *Silas Marner* (1861) is a lonely weaver whose life is brightened by the arrival of a lost child.

**Síle** see **Sheila**.

**Silvana** the feminine form of **Silvanus**.

**Silvanus, Sylvanus** (m) a Latin name, borne by the god of trees, forests, or uncultivated land and by the early Roman martyr St Silvanus. In parts of the New Testament St **Silas** is referred to as Silvanus. The name is rarely found in this form in the English-speaking world. See also **Selwyn**.
Variant: **Silas**.
Feminine form: **Silvana**.

**Silvester** see **Sylvester**.

**Silvia** see **Sylvia**.

**Sim** a diminutive of **Simon**, dating back to the Middle Ages.

**Simeon** [*simi*ŏn] (m) from Hebrew, meaning 'listening' or 'little hyena'; borne in the Old Testament by the second son of Jacob and Leah and in the New Testament by a devout old man who recognized the infant Jesus as the Messiah (Luke 2:25–35). The 5th-century monk St Simeon the Stylite, another early bearer of the name, spent the last 36 years of his life on a small platform at the top of a pillar. The name has never been common in this form in English-speaking countries.
Variant: **Simon**.

**Simon** [*sī*mŏn] a variant of **Simeon**, possibly influenced by Greek *simos* 'snub-nosed'. The name was borne by a number of New Testament characters, notably St **Peter**, the apostle St Simon the Zealot, and the sorcerer Simon Magus, whose attempt to buy the apostles' spiritual powers (Acts 8:18–23) gave rise to the word *simony*. Simon was a common name in medieval Britain; a number of surnames, such as *Simms*, *Simpkin*, and *Simpson*, are derived from its diminutive **Sim**. The name remained in frequent use until the Reformation and enjoyed a revival in the 20th century; it was particularly popular in the 1970s. Famous bearers include the 13th-century statesman Simon de Montfort, Earl of Leicester; the nursery-rhyme character Simple Simon; and the fictional hero Simon Templar, better known as 'The Saint', created by the 20th-century British writer Leslie Charteris.
Diminutive: **Sim**.
Feminine forms: **Simona, Simone**.

**Simona** a feminine form of **Simon**.

**Simone** the French feminine form of **Simon**. It has been publicized in the English-speaking world by the French writer Simone de Beauvoir and the French actress Simone Signoret.

**Sinclair** (m) from a Scottish surname derived from the French place name *Saint-Clair*; ultimately from the name of a Norman martyr, St Clair (or Clarus), meaning 'bright' or 'clear' (see **Clara**). *Sinclair* has been in occasional use as a first name since the late 19th century, a famous bearer being the US writer Sinclair Lewis (1885–1951).
Related name: **Clarence**.

**Sìne** see **Sheena**.

**Sinead** [shin*aird*] the Irish Gaelic form of **Jane**. The actress Sinead Cusack is a famous bearer of the name.

**Siobhan** [shŏv*awn*] the Irish Gaelic form of **Joan**. The actress Siobhan McKenna is a famous bearer of the name.

**Sisley** [*sis*li] a variant of **Cicely**.

**Sissy, Sissie** see **Cissy**.

**Solly** a diminutive of **Solomon**.

**Solomon** [*sol*ŏmŏn] (m) from Hebrew *shalom* 'peace'. The Solomon of the Old Testament, who succeeded his father David as king of Israel in the 10th century BC, is remembered for his great wisdom. The name was in regular use in Britain during the Middle Ages: the surname *Salmon* is derived from *Salamon*, a common medieval variant. *Solomon* was revived by the Puritans after the Reformation but is generally regarded as a Jewish name in modern times.
Related name: **Salome**.

**Sonia, Sonya, Sonja** [*son*yă] variants of **Sophia**, of Russian origin. The name has been in general use throughout the English-speaking world since the early 20th century, when it was popularized by the British writer Stephen McKenna's novel *Sonia* (1917).

**Sophia** [sŏ*fī*ă, sŏ*fee*ă] (f) from Greek, meaning 'wisdom'. The name was borne by a number of minor saints, one of whom is traditionally believed to have been martyred in the 2nd century with her three daughters, Faith, Hope, and Charity. Introduced into Britain in the 17th century, the name was popularized by King James I's granddaughter Sophia (1630–1714), mother of King George I, and became very fashionable in the 18th century. It began to fall from favour towards the end of the 19th century but remains in occasional use throughout the English-speaking world. The Italian actress Sophia Loren is a famous bearer of the name.
Variants: **Sonia, Sonja, Sonya, Sophie, Sophy**.

**Sophie, Sophy** [*sŏ*fi] variants of **Sophia** (*Sophie* is also the French form of the name). In the 18th and 19th centuries *Sophie* and *Sophy* were sometimes regarded as diminutives of *Sophia*; the spelling *Sophy* is still used for this purpose from time to time. *Sophie* has recently enjoyed a revival in Britain: since the 1960s the name has been more popular than *Sophia* itself.

**Sophronia** (f) from Greek, meaning 'prudent'. It is occasionally found in English-speaking countries but has never been common.

**Sophy** see **Sophie**.

**Sorcha** (f) an Irish name, meaning 'bright'; sometimes translated as **Sarah**.

**Spencer** (m) from a surname originally borne by a steward or butler; ultimately from the verb 'to dispense'. The name has been associated with the Churchill family (see **Winston**) since the 18th century, when one of the daughters of John Churchill, 1st Duke of Marlborough, married Charles Spencer, 3rd Earl of Sunderland. *Spencer* came into general use as a first name in the 19th century; famous bearers include the British prime minister Spencer Perceval, who was assassinated in 1812, and the US actor Spencer Tracy (1900–67).

**Stacey, Stacy** diminutives of **Anastasia** or **Eustace**, often used as independent names. The masculine name was probably influenced by the surname *Stacy* (or *Stacey*); the US actor Stacy Keach (born 1941) is a famous bearer. The name is now given almost exclusively to girls; it has been particularly popular since the 1970s.

**Stafford** (m) from a surname and place name; ultimately from Old English, meaning 'ford by a landing-stage'. It has been in occasional use as a first name since the 19th century, a famous bearer being the British politician Sir Stafford Cripps (1889–1952).

**Stan** a diminutive of **Stanley**. The comedian Stan Laurel, the thinner half of the Laurel and Hardy duo, was a famous bearer of the name.

**Stanford** (m) from a surname and place name; ultimately from Old English, meaning 'stony ford'.

**Stanislas, Stanislaus** [*stan*isläs] (m) from the Polish name *Stanislaw*, probably derived from two words meaning 'camp' and 'glory'. The name was borne by the 11th-century martyr St Stanislas (or Stanislaw), Bishop of Cracow, and by two 18th-century kings of Poland. It is occasionally used in the English-speaking world by families of Polish descent.

**Stanley** (m) from a surname and place name; ultimately from Old English, meaning 'stony field'. Its popularity as a first name in the late 19th and early 20th centuries has been attributed to the fame of the British explorer Sir Henry Morton Stanley (born John Rowlands), who was sent to Africa in search of Dr Livingstone in 1869. Famous bearers of the name include the British statesman Stanley Baldwin (1867–1947) and the British footballer Sir Stanley Matthews (born 1915).
Diminutive: **Stan**.

**Steenie** a Scottish diminutive of **Stephen**.

**Stefanie** see **Stephanie**.

**Stella** (f) from Latin, meaning 'star' (Roman Catholics use the title *Stella Maris*, meaning 'star of the sea', to invoke the Virgin Mary). The name occurs in a number of literary works, notably Sir Philip Sidney's sonnet cycle *Astrophel and Stella* and Jonathan Swift's *Journal to Stella* (Sidney's 'Stella' was Penelope Devereux, daughter of the 1st Earl of Essex; Swift's 'Stella' was his friend Esther Johnson). *Stella* came into general use as a first name during the 19th century and was particularly popular in Britain in the first half of the 20th century.

Related name: **Estella**.

**Stephanie, Stefanie** [*stef*äni] feminine forms of **Stephen**, of French origin. The name has been in regular use throughout the English-speaking world since the early 20th century.

**Stephen, Steven** [*steev*ĕn] (m) from Greek *stephanos* 'crown'. One of the earliest known bearers of the name was St Stephen, the first Christian martyr, who was stoned to death by the Jews (Acts 7:54–60). The name was subsequently borne by a number of other saints, by ten popes, and by an ineffectual king of England, grandson of William the Conqueror. It came into general use in Britain in the 11th century and was recorded in official documents, such as the Domesday Book of 1086, in the Latinized forms *Stefanus* and *Stephanus*. By the end of the Middle Ages *Stevyn* and *Steven* had established themselves as the most common forms of the name; they were subsequently replaced by *Stephen*, which remained in frequent use until the 19th century. In the latter half of the 20th century *Stephen* enjoyed a significant revival, becoming one of the most popular boys' names in the English-speaking world, and the spelling *Steven* was reintroduced.

Diminutives: **Steenie, Steve, Stevie**.

Feminine forms: **Stefanie, Stephanie, Stevie**.

**Steve** a diminutive of **Stephen**, sometimes used as a name in its own right.

**Steven** see **Stephen**.

**Stevie** a diminutive or feminine form of **Steven**. Its adoption as a girls' name was probably influenced by the 20th-century British poet Stevie Smith (born Florence Margaret Smith).

**Stew** a diminutive of *Stewart* (see **Stuart**).

**Stewart** see **Stuart**.

**Stirling** (m) from a surname and Scottish place name; made famous as a first name by the British motor-racing driver Stirling Moss (born 1929).

**St John** [*sin*jŏn] (m) from a surname derived from the French place name *Saint-Jean*; ultimately from the name of St **John** the Baptist or St John the Divine. It has been in regular use as a middle name since the 19th century.

**Stu** [stew] a diminutive of **Stuart**.

**Stuart, Stewart** (m) from a Scottish surname ultimately derived from Old English *stigweard* 'steward'. The name is generally associated with the

royal house of Stuart (or Stewart), the ruling dynasty of Scotland from 1371 to 1714 and of England from 1603 (the ancestors of the Stuart monarchs held the office of steward of Scotland). *Stewart* was the original form of the surname; 'the variant *Stuart*, adopted during the reign of Mary, Queen of Scots, is the more common form of the first name. Until the 20th century the use of *Stuart* or *Stewart* as a first name was largely confined to Scotland or to families of Scottish descent; since the 1950s, however, the name has been popular throughout the English-speaking world.
Diminutives: **Stew, Stu**.

**Sue** a diminutive of **Susan, Susannah, Suzanne**, or **Suzette**, sometimes used as a name in its own right.

**Sukey** a diminutive of **Susan** or **Susannah**, dating back to the 18th century.

**Susan** [*soozăn*] a variant of **Susannah**; in regular use since the 18th century. *Susan* was particularly popular in the mid-20th century, when it suddenly became one of the most common girls' names in the English-speaking world. Famous bearers include the US actress Susan Hayward (1918–75), whose real name was Edythe Marrener, and the British actress Susan Hampshire (born 1938).
Diminutives: **Sue, Sukey, Susie, Suzy**.

**Susannah, Susanna, Suzanna** [*soozănă*] (f) from Hebrew *shushannah* 'lily'; borne in the Old Testament Apocrypha by a virtuous and beautiful woman wrongly accused of adultery in the story of Susanna and the Elders. The name is also mentioned in the New Testament (Luke 8:3); it was revived by the Puritans after the Reformation and has been in regular use throughout the English-speaking world since then. Other famous bearers of the name include the heroine of the song 'Oh, Susanna', written by the 19th-century US composer Stephen Foster, and the British actress Susannah York (born 1942).
Variants: **Shushana, Shushanna, Susan, Susanne, Suzanne, Suzette**.
Diminutives: **Sue, Sukey, Susie, Suzy, Zana**.

**Susanne** see **Suzanne**.

**Susie, Suzy** diminutives of **Susan, Susannah, Suzanne**, or **Suzette**.

**Suzanna** see **Susannah**.

**Suzanne, Susanne** [*soozan*] variants of **Susannah**, of French origin. The name has been in regular use throughout the English-speaking world since the early 20th century.
Diminutives: **Sue, Susie, Suzy**.

**Suzette** [*soozet*] a variant of **Susannah**; originally a French diminutive of the name. The culinary term *crêpe suzette* describes a thin pancake cooked and served in an orange-flavoured sauce.
Diminutives: **Sue, Susie, Suzy**.

**Suzy**

**Suzy** see **Susie**.

**Swithin** (m) from Old English, meaning 'strong'; borne in the 9th century by St Swithin (or Swithun), Bishop of Winchester. The name is generally associated with the tradition that the weather on St Swithin's day (15th July) will last for forty days.

**Sybella** a variant of **Sybil**.

**Sybil, Sibyl** [*sibĭl*] (f) from a name or title borne in classical mythology by a number of prophetesses; ultimately from Greek *Sibulla*. The name was introduced into Britain during the Middle Ages in the Latin form *Sibylla* (or *Sibilla*), a famous medieval bearer being the wife of Robert Curthose, eldest son of William the Conqueror. *Sibyl* and *Sybil* came into regular use in the 15th century, the former being the more common spelling of the name until the publication of Benjamin Disraeli's novel *Sybil* in 1845. The name was further popularized in the first half of the 20th century by the British actress Dame Sybil Thorndike.
Variants: **Sibella, Sibilla, Sibylla, Sybella, Sybilla**.
Diminutives: **Sib, Sibbie, Sibby**.

**Sybilla** a variant of **Sybil**.

**Syd** see **Sid**.

**Sydney** see **Sidney** (m).

**Sylvanus** see **Silvanus**.

**Sylvester, Silvester** (m) from Latin, meaning 'of (or in) the woods'. The name was borne by the 4th-century pope St Silvester and by two of his successors in that office (St Silvester is traditionally believed to have baptized the emperor **Constantine** the Great and cured him of leprosy). It has been in occasional use in the English-speaking world since the Middle Ages; famous 20th-century bearers include a famous cartoon cat and the US actor Sylvester Stallone.

**Sylvia, Silvia** (f) from the Latin name *Silvius*; ultimately from *silva* 'wood'. According to legend, Rhea Silvia was the mother of Romulus and Remus, the traditional founders of Rome. The name was popularized in the English-speaking world by a character in Shakespeare's *The Two Gentlemen of Verona* (the song 'Who is Sylvia?' comes from this play); it subsequently occurred in a number of other literary works and was in frequent use as a first name during the 20th century.
Diminutive: **Sylvie**.

**Sylvie** a diminutive of **Sylvia**.

# T

**Tabitha** (f) from Aramaic, meaning 'gazelle', borne by a New Testament character also known as **Dorcas**. Adopted by the Puritans in the 17th century, the name remained in regular use until the end of the 19th century and enjoyed a slight revival in the 1960s.

**Tacey, Tacy** (f) from Latin *tacere* 'to be silent'. *Tace*, meaning 'hush!', was adopted by the Puritans as a feminine first name and remained in regular use until the 18th century; its variants *Tacey* and *Tacy* are still found from time to time in various parts of the English-speaking world.

**Taffy** a diminutive of **David**, used as a nickname or slang term for a Welshman.

**Talbot** (m) from an aristocratic surname of uncertain derivation: it may be from a medieval first name of Germanic origin or from the French nickname *taille-botte* (from *tailler* 'to cut' and *botte* 'bundle'). *Talbot* came into general use as a first name in the 19th century but has never been common.

**Taliesin** [taliesin] (m) a Welsh name, meaning 'radiant brow'. The name was borne by a Welsh bard of the 6th century, the supposed author of the *Book of Taliesin*; it is rarely used in modern times.

**Talitha** (f) from an Aramaic word meaning 'little girl'. The word occurs in the New Testament (Mark 5:41); it was adopted as a first name in the mid-19th century and has been in occasional use since then.

**Tallulah** (f) from an American Indian language, meaning 'running water'. The name is generally associated with the US actress Tallulah Bankhead (1903–68), who was famous for her wit, beauty, and extravagant lifestyle; it remains in occasional use in the USA but is rarely found in other English-speaking countries.

**Tam** a Scottish diminutive of **Thomas**. The hero of Robert Burns' poem *Tam o'Shanter* gave his name to a type of soft woollen cap, also known as a tammy.

**Tamar** [*tay*mar, *tay*mă] (f) from Hebrew, meaning 'palm tree'. The Tamar of the Old Testament, sister of Absalom, was raped by her half-brother Amnon (2 Samuel 13:1–14). The name was adopted by the Puritans after the Reformation; in modern times it is more frequently found in its variant form. *Tamar* is also the name of an English river, which marks the boundary between Devon and Cornwall.
Variant: **Tamara**.

# Tamara

**Tamara** (f) a Russian name; probably a variant of **Tamar**. *Tamara* is the title of a symphonic poem by the Russian composer Balakirev, written between 1867 and 1882. Famous bearers of the name include Queen Tamara of Georgia, who died in the early 13th century, and the Russian ballerina Tamara Karsavina (1885–1978). The name came into general use throughout the English-speaking world during the first half of the 20th century.
Diminutive: **Tammy**.

**Tamasine** a variant of **Thomasin**. See also **Tamsin**.

**Tammy** a diminutive of **Tamara**, **Tamsin**, or any other feminine name beginning with *Tam-*; often given as a name in its own right. In Scotland *Tammy* is sometimes used as a diminutive of **Thomas** (see also **Tam**).

**Tamsin** a variant of **Thomasin**, dating back at least to the 17th century. Largely confined to Cornwall until the mid-20th century, *Tamsin* and the less common **Tamasine** are now used throughout Britain. The name is rarely found in other English-speaking countries.
Diminutive: **Tammy**.

**Tancred** (m) from an Old German name derived from the words for 'think' and 'counsel', introduced into Britain at the time of the Norman Conquest. The name was borne in the 11th century by a hero of the first Crusade, whose exploits inspired a number of literary and musical works, notably Rossini's opera *Tancredi* (1813) and Disraeli's novel *Tancred* (1847).

**Tania** see **Tanya**.

**Tanith** (f) the name of the chief goddess of Carthage; in occasional use as a first name in Britain and other parts of the English-speaking world.

**Tansy** (f) from the flower name; ultimately from Greek *athanasia* 'immortality'.

**Tanya, Tania** diminutives of **Tatiana**, in regular use as independent names throughout the English-speaking world in the latter half of the 20th century.

**Tara** (f) from the name of a hill in County Meath, near Dublin, which is traditionally believed to have been the seat of the kings of Ireland until the 6th century. *Tara* came into general use as a first name in the mid-20th century; it was particularly popular in Britain in the 1970s.

**Tatiana** [tati*ah*nǎ] (f) the name of an early Christian martyr, venerated in the Eastern Orthodox Church. *Tatiana* is generally regarded as a Russian name; it is rarely used in this form in English-speaking countries.
Diminutives: **Tania**, **Tanya**.

**Taylor** (m) from a surname meaning 'tailor' (originally 'cutter'); in occasional use as a first name. *Taylor* was the middle name of the British poet S. T. Coleridge (1772–1834).

**Ted** a diminutive of **Edmund** or **Edward**, dating back to the 14th century.

**Teddy, Teddie** diminutives of **Edmund, Edward,** or **Theodore**.The Edwardian style of dress favoured by certain groups of young people in the 1950s gave rise to the term *teddy boy*. The English word *teddy*, referring to a child's toy bear, is derived from the name of the US president Theodore Roosevelt, whose many sporting activities included that of bear-hunting.

**Tegan** (f) a Welsh name, meaning 'beautiful'.

**Tegwen** (f) from two Welsh words meaning 'beautiful' and 'fair'.

**Tel** a diminutive of **Terry** (m).

**Temperance** (f) from the English word *temperance*; one of the many names of abstract qualities adopted by the Puritans after the Reformation. It enjoyed a slight revival in the 19th century but is rarely found in modern times.

**Terence, Terrence** [*terr*ĕns] (m) from the Roman clan name *Terentius*; borne in the 2nd century BC by the Roman dramatist Publius Terentius Afer (now known as Terence), a freed Carthaginian slave. Until the 19th century *Terence* was rarely found outside Ireland, where it was used to translate the Irish name *Turlough*, meaning 'like Thor (the Norse god of thunder)'. It became popular throughout the English-speaking world in the 20th century, a famous bearer being the British dramatist Sir Terence Rattigan (1911–77).
Diminutive: **Terry.**

**Teresa, Theresa** [tĕ*reez*ă, tĕ*rayz*ă] (f) a name of uncertain origin: it may be from *Therasia*, the name of an island in the Aegean Sea, or from a Greek word meaning 'reap'. In the form *Therasia* the name was borne by the Spanish wife of St Paulinus (353–431); other famous bearers include the Spanish mystic St Teresa of Avila (1515–82), St **Thérèse** of Lisieux, and the 20th-century missionary Mother Teresa, who was awarded the 1979 Nobel Peace Prize for her work with the destitute in India and elsewhere. Largely confined to Spain until the 16th century, the name gradually spread to other Roman Catholic countries and to Roman Catholic families in the English-speaking world; it came into more general use in the 19th century and was particularly popular in the 1960s and 1970s.
Variants: **Thérèse, Theresia, Tracey, Tracy.**
Diminutives: **Terri, Terry, Tess, Tessa, Tessie.**

**Terrence** see **Terence.**

**Terri** see **Terry** (f).

**Terry** (m) a variant of **Theodoric**, from the French form of the name, dating back to the Middle Ages. In modern times *Terry* is generally regarded and used as a diminutive of **Terence.**
Diminutive: **Tel.**

**Terry, Terri** (f) diminutives of **Teresa**, sometimes used as independent names.

**Tertius** [*ter*shiŭs] (m) from Latin, meaning 'third'.

**Tess, Tessa, Tessie** diminutives of **Teresa**. *Tess* and *Tessa* are often used as independent names; the former is generally associated with the unfortunate heroine of Thomas Hardy's novel *Tess of the D'Urbervilles* (1891).

**Tetty** a diminutive of **Elizabeth**; in regular use as an independent name in the 18th century but rarely found in modern times.

**Tex** (m) from the name of the American state of Texas. Generally used as a nickname for a Texan, *Tex* is occasionally given as a first name in the USA.

**Thaddeus** (m) possibly from Hebrew, meaning 'valiant'. The name occurs in the New Testament in the form *Thaddaeus* (see **Jude**); it is occasionally found in English-speaking countries, especially the USA and Ireland, but has never been common.

**Thea** [*thee*ă] a diminutive of **Dorothea**, sometimes used as a name in its own right.

**Thekla, Thecla** [*tek*lă, *thek*lă] (f) from two Greek words meaning 'god' and 'famous'. The 1st-century martyr St Thecla (or Thekla), venerated in the Eastern Orthodox Church, is traditionally believed to have been converted to Christianity by St Paul. The name is rarely found in the English-speaking world.

**Thelma** [*thel*mă, *tel*mă] (f) invented by the British writer Marie Corelli for her novel *Thelma* (1887); possibly influenced by a Greek word meaning 'will'. The name was popular throughout the English-speaking world during the first half of the 20th century.

**Theo** [*thee*ō] a diminutive of any name beginning with *Theo-*, sometimes used as a masculine name in its own right.

**Theobald** [*thee*ōbawld] (m) from the Old German name *Theudobald* (or its Old English equivalent), derived from *theuda* 'people' and *bald* 'bold'. In medieval Britain the name existed in a variety of forms, some of which reflect the former pronunciation [*ti*băld]. (The name *Tybalt*, which occurs in Shakespeare's play *Romeo and Juliet*, is probably a variant of *Theobald*.) Borne by a 12th-century Archbishop of Canterbury, patron of Thomas à Becket, the name remained in regular use until the end of the 17th century but is rarely found in modern times.

**Theodora** the feminine form of **Theodore**.
Variant: **Feodora**.
Diminutive: **Dora**.
Related name: **Dorothea**.

**Theodore** [*thee*ōdor] (m) from Greek, meaning 'God's gift'. The name was borne by a number of early saints, including a 7th-century Archbishop of

Canterbury; it was rarely used in the English-speaking world, however, until the 17th century. The US president Theodore Roosevelt popularized the name in the late 19th and early 20th centuries; it remains in regular use in the USA but is rarely found in Britain in modern times. See also **Tudor**.

Diminutives: **Teddie, Teddy**.

Feminine form: **Theodora**.

**Theodoric** [theeodŏrik] (m) from the Old German name *Thiudoricus*, derived from *theuda* 'people' and *ric* 'ruler'; borne by Theodoric the Great, King of the Ostrogoths and ruler of Italy in the early 6th century. The name has never been common in this form in the English-speaking world, despite a partial revival in the 18th century, but its variants remain in regular use.

Variants: **Derek, Derrick, Deryck, Deryk, Terry**.

**Theodosia** [theeŏdōsiä] (f) from Greek, meaning 'given by God'. The name has been in occasional use in Britain since the 17th century.

**Theophania** (f) from a Latin name for the Christian festival of the Epiphany; ultimately from Greek, meaning 'manifestation of God'. In medieval Britain the name was sometimes given to girls born on Twelfth Night (6th January).

Variant: **Tiffany**.

**Theophila** the feminine form of **Theophilus**.

**Theophilus** [theeofilŭs] (m) from Greek *theos* 'god' and *philos* 'loving'. The Theophilus of the New Testament, to whom St Luke's Gospel and the Acts of the Apostles are addressed, was probably an early Christian convert. The name was borne in the 2nd century by St Theophilus, Bishop of Antioch; it was adopted by the Puritans in the 17th century but is rarely found in modern times.

Feminine form: **Theophila**.

**Theresa** see **Teresa**.

**Thérèse** the French form of **Teresa**. Famous bearers of the name include the French nun St Thérèse (or Theresa) of Lisieux (1873–97) and the homicidal heroines of two major French novels, Emile Zola's *Thérèse Raquin* (1867) and François Mauriac's *Thérèse Desqueyroux* (1927). The name has been in regular use in English-speaking countries, usually in the anglicized form *Therese*, since the early 20th century.

**Theresia** a variant of **Teresa**.

**Thirsa** a variant of **Thirza**.

**Thirza** (f) from the biblical name *Tirzah*, of uncertain origin: it may be from a place name or from a Hebrew word meaning 'pleasantness' or 'acceptance'. The name has been in occasional use in English-speaking countries since the 17th century.

# Thom

Variant: **Thirsa**.

**Thom** a diminutive of **Thomas**, which gave rise to the surname *Thompson*. The variant spelling **Tom** has been the more common form of the name since the 14th century.

**Thomas** [*tom*ǎs] (m) from Aramaic, meaning 'twin'. The name was borne in the New Testament by St Thomas, one of the twelve apostles, whose refusal to accept the news of Jesus Christ's resurrection without evidence (John 20:24–28) gave rise to the phrase *doubting Thomas*, meaning 'sceptic'. *Thomas* has been in frequent use throughout the English-speaking world since the Middle Ages, when it was popularized by the martyr St Thomas à Becket (1118–70), Archbishop of Canterbury. (Becket's murder in Canterbury Cathedral at the instigation of King Henry II is the subject of a play by another famous bearer of the name, T. S. Eliot (1888–1965).) The name is also associated with the theologian St Thomas Aquinas (1225–74) and the humanist St Thomas More (1478–1535); it may be more familiar to modern children, however, through the Rev. W. Awdry's stories of Thomas the Tank Engine and his friends.
Diminutives: **Tam, Tammy, Thom, Tom, Tommy**.
Feminine forms: **Thomasin, Thomasina, Thomasine**.

**Thomasin, Thomasina, Thomasine** feminine forms of **Thomas**, dating back to the 14th century. *Thomasin* and *Thomasine* have been largely superseded by the variants **Tamsin** and **Tamasine**; *Thomasina*, the Latinized form of the name, was revived in the 19th century and remains in occasional use in various parts of the English-speaking world.
Variants: **Tamasine, Tamsin**.

**Thora** (f) a name of Scandinavian origin; probably derived from *Thor*, the name of the Norse god of thunder. It is occasionally found in English-speaking countries, a famous bearer being the British actress Thora Hird (born 1913).

**Thorley** (m) from a surname and place name; ultimately from Old English, meaning 'thorn wood (or clearing)'. It has been in occasional use as a first name since the 19th century.

**Thornton** (m) from a surname and place name; ultimately from Old English, meaning 'settlement among the thorns'. The US writer Thornton Wilder (1897–1975) was a famous bearer of the name.

**Thurstan, Thurston** (m) from an Old Norse name meaning 'Thor's stone'. Introduced into Britain by the Vikings, *Thurstan* survived the Middle Ages as a surname and was readopted as a first name in the 19th century. *Thurston*, a variant spelling of the first name and of the surname, may be derived from an English place name.

**Thyra** (f) a name of Scandinavian origin; probably derived from *Tyr*, the name of the Norse god of war.
Variant: **Tyra**.

**Tibby** a diminutive of **Isabel**.

**Tiffany** a variant of **Theophania**, of French origin. *Tiffany* was in regular use in medieval Britain and survived the Middle Ages as a surname; its re-adoption as a first name in the latter half of the 20th century has been attributed to the film *Breakfast at Tiffany's* (1961). The surname is generally associated with the US jeweller Charles L. Tiffany (1812–1902), father of the painter and craftsman Louis C. Tiffany.

**Tilda** a diminutive of **Matilda**.

**Tilly** a diminutive of **Matilda**, sometimes used as a name in its own right.

**Tim** a diminutive of **Timothy**, sometimes used as a name in its own right. In Charles Dickens' novel *A Christmas Carol* (1843) Tiny Tim is the crippled young son of Scrooge's employee Bob Cratchit.

**Timmy** a diminutive of **Timothy**.

**Timothea** a feminine form of **Timothy**.

**Timothy** [*tim*ŏthi] (m) from the Greek name *Timotheos*, derived from *time* 'honour' and *theos* 'god'. The name is borne in the New Testament by St Timothy, a Christian convert to whom two of St Paul's epistles are addressed. It came into general use as a first name in the 16th century and was popular throughout the English-speaking world in the latter half of the 20th century.
Diminutives: **Tim**, **Timmy**.
Feminine form: **Timothea**.

**Tina** [*teen*ă] a diminutive of **Christina** or any other name ending in *-tina*, often used as an independent name in the latter half of the 20th century.

**Tirzah** see **Thirza**.

**Tisha** a diminutive of **Letitia**, sometimes used as a name in its own right.

**Titus** [*tī*tŭs] (m) a Latin name of uncertain derivation; borne in the 1st century by the Roman emperor Titus Flavius Vespasianus and by the Christian convert St Titus, a disciple of St Paul. The name has been in occasional use in English-speaking countries since the Reformation but has never been common. Its lack of popularity may be due to the notoriety of Titus Oates (1649–1705), whose invention of the Popish Plot, a fictitious Jesuit conspiracy to assassinate King Charles II, led to the death of many innocent Roman Catholics.

**Tobias** [tŏb*ī*ăs] (m) from the Hebrew name *Tobiah*, meaning 'the Lord is good'. *Tobias*, the Greek form of the name, occurs in the Old Testament Apocrypha in the book of Tobit (Tobias is the son of Tobit). It came into general use after the Reformation but has never been as popular as the variant **Toby**. The 18th-century Scottish writer Tobias Smollett was a famous bearer of the name.
Variant: **Toby**.

# Toby

**Toby** [tōbi] the anglicized form of **Tobias**; sometimes regarded as a diminutive of the name. *Toby* may have been in use in Britain during the Middle Ages but it did not become popular until the 16th century, after the Reformation. Shakespeare gave the name to Sir Toby Belch in his play *Twelfth Night*; in the Punch and Judy puppet show *Toby* is the name of Punch's dog. The traditional Toby jug is believed to be named after a character called Toby Philpot in an 18th-century poem or play.

**Todd** (m) from a surname meaning 'fox'. It has been in occasional use as a first name in various parts of the English-speaking world, especially the USA, since the mid-20th century.

**Tolly** a diminutive of **Bartholomew**.

**Tom** a diminutive of **Thomas**, dating back to the 14th century; often used as a name in its own right. *Tom* has entered the English language in the phrase *every Tom, Dick, and Harry*; as a name for various male animals, especially the cat; and in such words as *tomboy* and *tomfoolery*. Famous bearers of the name in fiction include the fairy-tale dwarf Tom Thumb and the heroes of Henry Fielding's *Tom Jones* (1749), Thomas Hughes' *Tom Brown's Schooldays* (1857), and Mark Twain's *The Adventures of Tom Sawyer* (1876).

**Tommy** a diminutive of **Thomas**, sometimes given as a name in its own right. The use of *tommy* (or *Tommy Atkins*) as a colloquial term for a private soldier in the British army dates back to the early 19th century, when the name *Thomas Atkins* first appeared on specimen forms for enlistment. The name of the sub-machine-gun known as a Tommy gun is derived from a different source: the surname of its inventor J. T. Thompson.

**Toni** a diminutive of **Antoinette**, **Antonia**, or **Antonina**, sometimes used as a name in its own right.

**Tonia, Tonya** diminutives of **Antonia**, sometimes used as independent names.

**Tony** a diminutive of **Anthony**, dating back to the 17th century; often used as a name in its own right. Famous 20th-century bearers of the name include the US actor Tony Curtis, whose real name is Bernard Schwarz, and the British comedian Tony Hancock.

**Tonya** see **Tonia**.

**Topsy** (f) a name of uncertain origin, borne by a little black slave girl in Harriet Beecher Stowe's novel *Uncle Tom's Cabin* (1852). It is rarely given as a first name.

**Torquil** (m) from the Scottish Gaelic form of the Old Norse name *Thorketill*, probably meaning 'Thor's cauldron'.

**Totty** a diminutive of **Charlotte**.

**Tracy, Tracey** variants of **Teresa**. (The surname *Tracy*, borne by the US actor Spencer Tracy (1900–67) and the comic-strip detective Dick Tracy, is derived from a French place name.) *Tracy* was popularized in the mid-20th century by the rich heroine of the films *The Philadelphia Story* (1940) and its remake *High Society* (1956), played by Katharine Hepburn and Grace Kelly; in the late 1960s and early 1970s it was one of the most common feminine names in the English-speaking world.

**Travers** see **Travis**.

**Travis** (m) from a surname meaning 'crossing' or 'tollgate'. It is occasionally given as a first name in various parts of the English-speaking world, especially Australia. *Travers*, the original form of the surname, is also used from time to time.

**Trefor** see **Trevor**.

**Trev** a diminutive of **Trevor**.

**Trevor** [*trever*] (m) from a surname derived from the Welsh name *Trefor*; ultimately from a Welsh place name meaning 'large village'. *Trevor* came into general use as a first name in the 19th century; it was popularized throughout the English-speaking world in the mid-20th century by the British actor Trevor Howard.
Diminutive: **Trev**.

**Tricia, Trisha** [*trishă*] diminutives of **Patricia**, sometimes used as independent names.

**Trina** [*treenă*] a diminutive of **Catriona**, sometimes used as a name in its own right.

**Tris** a diminutive of **Beatrice**, **Tristan**, or **Tristram**.

**Trisha** see **Tricia**.

**Trissie** a diminutive of **Beatrice**.

**Tristan** (m) from the Celtic name *Drystan*, meaning 'din', influenced by French *triste* 'sad'. The medieval story of Tristan (or **Tristram**), nephew of King Mark of Cornwall, who falls in love with the Irish princess Isolde (or Iseult), his uncle's intended bride, has inspired a number of literary and musical works, notably Wagner's opera *Tristan und Isolde* (1865). The inhabitants of Tristan, one of the islands of Tristan da Cunha in the Atlantic Ocean, were temporarily evacuated to Britain after a volcanic eruption in 1961.
Variant: **Tristram**.
Diminutive: **Tris**.

**Tristram** a variant of **Tristan**; the usual form of the name in English-speaking countries since the 12th century. It occurs in a number of literary works based on the medieval story of Tristan and Isolde, such as Swinburne's poem *Tristram of Lyonesse* (1882), and was popularized in the 18th century by the hero of Laurence Sterne's novel *Tristram Shandy*.

**Trixie, Trix** diminutives of **Beatrix**. *Trixie* is often used as a name in its own right.

**Troy** (m) either from the name of the ancient city or from a surname of uncertain origin (the latter may be derived from an Irish name meaning 'foot soldier' or from the French place name *Troyes*). *Troy* is occasionally used as a first name but has never been common.

**Trudy, Trudie, Trudi** diminutives of **Ermintrude** or **Gertrude**, often used as independent names.

**Tryphena** (f) from Greek, meaning 'daintiness' or 'delicacy'. Mentioned in the New Testament (Romans 16:12), the name came into general use after the Reformation but is rarely found in modern times.

**Tudor** (m) from a surname derived from a Welsh variant of **Theodore**; in occasional use as a first name. It is generally associated with the royal house of Tudor, the ruling dynasty of England from the accession of King Henry VII in 1485 to the death of Queen Elizabeth I in 1603.

**Turlough** see **Terence**.

**Ty** a diminutive of **Tyrone**.

**Tybalt** see **Theobald**.

**Tyra** a variant of **Thyra**.

**Tyrone** (m) from the name of a county of Ireland; ultimately from Irish Gaelic, meaning 'Eoghan's land'. It was popularized as a first name by the US actor Tyrone Power (1913–58).
Diminutive: **Ty**.

# U

**Ulric** (m) from the Old English name *Wulfric* (or its Old German equivalent), a compound of *wulf* 'wolf' and *ric* 'ruler'. The name was borne by a number of saints, notably the 10th-century German bishop St Ulric (or Ulrich) of Augsburg. It remained in regular use in Britain until the end of the 13th century and was reintroduced into the English-speaking world from Germany several hundred years later.
Feminine form: **Ulrica**.

**Ulrica** the feminine form of **Ulric**.

**Ulysses** [*yoo*liseez] (m) from the Latin form of the Greek name *Odysseus*, possibly meaning 'hater', borne by the hero of Homer's *Odyssey*. Occasionally given as a first name in honour of the US president Ulysses S.

Grant (1822–85), *Ulysses* may also be associated with James Joyce's controversial novel of the same name, first published in 1922.

**Una** [*yoonă*, *oonă*] (f) an Irish name of unknown origin; sometimes associated with Irish *uan* 'lamb' or Latin *unus* 'one' (the latter interpretation dates back to the 16th century, when the name was given by Edmund Spenser to a character in his poem *The Faerie Queene*). No longer confined to Ireland, *Una* is found in most parts of the English-speaking world today. Variants: **Juno, Ona, Oona, Oonagh**.

**Unity** (f) from the English word *unity*; one of the many names of abstract qualities adopted by the Puritans after the Reformation. Unity Mitford (1914–48), sister of the writer Nancy Mitford, was notorious for her association with Adolf Hitler during World War II.

**Upton** (m) from a surname and place name; ultimately from Old English, meaning 'upper settlement'. *Upton* has been in occasional use as a first name since the 19th century; its most famous bearer was the US novelist Upton Sinclair, author of the series *World's End* (1940–53).

**Urban** (m) from Latin *urbanus* 'townsman' or 'citizen'. Mentioned in the New Testament (Romans 16:9), the name was borne by the 3rd-century pope St Urbanus I and by seven of his successors in that office. It is occasionally given as a first name in English-speaking countries but has never been common.

**Uriah** [*yoorīă*] (m) from Hebrew, meaning 'light of the Lord'; borne in the Old Testament by **Bathsheba**'s first husband Uriah the Hittite, whose death in battle was engineered by King David (2 Samuel 11:2–17). The name was adopted by the Puritans after the Reformation; since the mid-19th century it has been associated with the hypocritically servile clerk Uriah Heep in Charles Dickens' novel *David Copperfield* (1849–50).

**Ursula** [*ersewlă*] (f) from Latin *ursus* 'bear'. St Ursula, patron saint of the Ursuline order of nuns, is traditionally believed to have been a British princess martyred at Cologne with eleven thousand other virgins (this figure may be based on a misinterpretation of the name of one of the saint's companions). The name was popular in medieval Britain and enjoyed a revival in the 17th century; famous bearers include the heroine of Mrs Craik's immensely successful novel *John Halifax, Gentleman* (1856) and the Swiss-born actress Ursula Andress, who made her name in the film *Doctor No* (1962).

# V

**Val** a diminutive of **Valentine** or **Valerie**. The Irish singer Val Doonican (born 1932) is a famous male bearer of the name.

## Valda

**Valda** (f) from Old German *vald* 'power' or 'rule'. The name is occasionally found in English-speaking countries but has never been common.
Variant: **Velda**.
Masculine equivalent: **Waldo**.

**Valentina** a variant of **Valentine** (f).

**Valentine** (m *or* f) from Latin *valens* 'strong' or 'healthy'. The customs associated with St Valentine's day (14th February) are believed to be of pagan origin; they have no connection with either of the two Christian martyrs of that name. Borne in medieval romance by the twin brother of **Orson**, the name came into general use in Britain during the Middle Ages but has never been common. Although it is occasionally given to girls, *Valentine* is generally regarded as a masculine name, the 20th-century British actor Valentine Dyall being a famous bearer.
Variant: (f) **Valentina**.
Diminutive: **Val**.

**Valeria** [vălairiă, văleeriă] (f) from the Roman clan name *Valerius*; ultimately from Latin *valere* 'to be strong (or healthy)'. The name is rarely found in this form in the English-speaking world.
Variant: **Valerie**.

**Valerie** [valĕri] a variant of **Valeria**, of French origin; the usual form of the name in English-speaking countries since the late 19th century. It was particularly popular in the mid-20th century.
Diminutive: **Val**.

**Vanda** a variant of **Wanda**, reflecting the German pronunciation of the name. It has been in occasional use in Britain since the 19th century but is rarely found in other English-speaking countries.

**Vanessa** [vănesă] (f) invented by the 18th-century writer Jonathan Swift for his friend Esther Vanhomrigh (from the first syllable of her surname and *Essa*, a pet form of *Esther*). *Vanessa* was rarely given as a first name until the 20th century; it was popularized in the 1960s and 1970s by the British actress Vanessa Redgrave.

**Vashti** (f) a biblical name of uncertain origin; probably from Persian, meaning 'beautiful' or 'best'. Borne in the Old Testament book of Esther by the deposed Queen of Persia, the name was adopted by the Puritans in the 17th century and remains in occasional use today.

**Vaughan, Vaughn** [vawn] (m) from a surname derived from a Welsh word for 'little'; in regular use as a first name since the 19th century. In the world of music the name is generally associated with the English composer Ralph Vaughan Williams (1872–1958).

**Velda** (f) a name of uncertain origin; possibly a variant of **Valda**.

**Velma** (f) a name of uncertain origin; possibly a variant of **Wilhelmina**, influenced by **Selma** or **Thelma**.

**Venetia** [věneeshǎ] (f) probably from the Latin name for the Italian city of Venice, though some scholars favour a more complex derivation from the Welsh name **Gwyneth**. The name was popularized in the 17th century by Venetia Stanley, the beautiful wife of the British courtier and philosopher Sir Kenelm Digby, and in the 19th century by the heroine of Disraeli's novel *Venetia*. It is rarely found in modern times.

**Venus** [veenŭs] (f) the name of the Roman goddess of love. It has been in occasional use as a first name in various parts of the English-speaking world since the 16th century.

**Vera** [veerǎ] (f) from Russian, meaning 'faith'; sometimes associated with the feminine form of Latin *verus* 'true'. The name was introduced into the English-speaking world through two novels of the late 19th century, Ouida's *Moths* (1880) and Marion Crawford's *A Cigarette-Maker's Romance* (1890); it was particularly popular during the first half of the 20th century. The British singer Vera Lynn, the 'Forces' Sweetheart' of World War II, is a famous bearer of the name.

**Vere** (m) from the aristocratic surname *de Vere*, introduced into Britain by a companion of William the Conqueror (see **Aubrey**); ultimately from a French place name. It has been in occasional use as a first name since the 18th century.

**Verena** [věreenǎ] (f) the name of a 3rd-century saint, of uncertain origin. The cult of St Verena is particularly associated with Switzerland; the name may have been introduced into the English-speaking world by returning tourists.

**Verity** [verriti] (f) from the English word *verity*, meaning 'truth'; one of the many names of abstract qualities adopted by the Puritans after the Reformation.

**Verna** (f) probably from Latin *vernus* 'of spring'. The name is occasionally found in the USA and Britain but has never been common.

**Vernon** (m) from a surname derived from a French place name; ultimately from a Gaulish word meaning 'alder'. It has been in regular use as a first name since the 19th century.

**Verona** [věrōnǎ] (f) from the name of the Italian city of Verona; sometimes regarded as a variant of **Veronica**.

**Veronica** [věronikǎ] (f) from Latin, meaning 'true image'; the name of a cloth that is said to bear a representation of Christ's features (according to legend, St Veronica used the cloth to wipe Jesus' face on his way to Calvary). Introduced into Scotland in the 17th century, *Veronica* was rarely given as a first name in other parts of Britain until the late 19th century. It was in regular use throughout the English-speaking world during the first half of the 20th century and was further popularized in the

1940s by the US actress Veronica Lake. The name is sometimes erroneously associated with **Berenice**.
Variants: **Verona**, **Véronique**.

**Véronique** the French feminine form of **Veronica**; occasionally found in English-speaking countries.

**Vi** [vī] a diminutive of **Viola** or **Violet**.

**Vic**, **Vick** diminutives of **Victor**.

**Vicky**, **Vicki**, **Vickie**, **Vikki** diminutives of **Victoria**, sometimes used as independent names.

**Victor** (m) from Latin, meaning 'conqueror'. Borne by three popes and a number of minor saints, *Victor* was occasionally given as a first name in medieval Britain but did not come into regular use in the English-speaking world until the latter half of the 19th century, when it may have been regarded as a masculine form of **Victoria**. Famous 20th-century bearers of the name include the US actor Victor Mature and the Danish entertainer Victor Borge.
Diminutives: **Vic**, **Vick**.
Feminine form: **Victorine**.

**Victoria** (f) from Latin, meaning 'victory'. The name was popularized in a number of European countries by the cult of the early Christian martyr St Victoria; in the English-speaking world, however, it is generally associated with Queen Victoria (1819–1901), who was named after her mother Princess Maria Louisa Victoria of Saxe-Coburg-Gotha. The name came into regular use during Victoria's 64-year reign and enjoyed a revival in the latter half of the 20th century. See also **Queenie**.
Diminutives: **Vicki**, **Vickie**, **Vicky**, **Vikki**, **Vita**.

**Victorine** a feminine form of **Victor**, of French origin.

**Vida** a diminutive of **Davida**, sometimes used as a name in its own right.

**Vikki** see **Vicky**.

**Vilma** a variant of **Wilhelmina**.

**Vin** a diminutive of **Vincent**.

**Vina** a diminutive of **Davina**, **Lavina**, or any other name ending in *-vina*; sometimes used as a name in its own right.

**Vince** a diminutive of **Vincent**.

**Vincent** (m) from Latin *vincens* 'conquering'. The name was borne by a number of saints, notably the Spanish martyr St Vincent of Saragossa, who died in the early 4th century, and the 17th-century French priest St Vincent de Paul, remembered for his charitable work. *Vincent* was a fairly common name in Britain during the latter half of the Middle Ages; it enjoyed a revival in the 19th century and has been in regular use throughout the English-speaking world since then. Famous bearers of the name

Include the Dutch painter Vincent Van Gogh (1853–90) and the US actor Vincent Price (born 1911).
Diminutives: **Vin, Vince, Vinnie, Vinny.**
Feminine form: **Vincentia.**

**Vincentia** the feminine form of **Vincent.**

**Vinnie, Vinny** diminutives of **Lavinia** or **Vincent.**

**Viola** [vīōlă] (f) from Latin, meaning 'violet'; borne by one of the heroines of Shakespeare's play *Twelfth Night. Viola* is occasionally given as a first name in various parts of the English-speaking world but has never been as popular as **Violet.** See also **Yolande.**
Variants: **Violetta, Violette.**
Diminutive: **Vi.**
Related name: **Violet.**

**Violet** [vīōlĕt] (f) from the flower name; ultimately from Latin *viola.* The name was largely confined to Scotland until the latter half of the 19th century, when it became fashionable throughout Britain and in other English-speaking countries. It remained in frequent use until the 1930s but is rarely found in modern times.
Variants: **Violetta, Violette.**
Diminutive: **Vi.**
Related name: **Viola.**

**Violetta** a variant of **Viola** or **Violet**; originally an Italian diminutive of **Viola.** Made famous by the consumptive heroine of Verdi's opera *La Traviata* (1853), *Violetta* is sometimes given as a first name in the English-speaking world.

**Violette** the French form of **Viola** or **Violet**; occasionally found in English-speaking countries.

**Virgil** [verjil] (m) from the Roman clan name *Vergilius*; borne in the 1st century BC by the Roman poet Publius Vergilius Maro (better known as Virgil), author of the *Aeneid. Virgil* is sometimes given as a first name in the USA but is rarely found in other parts of the English-speaking world (the 8th-century Irish abbot St Virgil of Salzburg originally bore the Gaelic name *Fergal*).

**Virginia** [verjiniă] (f) from the Roman clan name *Verginius*, of uncertain origin. The name is popularly associated with Latin *virgo* 'virgin' (the American state of Virginia was named after Elizabeth I, the 'Virgin Queen'). The first child to be born of British parents in the New World (on Roanoke Island, 18th August 1587) was given the name *Virginia*; until the 20th century the name was far more common in the USA than in other English-speaking countries. Famous British bearers include the actress Virginia McKenna (born 1931) and the tennis player Virginia Wade (born 1945).
Diminutives: **Ginger, Ginny, Jinny.**

**Vita** (f) from Latin, meaning 'life'. The name is also used as a diminutive of **Victoria**, the British writer Vita Sackville-West (1892–1962) being a famous example.

**Vitus** see **Guy**.

**Viv** a diminutive of **Vivian** or any of its variant forms.

**Viva** (f) from Latin *vivus* 'alive'.
Variant: **Vivia**.

**Vivia** a variant of **Viva** or **Vivian** (f).

**Vivian** (m *or* f), **Vivien** (f), **Vyvyan** (m) from the Latin name *Vivianus*, of uncertain origin; probably from *vivus* 'alive'. The masculine name came into general use in Britain during the Middle Ages but has never been common: famous bearers include the hero of Disraeli's novel *Vivian Grey* (1826–27) and the British explorer Sir Vivian Fuchs (born 1908). *Vivien*, the more familiar spelling of the feminine name, became fashionable in the latter half of the 19th century, having featured in one of Tennyson's *Idylls of the King* (*Vivien* is Tennyson's name for the Lady of the Lake, who seduces and imprisons the wizard Merlin). The name was further popularized in the 20th century by the British actress Vivien Leigh (1913–67). *Vyvyan*, a variant spelling of the surname *Vivian*, was adopted as a first name in the 19th century. See also **Ninian**.
Variants: (f) **Vivia**, **Viviana**, **Vivienne**.
Diminutive: **Viv**.

**Viviana** a variant of **Vivian** (f), dating back to the Middle Ages; originally a feminine form of the masculine name.

**Vivien** see **Vivian**.

**Vivienne** [*vivi*ĕn, *vivi*ĕn] the French feminine form of **Vivian**; in regular use in Britain and other parts of the English-speaking world since the early 20th century.

**Vyvyan** see **Vivian**.

# W

**Wade** (m) from a surname of uncertain origin: it may be from the name of a legendary hero, mentioned in medieval literature, or from a place name meaning 'ford'. *Wade* has been in regular use as a first name since the 19th century.

**Wal** a diminutive of **Wallace** or **Walter**.

**Walburga** (f) from the Old German or Old English words for 'power' and 'protection'; borne by the 8th-century abbess St Walburga (or Waldburg). The eve of St Walburga's feast day (1st May), known in German folklore as Walpurgis Night, is associated with witchcraft.

**Waldo** [*wawl*do, *wol*do] (m) from Old German *vald* 'power' or 'rule'. The US philosopher Ralph Waldo Emerson (1803–82) is the best-known bearer of the name in the English-speaking world.
Feminine equivalent: **Valda**.

**Wallace** (m), **Wallis** (m *or* f) [*wol*is] from a surname ultimately derived from a Germanic word for 'foreign' (the Old English equivalent of this word gave rise to the place name *Wales*). *Wallace*, the usual form of the surname in Scotland, was adopted as a first name in honour of the Scottish national hero Sir William Wallace, who was executed in 1305; it has been in regular use throughout the English-speaking world since the 19th century. The feminine name *Wallis* is generally associated with Mrs Wallis Simpson, for whom King Edward VIII abdicated in 1936.
Diminutives: **Wal, Wally**.

**Wally** [*wol*i] a diminutive of **Wallace** or **Walter**, which has degenerated into a slang term for a foolish person.

**Walt** [wawlt, wolt] a diminutive of **Walter**. The creator of Mickey Mouse, Donald Duck, and a host of other cartoon characters, Walt Disney (1901–66), is probably the best-known bearer of the name.

**Walter** [*wawl*ter, *wol*ter] (m) from the Old German name *Waldhar*, derived from *vald* 'power' or 'rule' and *harja* 'people', rendered in Old English as *Wealdhere*. *Walter* was introduced into Britain at the time of the Norman Conquest and remained in regular use throughout the English-speaking world until the mid-20th century. The name existed in a variety of forms during the Middle Ages; the variant *Water*, which was last used in the 19th century, reflects an early alternative pronunciation. Famous bearers of the name include the explorer Sir Walter Raleigh (1554–1618), the writer Sir Walter Scott (1771–1832), and several 20th-century actors, such as Walter Pidgeon and Walter Matthau.
Diminutives: **Wal, Wally, Walt, Wat**.

**Wanda** [*won*dă] (f) a name of uncertain origin; it may be from an Old German word meaning 'family' or it may be related to the name of the Germanic people whose acts of destruction gave rise to the English word *vandalism*. Borne by the heroine of Ouida's novel of the same name, published in 1883, *Wanda* came into general use throughout the English-speaking world during the 20th century.
Variants: **Vanda, Wenda**.

**Ward** (m) from a surname originally borne by a guard or watchman; in occasional use as a first name since the 19th century.

**Warner** (m) from an Old German name derived from *Varin* (see **Warren**) and *harja* 'people'; introduced into Britain at the time of the Norman Conquest. *Warner* survived the Middle Ages as a surname and was re-adopted as a first name in the 19th century.

# Warren

**Warren** (m) from the Old German name *Varin*, ultimately from the verb 'to protect'. The name was introduced into Britain at the time of the Norman Conquest in the forms *Warin* and *Guarin*, which gave rise to such surnames as *Warren* and *Garnett* (the surname *Warren* may also be derived from a French place name). *Warren* was subsequently readopted as a first name; famous bearers include Warren Hastings (1732–1818), first governor general of India, the US president Warren G. Harding (1865–1923), and the actors Warren Mitchell and Warren Beatty.

**Warwick** [*wo*rrik] (m) from a surname and place name; in occasional use as a first name since the 19th century. It was particularly popular in Australia in the mid-20th century.

**Washington** (m) from the surname of George Washington (1732–99), first president of the USA; ultimately from an English place name meaning 'settlement of Wassa's people'. The US writer Washington Irving (1783–1859), author of 'Rip van Winkle', was a famous bearer of the name.

**Wat** [wot] a former diminutive of **Walter**, which gave rise to such surnames as *Watkins*, *Watson*, and *Watt*. The name was borne by the rebel Wat Tyler, one of the leaders of the Peasants' Revolt (1381).

**Wayne** (m) from a surname originally borne by a maker (or driver) of wagons. The adoption of *Wayne* as a first name has been attributed to the popularity of the US actor John Wayne (1907–79); it has been in regular use throughout the English-speaking world since the mid-20th century.

**Wenda** a variant of **Wanda** or **Wendy**.

**Wendell** (m) from a surname of Germanic origin, meaning 'wanderer'. *Wendell* has been in occasional use as a first name since the 19th century, when it was borne by the US writer Oliver Wendell Holmes and his son, a judge of the US Supreme Court. (The former was named after his maternal grandfather, Oliver Wendell.)

**Wendy** (f) invented by the writer Sir J. M. Barrie for one of the central characters of his play *Peter Pan* (1904). Barrie is believed to have derived the name from *friendy-wendy*, a term of endearment applied to him by the young daughter of a friend. The name has been in regular use throughout the English-speaking world since the 1920s; it was particularly fashionable in Britain in the 1960s, perhaps influenced by the popular actresses Wendy Hiller and Wendy Craig.

Variant: **Wenda**.

**Wesley** (m) from the surname of the 18th-century clergymen John and Charles Wesley, founders of Methodism; ultimately from Old English, meaning 'west meadow'.

**Wilbert** (m) from an Old English or Old German name derived from the words for 'will' and 'bright'. It is still used from time to time in various parts of the English-speaking world, especially the USA.

**Wilbur** (m) from a surname derived from an Old English or Old German feminine name; ultimately from the words for 'will' and 'defence'. *Wilbur* was readopted as a first name in the 19th century, a famous bearer being the US aviator Wilbur Wright (1867–1912), brother of **Orville**; it remains in occasional use in the USA but is rarely found in other English-speaking countries.

**Wilf** a diminutive of **Wilfred**.

**Wilfred, Wilfrid** (m) from the Old English name *Wilfrith*, derived from *will* 'will' and *frith* 'peace'; borne in the 7th century by St Wilfrid, Bishop of York. The name was revived in the 19th century and remained in regular use until the mid-20th century; famous bearers include the hero of Sir Walter Scott's novel *Ivanhoe* (1819) and the British actors Wilfrid Lawson and Wilfrid Hyde White.
Diminutive: **Wilf**.
Feminine forms: **Wilfreda, Wilfrida**.

**Wilfreda** see **Wilfrida**.

**Wilfrid** see **Wilfred**.

**Wilfrida, Wilfreda** feminine forms of **Wilfred**.

**Wilhelmina** [wilĕmeenă, wilhelmeenă] a feminine form of **William**, of German origin. The name has been in general use in English-speaking countries, especially Scotland, since the 18th century.
Variants: **Velma, Vilma, Willa, Wilma**.
Diminutives: **Ilma, Mina, Minna, Minnie**.

**Will** a diminutive of **William**, dating back to the Middle Ages; sometimes used as a name in its own right. Robin Hood's companion Will Scarlet was a famous bearer of the name.

**Willa** a variant or diminutive of **Wilhelmina**.

**Willard** (m) from a surname derived from an Old English name meaning 'bold resolve'; in occasional use as a first name, especially in the USA.

**William** (m) from the Old German name *Willahelm*, derived from *vilja* 'will' and *helma* 'helmet', rendered in modern German as *Wilhelm*. Introduced into Britain in the 11th century by William the Conqueror and a number of his companions, *William* rapidly became one of the most common masculine names in the English-speaking world (a position it retained until the early 20th century); its many diminutives gave rise to such surnames as *Wilcox, Wilkins, Wilmot*, and *Wilson*. The name was subsequently borne by three other British kings and by several saints, notably St William Fitzherbert, Archbishop of York, who died in 1154; famous bearers in the literary world include William Shakespeare (1564–1616) and William Wordsworth (1770–1850). In modern times the name has been popularized by the mischievous young hero of Richmal Crompton's *Just William* stories and by Prince William (born 1982), elder son of the Prince and Princess of Wales.

Variants: **Gwilym, Gwylim, Liam.**

Diminutives: **Bill, Billie, Billy, Will, Willie, Willy.**

Feminine forms: **Gulielma, Wilhelmina, Williamina.**

**Williamina** a feminine form of **William**; rarely found outside Scotland.

**Willie, Willy** diminutives of **William**, sometimes used as independent names.

**Willis** (m) from a surname meaning 'son of **Will**'; in occasional use as a first name since the 19th century.

**Willoughby** [*wilŏ*bi] (m) from a surname and place name meaning 'farm among the willows'; adopted as a first name in the 19th century.

**Willy** see **Willie**.

**Wilma** a variant or diminutive of **Wilhelmina**. In Britain the name is largely confined to Scotland; it is also found in the USA and Canada.

**Wilmer** (m) from an Old German name derived from the words for 'will' and 'fame'. It has never been common in the English-speaking world.

**Wilmot** (m) from a surname derived from a medieval diminutive of **William**. It was readopted as a first name in the 19th century and remains in occasional use in various parts of the English-speaking world.

**Win** a diminutive of **Winifred, Winston**, or **Winthrop**.

**Windsor** [*winz*er] (m) from a surname and place name; ultimately from Old English, meaning 'riverbank with a winch'. *Windsor* has been the surname of the ruling dynasty of the United Kingdom since 1917. It was adopted as a first name in the 19th century; the Welsh actor Windsor Davies is a famous bearer.

**Winefred** see **Winifred**.

**Winfred, Winfrid** (m) from the Old English name *Winfrith*, derived from *wine* 'friend' and *frith* 'peace'. It is rarely found in modern times. See also **Boniface**.

**Winifred, Winnifred, Winefred** (f) from the Welsh name *Gwenfrewi*, meaning 'blessed reconciliation', influenced by the masculine name **Winfred**. St Winifred, one of the earliest known bearers of the name, is traditionally believed to have been beheaded and restored to life in the 7th century; the Welsh town of Holywell is named after the spring of healing water that is said to mark the spot where her head fell. The name came into general use throughout the English-speaking world in the 16th century; it was particularly popular in Britain in the late 19th and early 20th centuries.

Diminutives: **Freda, Win, Winnie.**

**Winnie** a diminutive of **Winifred** or **Winston**. The character of Winnie-the-Pooh, one of the best-known bears in children's literature, was created by A. A. Milne in the 1920s in a series of stories and poems written for his son Christopher Robin.

**Winnifred** see **Winifred**.

**Winston** (m) from a surname derived from a Gloucestershire place name; ultimately from Old English, meaning 'friend's settlement'. *Winston* was adopted as a first name by the Churchill family in the early 17th century; since the first half of the 20th century it has been associated with the British statesman Sir Winston Leonard Spencer Churchill (1874–1965), remembered for his great leadership during World War II. This illustrious bearer does not appear to have popularized the name, however; it has never been common in Britain or any other part of the English-speaking world.
Diminutives: **Win**, **Winnie**.

**Winthrop** (m) from a surname and place name, ultimately from Old English, meaning 'friend's farm (or village)'. *Winthrop* is occasionally given as a first name in the USA but is rarely found in other English-speaking countries.
Diminutive: **Win**.

**Woodrow** (m) from a surname and place name; ultimately from Old English, meaning 'row of houses in a wood'. It was popularized as a first name by the US president Woodrow Wilson (1856–1924), who was named after his maternal grandfather, Thomas Woodrow.

**Wyatt** (m) from a surname derived from a medieval diminutive of **Guy**. It was readopted as a first name in the 19th century, a famous bearer being the US frontier marshal Wyatt Earp (1848–1929), hero of numerous westerns.

**Wybert** (m) from Old English *wig* 'battle' and *beorht* 'bright'. It is rarely found in modern times.

**Wyndham** (m) from a surname and place name; ultimately from Old English, meaning 'Wyman's settlement' (*Wyman*, an Anglo-Saxon name, is derived from *wig* 'battle' and *mund* 'protection'). *Wyndham* was borne as a middle name by two 20th-century British writers: Wyndham Lewis (1882–1957), whose full name was Percy Wyndham Lewis, and John Wyndham Harris (1903–69), better known as John Wyndham.

**Wynford** (m) from a surname and place name, meaning 'white (or holy) stream'; in occasional use as a first name since the early 20th century. The Welsh writer and broadcaster Wynford Vaughan-Thomas (born 1908) is a well-known bearer.

**Wynn**, **Wynne** (m *or* f) from a surname derived either from Welsh, meaning 'white' or 'fair', or from Old English, meaning 'friend'.

## Wystan

**Wystan** (m) from the Old English name *Wigstan*, a compound of *wig* 'battle' and *stan* 'stone'. *Wystan* was the first name of the British poet W. H. Auden (1907–73).

# X

**Xanthe** [*zan*thi] (f) from Greek *xanthos* 'yellow' (a reference to the colour of the bearer's hair).

**Xavier** [*zay*vier] (m) from the name of the Jesuit missionary St Francis Xavier (1506–52), of Basque origin. Its occasional use as a first name in the English-speaking world is largely confined to Roman Catholic families.

**Xenia** [*zee*niă] (f) from Greek, meaning 'hospitable'.
Variant: **Zena**.

# Y

**Yasmin** a variant of **Jasmine** (*yasmin* is the Persian word from which the flower name is derived). The name was publicized in the first half of the 20th century by the heroine of James Elroy Flecker's play *Hassan* (1922).

**Yehudi** [ye*hoo*di] the Hebrew form of **Judah**. In the English-speaking world the name is generally associated with the US violinist Yehudi Menuhin (born 1916).

**Yolande, Yolanda** variants of **Iolanthe**, of French origin; influenced by *Violante*, an Italian form of **Viola**.

**Yorath** an anglicized form of **Iorwerth**.

**Yves** [eev] the French form of **Ivo**, made famous in the English-speaking world by the French couturier Yves Saint-Laurent (born 1936).

**Yvette** [ee*vet*] a feminine form of **Ivo**, of French origin; occasionally found in English-speaking countries.

**Yvonne** [ee*von*] a feminine form of **Ivo**, of French origin; in regular use throughout the English-speaking world since the beginning of the 20th century. The alternative spelling *Evonne* was made famous in the early 1970s by the Australian tennis player Evonne Goolagong (now Evonne Cawley).

# Z

**Zacchaeus** [za*keeŭs*] (m) a biblical name of uncertain origin; it may be from Aramaic, meaning 'pure', or it may simply be a variant of **Zachariah**. Borne in the New Testament by a wealthy tax-collector (Luke 19:1–8), the name came into general use in the English-speaking world in the 17th century.

**Zachariah** [zakă*rīă*] (m) from Hebrew, meaning 'the Lord has remembered', borne in the Authorized Version of the Old Testament by one of the kings of Israel (2 Kings 15:8; see also **Zechariah**). The name was adopted by the Puritans after the Reformation but is rarely found in this form in modern times.
Variants: **Zacchaeus, Zacharias, Zachary, Zechariah.**

**Zacharias** [zakă*rīăs*] a variant of **Zachariah**. The name is borne in the Authorized Version of the New Testament by the father of John the Baptist (Luke 1; see also **Zechariah**) and in the Douai Bible by the Old Testament prophet Zechariah. See also **Zachary**.

**Zachary** [*zak*ări] a variant of **Zachariah**; the usual form of the name in English-speaking countries. Famous bearers include the 8th-century pope St Zachary (or Zacharias), the US president Zachary Taylor (1784–1850), and the US actor Zachary Scott (1914–65).
Diminutives: **Zack, Zak.**

**Zak, Zack** diminutives of **Isaac** or **Zachary**, sometimes used as independent names.

**Zana** (f) a name of uncertain origin: it may be from Persian, meaning 'woman', or it may simply be a diminutive of **Susannah**.

**Zandra** a diminutive of **Alexandra** or a variant of **Sandra**, made famous by the British fashion designer Zandra Rhodes (born 1940).

**Zane** (m) from a surname of uncertain origin. Zanesville, Ohio, was the birthplace of the US novelist Zane Grey (1875–1939); both the city and the writer were named after Grey's ancestor Ebenezer Zane. The name remains in occasional use in the USA but is rarely found in other English-speaking countries.

**Zara** (f) a name of uncertain origin: it may be from Arabic, meaning 'eastern splendour', or it may simply be a variant of **Sarah**. The name occurs in a number of literary works, notably Congreve's play *The Mourning Bride* (1697), in which it is borne by a Moorish queen. Rarely given as a first name until the 1970s, it was further publicized by the birth of Princess Anne's daughter Zara in 1981.

**Zechariah** [zekă*rīă*] a variant of **Zachariah**; borne by an Old Testament prophet of the 6th century BC. In many versions of the Bible *Zechariah* replaces *Zachariah* (in the second book of Kings) and **Zacharias** (in St

Luke's Gospel). The name was adopted by the Puritans after the Reformation but is rarely found in modern times.

**Zedekiah** [zedĕkīǎ] (m) from Hebrew, meaning 'the Lord is righteous'. Borne in the Old Testament by the last king of Judah (2 Kings 24:18), the name came into general use in the English-speaking world in the 17th century.

**Zeke** a diminutive of **Ezekiel**.

**Zelda** a diminutive of **Griselda**, often used as a name in its own right. It was borne by the schizophrenic wife of the 20th-century US writer F. Scott Fitzgerald.

**Zelma** a diminutive of **Anselma**, often used as a name in its own right.

**Zena** (f) a name of uncertain origin: it may be from Persian, meaning 'woman', or it may simply be a variant of **Xenia**.

**Zenobia** [zenōbiǎ] (f) the name of a 3rd-century ruler of Palmyra; probably of Greek origin. *Zenobia* is occasionally given as a first name in various parts of the English-speaking world but has never been common.

**Zephaniah** [zefǎnīǎ] (m) from Hebrew, meaning 'the Lord has concealed (or protected)'; borne by an Old Testament prophet of the 7th century BC. The name was adopted by the Puritans after the Reformation but is rarely found in modern times.

**Zillah** (f) from Hebrew, meaning 'shade'; the name of one of the wives of Lamech in the Old Testament (Genesis 4:19). It has been in general use in English-speaking countries since the 16th century.

**Zinnia** (f) from the flower name; in occasional use as a first name during the 20th century.

**Zita** (f) the name of a 13th-century saint, of uncertain origin. St Zita is the patroness of domestic servants; her name is used from time to time in various parts of the English-speaking world but has never been common.

**Zoë, Zoe** [zōi] (f) from Greek, meaning 'life'; a translation of the Hebrew name from which **Eve** is derived. The name was borne by the 3rd-century Roman martyr St Zoë and by a Byzantine empress of the 11th century. It came into general use in the English-speaking world in the 19th century and enjoyed a revival in the 1970s.

**Zola** (f) possibly from the surname of the 19th-century French writer Emile Zola; in occasional use as a first name. It was publicized in the 1980s by the athlete Zola Budd.

**Zora, Zorah** (f) a name of uncertain origin: it may be from Arabic, meaning 'dawn', or from an Old Testament place name.

**Zuleika** [zoolaykǎ, zoolīkǎ] (f) from Persian, meaning 'brilliant beauty'. Some scholars believe the name to have been borne by Potiphar's wife, whose false accusations led to Joseph's imprisonment (Genesis 39). Made famous by the beautiful heroines of Lord Byron's poem *The Bride of*

*Abydos* (1813) and Sir Max Beerbohm's novel *Zuleika Dobson* (1911), it is occasionally given as a first name in Britain and other parts of the English-speaking world.

# CALENDAR OF SAINTS

## JANUARY

1  Basil, Justin.
2  Abel, Caspar.
3  Daniel, Frances, Geneviève.
4  Benedicta, Roger.
5  Paula, Simeon.
6  Balthasar, Gaspar (or Caspar), Raphaela.
7  Crispin, Lucian, Reinold (or Reynold), Valentine.
8  Lucian.
9  Adrian, Alix, Peter.
10  William.
11  Brandan.
12  Benedict, Tatiana.
13  Godfrey.
14  Felix, Hilary, Kentigern (or Mungo), Malachi.
15  Isidore, Ita, Micah, Paul.
16  Henry, Marcellus, Otto, Priscilla (or Prisca).
17  Antony, Roseline.
18  Dermot, Faustina, Priscilla (or Prisca), Susanna.
19  Gerontius, Henry, Marius, Martha, Pia.
20  Fabian, Sebastian.
21  Agnes, Josepha.
22  Dominic, Vincent.
23  Aquila, Bernard (or Barnard), Raymond.
24  Timothy.
25  Artemas, Joel.
26  Alberic (or Aubrey), Conan, Paula.
27  Candida, John, Julian, Marius, Theodoric.
28  Peter.
29  Francis.
30  Hyacintha, Martina, Matthias.
31  Adamnan, Aidan, Cyrus, Julius, Marcella, Tryphena.

## FEBRUARY

1  Brigid (or Bridget or Bride), Ignatius.
2  Joan (or Jane), Theodoric.
3  Blase (or Blasius), Ia (or Ives), Laurence, Margaret, Oliver.
4  Andrew, Gilbert, Isidore, Joan (or Jane), Joseph, Nicholas, Theophilus.
5  Adelaide, Agatha, Caius, Joachim, Matthias.
6  Dorothea (or Dorothy), Gerald, Luke, Mel, Silvanus, Titus.
7  Juliana, Luke, Moses, Richard, Theodore.
8  Isaiah, Sebastian, Stephen.

    9 Apollonia, Cyril.
   10 Hyacinth, Silvanus.
   11 Benedict, Gregory, Jonas, Lazarus, Lucius, Theodora, Victoria.
   12 Alexis, Eulalia, Julian, Marina.
   13 Beatrice (or Beatrix), Catherine.
   14 Abraham, Adolf (or Adolphus), Valentine.
   15 Claud (or Claudius), Georgia, Jordan, Sigfrid.
   16 Elias, Gilbert, Jeremy, Juliana, Philippa, Samuel.
   17 Reginald.
   18 Simeon.
   19 Boniface, Conrad.
   20 Amata, Wulfric (or Ulric).
   21 George.
   22 Margaret.
   23 Lazarus, Martha, Mildburh (or Mildburga), Milo.
   24 Adela, Lucius, Matthias.
   25 Ethelbert, Walburga.
   26 Alexander, Isabel (or Isabelle), Victor.
   27 Gabriel, Leander.
   28 Antonia, Hedwig, Hilary (or Hilarus), Louisa, Oswald.

# MARCH

    1 Albinus, David, Felix, Roger.
    2 Agnes, Chad (or Ceadda).
    3 Anselm, Camilla, Marcia, Owen.
    4 Adrian, Casimir, Humbert, Lucius, Peter.
    5 Kieran (or Ciaran), Piran, Virgil.
    6 Colette, Cyril, Felicity, Jordan, Perpetua.
    7 Paul, Thomas.
    8 Beata, Felix, Humphrey (or Hunfrid), Julian, Philemon, Stephen.
    9 Catherine, Dominic, Frances, Gregory.
   10 Anastasia, Caius.
   11 Alberta, Aurea, Constantine, Teresa.
   12 Bernard, Gregory, Maximilian, Paul, Seraphina.
   13 Gerald, Patricia, Roderick, Solomon.
   14 Eustace, Matilda.
   15 Clement, Louise, Lucretia, Zachary (or Zacharias).
   16 Abraham, Julian, René.
   17 Gertrude, Joseph, Patrick, Paul.
   18 Alexander, Anselm, Christian, Cyril, Edward, Egbert, Narcissus, Salvator.
   19 Joseph.

20 Alexandra, Claudia, Cuthbert, Euphemia, Herbert, Hippolytus, Martin, Sebastian, Theodosia.
21 Benedict, Clementia.
22 Basil, Octavian.
23 Aquila, Theodosia.
24 Catherine, Gabriel, Simon.
25 Harold, Humbert, Lucy, Richard.
26 Basil, Emmanuel.
27 Augusta, John, Lydia, Matthew.
28 Gwendoline, John.
29 Berthold, Gladys (or Gwladys), Jonas, Mark, Rupert.
30 John.
31 Aldo, Amos, Benjamin, Cornelia, Guy.

## APRIL
1 Gilbert, Hugh, Ludovic.
2 Constantine, Drogo, Francis, Leopold, Mary, Theodosia, Urban.
3 Alexandrina, Irene, Richard.
4 Benedict, Isidore.
5 Gerald, Vincent.
6 Celestine, William.
7 George, Herman, Llewellyn (or Llywelyn).
8 Dionysius, Walter.
9 Hugh, Mary, Reginald.
10 Ezekiel, Fulbert, Hedda, Michael, Terence.
11 Gemma, Hildebrand, Isaac, Leo.
12 Damian, Julius.
13 Ida.
14 Bernard, Caradoc, Eustace, Justin, Lambert.
15 Anastasia, Silvester.
16 Benedict, Bernadette, Drogo, Hervé, Lambert, Magnus.
17 Elias, Robert, Stephen.
18 Andrew, James.
19 Leo.
20 Agnes.
21 Anselm, Conrad, Simeon.
22 Caius, Theodore.
23 Fortunatus, George, Gerard, Giles, Helen.
24 Egbert, Ives (or Ivo).
25 Mark.
26 Alda, Franca, Stephen.
27 Zita.
28 Louis, Patrick, Paul, Theodora, Valeria.

29   Antonia, Ava, Hugh, Robert, Wilfrid.
30   Catherine, Hildegard, James, Miles, Sophia.

## MAY

1   Bertha, Isidora, Joseph, Peregrine, Sigismund, Walburga.
2   Zoë.
3   Antonina, Maura, Philip, Timothy.
4   Ethelred, Florian, Monica, Silvanus.
5   Angelo (or Angelus), Hilary.
6   Benedicta, Prudence.
7   Augustus, Flavia, Gisela (or Giselle), Stanislas (or Stanislaw).
8   Benedict, Boniface, Michael, Peter, Victor.
9   Gerontius.
10   Aurelian, Beatrice (or Beatrix), Job.
11   Aloysius, Ignatius, James, Philip, Walter.
12   Dominic, Gemma.
13   Robert.
14   Carthach (or Carthage), Giles, Mary, Michael, Petronilla.
15   Bertha, Dionysia, Dympna, Hilary, Isidore, Magdalen, Rupert, Silvanus.
16   Brendan, Peregrine, Simon.
17   Basilla, Paschal.
18   Alexandra, Camilla, Claudia, Eric, Julitta.
19   Celestine, Dunstan, Ivo (or Yves).
20   Aquila, Basilissa (or Basilla), Ethelbert, Orlando.
21   Theobald, Theophilus.
22   Julia, Rita.
23   Ivo, William.
24   David, Joanna, Patrick, Susanna, Vincent.
25   Aldhelm, Dionysius, Gregory, Madeleine, Urban.
26   Augustine (or Austin), Lambert, Philip, Zachary.
27   Frederick, John, Julius.
28   Augustine (or Austin), Bernard.
29   Theodosia, William.
30   Felix, Ferdinand, Hubert, Isaac, Joan.
31   Camilla, Petronilla.

## JUNE

1   Angela, Simeon, Theobald.
2   Erasmus (or Elmo), Eugene, Nicholas.
3   Charles, Clotilda, Isaac, Kevin, Matthias, Paula.
4   Cornelius, Francis, Vincentia, Walter.
5   Boniface (or Winfrid), Ferdinand, Franco, Marcia, Valeria.

247

6  Claud (or Claudius), Felicia, Norbert, Philip.
7  Robert.
8  Melania, William.
9  Amata, Cecilia, Columba, Diana, Richard.
10  Margaret, Olive, Zachary.
11  Barnabas, Fortunatus.
12  Antonia (or Antonina), Christian, Leo, Onuphrius (or Humphrey).
13  Antony, Lucian.
14  Basil.
15  Alice, Germaine, Vitus (or Guy), Yolanda.
16  Aurelian, Julitta.
17  Botolph (or Botulf), Emily, Harvey (or Hervé), Manuel, Sanchia, Teresa.
18  Elizabeth, Fortunatus, Guy, Marina, Mark.
19  Bruno (or Boniface), Gervase, Juliana, Odo.
20  John.
21  Alban (or Albinus), Aloysius, Lazarus, Ralph (or Raoul), Terence.
22  Alban, Eberhard (or Everard).
23  Audrey (or Etheldreda).
24  Bartholomew, Ivan, John.
25  Solomon, William.
26  John.
27  Ferdinand, Madeleine, Samson.
28  Marcella, Paul.
29  Emma, Judith, Paul, Peter, Salome.
30  Bertrand, Lucina, Theobald.

## JULY

1  Aaron, Simeon, Theodoric.
2  Marcia, Otto, Reginald.
3  Aaron, Julius, Leo.
4  Andrew, Aurelian, Bertha, Odo, Ulric.
5  Antony, Grace, Gwen (or Blanche), Philomena, Zoë.
6  Isaiah.
7  Cyril, Heddda.
8  Adrian, Aquila, Arnold, Edgar, Elizabeth, Morwenna, Priscilla (or Prisca), Raymund.
9  Alberic, Barnabas, Cornelius, Everild, Godfrey, Jerome, Nicholas, Thomas, Veronica.
10  Amalburga (or Amelia), Emmanuel, Maurice.
11  Olga, Oliver.
12  Fortunatus, Jason, John, Monica, Veronica.
13  Eugene, Joel, Mildred, Silas (or Silvanus).

14 Humbert, Ulric.
15 Baldwin, David, Donald, Edith, Henry, Swithin (or Swithun).
16 Eustace, Milo, Valentine.
17 Alexis, Antoinette, Kenelm, Leo, Nahum.
18 Bruno, Camillus, Edith, Frederick, Marina.
19 Ambrose, Aurea, Jerome, Vincent.
20 Elias, Elijah, Jerome, Margaret (or Marina).
21 Angelina, Constantine, Daniel, Julia, Laurence, Victor.
22 Joseph, Mary Magdalene, Theophilus.
23 Anne (or Susanna), Balthasar, Gaspar (or Caspar).
24 Boris, Christiana, Christina, Declan, Felicia.
25 Christopher, James, Thea, Valentina.
26 Anne.
27 Berthold, Celestine, Natalia, Rudolph, Theobald.
28 Samson, Victor.
29 Beatrice (or Beatrix), Felix, Flora, Lucilla, Martha, Olaf, Urban.
30 Everard, Julitta.
31 Helen, Ignatius.

## AUGUST
1 Charity, Eiluned (or Elined), Faith, Hope, Justin, Kenneth.
2 Alphonsus, Stephen.
3 Gamaliel, Lydia, Nicodemus.
4 Dominic, Perpetua.
5 Afra, Oswald.
6 Octavian.
7 Albert, Claudia.
8 Myron.
9 Oswald, Samuel.
10 Gerontius (or Geraint), Lawrence (or Laurence), Philomena.
11 Alexander, Blane (or Blaan), Lelia, Susanna.
12 Clare (or Clara), Murtagh.
13 Hippolytus.
14 Marcellus.
15 Mary, Napoleon, Stanislaus.
16 Joachim, Serena, Titus.
17 Benedicta, Cecilia, Clare, Hyacinth, Myron, Septimus.
18 Evan, Helena (or Helen), Milo.
19 Louis, Magnus, Thecla, Timothy.
20 Bernard, Herbert, Oswin, Philibert, Ronald, Samuel.
21 Abraham, Jane.
22 Andrew, Hippolytus, Sigfrid, Timothy.
23 Claudius, Eleazar, Eugene (or Eoghan), Philip, Zacchaeus.

24  Alice, Bartholomew (or Nathanael), Emily, Joan (or Jane).
25  Louis, Lucilla, Patricia.
26  Elias, Elizabeth.
27  Gabriel, Hugh, Margaret, Rufus.
28  Adelina, Alexander, Augustine, Julian, Moses, Vivian.
29  Basilla, Medericus (or Merry), Sabina.
30  Felix, Rose.
31  Aidan, Raymund.

## SEPTEMBER
1  Anna, Augustus, Gideon, Giles, Joshua, Verena.
2  René, Stephen, William.
3  Dorothy, Euphemia, Gabriel, Gregory, Phoebe, Simeon.
4  Boniface, Candida, Hermione, Ida, Marcellus, Moses, Rosalia, Rose.
5  Laurence, Urban, Vitus.
6  Beata, Magnus, Zechariah.
7  Eustace, Regina (or Reine).
8  Adrian, Natalia, Sergius.
9  Isaac, Kieran (or Ciaran), Louise, Seraphina, Wilfrida.
10  Aubert, Candida, Isabel, Nicholas.
11  Daniel, Hyacinth, Theodora.
12  Guy.
13  Amatus.
14  Cormac.
15  Albinus, Catherine, Roland.
16  Cornelius, Cyprian, Edith, Eugenia, Euphemia, Lucy, Ninian, Victor.
17  Ariadne, Columba, Hildegard, Justin, Lambert, Narcissus, Theodora.
18  Irene, Sophia.
19  Constantia, Emily, Susanna, Theodore.
20  Candida, Eustace, Philippa, Vincent.
21  Jonah, Matthew, Maura.
22  Felix, Jonas, Maurice, Thomas.
23  Adamnan, Helen, Thecla (or Thekla).
24  Gerard.
25  Albert, Aurelia, Herman.
26  Cyprian, Justina, René.
27  Adolphus, Caius, Cosmas, Damian, Terence.
28  Solomon.
29  Michael.
30  Jerome, Simon, Sophia.

## OCTOBER

1   Francis, Nicholas.
2   Theophilus.
3   Gerard, Thérèse (or Theresa).
4   Aurea, Berenice, Francis.
5   Flavia, Flora.
6   Aurea, Bruno, Faith, Magnus, Mary.
7   Augustus, Julia, Justina, Mark.
8   Birgitta (or Bridget), Laurentia, Sergius, Simeon.
9   Abraham, Denys (or Denis), Dionysius, Gunther, Louis.
10   Daniel, Francis, Samuel.
11   Bruno, Canice (or Kenneth), Juliana.
12   Cyprian, Edwin, Maximilian, Wilfrid.
13   Edward, Gerald, Magdalen, Maurice, Theophilus.
14   Dominic.
15   Aurelia, Leonard, Teresa, Thecla, Willa.
16   Baldwin, Bertrand, Gerard, Hedwig.
17   Margaret, Rudolph.
18   Gwen (or Candida or Blanche), Gwendoline, Luke.
19   Cleopatra, Laura, Lucius, Peter.
20   Adelina, Andrew, Irene, Martha.
21   Ursula.
22   Philip.
23   Bartholomew, Ignatius, Josephine.
24   Antony, Martin, Raphael, Septimus.
25   Balthasar, Crispin, Crispinian, Dorcas (or Tabitha), George, Thaddeus, Theodoric.
26   Albinus, Cuthbert, Damian, Lucian.
27   Antonia, Sabina.
28   Anastasia, Godwin, Jude (or Thaddaeus), Simon.
29   Narcissus, Terence.
30   Alphonsus, Artemas, Dorothy, Marcellus, Zenobia.
31   Quentin (or Quintinus).

## NOVEMBER

1   Cledwyn, Mary.
2   Maura, Tobias.
3   Hubert, Malachy, Sylvia, Valentine, Winifred.
4   Charles, Frances.
5   Cosmo (or Cosimo), Elizabeth, Martin, Zacharias (or Zechariah).
6   Leonard.
7   Carina, Florentius, Gertrude, Rufus.

8   Godfrey.
9   Theodore.
10   Florentia (or Florence), Tryphena.
11   Bartholomew, Martin, Theodore.
12   Martin, Matthew, René.
13   Brice (or Britius), Eugene, Nicholas, Stanislaus.
14   Laurence.
15   Albert, Leopold.
16   Agnes, Edmund, Gertrude, Margaret.
17   Dionysius, Gregory, Hilda, Hugh, Victoria, Zacchaeus.
18   Constant, Odo.
19   Crispin, Elizabeth.
20   Edmund, Octavius, Silvester.
21   Albert, Rufus.
22   Cecilia, Philemon.
23   Clement, Felicity, Lucretia.
24   Flora, John, Thaddeus.
25   Catherine, Moses.
26   Conrad, Leonard, Peter, Silvester.
27   Fergus, James, Virgil.
28   James, Stephen.
29   Blaise, Brendan, Cuthbert, Frederick.
30   Andrew, Maura.

## DECEMBER
1   Nahum, Natalia, Ralph.
2   Aurelia, Bibiana (or Viviana).
3   Claudius, Francis Xavier, Jason, Lucius.
4   Ada, Barbara, Bernard, Osmond (or Osmund).
5   Bartholomew.
6   Abraham, Dionysia, Gertrude, Nicholas, Tertius.
7   Ambrose, Josepha.
8   Mary.
9   Peter.
10   Brian, Eulalia, Gregory, Julia, Sidney.
11   Daniel, Franco.
12   Agatha, Cormac, Dionysia.
13   Aubert, Judoc (or Judocus or Josse), Lucia (or Lucy), Ottilia (or Odilia).
14   Conrad.
15   Christiana, Mary.
16   Adelaide, Albina, Azariah.
17   Florian, Lazarus, Olympias.

18 Rufus.
19 Thea, Urban.
20 Dominic.
21 Thomas.
22 Adam.
23 Victoria.
24 Adam, Adela, Eve.
25 Anastasia, Eugenia.
26 Christina, Dionysius, Stephen, Vincentia.
27 John, Theodore.
28 Theophila.
29 David, Marcellus, Thomas.
30 Sabinus.
31 Columba, Cornelius, Fabian, Melania, Sextus, Silvester.

### Audrey Eyton's F-Plus   Audrey Eyton

'Your short-cut to the most sensational diet of the century' – *Daily Express*

### Caring Well for an Older Person   Muir Gray and Heather McKenzie

Wide-ranging and practical, with a list of useful addresses and contacts, this book will prove invaluable for anyone professionally concerned with the elderly or with an elderly relative to care for.

### Baby and Child   Penelope Leach

A beautifully illustrated and comprehensive handbook on the first five years of life. 'It stands head and shoulders above anything else available at the moment' – Mary Kenny in the *Spectator*

### Woman's Experience of Sex   Sheila Kitzinger

Fully illustrated with photographs and line drawings, this book explores the riches of women's sexuality at every stage of life. 'A book which any mother could confidently pass on to her daughter – and her partner too' – *Sunday Times*

### Food Additives   Erik Millstone

Eat, drink and be worried? Erik Millstone's hard-hitting book contains powerful evidence about the massive risks being taken with the health of consumers. It takes the lid off the food we eat and takes the lid off the food industry.

### Pregnancy and Diet   Rachel Holme

It *is* possible to eat well and healthily when pregnant while avoiding excessive calories; this book, with suggested foods, a sample diet-plan of menus and advice on nutrition, shows how.

## PENGUIN HEALTH

### Medicines: A Guide for Everybody   Peter Parish

This fifth edition of a comprehensive survey of all the medicines available over the counter or on prescription offers clear guidance for the ordinary reader as well as invaluable information for those involved in health care.

### Pregnancy and Childbirth   Sheila Kitzinger

A complete and up-to-date guide to physical and emotional preparation for pregnancy – a must for all prospective parents.

### The Penguin Encyclopaedia of Nutrition   John Yudkin

This book cuts through all the myths about food and diets to present the real facts clearly and simply. 'Everyone should buy one' – *Nutrition News and Notes*

### The Parents' A to Z   Penelope Leach

For anyone with a child of 6 months, 6 years or 16 years, this guide to all the little problems involved in their health, growth and happiness will prove reassuring and helpful.

### Jane Fonda's Workout Book

Help yourself to better looks, superb fitness and a whole new approach to health and beauty with this world-famous and fully illustrated programme of diet and exercise advice.

### Alternative Medicine   Andrew Stanway

Dr Stanway provides an objective and practical guide to thirty-two alternative forms of therapy – from Acupuncture and the Alexander Technique to Macrobiotics and Yoga.

## PENGUIN HEALTH

### A Complete Guide to Therapy Joel Kovel

The options open to anyone seeking psychiatric help are both numerous and confusing. Dr Kovel cuts through the many myths and misunderstandings surrounding today's therapy and explores the pros and cons of various types of therapies.

### Pregnancy Dr Jonathan Scher and Carol Dix

Containing the most up-to-date information on pregnancy – the effects of stress, sexual intercourse, drugs, diet, late maternity and genetic disorders – this book is an invaluable and reassuring guide for prospective parents.

### Yoga Ernest Wood

'It has been asked whether in yoga there is something for everybody. The answer is "yes"' Ernest Wood.

### Depression Ross Mitchell

Depression is one of the most common contemporary problems. But what exactly do we mean by the term? In this invaluable book Ross Mitchell looks at depression as a mood, as an experience, as an attitude to life and as an illness.

### Vogue Natural Health and Beauty Bronwen Meredith

Health foods, yoga, spas, recipes, natural remedies and beauty preparations are all included in this superb, fully illustrated guide and companion to the bestselling *Vogue Body and Beauty Book*.

### Care of the Dying Richard Lamerton

It is never true that 'nothing more can be done' for the dying. This book shows us how to face death without pain, with humanity, with dignity and in peace.

### The Penguin Encyclopaedia of Nutrition   John Yudkin

This book cuts through all the myths about food and diets to present the real facts clearly and simply. 'Everyone should buy one' – *Nutrition News and Notes*

### The Prime of Your Life   Dr Miriam Stoppard

The first comprehensive, fully illustrated guide to healthy living for people aged fifty and beyond, by top medical writer and media personality, Dr Miriam Stoppard.

### A Good Start   Louise Graham

Factual and practical, full of tips on providing a healthy and balanced diet for young children, *A Good Start* is essential reading for all parents.

### How to Get Off Drugs   Ira Mothner and Alan Weitz

This book is a vital contribution towards combating drug addiction in Britain in the eighties. For drug abusers, their families and their friends.

### The Royal Canadian Airforce XBX Plan for Physical Fitness for Men and The Royal Canadian Airforce XBX Plan for Physical Fitness for Women

Get fit and stay fit with minimum fuss and maximum efficiency, using these short, carefully devised exercises.

### Pregnancy and Childbirth   Sheila Kitzinger

A complete and up-to-date guide to physical and emotional preparation for pregnancy – a must for prospective parents.

### Alternative Medicine   Andrew Stanway

Dr Stanway provides an objective and practical guide to thirty-two alternative forms of therapy – from Acupuncture and the Alexander Technique to Macrobiotics and Yoga.

### Jane Grigson's Vegetable Book   Jane Grigson

The ideal guide to the cooking of everything from artichoke to yams,
written with her usual charm and depth of knowledge by 'the most
engaging food writer to emerge during the last few years' – *The Times*

### More Easy Cooking for One or Two   Louise Davies

This charming book, full of ideas and easy recipes, offers even the novice
cook good wholesome food with the minimum of effort.

### The Cuisine of the Rose   Mireille Johnston

Classic French cooking from Burgundy and Lyonnais, including the most
succulent dishes of meat and fish bathed in pungent sauces of wine and
herbs.

### Good Food from Your Freezer   Helge Rubinstein and Sheila Bush

Using a freezer saves endless time and trouble and cuts your food bills
dramatically; this book will enable you to cook just as well – perhaps even
better – with a freezer as without.

### An Invitation to Indian Cooking   Madhur Jaffrey

A witty, practical and delightful handbook of Indian cookery by the much
loved presenter of the successful television series.

### Budget Gourmet   Geraldene Holt

Plan carefully, shop wisely and cook well to produce first-rate food at
minimal expense. It's as easy as pie!

## GARDENING IN PENGUINS

### The Adventurous Gardener  Christopher Lloyd

Prejudiced, delightful and always stimulating, Christopher Lloyd's book is essential reading for everyone who loves gardening. 'Get it and enjoy it' – *Financial Times*

### The Magic Garden  Shirley Conran

*The* gardening book for the absolute beginner. 'Whether you have a window box, a patio, an acre or a cabbage patch . . . you will enjoy this' – *Daily Express*

### The Cottage Garden  Anne Scott-James

'Her history is neatly and simply laid out; well-stocked with attractive illustrations' – *The Times*. 'The garden book I have most enjoyed reading in the last few years' – *Observer*

### Growing Fruit  Mary Spiller

From blossom to harvest, through planting, pruning, picking and storing, in a small or large garden, plot or pot, here is an illustrated step-by-step guide to growing fruit of all kinds.

### The Illustrated Garden Planter  Diana Saville

How to choose plants for your garden – to cover a wall, creep between paving, provide colour in summer – and to plan for collective effect or to overcome a difficult site. 650 plants are illustrated, in all over 900 described.

### Organic Gardening  Lawrence D. Hills

The classic manual on growing fruit and vegetables without using artificial or harmful fertilizers. 'Enormous value . . . enthusiastic writing and off-beat tips' – *Daily Mail*